Foreign Jack Tars

The British Royal Navy of the French Wars (1793–1815) is an enduring national symbol, but we often overlook the tens of thousands of foreign seamen who contributed to its operations. *Foreign Jack Tars* presents the first in-depth study of their employment in the Navy during this crucial period. Based on sources from across Britain, Europe, and the USA, and blending quantitative, social, cultural, economic, and legal history, it challenges the very notions of 'Britishness' and 'foreignness'. The need for manpower during wartime meant that naval recruitment regularly bypassed cultural prejudice, and even legal status. Temporarily outstripped by practical considerations, these categories thus revealed their artificiality. The Navy was not simply an employer in the British maritime market, but a nodal point of global mobility. Exposing the inescapable transnational dimensions of a quintessentially national institution, the book highlights the instability of national boundaries, and the compromises and contradictions underlying the power of modern states.

Sara Caputo is Affiliated Lecturer at the Faculty of History, University of Cambridge, and Research Fellow at Magdalene College. Her work has won the Prince Consort and Thirlwall Prize and Seeley Medal for a historical doctoral thesis completed at the University of Cambridge and the British Commission for Maritime History Prize for best UK thesis on maritime history. She has also been awarded the international Ideas Prize, the Sir Julian Corbett Prize in Modern Naval History, and the Scottish History Society Rosebery Prize. She has published several articles on maritime social and cultural history and held visiting fellowships at various institutions in Britain, Germany, and the USA.

Modern British Histories

Series Editors:

Deborah Cohen, *Northwestern University*
Margot Finn, *University College London*
Peter Mandler, *University of Cambridge*

'Modern British Histories' publishes original research monographs drawn from the full spectrum of a large and lively community of modern historians of Britain. Its goal is to keep metropolitan and national histories of Britain fresh and vital in an intellectual atmosphere increasingly attuned to, and enriched by, the transnational, the international and the comparative. It will include books that focus on British histories within the UK and that tackle the subject of Britain and the world inside and outside the boundaries of formal empire from 1750 to the present. An indicative – not exclusive – list of approaches and topics that the series welcomes includes material culture studies, modern intellectual history, gender, race and class histories, histories of modern science and histories of British capitalism within a global framework. Open and wide-ranging, the series will publish books by authoritative scholars, at all stages of their career, with something genuinely new to say.

A complete list of titles in the series can be found at:
www.cambridge.org/modernbritishhistories

Foreign Jack Tars

The British Navy and Transnational Seafarers during the Revolutionary and Napoleonic Wars

Sara Caputo

University of Cambridge

CAMBRIDGE
UNIVERSITY PRESS

Shaftesbury Road, Cambridge CB2 8EA, United Kingdom

One Liberty Plaza, 20th Floor, New York, NY 10006, USA

477 Williamstown Road, Port Melbourne, VIC 3207, Australia

314–321, 3rd Floor, Plot 3, Splendor Forum, Jasola District Centre,
New Delhi – 110025, India

103 Penang Road, #05–06/07, Visioncrest Commercial, Singapore 238467

Cambridge University Press is part of Cambridge University Press & Assessment,
a department of the University of Cambridge.

We share the University's mission to contribute to society through the pursuit of
education, learning and research at the highest international levels of excellence.

www.cambridge.org
Information on this title: www.cambridge.org/9781009199797

DOI: 10.1017/9781009199841

First published 2023

A catalogue record for this publication is available from the British Library

Library of Congress Cataloging-in-Publication Data
Names: Caputo, Sara, author.
Title: Foreign jack tars : the British Navy and transnational seafarers during the
   Revolutionary and Napoleonic Wars / Sara Caputo, University of Cambridge.
Other titles: British Navy and transnational seafarers during the Revolutionary
   and Napoleonic Wars
Description: Cambridge, United Kingdom ; New York, NY : Cambridge
   University Press, 2023. | Series: Modern British histories | Includes
   bibliographical references and index.
Identifiers: LCCN 2022033911 (print) | LCCN 2022033912 (ebook) |
   ISBN 9781009199797 (hardback) | ISBN 9781009199810 (paperback) |
   ISBN 9781009199841 (epub)
Subjects: LCSH: Great Britain. Royal Navy–History–18th century. | Foreign
   enlistment–Great Britain–History–18th century. | Mercenary troops–Great
   Britain–History–18th century.
Classification: LCC DA87 .C37 2023 (print) | LCC DA87 (ebook) |
   DDC 359.00941–dc23/eng/20220719
LC record available at https://lccn.loc.gov/2022033911
LC ebook record available at https://lccn.loc.gov/2022033912

ISBN 978-1-009-19979-7 Hardback

For Mum and Dad

Contents

Figures

Tables

Acknowledgements

Every historian could fill volumes with their archival adventures, and recounting them here would be self-indulgent. In my mind, however, it is not the picturesque or the uncanny (much of both was encountered) that stands out the most: along the way, I have met so many kind and helpful people that the thought is overwhelming. It has been an absolute privilege.

Many individuals and institutions are due gratitude. To begin with, I owe huge thanks to Renaud Morieux, my PhD supervisor. Infallibly pointing out inconsistencies and weaknesses in my work, he helped me hammer my thinking into better shape, and provided exceptional and ongoing support. The book has changed since then, and, as per the usual formula, all remaining blunders are mine. I could not have hoped for a better doctoral supervisor.

Liam Gauci in Malta, Biagio Passaro, Angelo Odore, and Massimo Maresca in Naples and Sorrento, and Nicholas Rodger in Oxford were incredibly generous and hospitable, making me feel at home during my visits and providing much useful information. I remain in their debt. Gareth Atkins was a wonderful advisor, and Melissa Calaresu and Stephen Conway were exceptional examiners. Every single one of their thoughtful suggestions has helped me shape my thesis into this book. The ever-kind Callum Easton shared sources, ideas, and words of encouragement. Joan Abela, Emmanuel Buttigieg, Maroma Camilleri, Simona Cerutti, Noel D'Anastas, Berit Eide Johnsen, Irene Galandra Cooper, Mary Laven, Silvia Marzagalli, James Raven, and Jakob Seerup, via email or in person, provided valuable indications and sources that have shaped the direction of this project. Mark Williams, Paul Webster, Tracey Loughran, Federica Ferlanti, Lloyd Bowen, Anna Groundwater, and Gordon Pentland were fantastic teachers, mentors, and believers before, during, and after this journey. Nicole Janz and the Social Sciences Research Methods Programme at Cambridge trained me from scratch in the use of inferential statistical methods and R. The brilliant Claire Simons, too, cannot be thanked enough for all her kindness and expertise, for reading my quantitative chapter, and for texting over stunningly fast and spot-on solutions if my code defeated me. The editors, series editors, and anonymous readers at Cambridge University Press offered excellent and generous feedback and advice. Students, as ever, and in particular the school pupils whom I had the privilege to meet through the Brilliant Club, kept the enthusiasm and inspiration alive.

Many, many more people are owed thanks for their assistance, suggestions, support, encouragement, for interesting conversations, or for triggering new ideas and insights, or sharing individual sources and literature. I am certain that this will not be a comprehensive list, but here are many of their names – in alphabetical order, as I could not begin to think of a fair way of 'ranking' them: Sarah Atkins, Catherine Beck, Sandy Biery, Erica Charters, Nicholas Chiasson, Gaetano Damiano, Jeremiah Dancy, James Davey, J. D. Davies, Renata De Lorenzo, Nicholas Dixon, Saul Dubow, Jake Dyble, Elisa Ercolin, Amy Erickson, Christina Faraday, Simon Gallaher, Fernanda Gallo, Ben Gilding, Yonatan Glazer-Eytan, Ben Griffin, Nick Guyatt, Cath, Craig, and Carrie Holloway, Josh Ivinson, Walter Jansson, Lawrence Klein, Roger Knight, Emily Manson, Dániel Margócsy, Madison Marshall, Louise Moschetta, Elaine Murphy, Barbara Naddeo, Bruno Pappalardo, Sarah Pearsall, Vincent Peresso, Anna Maria Rao, Alexander Ray, Olesya Razuvayevskaya, Glauco Schettini, Ruth Schilling, Sujit Sivasundaram, Christina Skott, Fred Smith, Mary Stewart, Alistair Swiffen, Deborah Thom, Louis Volkmer, Sarah Watkinson, Callie Wilkinson, and Evan Wilson.

This project was originally funded by a Robinson College Lewis – Arts and Humanities Research Council studentship and by a twelve-month Scouloudi Fellowship at the Institute of Historical Research, London. My research trips to archives in Britain, Italy, Malta, and the Netherlands, as well as attendance at conferences and workshops, were generously funded by an Arts and Humanities Research Council RTSG grant, by the Cambridge History Faculty Fieldwork Fund, Members' History Fund, Specialist Archive Travel Fund, and Conference Attendance Fund, by four Academic Expenses grants from Robinson College, by the IHR Power and Postan Fund, and by two conference attendance bursaries from the Economic History Society. Fellowships at Magdalene College, Cambridge, the Deutsches Schifffahrtsmuseum in Bremerhaven, and the Huntington Library in San Marino, CA, gave me much-needed mind space, time, and new resources to turn my thesis into this book.

I would also like to express my gratitude for the help of staff at the Cambridge Faculty of History, Robinson College and Magdalene College, and at the various archives and libraries I visited: from nearest to furthest, the Cambridge University Library and affiliated libraries,

Robinson College Library, Magdalene College Library, the Jerwood Library of Trinity Hall, the British Library, Senate House Library, and Parliamentary Archives in London, the Caird Library of the Greenwich National Maritime Museum, the National Archives in Kew, the University of Nottingham Manuscripts and Special Collections, the Portsmouth Museum of the Royal Navy Library, the Devon Archives and Local Studies Service, the Koninklijk Huisarchief and the Nationaal Archief in The Hague, the Deutsches Schifffahrtsmuseum library, the Archivio di Stato in Naples and Pizzofalcone, the National Library of Malta and Notarial Archive in Valletta, the Archives of the Metropolitan Cathedral and National Archives of Malta in Mdina, and the Huntington Library in San Marino, California.

Finally, I need to thank Elisa, who has put up with me for a very long time; Mum and Dad, for being there for me at any hour and anyway; and Cameron, for his stalwart support and patient love.

Older versions of some parts of this book (especially the Introduction and Chapter 7) have appeared in print in a short historiographical piece:

Sara Caputo, "Vers une histoire transnationale de la marine britannique au XVIIIe siècle" in *Annales historiques de la Révolution française*, 2019/3 (no. 397), pp. 13–32, © Armand Colin. Armand Colin est une marque de Dunod Éditeur, Malakoff.

A previous incarnation of Chapter 2, also containing some fragments from the Introduction, was published in the *Historical Journal*:

Sara Caputo, 'Alien Seamen in the British Navy, British Law, and the British State, *c*.1793–*c*.1815', *The Historical Journal* 62:3 (2019), 685–707.

This material is reproduced here by kind permission of the two publishers.

Introduction

> It would be difficult to give any adequate idea of the scenes these decks presented to any one who has not witnessed them. To the eye were presented complexions of every varied hue, and features of every cast, from the jetty face, flat nose, thick lips and frizzled hair of the African, to the more slender frame and milder features of the Asiatic. The rosy complexion of the English Swain and the sallow features of the sun-burnt Portuguese. (...) Costumes of the most various hues presented themselves from the Kilted Highlander to the quadruple breeched sons of Holland. From the shirtless sons of the British prison-house to the knuckle ruffles of the haughty Spaniard. (...) To the ear was addressed a hubub [*sic*] little short of that which occurred at Babel. Irish, Welsh, Dutch, Portuguese, Spanish, French, Swedish, Italian and all the provincial dialects which prevail between Landsend and John O'Groats, joined their discordant notes.[1]

Contrary to appearances, this is not the description of a bustling public quay. It is a Scottish boy's first impression of a Royal Navy recruitment guard ship, anchored at Plymouth in 1803. His memoirs were written seventeen years later, no doubt influenced by nostalgia and the picturesque flourishes of the genre: this passage rings with clear echoes of a classic trope, the 'motley crew'.[2] However, Hay's vignette is not purely the product of literary fancy. At the turn of the nineteenth century, the boundaries between a national military institution like the British Navy and the rest of the maritime world were far from impermeable.

As N. A. M. Rodger once wrote, referring to the period of the Seven Years' War (1756–1763), 'there were men from every nation under Heaven in the Navy'.[3] The statement still applied half a century later. During the French Revolutionary and Napoleonic Wars (1793–1815),

---

[1] Robert Hay, *Landsman Hay: The Memoirs of Robert Hay 1789–1847*, ed. M. D. Hay (London: Rupert Hart-Davis, 1953), 43–4.
[2] Marcus Rediker, 'Afterword: Reflections on the Motley Crew as Port City Proletariat', *International Review of Social History* 64 (2019), 255–62.
[3] N. A. M. Rodger, *The Wooden World: An Anatomy of the Georgian Navy* (London: William Collins, 1986), 158.

1

likely between one-twelfth and one-seventh of the fleet was foreign-born.[4] Thousands of sailors from all over Europe, the Americas, Africa, the Indian Ocean, and as far away as China feature again and again in the sources. Most of them were not British subjects. However, constructions of foreignness do not stop at origin or legal status. Large numbers of seamen in British men-of-war did not conform to the Anglo–American cultural stereotype of the 'Jack Tar', the flattening symbol of British (or in fact English) national character that became ubiquitous precisely during the 'French Wars'.[5] Many 'British tars' spoke no English; many were devout Catholics; many were of African or Asian descent, racialised as Black, and survivors of enslavement; many had grown up, lived, and worked all over the world, and had complex allegiances and personal trajectories.

The service of 'foreigners' in the eighteenth- and early nineteenth-century Navy is a well-established fact, often mentioned in passing in the historiography, and even referenced in popular culture.[6] It is also a fact that is often stated, but rarely discussed. The word 'foreigner' was and is used flatly, mainly as an implicit synonym of that supremely ambiguous concept – 'from abroad'. In 1792, the tenth edition of Samuel Johnson's English *Dictionary* defined a foreigner as 'a man that comes from another country; not a native; a stranger', and a 1795 pocket edition offered the even more vague 'one of another country', blending origin, ownership, and belonging into one ambiguous preposition.[7] As a modish Graecism, 'foreigner' was listed as one of the possible meanings of 'barbarian'.[8] Several dictionaries contained prefaces addressed to 'foreigners', this time assuming 'foreigner' as a synonym for a non-English speaker who needed

---

[4] See Chapter 1.

[5] James Davey and Richard Johns, *Broadsides: Caricature and the Navy 1756–1815* (Barnsley: Seaforth Publishing, 2012), 30–9.

[6] Michael Lewis, *A Social History of the Navy 1793–1815*, new ed. (London and Mechanicsburg, PA: Chatham Publishing, 2004 [1960]), 127–33; Stephen F. Gradish, *The Manning of the British Navy during the Seven Years' War* (London: Royal Historical Society, 1980), 79–81; Kevin McCranie, 'The Recruitment of Seamen for the British Navy, 1793–1815: "Why Don't You Raise More Men?"', in Donald Stoker, Frederick C. Schneid, and Harold D. Blanton (eds.), *Conscription in the Napoleonic Era: A Revolution in Military Affairs?* (London and New York: Routledge, 2009), 84–101, at 85, 95; Christopher Lloyd, *The British Seaman 1200–1860: A Social Survey* (London: Collins, 1968), 122, 158–9, 196, 212–20, 267; Stephen Conway, *Britannia's Auxiliaries: Continental Europeans and the British Empire, 1740–1800* (Oxford: Oxford University Press, 2017), 30–1. For examples in popular culture, see *Horrible Histories*, series 4, episode 12, written by Laurence Ricard (BBC, 2012); *Bloody Foreigners: The Untold Battle of Trafalgar*, series 1, episode 3 (Channel 4, 28 June 2010).

[7] Samuel Johnson, *A Dictionary of the English Language*, 10th ed. (London: various, 1792), n.p.; *Johnson's Dictionary of the English Language in Miniature* (London: S. Jordan, 1795), 89.

[8] Johnson, *Dictionary*, n.p.

pronunciation advice; although 'the Provincials' (Irish, Scots, and Welsh) were treated as a separate category, the distinction was self-evidently arbitrary.[9] 'Foreign' also had a raft of other meanings, which would seem to turn a 'foreign Royal Navy sailor' into a living oxymoron: 'remote', 'not allied', 'not belonging'; 'excluded', 'not admitted', 'held at a distance'; and 'extraneous'.[10] This jumble of the geographical, the legal, the pejorative, the linguistic, and the extrinsic has filtered into a blurry historiographical presence. We still know very little about who exactly these 'foreigners' were: on their experiences, demographic traits, social and legal status, cultural diversity, motivations, and on the ways in which the Navy integrated and utilised them. That the 'foreigner' has remained out of focus, I argue, is more than an accident. It is constitutive of the original essence of both naval and national history.

Maritime communities, seafaring work, and oceanic trade and travel are now firmly associated with transnational history.[11] Yet, few fields have traditionally plotted their course further away from transnational history than British naval history. By the end of the eighteenth century, the Royal Navy had come to symbolise Britannia herself and her might, and ever since then, it has remained a powerful focus of national pride. The French Wars marked a crucial moment: especially in the wake of victories, in public discourse and collective imagination, Jack Tar *was* the nation, manly, sturdy, well-fed, and punching weak foreign enemies across the globe (see **Figure I.1**). Jack Tar was anything but a 'foreigner' and had nothing in common with foreigners (**Figure I.2**). Britain's superiority at sea and the mythology of Britons' unique, racialised predisposition to seafaring became deeply intertwined with national self-identification, and naval history formed the core of this system of beliefs.[12] In the nineteenth and early twentieth centuries, histories of the British Navy

[9] Thomas Sheridan, *A Complete Dictionary of the English Language, both with regard to Sound and Meaning*, 2nd ed. (London: Charles Dilly, 1789), xviii, liii-[lxii].

[10] Johnson, *Dictionary*, n.p.

[11] Some key examples: Marcus Rediker, *Between the Devil and the Deep Blue Sea: Merchant Seamen, Pirates, and the Anglo-American Maritime World, 1700–1750* (Cambridge: Cambridge University Press, 1987); Maria Fusaro and Amélia Polónia (eds.), *Maritime History as Global History* (St John's, Newfoundland: International Maritime Economic History Association, 2010); Renaud Morieux, *The Channel: England, France and the Construction of a Maritime Border in the Eighteenth Century* (Cambridge: Cambridge University Press, 2016).

[12] Cynthia Fansler Behrman, *Victorian Myths of the Sea* (Athens, OH: Ohio University Press, 1977); Morieux, *Channel*, 6–9. On Britain's maritime commercial identity, see also Geoff Quilley, '"All Ocean Is Her Own": The Image of the Sea and the Identity of the Maritime Nation in Eighteenth-Century British Art', in Geoffrey Cubitt (ed.), *Imagining Nations* (Manchester and New York: Manchester University Press, 1998), 132–52.

Figure I.1 James Gillray, *Fighting for the Dunghill: – or – Jack Tar Settl'ing Buonaparte* (20 November 1798).
Image: Bodleian Libraries, University of Oxford, Bodleian Library Curzon b.18(82), CC BY-NC-SA 3.0 https://digital.bodleian.ox.ac.uk/objects/117e5402–9b4a–42c2–8a7f–93c6b0e6d7b9/.

were biographies of admirals and captains, sweeping accounts of battles and campaigns, or ambitious descriptions of the Navy's historical and strategic trajectory.[13] Later, new studies of the administrative, logistical, and technological aspects of naval power began to appear.[14] The focus of this scholarship was ultimately the same as that advocated by J. K. Laughton in 1898, at the height of the 'New Navalism' movement: exploring 'the lessons of national importance which are to be sought for in the history of our navy, "the wall and fence of the kingdom"'.[15]

[13] For two examples of the latter, see William James, *The Naval History of Great Britain, from the Declaration of War by France, in February 1793; to the Accession of George IV. in January 1820*, 6 vols., new ed. (London: Richard Bentley, 1886); A. T. Mahan, *The Influence of Sea Power upon the French Revolution and Empire, 1793–1812*, 2 vols. (Boston: Little, Brown, and Company, 1892).

[14] See, for example, Daniel A. Baugh, *British Naval Administration in the Age of Walpole* (Princeton, NJ: Princeton University Press, 1965). For an overview, see Roger Knight, 'Changing the Agenda: The "New" Naval History of the British Sailing Navy', *The Mariner's Mirror* 97:1 (2011), 225–42.

[15] J. K. Laughton, 'The National Study of Naval History', *Transactions of the Royal Historical Society* 12 (1898), 81–93, at 81. On 'New Navalism', see W. Mark Hamilton, *The Nation and the Navy: Methods and Organization of British Navalist Propaganda, 1889–1914* (New York and London: Garland Publishing Inc., 1986).

Figure I.2 G. M. Woodward, *An English Sailor at a French Eating House* (30 May 1805).
Image: Bodleian Libraries, University of Oxford, Bodleian Library Curzon b.24(26), CC BY-NC-SA 3.0 https://digital.bodleian.ox.ac.uk/objects/1b14e8f7–0388–4bd7–b219–720613876b4c/.

Much has changed, of course, in the past few decades, and only uninformed observers could deny the current sophistication of the field.[16] Recent studies have explored in detail the functioning of various departments of naval administration, as arms of the eighteenth-century British state: naval history has thus become a fruitful branch of political and financial history.[17] From the 1960s onwards, thanks to pioneers such as Michael Lewis and Nicholas Rodger, naval social history has also received much attention.[18] Fresh and detailed research has now appeared on many aspects of life in the Navy – patronage, discipline, gender, sexuality, health, and religion, to name but a few.[19] Cultural

[16] The best example is perhaps Quintin Colville and James Davey (eds.), *A New Naval History* (Manchester: Manchester University Press, 2018).
[17] See, for example, Clive Wilkinson, *The British Navy and the State in the Eighteenth Century* (Woodbridge: The Boydell Press, 2004); Roger Knight and Martin Wilcox, *Sustaining the Fleet, 1793–1815: War, the British Navy and the Contractor State* (Woodbridge: The Boydell Press, 2010).
[18] Rodger, *Wooden World*; Lewis, *Social History*; N. A. M. Rodger, *The Command of the Ocean: A Naval History of Britain, 1649–1815* (London: Allen Lane, 2004).
[19] Examples include Evan Wilson, *A Social History of British Naval Officers, 1775–1815* (Woodbridge: The Boydell Press, 2017); John Morrow, *British Flag Officers in the French Wars, 1793–1815: Admirals' Lives* (London and New York: Bloomsbury Academic,

historians, in turn, have analysed public representations and perceptions of the Navy.[20] Yet, all of these topics, and related debates, have once again been tackled entirely within the framework of national history. That naval history is inescapably *inter*national has long been pointed out, and some historians have successfully deployed comparative approaches, but almost no one has attempted to go further, focusing on cross-national movement, or testing the edges of the national itself.[21]

Given that the Royal Navy is a national institution, this would seem relatively unproblematic. Whilst its ships travelled all over the world, they remained legally national territory,[22] and directly controlled by a branch of the British state, fighting to defend national interest. The aim here is not to suggest that the British Navy ultimately was not British, or that the national framework does not remain the most simple and obvious way of approaching its study. However, a national and a transnational perspective are not contradictory. They only clash if we overemphasise either fluidity of movement or the importance and autonomy of 'nation-states'.[23] Eighteenth-century Britain was not a self-contained island: it maintained

2018); S. A. Cavell, *Midshipmen and Quarterdeck Boys in the British Navy, 1771–1831* (Woodbridge: The Boydell Press, 2012); B. R. Burg, *Boys at Sea: Sodomy, Indecency, and Courts Martial in Nelson's Navy* (Basingstoke: Palgrave Macmillan, 2007); Laurence Brockliss, John Cardwell, and Michael Moss, *Nelson's Surgeon: William Beatty, Naval Medicine, and the Battle of Trafalgar* (Oxford: Oxford University Press, 2005); Richard Blake, *Evangelicals in the Royal Navy 1775–1815: Blue Lights & Psalm-Singers* (Woodbridge: The Boydell Press, 2008).

[20] See, for example, Isaac Land, *War, Nationalism, and the British Sailor, 1750–1850* (New York: Palgrave Macmillan, 2009); Margarette Lincoln, *Representing the Royal Navy: British Sea Power, 1750–1815* (Aldershot and Burlington, VT: Ashgate, 2002); Timothy Jenks, *Naval Engagements: Patriotism, Cultural Politics, and the Royal Navy 1793–1815* (Oxford and New York: Oxford University Press, 2006).

[21] One very recent exception, on which see more below, is Niklas Frykman, *The Bloody Flag: Mutiny in the Age of Atlantic Revolution* (Oakland, CA: University of California Press, 2020). For examples of comparative naval history, see Jan Glete, *Navies and Nations: Warships, Navies and State Building in Europe and America, 1500–1860*, 2 vols. (Stockholm: Almqvist & Wiksell International, 1993); Evan Wilson, AnnaSara Hammar, and Jakob Seerup (eds.), *Eighteenth-Century Naval Officers: A Transnational Perspective* (Cham: Palgrave Macmillan, 2019).

[22] James Fulton Zimmerman, *Impressment of American Seamen* (New York: [NA], 1925), 19–20; A. D. Watts, 'The Protection of Alien Seamen', *The International and Comparative Law Quarterly* 7:4 (1958), 691–711, at 703, 708; *Letters by Historicus on Some Questions of International Law* (London and Cambridge: Macmillan and Co., 1863), 201–12.

[23] Andreas Wimmer and Nina Glick Schiller, 'Methodological Nationalism and Beyond: Nation-State Building, Migration and the Social Sciences', *Global Networks* 2:4 (2002), 301–34. For a balanced defence of the nation-state framework, see, for example, Rogers Brubaker, 'In the Name of the Nation: Reflections on Nationalism and Patriotism', *Citizenship Studies* 8:2 (2004), 115–27, at 118–20; Michael McGerr, 'The Price of the "New Transnational History"', *The American Historical Review* 96:4 (1991), 1056–67; Morieux, *Channel*, 18.

deep ties not only with its empire, but also with continental Europe – politically, intellectually, and through the movement of individuals.[24] The Navy itself was pervious to such influences and movements.

In Pierre-Yves Saunier's definition, one of the roles of transnational history is to acknowledge and assess 'foreign contributions to the design, discussion and implementation of domestic features'.[25] Casting foreigners' service as a 'contribution' undoubtedly has its value, as well as important implications in the current political climate. The presence of sailors from every corner of the world in an institution that had come to represent Britons' special maritime vocation and self-sufficiency draws attention to a glaring contradiction, between reality and the crudest forms of mythology.[26] Yet, examining these men's employment also allows us to explore larger issues. Transnational history, as Sven Beckert puts it, is a 'way of seeing'.[27] Integrating 'foreigners' into the study does not simply add one little tile to the history of the British Navy; it significantly shifts the paradigm by which many historiographical debates on it are conducted. The opposite is also true: the cosmopolitanism of the Navy can be deployed as a case study to cast light on the functioning of transnational processes and state power. This book is not a history *of* the Navy, as much as a history *through* the Navy: by locating the transnational in the depths of the national, I want to question the very categories on which this distinction is built. Peering into the meaning of 'foreignness', that mysterious dark matter defined by otherness and absence, also spills a mordant puddle of light on its complementary – the comforting notion of national belonging. The conceptual instability of the nation is well known.[28] More can be said, however, by analysing what it is supposedly defined against.

1.1 Mercenaries, Sailors, and Foreigners

In British eighteenth-century naval historiography, only three categories of 'foreign' sailors have ever been examined in some detail, and mostly

---

[24] Stephen Conway, *Britain, Ireland, and Continental Europe in the Eighteenth Century: Similarities, Connections, Identities* (Oxford: Oxford University Press, 2011); idem, 'Continental Connections: Britain and Europe in the Eighteenth Century', *History* 90:299 (2005), 353–74; idem, *Britannia's Auxiliaries*.

[25] Pierre-Yves Saunier, *Transnational History* (Basingstoke: Palgrave Macmillan, 2013), 3.

[26] This tension is also mentioned in Conway, *Britain, Ireland, and Continental Europe*, 254.

[27] C. A. Bayly et al., '*AHR* Conversation: On Transnational History', *The American Historical Review* 111:5 (2006), 1441–64, at 1459.

[28] The classics in a truly immense literature include, for example, Benedict Anderson, *Imagined Communities: Reflections on the Origin and Spread of Nationalism*, 2nd ed. (London and New York: Verso, 1991); E. J. Hobsbawm, *Nations and Nationalism since 1780: Programme, Myth, Reality*, 2nd ed. (Cambridge: Cambridge University Press, 1990); Ernest Gellner, *Nations and Nationalism* (Oxford: Blackwell Publishers, 1983).

because their situation tied into broader themes. First, we have a legal type of 'foreigner': the impressment (forced recruitment) of American citizens has been widely discussed, as a catalyst for the War of 1812, and potentially, earlier on, the American Revolution.[29] This scholarship examines the origins of US citizenship and diplomacy, or the culture of American seamen specifically. The perspective of the British Navy itself is rarely central. Second, some research has focused on Black sailors, mainly in the context of Atlantic history, and, again, of American shipping and nation-building, although the British naval service is also considered.[30] Finally, several studies have appeared on the European employment of seamen from the Indian Ocean (called 'Lascars'), examining their legal status, organised recruitment, language, religion, work practices, and resistance.[31] However, this literature mostly concentrates on the nineteenth century, and it deals with British shipping at large, rather than the Navy.

If much is left to be written on Americans, Black men, and Lascars, other 'foreign' groups remain almost totally obscure: most notably, continental European seamen in the British Navy are still virtually unstudied, even though, I will show, they were the single largest group of 'foreigners' employed. We are also missing the big picture, one that can incorporate all these men not simply as distinct groups, but as an integral

[29] Lewis, *Social History*, 434–9; Paul A. Gilje, *Free Trade and Sailors' Rights in the War of 1812* (Cambridge: Cambridge University Press, 2013); Zimmerman, *Impressment*; Nathan Perl-Rosenthal, *Citizen Sailors: Becoming American in the Age of Revolution* (Cambridge, MA and London: The Belknap Press of Harvard University Press, 2015); Joshua Wolf, '"To Be Enslaved or Thus Deprived": British Impressment, American Discontent, and the Making of the *Chesapeake-Leopard* Affair, 1803–1807', *War & Society* 29:1 (2010), 1–19. On impressment in the Atlantic world, see Denver Brunsman, *The Evil Necessity: British Naval Impressment in the Eighteenth-Century Atlantic World* (Charlottesville, VA and London: University of Virginia Press, 2013); Christopher P. Magra, *Poseidon's Curse: British Naval Impressment and Atlantic Origins of the American Revolution* (Cambridge: Cambridge University Press, 2016).

[30] See, for example, W. Jeffrey Bolster, *Black Jacks: African-American Seamen in the Age of Sail* (Cambridge, MA and London: Harvard University Press, 1997); Charles R. Foy, 'The Royal Navy's Employment of Black Mariners and Maritime Workers, 1754–1783', *The International Journal of Maritime History* 28:1 (2016), 6–35.

[31] Conrad Dixon, 'Lascars: The Forgotten Seamen', in Rosemary Ommer and Gerald Panting (eds.), *Working Men Who Got Wet: Proceedings of the Fourth Conference of the Atlantic Canada Shipping Project July 24–July 26* (St. John's, Newfoundland: Memorial University of Newfoundland, 1980), 263–81; Michael H. Fisher, 'Working across the Seas: Indian Maritime Labourers in India, Britain, and in Between, 1600–1857', *International Review of Social History* 51 (2006), 21–45; Aaron Jaffer, *Lascars and Indian Ocean Seafaring, 1780–1860: Shipboard Life, Unrest and Mutiny* (Woodbridge: The Boydell Press, 2015); Marika Sherwood, 'Race, Nationality and Employment among Lascar Seamen, 1660 to 1945', *Journal of Ethnic and Migration Studies* 17:2 (1991), 229–44; Jesse Ransley, 'Introduction: Asian Sailors in the Age of Empire', *Journal for Maritime Research* 16:2 (2014), 117–23.

part of a diverse workforce. Transnational approaches, however, have blossomed in two close historiographical areas: the study of eighteenth-century armies, on the one hand, and maritime trade and employment, on the other. Naval sailors had a foot in each of these worlds, and this is key to understanding how the Navy related to either.

Early modern European militaries were often very cosmopolitan. Fully 'autarkic' models of the 'fiscal-military' state fail to remind us how warfare could only be waged with the help of external resources, material, economic, and human.[32] Much has now been written on the role of foreigners, particularly Germans, within the Georgian British Army.[33] Eighteenth-century non-native forces fought mostly as separate 'auxiliary' units for hire, but also as foreign regiments, or as 'subsidy troops' provided by financially weaker allies.[34] As we shall see, these models of enlistment were only adopted by the British Navy in some specific cases. Because of the military functions of a fleet, however, there are some obvious parallels to be drawn. Both the term 'mercenary' (presupposing 'financial gain' as a soldier's 'dominant motive') and the more generic 'international volunteer' can apply to many of the seamen who served in the Navy, joining as individuals for a multiplicity of reasons.[35] These concepts are undoubtedly useful, in particular, when we examine the British state's perspective on 'foreigners'' recruitment.

Nevertheless, I would further argue that military skill was secondary to these men's professional seafaring skill. The same sailors moved between

---

[32] Peter H. Wilson, '"Mercenary" Contracts as Fiscal-Military Instruments', in Svante Norrhem and Erik Thomson (eds.), *Subsidies, Diplomacy, and State Formation in Europe, 1494–1789; Economies of Allegiance* (Lund: Lund University Press, 2020), 68–92.

[33] See, for example, Rodney Atwood, *The Hessians: Mercenaries from Hessen-Kassel in the American Revolution* (Cambridge: Cambridge University Press, 1980); Stephen Conway, 'Continental European Soldiers in British Imperial Service, c.1756–1792', *English Historical Review* 129:536 (2014), 79–106; idem, 'Continental Connections', 365, 368–9.

[34] Wilson, '"Mercenary" Contracts', 80–91; Chen Tzoref-Ashkenazi, 'German Auxiliary Troops in the British and Dutch East India Companies', in Nir Arielli and Bruce Collins (eds.), *Transnational Soldiers: Foreign Military Enlistment in the Modern Era* (Basingstoke: Palgrave Macmillan, 2013), 32–49, esp. at 32–4; Atwood, *Hessians*, 1.

[35] For the debate on the concepts of 'mercenary' and 'international volunteer', see Sarah V. Percy, 'Mercenaries: Strong Norm, Weak Law', *International Organization* 61 (2007), 367–97, esp. 371–2; Juan Carlos Zarate, 'The Emergence of a New Dog of War: Private International Security Companies, International Law, and the New World Disorder', *Stanford Journal of International Law* 34:75 (1998), 75–162, at 79, 120–5; Janice E. Thomson, *Mercenaries, Pirates, and Sovereigns: State-Building and Extraterritorial Violence in Early Modern Europe* (Princeton, NJ: Princeton University Press, 1994), esp. ch. 4; Nir Arielli and Bruce Collins, 'Introduction: Transnational Military Service since the Eighteenth Century', in eidem, *Transnational Soldiers*, 1–12.

the naval and the merchant service of various countries in an entirely seamless fashion, repeatedly throughout their working lives. As such, they are better understood as international and transnational migrant labourers. Their migration was transnational because, in many cases, it did not consist of one simple movement across borders, from Country A to Country B, but it involved a complex network of connections, disconnections, uprootings, and returns.[36]

Marcus Rediker, nearly forty years ago, theorised that eighteenth-century maritime labourers shared a sense of seafaring working class identity, cutting across national borders.[37] Of particular interest is his point that 'the seaman's international life and labor require an international history'.[38] Here, he used 'international' as a synonym for 'transnational': he was not concerned with interactions between countries, but with the individuals and ideas that slip and live across their borders. His methodology led him 'to adopt... [Jack Tar's] almost nomadic mobility and to follow him from port to port around the globe' – although it has to be observed that the Jack Tar he followed was almost exclusively the British and North American seaman.[39] Rediker's hypotheses have been pursued only occasionally in naval historiography, and specifically by scholars like Niklas Frykman, focusing on the impact of sailors' cosmopolitanism on national disaffection and mutiny.[40]

Even leaving aside the discussion of class formation and rebellion, it is now clear that seamen, in the merchant service even more than in navies, often moved on an international rather than narrowly national employment market. Recent quantitative studies, somewhat undermining Rediker's more extreme claims, have shown that national recruitment

---

[36] For a critique of simplistic equations between migration and 'uprooting', see Nina Glick Schiller, Linda Basch, and Cristina Szanton Blanc, 'From Immigrant to Transmigrant: Theorizing Transnational Migration', *Anthropological Quarterly* 68:1 (1995), 48–63.

[37] Rediker, *Between the Devil and the Deep Blue Sea*; Peter Linebaugh and Marcus Rediker, *The Many-Headed Hydra: Sailors, Slaves, Commoners, and the Hidden History of the Revolutionary Atlantic* (London and New York: Verso, 2000).

[38] Rediker, *Between the Devil and the Deep Blue Sea*, 7–8.   [39] ibid.

[40] Frykman, *Bloody Flag*; idem, 'The Mutiny on the Hermione: Warfare, Revolution, and Treason in the Royal Navy', *Journal of Social History* 44:1 (2010), 159–87; idem, 'Seamen on Late Eighteenth-Century European Warships', *International Review of Social History* 54 (2009), 67–93; idem, 'Connections between Mutinies in European Navies', in Clare Anderson, Niklas Frykman, Lex Heerma van Voss, and Marcus Rediker (eds.), *Mutiny and Maritime Radicalism in the Age of Revolution* (Cambridge: Press Syndicate of the University of Cambridge, 2013), 87–107; Nicole Ulrich, 'International Radicalism, Local Solidarities: The 1797 British Naval Mutinies in Southern African Waters', in Anderson et al., *Mutiny and Maritime Radicalism*, 61–85.

remained paramount, especially on intra-European and protected Atlantic routes.[41] Still, migratory movements of seafarers across borders are far from a 'recent' phenomenon, as is claimed by some sociologists.[42] For example, the Dutch Republic absorbed large amounts of seafaring workforce, up until the middle of the eighteenth century, particularly from Norway.[43] Maritime spaces were often zones of transnational circulation and exchange.[44] As pointed out by Stephen Conway, something akin to a 'maritime international' drew together seamen from across Europe: its pillars were a shared market of employment and broad similarity in customs, professional competence, and cultural background.[45] Cross-border movement extended to navies, as well, and for some it has received more scholarly attention than for the British.[46]

[41] Matthias van Rossum, Lex Heerma van Voss, Jelle van Lottum, and Jan Lucassen, 'National and International Labour Markets for Sailors in European, Atlantic and Asian Waters, 1600–1850', in Fusaro and Polónia, *Maritime History as Global History*, 47–72 (53–4 for Britain); Perl-Rosenthal, *Citizen Sailors*, 25–33. Cf. Rediker, *Between the Devil and the Deep Blue Sea*, 80.

[42] Helen Sampson, *International Seafarers and Transnationalism in the Twenty-First Century* (Manchester and New York: Manchester University Press, 2013), 11. For a criticism of this modernist trend in the sociology of transnationalism, see also Nancy L. Green, *The Limits of Transnationalism* (Chicago, MI and London: The University of Chicago Press, 2019), ch. 2.

[43] Sølvi Sogner, 'Norwegian-Dutch Migrant Relations in the Seventeenth Century', in Louis Sicking, Harry de Bles, and Erlend des Bouvrie (eds.), *Dutch Light in the 'Norwegian Night': Maritime Relations and Migration across the North Sea in Early Modern Times* (Hilversum: Uitgeverij Verloren, 2004), 43–56; Ivonne Lucker, 'Jacob Dirksen: A Norwegian Sailor in the Dutch Republic (1727–1754)', ibid., 81–91; Jelle van Lottum, *Across the North Sea: The Impact of the Dutch Republic on International Labour Migration, c. 1550–1850* (Amsterdam: Aksant, 2007), 28–36, 61–2, 67–9, 76, 80–2, 86, 93.

[44] Morieux, *Channel*; idem, 'Diplomacy from Below and Belonging: Fishermen and Cross-Channel Relations in the Eighteenth Century', *Past & Present* 202 (2009), 83–125; David Abulafia, 'Mediterraneans', in W. V. Harris (ed.), *Rethinking the Mediterranean* (Oxford: Oxford University Press, 2005), 64–93; van Lottum, *Across the North Sea*, 15–17; Juliette Roding and Lex Heerma van Voss (eds.), *The North Sea and Culture (1550–1800): Proceedings of the International Conference Held at Leiden 21–22 April 1995* (Hilversum: Verloren, 1996).

[45] Conway, *Britain, Ireland, and Continental Europe*, 245–65. For detailed comparisons, see Paul van Royen, Jaap Bruijn, and Jan Lucassen (eds.), *'Those Emblems of Hell'? European Sailors and the Maritime Labour Market, 1570–1870* (St John's, Newfoundland: International Maritime Economic History Association, 1997).

[46] Jaap R. Bruijn, *The Dutch Navy of the Seventeenth and Eighteenth Centuries* (St. John's, Newfoundland: International Maritime Economic History Association, 2011), 48–9, 116–18, 121, 160–1, 177–9, 189, 193; Luca Lo Basso, 'Lavoro marittimo, tutela istituzionale e conflittualità sociale a bordo dei bastimenti della Repubblica di Genova nel XVIII secolo', *Mediterranea* 12 (2015), 147–68; Dmitry Fedosov, 'Under the Saltire: Scots and the Russian Navy, 1690s–1910s', in Mark Cornwall and Murray Frame (eds.), *Scotland and the Slavs: Cultures in Contact 1500–2000* (Newtonville, MA: Oriental Research Partners, 2001), 21–53; Anthony Cross, 'The Elphinstones in Catherine the Great's Navy', ibid., 55–71; K. L. Koziurenok, 'Голландске офицеры в Российском

No study, however, has yet explored the implications of this phenomenon. Naval service was more strictly regulated and anchored in the structures of the state than service in merchant marines, and it was invested with more explicit national and patriotic meaning, most evidently in the British case. It is this peculiar middling status, halfway between the nation and the 'deep blue sea', that allows a study of transnationalism from within the national: how could socially and culturally 'motley crews' also develop at the heart of the most national of institutions?

'Foreign Jack Tars', we may say, simultaneously belonged to three social categories: they were transnational maritime labourers; they were supplementary military manpower; and they were, by a multiplicity of varying definitions, 'foreigners'. This takes us to the three main aims of this book.

I.2   A Transnational Navy, State Boundaries, and the Meanings of Foreignness

First, and most generally, integrating 'foreign seafarers' in a study of the late eighteenth-century Royal Navy helps us to integrate the Navy itself into maritime history. Simply taking for granted its overall 'Britishness' leaves us with an incomplete understanding of its functioning and social history. Because the Navy was a national institution, too often we tend to forget that it was also part and parcel of the cosmopolitan maritime world. If Britain and its Navy did not exist in an isolated bubble, but in a global labour marketplace, studying naval history transnationally can be enlightening, and it complicates, for example, current debates on the quality of shipboard life and on modalities of recruitment. Understanding 'foreign' tars as migrant workforce invites us to see the Navy as they (and many of their British colleagues) did, from the inside out and from the outside in, as an employer among many others. As a corollary, it also refines our perception of the Navy's relationship to 'Britishness' itself, which was far from straightforward: by some definitions, 'foreignness' could encompass recruits from various parts of the British Isles and Ireland, and this complexity remains relatively understudied by naval historians – particularly if we consider that the Royal

Военно-морском флоте (вторая половина XVIII – начало XIX в.)', in Yu. N. Bespiatykh, Ia. V. Veluvenkamp, and L. D. Popova (eds.), *Нидерланды и северная Россия* (Saint Petersburg: Русско–Балтийский информационный центр, 2003), 299–324.

Navy was one of the largest centralised institutions spanning across the 'Four Nations'.[47]

Second, by also looking at foreign tars as imported military force, this book highlights some cracks in the power of the late eighteenth- and early nineteenth-century state. These cracks are especially visible when we observe the cross-border movement of individuals and the compromises that governments were forced to make for the state's survival. One of the 'parameters' of eighteenth-century naval power was the availability of seamen, especially skilled and trained: manpower was always a scarce commodity during wartime, much in demand.[48] Thus, throughout the French Wars, searching for hands and putting each man to use in the best possible way were constant preoccupations of the British naval administration and officer classes. This was an endeavour complicated not only by the fact that Britain's population did not suffice to crew both its merchant marine and its Navy, but also by Parliament's refusal to adopt seafarers' systematic registration and conscription, common in other contemporary European countries.[49] Recruitment and management, therefore, adopted 'utilitarian' principles in order to maximise efficiency with the available resources.[50] This very pragmatism, I will argue, is what led to significant numbers of 'foreigners' being entered into the fleet, and it is a leitmotif in every chapter. It reveals the inherent flexibility and weakness of categorisations, not only cultural but also legal, based on 'foreignness' or 'nativity'. The compromise made by a

---

[47] For existing work on the subject, see Patrick Walsh, 'Ireland and the Royal Navy in the Eighteenth Century', in John McAleer and Christer Petley (eds), *The Royal Navy and the British Atlantic World, c. 1750–1820* (London: Palgrave Macmillan, 2016), 51–76; Brian Lavery, *Shield of Empire: The Royal Navy and Scotland* (Edinburgh: Birlinn, 2007); Sara Caputo, 'Scotland, Scottishness, British Integration and the Royal Navy, 1793–1815', *The Scottish Historical Review* 97:1 (2018), 85–118; J. D. Davies, *Britannia's Dragon: A Naval History of Wales* (Stroud: The History Press, 2013); J. D. M. Robertson, *The Press Gang in Orkney and Shetland* (Kirkwall: Orcadian (Kirkwall Press), 2011); Donald John Macleod, 'Hebridean Service with the Royal Navy', in The Islands Book Trust, *Island Heroes: The Military History of the Hebrides* (Isle of Lewis: Islands Book Trust, 2010), 73–90.

[48] Nicholas Rodger, '"A Little Navy of Your Own Making": Admiral Boscawen and the Cornish Connection in the Royal Navy', in Michael Duffy (ed.), *Parameters of British Naval Power 1650–1850* (Exeter: University of Exeter Press, 1992), 82–92, at 82–4; Baugh, *British Naval Administration*, 147–240.

[49] Jaap R. Bruijn, 'Seafarers in Early Modern and Modern Times: Change and Continuity', *International Journal of Maritime History* 17:1 (2005), 1–16, at 4–6; Baugh, *British Naval Administration*, 170, 233–40; Frykman, 'Seamen', 67–70. For an overview of the British manning problem, see J. Ross Dancy, *The Myth of the Press Gang: Volunteers, Impressment and the Naval Manpower Problem in the Late Eighteenth Century* (Woodbridge: The Boydell Press, 2015).

[50] Roger Morriss, *The Foundations of British Maritime Ascendancy: Resources, Logistics and the State, 1755–1815* (Cambridge: Cambridge University Press, 2011), 223–70.

state ignoring the boundaries of subjecthood in its recruitment helped the Navy to keep its ships at sea. Theoretically, however, this compromise opened to question the state's own self-definition. Christopher Tozzi has shown that the need for men during the French Wars forced even a state like France, which, he argues, was explicitly 'nationalising' its armies and 'purging' them of foreigners, to continue its use of them.[51] The British state, as far as the wartime Navy was concerned, had no such gatekeeping policies or rhetoric in place: its open welcoming of foreign manpower was not done hypocritically, covertly, or ashamedly – it explicitly blurred the frontiers of subjecthood.

Foreign mercenaries in general are sometimes described as 'surrogates for state power', in a Weberian sense.[52] They are, therefore, intrinsically problematic for the self-styled modern 'nation-state'. The use of Hessian troops during the American Revolution, for example, offered a powerful rhetorical tool to rival states, which accused Britain of ruthless exploitation and national insufficiency; for similar reasons, British patriotic narratives routinely elided foreign recruits during the French Wars.[53] However, naval 'mercenaries' are a very special case. While non-British soldiers in the Army were usually arranged into special regiments,[54] the eighteenth-century Navy fully integrated most foreigners. This peculiarity makes it an especially valuable context for exposing fissures in a state's self-definition. Often, forces recruited outside a country remain distinguishable from native troops, and thus justifiable, because they serve specific functions, diplomatic, political, and strategic. Ancien Régime foreign regiments brought 'prestige' and diplomatic connections to a monarch.[55] This was rarely the case for foreign sailors enlisted in the Navy – if anything, their recruitment soured international relations with countries like the United States. Furthermore, mercenaries have historically been hired either as disposable or as uniquely effective, specially trained units.[56] Many of Napoleon's foreign regiments in the 1800s and 1810s were cannon fodder to spare Frenchmen, as he did not hesitate to

---

[51] Christopher J. Tozzi, *Nationalizing France's Army: Foreign, Black, and Jewish Troops in the French Military, 1715–1831* (Charlottesville, VA and London: University of Virginia Press, 2016).

[52] Zarate, 'Emergence of a New Dog of War', 81.

[53] H. D. Schmidt, 'The Hessian Mercenaries: The Career of a Political Cliché', *History* 43:149 (1958), 207–12; Sarah Percy, *Mercenaries: The History of a Norm in International Relations* (Oxford: Oxford University Press, 2007), 123–8; Kevin Linch, 'The Politics of Foreign Recruitment in Britain during the French Revolutionary and Napoleonic Wars', in Arielli and Collins, *Transnational Soldiers*, 50–66, at 61–3.

[54] For some exceptions, see Conway, 'Continental European Soldiers', 90. For the French case, see Tozzi, *Nationalizing France's Army*, 18.

[55] Tozzi, *Nationalizing France's Army*, 28–30.   [56] Ibid., 30.

admit.[57] Later, the 1831 French Foreign Legion was intended as a politically 'expendable' corps, which could be sacrificed instead of citizen manpower on remote dangerous frontlines.[58] This book, however, finds few patterns of discrimination or preference in the way in which the Royal Navy treated and deployed its British or foreign men. Again, this stems from the fact that, whilst a regiment could be fully foreign, ships were nearly always mixed communities, each only comprising a more or less significant *minority* of foreigners. Most foreigners in the Navy were intended as recruits like any other man, qualitatively not too different, naval officers hoped, from the average British sailor. They were not, in this sense, an 'outsider' force. In every respect, for as long as the war lasted, the British state opened its doors to them. It is for this reason that they can serve well to highlight some of its institutional contradictions.

Linked to this, the final and core intent of this book is using the Royal Navy at the turn of the nineteenth century as a case study for deconstructing various meanings and facets of the term 'foreigner'. Escaping the reification of nations and 'nation-states' can be especially difficult for the historian setting out to examine 'non-British' sailors in the British Navy, an object already identified a priori through the framework of national and state categories. When interrogated in front of prize courts, early modern seamen were asked to specify their birthplace, residence, citizenship(s), and to which sovereign they believed they owed allegiance.[59] Someone could theoretically give a different answer to each of these points, yet it was, and is, all too easy to conflate them bluntly into labels of state belonging, and – as we saw from contemporary dictionaries – into the term 'foreigner' itself. This is even before we begin to consider cultural or ethnic understandings of the word. Some men could be born abroad, but be British subjects, owing to the *jus sanguinis* rule (being children of British men); some could be born in Britain, or be subjects, but speak little English, as in the case of many from the so-called Celtic Fringe. Looking at each of these traits separately – birthplace, subjecthood, allegiance, language, culture, racialised identification, residence, and social integration – allows us to assess the weight of different components of foreignness.

This framing of the issue draws inspiration from the work of various scholars. Simona Cerutti has shown that, in early modern communities,

[57] Guy C. Dempsey, Jr., *Napoleon's Mercenaries: Foreign Units in the French Army under the Consulate and Empire, 1799–1814* (London and Mechanicsburg, PA: Greenhill Books and Stackpole Books, 2002), 21–2.

[58] Tozzi, *Nationalizing France's Army*, 218–19.

[59] Van Rossum et al., 'National and International Labour Markets', 67.

the word *étranger* did not necessarily signify coming from the outside: being a 'foreigner', or a 'stranger', could be the result of religious or familial extraneity, or lack of stakes, property, investment, or settlement in the local community – social and cultural factors often independent of one's provenance.[60] Jan Lucassen and Rinus Penninx have also highlighted the difference between legal, cultural, and social meanings of the term 'newcomer' in Dutch immigration history, and how it could reflect different realities.[61] Sociologist Rogers Brubaker has suggested ways of bypassing the fallacious reification of categories of analysis like 'ethnicity', 'race', and 'nation' into 'groups': from a cognitivist position, he treats these terms as expressing 'perspectives on the world rather than entities in the world'. As he warns, adopting this approach to studying ethnicity, 'we may end up not studying ethnicity at all' – something that is true of most of *Foreign Jack Tars*.[62] Finally, Norbert Elias has argued that the fundamental social tension between 'the established' and 'the outsiders' undergirds more superficial class, ethnic, and racial conflict: greater or lesser social 'cohesion', in his view, is the true key to explaining group power differentials.[63] In naval crews that were 'melting pots' of origins and backgrounds, and in which experience and skill were the currency of respect, Elias's theory can probably explain shipboard interactions, and in fact official policy, better than abstract notions of national belonging. It also explains how and why these melting pots, 'prefabricated communities' of 'interchangeable' parts, to use James Belich's definition of a 'crew', were splintered by national rhetoric as soon as the peace slashed the job market in 1815.[64]

This book, then, examines, in turn, different types of 'foreign seamen': foreign seamen identified as such by their birthplace abroad, by legal alienhood, by linguistic or religious extraneousness, by culturally constructed physical differences, and finally simply by the fact of being 'immigrants' or 'refugees', with the core of their interests, their domicile, and 'home' situated away from British territory and jurisdiction. The question 'How did a foreigner fit in the late Hanoverian British Navy?' is

---

[60] Simona Cerutti, *Étrangers: Étude d'une condition d'incertitude dans une société d'Ancien Régime* (Montrouge Cedex: Bayard, 2012).

[61] Jan Lucassen and Rinus Penninx, *Newcomers: Immigrants and Their Descendants in the Netherlands, 1550–1995* (Amsterdam: Het Spinhuis, 1997), 7–17.

[62] Rogers Brubaker, *Ethnicity without Groups* (Cambridge, MA and London: Harvard University Press, 2004), quotes at 4, 27.

[63] Norbert Elias and John L. Scotson, *The Established and the Outsiders: A Sociological Enquiry into Community Problems*, 2nd ed. (London: SAGE, 1994).

[64] On the notion of 'crew culture' see James Belich, *Making Peoples: A History of the New Zealanders from Polynesian Settlement to the End of the Nineteenth Century* (Auckland: Penguin Books, 1996), 428–36.

not answered by looking at different traits of a blurry 'foreigner' character, but rather, it is answered multiple times, in slightly different ways, with regards to multiple possible understandings of what 'foreignness' meant. Wartime pressures, I argue, ensured that legal and cultural differences were easily accommodated by a needy state. Not so, however, for the consequences of the physical and social displacement brought by migration, which the Navy could attempt to compensate, but was unable to erase. The story of 'foreign' Jack Tars is not simply one of romantic citizenship of the sea, of fluid movement and advantageous freedom from barriers and conventions: it alerts us to the fundamental harshness of transnational lives, not only, as other historians have warned, when migrants face the contrasting claims and rules of multiple states,[65] but *even* when states do not actually interfere, and, in fact, try to encourage transnationality.

The choice of focusing on the Revolutionary and Napoleonic Wars reflects the fact that this conflict marked, in many ways, the culmination and the end of a specific phase in British naval history. Recruitment practices radically changed thereafter: impressment, which had branded naval social relations and power structures, attracted increasing stigma and was never deployed again.[66] As discussed in the Conclusion, the Navy did not stop employing foreigners in 1815, but no other British war before the twentieth century reached a scale demanding recruitment measures as desperate as the large, systematic, and indiscriminate use of aliens. When such a war eventually came along, a new model based on 'citizen armies' had reached full maturity even in Britain. Nineteenth-century colonial developments also supplied the British military and shipping services with cheap workforce on a completely different basis, as would have been impossible in the late eighteenth century.

Looking backwards instead of forwards, the boundaries are more blurred, but not invisible. Classic naval historiography, reflecting interpretations of the English mid-eighteenth century as a socially and politically stable period, posits a substantial shift in models of shipboard organisation: the collaborative and 'negotiated' order of the 1750s and 1760s, it is argued, eventually gave way to stricter forms of top-down discipline and hierarchy by the end of the century.[67] If the earlier Navy was such an organically balanced system, focusing on the Seven Years'

---

[65] See most recently Green, *Limits of Transnationalism*.
[66] C. J. Bartlett, *Great Britain and Sea Power 1815–1853* (Oxford: Clarendon Press, 1963), 48–9, 305–7; Michael Lewis, *The Navy in Transition 1814–1864: A Social History* (London: Hodder and Stoughton, 1965).
[67] Rodger, *Wooden World*, 12, 205–11.

War (1756–1763) instead of the French Wars may well lead to different conclusions on the institutional fit of individuals who were in any way perceived as outsiders. Officers' notions of order and discipline, we shall see, played a crucial role in their perception of 'foreign' hands. Equally, while it is undeniable that several themes discussed in this book can be traced back especially to the time of the American War (1775–1783), important differences also intervened between the 1780s and the 1790s. The French Wars were characterised not only by a spike in national feeling, explicitly appropriating the figure of 'Jack Tar', but also by a mobilisation of manpower and resources that was unprecedented in 'scope and intensity', and was accompanied by a new 'culture of war'.[68] Following the ebb and flow of conflict, overall, the British Navy mushroomed throughout the second half of the eighteenth century, peaking during these two decades: after the end of the American War, in 1785, Navy Office figures put it at 438 ships; this was relatively similar to the 357 of 1765, but little more than half of the 800 it was to count in 1805.[69] Already by 1796, with over 114,000 seamen mobilised, the fleet had topped by 7,000 its previous high figure of 1783: seamen borne for wages were to reach a staggering 142,000 in 1810.[70] In that year, the Royal Navy surpassed the size of all other European fleets combined.[71] Therefore, we can postulate that this period represents an especially vivid context for observing the ways in which the British state negotiated its use of external resources, and individuals navigated the boundaries between countries at war.

Our main concern here are the 'common seamen', the 'hands' who dwelled 'before the mast'. A running theme, we shall see, is that much of what applied to them did not apply to officers, who were in far less demand, and bound by different social and cultural norms.[72] The principal characters in this book are also, for the vast majority, men. The Navy and its men were heavily indebted to the labour of women, but, for this very reason, 'foreign Poll' and 'foreign Jenny Tar' deserve their own book(s), which I very much hope that someone will write soon.[73] The evidence deployed in what follows varies widely from chapter to chapter:

---

[68] David Bell, *The First Total War: Napoleon's Europe and the Birth of Modern Warfare* (London: Bloomsbury, 2007), specific quotes at 7, 12.

[69] Morriss, *Foundations*, 132.   [70] Ibid., 226–7.

[71] Glete, *Navies and Nations*, II, 376–9.

[72] On officers, see Sara Caputo, 'Mercenary Gentlemen? The Transnational Service of Foreign Quarterdeck Officers in the Royal Navy of the American and French Wars, 1775–1815', *Historical Research* 94:266 (2021), 806–26.

[73] For existing work on naval women, see Margarette Lincoln, *Naval Wives & Mistresses* (London: National Maritime Museum, 2007); Suzanne J. Stark, *Female Tars: Women aboard Ship in the Age of Sail*, 2nd ed. (London: Pimlico, 1998).

it includes memoirs and personal letters, material and iconographic sources, and most of all the rich records of the British, Dutch, and Neapolitan governments and admiralties – which themselves range from lists of persons to official certificates, from vast amounts of detailed correspondence to court martial records and shipboard journals. The collective regulating voices of the Navy and the state tower powerfully across this study, but those of many individuals emerge with equal force. *Foreign Jack Tars*, then, is structured to flow from the general to the particular. It begins with the most 'impersonal' types of history – quantitative and legal – concerned with the flattening, classificatory gaze and official language of the state. In the central section, the principal actors are the Navy officers who made decisions on seamen's recruitment and management, often influenced by stereotypes of national character. We observe their ideas, feelings, beliefs, and practices at first generally, and then through two specific geographical studies, drawing on fragments of microhistories. Finally, we turn to the seamen themselves, and their motivations and experience.

Chapter 1 tackles 'foreigners' defined as such on the basis of their birthplace, as recorded in naval musters. Questioning the meaningfulness of this type of categorisation, I deploy it as a working hypothesis: through quantitative methodologies, I compare the rating, numeracy, and age of various groups of foreign-born men in the Navy to those of British- and Irish-born shipmates. The results show that Irish seamen, rather than foreigners, displayed the most distinctive patterns: a line sharply drawn between the men born in the British Isles and Ireland and those born abroad is a relatively poor predictor of demographic or employment differences.

The 'foreigners' discussed in Chapter 2 were 'aliens' by law. Legal distinctions ultimately mattered little to the Navy. Britain was rather open to immigration, and, during wartime, most residual disabilities of non-subjects were eased for common sailors, who were needed and overall welcome. At the same time, military necessity meant that any advantages which their status as subjects of a different sovereign should have granted them, most notably protection from impressment, were often ignored in practice. In courts martial, special accommodations and concessions were granted informally, as a result of perceived cultural ignorance, rather than on the basis of legal status. Finally, naturalisation was liberally bestowed on naval seamen, but it was, I argue, an unstable and largely irrelevant benefit.

Chapters 3 and 4 examine three features that were deemed expressions of 'national characters' in the eighteenth and nineteenth centuries: language and religion (Chapter 3) and racialised physical traits, including both phenotype and supposed medical predisposition or resistance to specific diseases and climates (Chapter 4). Chapter 4 also tackles concepts of filthiness and hygiene, which straddled the line between cultural and racial prejudice. Racism certainly had a strong impact on individual lives. However, it was in the nature of the service to pursue efficiency: naval organisation and discipline were very efficacious at smoothing, ignoring, or accommodating diversity or assumed diversity, to maximise the exploitation of human resources.

Chapters 5 and 6 are case studies, further exploring the conclusions of Chapters 3 and 4, and dissecting some of the long-standing stereotypes through which Britons have imagined 'northern' and 'southern' continental Europeans. First, we analyse an example of 'hard-to-integrate' foreigner: British officers and policymakers saw southern Italian sailors through the lens of substantial racial prejudice, stemming from cultural, linguistic, and religious differences, mutual unfamiliarity, and the Mediterranean's geographical distance from the British world. This does not mean that it was deemed impossible to turn Neapolitans and Sicilians into useful and respected crewmembers. However, it did mean that, if this was to happen, they needed to be completely removed from the structures of their own state, and particularly from the influence and perceived corruption and inefficiency of Neapolitan and Sicilian officers.

In contrast to southern European sailors, men from the North Sea basin were Britain's cultural and geographical neighbours, as discussed in Chapter 6: their linguistic integration was smoother, and the stereotypes surrounding them more positive. Unlike the Neapolitan, the leadership and administration of the old Dutch Admiralties had much in common with the British. In an unusual experiment, mimicking the Army's tradition of segregating foreigners into special regiments, four ships entirely manned by Dutch men and officers were even allowed into the British service, in 1800. A microhistory of this episode illustrates how similar institutional cultures facilitated this kind of integration and administrative translation. The Admiralty also held individual sailors from Denmark and Norway in high esteem, as reliable and skilled manpower. At the same time, the very qualities of these men made them potentially formidable rivals and enemies, meaning that their recruitment caused diffidence and concerns among British elites and seafarers. In a way, then, the problems that the Navy had to grapple with when recruiting southern and northern European men were specular to each other: prejudice held the former as poor workforce, and thus of little use, and the latter as exceptional workforce, and therefore dangerous. In neither case, I argue, did the negative implications ultimately carry much weight for an institution that was only concerned with sustaining a strenuous war effort.

Finally, Chapter 7 aims to reframe the ways in which we discuss the social history of naval crews, by looking at their geographical displacement. Being foreign 'by provenance', an immigrant or refugee, changed a man's experience in and of the Navy and conferred completely different weight and meaning to the supposed advantages and disadvantages of the service. The historiographical debate on standards of living and pay in the Navy needs to be expanded, not simply looking at the difference between the British Navy and the British merchant service, but also at the options seamen would have on other countries' seafaring markets. Moreover, supposed perks of naval employment, such as pensions and wage payments to families, were only attractive and valuable if the place of residence of a wife or widow or the place of retirement of the sailor himself lay within reach of the British administrative machine. Some motivations for enlistment also elude the relatively neat dichotomy between 'volunteer' and 'pressed man', which is the usual focus of debate: being 'loaned' by another monarch, or enslaver; escaping indefinite confinement in a British war prison; seeking freedom from enslavement; and exile. These nuanced situations and motives only become visible when we look at Navy crews as 'motley crews', social and cultural mixtures of mobile and uprooted individuals often transcending the traditional image of the British 'Jack Tar', and very different from the modern model of citizen serviceman. Overall, labels of foreignness based on birthplace, subjecthood, or cultural difference may have been easily neglected when the Navy aimed at efficiency and maximising the available manpower. But this could not erase practical circumstances. The material, concrete aspects of social and geographical displacement left deep marks on the lives of Foreign Jack Tars.

Part I

The State

1 Countable 'Foreigners'
Birthplace and Demographic Profiles

'Were there many?' The question immediately confronts any historian who sets out to study 'foreigners' in the Navy. Because the Navy's transnational recruitment has been neglected in common narratives, the very existence of the topic needs to be justified. Was the 'foreign' presence at all significant? How large was it, exactly? We often take proportions and hard figures as synonyms for relevance. Yet, this question requires, first of all, that we choose a definition of 'foreignness'. Were there many *of what*?

The only way in which 'foreign' seamen can be even partially quantified, on the basis of the existing sources, is by looking at foreignness by birthplace, as stated in naval records: in other words, at how many men were born abroad. This is highly problematic. The legal definition of a foreigner, grounded in the language of state regulations and bureaucracy, does not necessarily overlap with cultural and social definitions. Most importantly, birthplace does not fully coincide with legal status itself, either: men born of a British father were British subjects, regardless of location, and naturalisation and imperial conquest nominally reshuffled many sailors' situations.[1] These complexities frequently surface in the sources. In 1814, for example, when Admiral Bickerton forwarded to the Admiralty a list of 'foreigners' requesting discharge, their applications came under heavy scrutiny. Despite their foreign birth, the Lords Commissioners observed, 'most of these men appear by their Christian & sur names to be british'; they were 'not to be discharged', it was ruled, 'till by minute inquiry it shall be ascertain'd that they are really foreigners'. If the weight of birthplace as a personal characteristic was problematic, so was its exact classification: as the response to Bickerton continued, 'their Lords do not see why a native of H M. Island of Jamaica is call'd a foreigner'.[2]

---

[1] See Chapter 2.
[2] UK National Archives, Kew [henceforth TNA], ADM 1/1236, Letters from Commanders-in-Chief, Portsmouth, 1814, nn. 802–900, 812, Richard Bickerton to John Wilson Croker, 12 May 1814.

In spite of these ambiguities, however, which I discuss in more detail in Chapter 2, geographical birthplace remained the proxy that the British state and Admiralty most frequently used to account for their seamen's provenance and national belonging, as a convenient legal and administrative shortcut. Naval personnel registers were mainly designed for British seamen. This book argues that the Navy was one of the earliest and largest transnational institutions, but it was also one of the earliest and largest nationwide institutions: in an era pre-dating systematic and 'reliable' personal documentation, placing each man by parish and county of birth (assimilated to residence) likely helped to perform very practical bureaucratic functions, such as tracking down deserters or persons owed wage and pension payments. The result was that, from the second half of the eighteenth century, it was birthplace that served as a meaningful way to identify a naval seaman officially, over and above, for example, allegiance, subject status, language spoken, religion, or racialised appearance, which were not mentioned. We shall focus on these other aspects later in the book, using more traditional qualitative sources.

This chapter, instead, applies inferential statistical methods to analyse a sample of 4,392 men, drawn from Navy 'muster books'. In each vessel, a new muster was compiled every two months, reporting, on a pre-printed template, information on most crew members' date and mode of entry, name, rank or rating, discharge, and, from the 1760s onwards, birthplace and age.[3] These data allow us to ask not only how many foreign-born men served in the wartime Navy (a point which, we shall see, cannot be fully answered after all), and whether this changed over time or across stations, but also some further questions: were they more or less professionally experienced than Britons and Irishmen? Were they rated on average in the same way? Were they older or younger? What were the variations between foreign groups? In short, how far did being born abroad *matter*?

1.1   Birthplace as a Category of Analysis

Classifying individuals by birthplace is not a straightforward task. The musters only partially deploy the language of states: often sailors are listed with their hometowns ('Gottenburgh', 'Naples', 'Oporto') or geo-graphical areas that were not political units at the time ('East Indies', 'Germany', 'Italy'). Some Londoners even indicated their address:

---

[3] These survive in TNA, ADM 36 and 37. For more details, see N. A. M. Rodger, *Naval Records for Genealogists* (Kew: PRO Publications, 1998), 45–55.

'Monmouth Street London', 'Prescot Street Goodmanfields', 'Grosvenor Street London', 'City Road London'.[4] As noted by Walker Connor, mass self-identification with modern 'nations' was far from natural and complete even into the twentieth century, with many people across Europe privileging regional or local belonging.[5] The muster annotations are the product of a hybrid series of inputs and interpretations, to which the official language of the state, the state's servants (ship clerks), and the individual sailors all contributed in proportions nearly impossible to reconstruct. Birthplace, or, more precisely, 'Place and County where born', assuming a British or Irish locality, was requested by the printed template of the muster, regardless of its pertinence or importance to the individual; the individual chose the form in which to declare it, or perhaps was left at a loss, but the clerk then further reinterpreted this, often misunderstanding, simplifying, or asking for clarifications. Thus, a complex chain of imperfect communication in most cases scrambles any evidence of individual perspectives. If, on the one hand, we find street names, on the other, there are entire musters in which the names of Scottish or Welsh places are replaced with a generic 'Scotland' and 'Wales', clearly showing a bureaucratic levelling hand.[6] This creates a fundamental methodological problem, because pieces of information that are qualitatively different from one another, in terms of scale, purpose, and even origin (who chose the final formulation, the sailors or the clerk?) must be reduced to 'categories of equivalence' for the purpose of statistical analysis.[7]

As a result of these difficulties, the categories into which I have grouped the men are sometimes arbitrarily defined, to make analysis viable and avoid excessive fragmentation. This might seem an undue interpretative intrusion.[8] In particular, it will appear strikingly simplistic to the global historian that even small European countries receive a separate identification, whilst immense, conceptually nebulous territorial units like 'Africa', 'East Indies', 'West Indies', and 'America' are deployed as equivalent. In most cases, however, this classification is based on categories 'indigenous'

---

[4] TNA, ADM 36/15379, Muster Book of HMS *Centurion*, February–March 1802, ff. 18, 28, 36, 37.

[5] Walker Connor, *Ethnonationalism: The Quest for Understanding* (Princeton, NJ: Princeton University Press, 1994), 220–4.

[6] Caputo, 'Scotland, Scottishness, British Integration and the Royal Navy' (2018), 93–6.

[7] On this process, see Alain Desrosières, *The Politics of Large Numbers: A History of Statistical Reasoning*, trans. Camille Naish (Cambridge, MA and London: Harvard University Press, 1998).

[8] For a discussion of this pitfall, see A. W. Carus and Sheilagh Ogilvie, 'Turning Qualitative into Quantitative Evidence: A Well-Used Method Made Explicit', *Economic History Review* 62:4 (2009), 893–925, at 913–14.

to the sources.[9] Apart from 'Guinea', no specific birthplace was used in the musters for African-born sailors, and terms like 'West Indies' or 'East Indies' recur throughout (admittedly together with 'Jamaica', 'Nevis', 'Martinique', 'India', or 'Bengal').[10] 'America' or 'N. America' is also an extremely frequent label, and in no instance is the term 'United States' deployed. 'Italy' and 'Germany', too, occasionally appear in the musters, showing that either the sailors themselves, or the clerks who listed them, subscribed to such notions. At the same time, there was no instance of a sailor born in 'Europe', as there was none of men from 'England' or 'Great Britain'. Details and focus got blurrier further away from the fleet's institutional home.

As pointed out by Alain Desrosières, while the conventions and objects on which statistical analysis is performed are necessarily constructed, this does not mean that they cannot be valid, if a large enough 'investment' was put into their meaning by those who produced the sources.[11] Grouping 'foreigners' by specific birthplaces, then, can in itself become a working hypothesis: this chapter will test the value of such groupings, and how far they reflected genuine differences in demographic traits or rating.

1.2   Missing Information

I mentioned before that the exact numbers of foreign-born men in the Navy are likely impossible to establish. This is because musters lack birthplace data for three important categories: officers (commissioned and warrant), supernumeraries (men in excess of the established crew size), and Royal Marines (shipboard soldiers). We do know that, legally, only subjects could receive commissions and warrants, so a large proportion of officers likely came from Britain, Ireland, or, at most, British imperial territories, even allowing for the imperfect birthplace–subjecthood overlap.[12] However, qualitative evidence suggests that thousands of foreign-born men served as supernumeraries and Marines. When in 1794 Lord Hood obtained at least 440 seamen 'on loan' from Malta, his flagship's muster showed no significant increase in the number

---

[9] For this use of the term, see Renaud Morieux, 'Indigenous Comparisons', in John H. Arnold, Matthew Hilton, and Jan Rüger (eds.), *History after Hobsbawm: Writing the Past for the Twenty-First Century* (Oxford: Oxford University Press, 2017), 50–75.

[10] On the European tendency to flatten 'Africa' into one undifferentiated unit, see Nicholas Hudson, 'From "Nation" to "Race": The Origin of Racial Classification in Eighteenth-Century Thought', *Eighteenth-Century Studies* 29:3 (1996), 247–64, esp. 249–51, 258.

[11] Desrosières, *Politics*, 12, 333, 337.

[12] Some officers' birthplace can be reconstructed from alternative records. For data, see Lewis, *Social History*, 60–80; Wilson, *Social History*, 16–17, 67–9.

of Maltese in the main complement. Yet, the 'Supernumeraries for Victuals and Wages' section contains at least twenty able seamen marked as 'Maltese volunteers', all enlisted in February 1794, as well as several other Italian names and men from Corsican gunboats, entered in the following months and all later discharged together.[13] Similar circumstantial evidence exists for Royal Marines: in October 1795, the Chatham Marine division reported to the Admiralty that 'nearly the whole of the Recruits at Head Quarters' were Dutch.[14]

Quantitative studies of birthplace, then, remain necessarily constrained. However, mine and other scholars' figures provide a minimum point of reference in terms of 'head counts' by country. Moreover, Marines were rather different from seamen, demographically and professionally, so a study excluding them wholesale remains valid when assessing biases in 'foreigners'' rating. Supernumeraries were less distinguishable, but their employment was sometimes, by definition, extraordinary and/or temporary. The lack of data on them does not invalidate our statistical analysis of the main complement.

1.3   Numbers of Foreigners: Existing Studies

Bearing in mind these caveats, can we even roughly estimate how many foreign-born men served in the Navy? According to some Admiralty returns, the fleet employed 14,732 'foreigners', between seamen and Marines, in 1811; 12,324 in 1812; and 13,205 in 1813; this amounted to nearly 10% of the whole establishment.[15] In a few ships, however, the figure was far higher: for example, between 1798 and 1801, about 42.8% of the sailors who served in HMS *Santa Dorotea*, in the Mediterranean, were born outside Britain and Ireland.[16] Some scholars, most notably Nick Slope and J. Dancy, have conducted quantitative analysis on select muster books, for various purposes: together, this body of work indicates a foreign presence oscillating between 3% and 18% of each ship's complement (see **Table 1.1**).

The total sample is large and drawn from a range of stations and moments of the French Wars. Further study is needed, however, because none of the ships analysed were selected specifically with the question of foreigners in mind. Moreover, collating several unrelated studies to reach

---

[13] TNA, ADM 36/11578, Muster Book of HMS *Victory*, May–October 1794, ff. 91–107. See also Section 5.1.2.

[14] TNA, ADM 12/67, Admiralty Digest 1795 – Part 2, 63.14, summary of letter from Lieut. Colonel Elliot, 20 October 1795.

[15] Morriss, *Foundations*, 230, 248.

[16] TNA, ADM 36/14389, Muster Book of HMS *Santa Dorotea*, January–February 1801.

Table 1.1. *Proportions of foreigners in existing studies of musters*

Study	Foreigners	Crew total	Percentage of foreigners
J. Dancy sample, Revolutionary Wars[1]			8
Trafalgar, 1805[2]	1,352	c.21,500	6
Vessels at Plymouth, 1804–5[3]		4,474	11
HMS *Bellerophon*, 1812[4]			8
HMS *Caledonia*, 1810[5]	51	585	9
HMS *Emerald* – 1, 1795–1805[6]	137	782	18
HMS *Emerald* – 2, 1806–11[7]	77	441	18
HMS *Glenmore*, 1796–1803[8]	37	438	9
HMS *Implacable*, 1808[9]	81	563	14
HMS *San Domingo*, 1812[10]	62	439	14
HMS *Trent*, 1796–1803[11]	74	827	9
HMS *Warspite*, 1812[12]	97		>17
North Sea, 1797[13]			
HMS *Ardent*	43	531	8
HMS *Belliqueux*	50	450	11
HMS *Circe*	9	167	5
HMS *Monmouth*	52	528	10
HMS *Montagu*	63	597	11
HMS *Venerable*	17	517	3

[1] Dancy, *Myth*, 50. This is out of a total including men with ambiguous or missing birthplaces.

[2] Rodger, *Command*, 498. This percentage is so low compared to others because the total includes officers.

[3] Ibid.

[4] David Cordingly, *Billy Ruffian – The Bellerophon and the Downfall of Napoleon: The Biography of a Ship of the Line, 1782–1836* (London: Bloomsbury, 2003), 210. A man from the Isle of Man and one from Guernsey are included in the 8% of foreigners, unlike in my sample.

[5] Brian Lavery (ed.), *Shipboard Life and Organisation, 1731–1815* (Aldershot and Brookfield, VT: Ashgate, 1998), 451. But compare Lavery, *Shield of Empire*, 148–9.

[6] Nick Slope, 'Serving in Nelson's Navy: A Social History of Three Amazon Class Frigates Utilising Database Technology' (unpublished PhD thesis, University of West London, 2006), 125–7.

[7] Ibid., 137–8.

[8] Ibid., 147–9.

[9] Lewis, *Social History*, 129. Lewis lists one Canadian as 'British', but I have shifted him to 'Others'.

[10] J. S. Bromley (ed.), *The Manning of the Royal Navy: Selected Public Pamphlets 1693–1873* (London: Navy Records Society, 1974), 352–3.

[11] Slope, 'Serving', 114–15.

[12] Lewis, *Social History*, 131.

[13] Sara Caputo, 'Scotland, Scottishness and the British Navy, c.1793—1815' (unpublished MSc dissertation, The University of Edinburgh, 2015), 61–6.

a general conclusion has the advantage of breadth, but it will inevitably result in haphazard coverage. Some of these databases include Royal Marines (where their birthplace information has exceptionally survived) and commissioned officers, others do not, and there is a heavy bias towards ships present at pivotal battles or in certain periods of the war. Precisely because of the subjectivity inevitable in quantification, different researchers will interpret and classify categories in different ways, making their work not fully commensurable.[17] Finally, again because they were not interested in foreigners specifically, almost none of these projects went on to compare demographic characteristics by birthplace. This issue is compounded by the fact that no inferential statistical method has ever been applied to the data to test its significance. This is what we can attempt here, using a fresh sample designed for the purpose.

1.4   Sampling Criteria

The first criterion I used for selection was picking ships during service in a remote foreign station. In future, a very large separate project might attempt to sample evenly across the fleet, in both foreign and home stations, but for the present, I am specifically concerned with extremes, because the only extensive study of musters, Dancy's, focuses instead on home waters.[18] Ships serving in foreign parts, we may assume, would tend to have higher proportions of foreign-born seamen, owing to manning necessities and the limited options to fulfil them abroad.[19] In order to maximise this effect, the three stations I selected were those situated the furthest away from Britain (East Indies, Jamaica, and the Cape of Good Hope, the latter replaced by the Leeward Islands for 1793, when it was still a Dutch colony) and known for having high mortality rates connected to climate and disease. Furthermore, within each of these stations, I chose the ship which had sailed from England the longest time before, using Admiralty ship lists (see **Table 1.2**).[20] This had two

---

[17] Pat Hudson and Mina Ishizu, *History by Numbers: An Introduction to Quantitative Approaches*, 2nd ed. (London and New York: Bloomsbury, 2017), 17–18.

[18] Dancy, *Myth*.

[19] Slope, 'Serving', 125–7; John Rankin, 'Nineteenth-Century Royal Navy Sailors from Africa and the African Diaspora: Research Methodology', *African Diaspora* 6 (2013), 179–95, at 183; Christian Buchet, 'La Royal Navy et les levées d'hommes aux Antilles (1689–1763) : difficultés rencontrées et modalités évolutives', *Histoire, économie et société* 4 (1990), 521–43; Baugh, *British Naval Administration*, 215–24.

[20] TNA, ADM 8/69, The Present Disposition of His Majesty's Ships and Vessels in Sea Pay, 1 December 1793; ADM 8/83, The Present Disposition of His Majesty's Ships and Vessels in Sea Pay, 1 March 1802; ADM 8/100, The Present Disposition of His Majesty's Ships and Vessels in Sea Pay, 1 July 1813.

Table 1.2. *Ships included in the sample*

Date of the muster	Station	Ship	Rate and complement	Date of commissioning	Date of sailing from England
December 1793	East Indies	HMS *Minerva*	5th (38 guns), 297	May 1790	December 1790
	Jamaica	HMS *Penelope*	5th (32 guns), 220	August 1792	October 1792
	Leeward Islands	HMS *Blanche*	5th (32 guns), 220	September 1792	November 1792
March 1802	East Indies	HMS *Centurion*	4th (50 guns), 343	November 1792	November 1793
	Jamaica	HMS *Quebec*	5th (32 guns), 254	January 1799	April 1799
	Cape of Good Hope	HMS *Jupiter*	4th (50 guns), 343	July 1794	April 1796
July 1813	East Indies	HMS *Bucephalus*	5th (32 guns), 270	March 1807	November 1807
	Jamaica	HMS *Garland*	6th (22 guns), 175	March 1807	November 1807
	Cape of Good Hope	HMS *Astrea*	5th (36 guns), 284	June 1810	October 1810

advantages: it further enhanced any effect of foreign stationing on crew composition, and expanded the sample of men. The ships within which the selection was performed were all, for the sake of sample uniformity, broadly defined 'frigates', from sixth to fourth rate.[21]

The sampled musters were extracted from three specific points in time. The first is December 1793: this date is chosen to represent the beginning of the Revolutionary Wars and was selected instead of February (the actual commencement of the conflict) so that ships could have time to be commissioned and sail to their respective stations. In fact, in all three cases, the date of sailing from England precedes the start of hostilities (December 1790, and October and November 1792).[22] This sample, then, gives us a picture of the initial status quo before the war and during its first few months. The second moment is March 1802, marking the end of the Revolutionary Wars. In this case, the three ships had been in their respective stations for between three and almost nine years.[23] Because of the way in which musters were compiled, with all names being retained on them even after their owners had been discharged, the sample thus returns the overall composition of crews throughout an extended portion of the Revolutionary Wars. Similar considerations apply to the third and final cluster, consisting of three ship musters from July 1813: the discharge dates of some men go back to 1807.[24] July 1813 stands in for the end of the war, instead of June 1815, because subsequent Admiralty list books are now lost.[25]

As can be deduced from the above, the numbers of men per ship, year, and station range widely, from 237 valid names on the HMS *Blanche* muster to 850 on HMS *Centurion*'s. This depends on how long each ship had been in commission, how large a turnover of men it had experienced, and its initial nominal complement size (with a variation of about 130 men between the smallest and the largest). Obtaining equal samples,

---

[21] Fourth rates under sixty guns were not deemed line-of-battle ships, so I have included them. See Rodger, *Command*, xxvii.

[22] TNA, ADM 36/11194, Muster Book of HMS *Minerva*, November–December 1793; ADM 36/11981, Muster Book of HMS *Penelope*, November–December 1793; ADM 36/ 12177, Muster Book of HMS *Blanche*, August–December 1793.

[23] TNA, ADM 36/15379, Muster Book of HMS *Centurion*, February–March 1802; ADM 36/14781, Muster Book of HMS *Quebec*, March–April 1802; ADM 36/15330, Muster Book of HMS *Jupiter*, March–April 1802.

[24] TNA, ADM 37/3701, Muster Book of HMS *Bucephalus*, June–July 1813; ADM 37/ 4303, Muster Book of HMS *Garland*, June–July 1813; ADM 37/4214, Muster Book of HMS *Astrea*, July–August 1813.

[25] Alternative methods of reconstructing the disposition of ships did not allow performance of the sampling according to the same criteria.

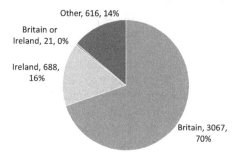

Sailors' origins (1793, 1802, and 1813 samples)

Other, 616, 14%

Britain or Ireland, 21, 0%

Ireland, 688, 16%

Britain, 3067, 70%

Figure 1.1 Origins of crews (1793, 1802, and 1813 samples).

however, was not a priority, as statistical tests can control for such differences in size. Several men also had to be expunged, because their birthplace was either missing or ambiguous.[26]

1.5   How Many Foreigners in Foreign Stations?

Overall, across the nine ships, men born outside Britain, Ireland, and the Channel Islands amounted to 14% of the total (**Figure 1.1**). There was, however, a significant variation from one period to the next, with their proportion rising from 6% in the 1793 sample to 15% in the 1802 sample, and 18% in the 1813 sample (**Figure 1.2**).[27] This trend clearly reflects the increasing difficulty of securing manpower from Britain, as the ongoing conflict drained national resources. Enlisting unskilled

---

[26] See Appendix 1.

[27] H_0: no association between origin and presence aboard RN ships at different stages of the war; $\chi^2(1) = 94.50348$, $p < .01$, $\varphi_c = 0.104$. Pearson's chi-square test serves to check whether an association exists between the membership of various categories (here, origin and stage of the war) that is stronger than that which chance would dictate. This depends on an assessment of the probability distribution of frequencies and is expressed by the value of p (anything under 0.01 signals high significance of the result). φ_c, ranging from 0 to 1, denotes the strength of the association. All the statistical tests in this and subsequent chapters were carried out through R and R Studio, using the following packages and previous versions of the same, from 2015 to 2021: Gregory R. Warnes, Ben Bolker, Thomas Lumley, and Randall C. Johnson, *gmodels: Various R Programming Tools for Model Fitting* (2018, version 2.18.1) https://cran.r-project.org/web/packages/gmodels/index.html; David Meyer, Achim Zeileis, and Kurt Hornik, *vcd: Visualizing Categorical Data* (2021, version 1.4-9) https://cran.r-project.org/web/packages/vcd/index.html. For an explanation of the mathematical concepts, see Andy Field, Jeremy Miles, and Zoë Field, *Discovering Statistics Using R* (London: SAGE Publications, 2012), 813–28. I am also indebted to Dr Nicole Janz and her course on *Basic Quantitative Analysis*.

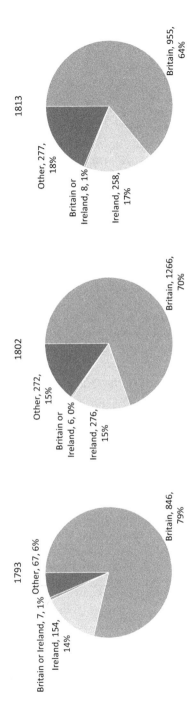

Figure 1.2 Origins of crews by time period.

so-called landsmen (non-sailors) to pad out crews could in the long run augment the pool of trained seamen, as even the greenest recruit gradually learned his ropes. However, even landsmen willing to join were not unlimited, given the parallel demands of the Army, militia, and wartime industry; simultaneously, thousands of professional seamen died in service, while the Navy kept growing and growing.

The number of foreigners also slightly varied by station, although, statistically, the effect size was almost negligible. They were fewest in the East Indies (11%), but 18% and 19%, respectively, at the Cape of Good Hope and Jamaica (**Figure 1.3**).[28] It is difficult to explain why the East Indies, which was the furthest station from Britain, should also have the lowest representation of foreign-born seamen. A conclusive answer will need further study of specific Indian Ocean naval recruitment practices. In merchant shipping, Lascar sailors, like African 'Kroomen' later in the nineteenth century, were recruited and contracted in groups, led by their own petty officers: it may well be that the Navy, too, listed them separately as supernumeraries.[29]

Overall, as can be seen from a breakdown of individual ships (**Figure 1.4**), the proportions of foreign-born men ranged widely, going from a mere 5% in HMS *Minerva* in the East Indies in 1793 to a rather impressive 23% for HMS *Garland* in Jamaican waters in 1813. This helps us to remember that a general study of the 'Navy' will always have to take into account the stark differences between ships, and the social specificity of these self-contained communities.

1.6   From Every Corner of the World

Where did these people come from? The United States (individual places, or 'America') is the single best represented country in the sample (**Figure 1.5**). This category is very problematic: aside from men whose subjecthood was contested, we know that impressed British sailors often tried to pass themselves off as Americans, hoping for discharge. At the same time, however, many American-born seamen were probably not listed as such, because their officers refused to acknowledge their

---

[28] $\chi^2(1) = 64.34136$, $p < .01$, $\varphi_c = 0.088$. The one Leeward Islands ship was not considered here.

[29] For data on Asian employment in European shipping, see van Rossum et al., 'National and International Labour Markets', 60–3. On Kroomen, see Rankin, 'Nineteenth-Century Royal Navy Sailors', 184–5.

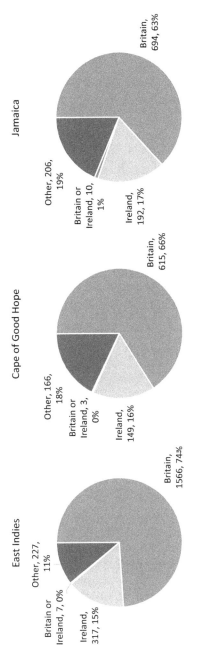

Figure 1.3 Origins of crews by station.

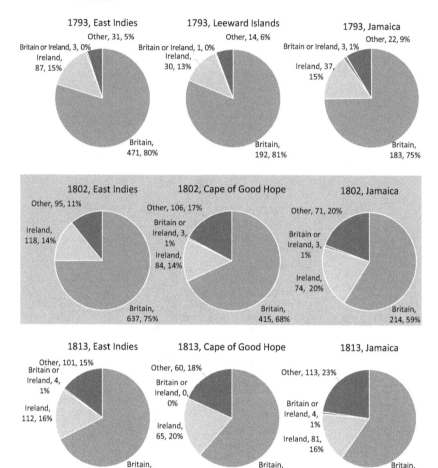

Figure 1.4 Origins of crews by ship.

origin.[30] Numerically, these two trends might go some way towards offsetting each other.

Whether skewed or not, the substantial number of Americans does not come as a surprise. Contrary to what we have learned to expect since the late nineteenth century, however, nearly half of foreign-born manpower was not provided by imperial or ex-imperial territories: it came from continental Europe. This is all the more significant if we remember that

[30] See Section 2.2.

Origins of Foreign Sailors (1793, 1802, and 1813)

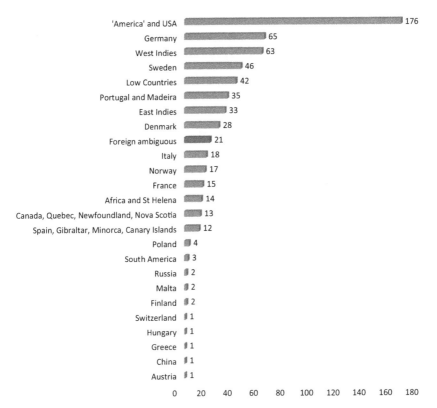

Figure 1.5 Origins of foreign sailors (1793, 1802, and 1813 samples) (n = 616).

the sample did not contain ships deployed in European waters. Sailors from Scandinavia – Swedes, Danes, Norwegians, and Finns (listed as such, even though Norway was then part of Denmark, and Finland of Sweden) – were the second largest origin group. Adding to these Germans and Dutchmen/Flemings, we see that seamen from Northern Europe actually outnumber even the Americans. Of all these birthplaces, 'Germany' was the most common, occasionally even listed as such. Whilst many men came from ports like Hamburg and the Hanseatic Towns, or Prussia, some were also from the hinterland: for example, Bavaria, Hanover, and Rhineland. Apart from the direct link between Hanover and Britain, we can likely trace this trend to the weakness and fragmentation of German states in the eighteenth century, which made them prime recruiting ground for other European forces – including the Dutch fleet and the British and Dutch East India Companies.[31] Additionally, the economic prospects of young labourers in northern German towns were scarce. As a result, local shipping was never short of recruits and paid extremely low wages: the lure of emigration to better-remunerated foreign service was strong.[32]

Third comes a category that I broadly framed as 'West Indies': very occasionally, this is all that was reported. Even when individual islands were listed, breaking down the sample along those lines would have made the figures very small and difficult to grasp. Organising seamen by imperial possessions would have been meaningless, too, given the frequency with which individual localities changed hands in those years. The musters, we should note, have little to say on the most meaningful social divides in the eighteenth-century Caribbean: not exact island of birth, but race and enslavement.

After West Indians, ranking relatively high on the list, are seamen from neutral or allied European countries, like Portugal and the various Italian states. We also encounter several men from parts of the world that were landlocked or remote from naval operations, including China, Austria, Hungary, and even Switzerland. Most important of all, however, is the fact that birthplace in a country nominally at war with Britain did not seem to preclude service: these crews counted many Danes, Dutchmen, and even Frenchmen.

On the whole, this sample of origins shows a remarkable geographical span. It questions established narratives of intra-imperial preference and displays the European contribution, even in extra-European stations. It also qualifies assumptions on the rigidity of state boundaries, national loyalties, and especially wartime allegiances. These themes will be elaborated in the rest of the book, but for now we may turn to testing whether origin translated into any form of demographic difference.

1.7   Skill, Numeracy, and Rating

Men aboard Royal Navy ships were rated and paid according to their experience: those relatively new to the profession were classed as 'lands-men', whereas seasoned sailors could be, in increasing order of ability,

---

[31] Arielli and Collins, 'Introduction', 3; Tzoref-Ashkenazi, 'German Auxiliary Troops', esp. 36; Atwood, *Hessians*, 7–21. On Dutch naval recruitment, see Frykman, 'Seamen', 73, 75.

[32] Walter Ried, *Deutsche Segelschiffahrt seit 1470* (Munich: J. F. Lehmanns Verlag, 1974), 138, 141.

'ordinary seamen' or 'able seamen'. Other categories aboard included boys (second or third class, depending on age), warrant officers (boatswain, carpenter, sailmaker, gunner, cook, cooper, schoolmaster, surgeon, master, and chaplain), their mates and crews, and other men in positions of some responsibility (petty officers), young gentlemen training to be commissioned officers (volunteers first class, midshipmen, and master's mates), and finally the commissioned officers themselves (lieutenants and the captain).[33] Many of the men cycled from one rating to the next in the same muster, being promoted or demoted, often multiple times. For the purpose of this study, I uniformly used the highest rating achieved.

The literature cautiously advances the hypothesis that foreigners would tend to be hired above a certain skill level (hence not as 'landsmen'), but at the same time not rise very often to the rank of petty officer, which carried responsibilities and required 'skill, trust and language skill'.[34] In Dancy's sample, foreigners were 5% of landsmen, 9% of ordinary seamen, 11% of able seamen, and 8% of petty officers.[35] These results might in good part depend on the fact that his study targeted ships picked at the moment they first sailed from England.[36] Presumably, as he points out, most foreign-born sailors who had reached Britain would have had at least some experience of seafaring. By looking at the opposite case – ships as far away from Britain as possible, and after as long a time as possible since commissioning – my study offers a complementary, if smaller, sample.

As shown in **Figure 1.6**, in the nine frigates selected, foreign-born sailors represented 16% of landsmen, 20% of ordinary seamen, and only 14% of able seamen. 13% of the foreigners were landsmen, as opposed to 10% of the Britons (**Figure 1.7**). Frigates' crews were generally the most skilled and 'elite', so this suggests that even larger numbers of foreign landsmen, in stations abroad, may have found their way onto the decks of other classes of vessel – ships of the line and sloops.[37] Away from British shores, the Navy's apparent hesitation to hire unskilled foreigners vanished. As we shall see when analysing age, it is unlikely that these foreign 'landsmen' were in reality underpaid and underrated sea wolves.

One further category, grouping together petty and warrant officers, as well as specialist artisans, saw the lowest representation of foreigners, at 10% only, this time closer to Dancy's findings. Foreign-born men were

[33] For a detailed overview, see Lewis, *Social History*, 86–90, 256–80.
[34] Dancy, *Myth*, 52.   [35] Ibid.   [36] Ibid., 6.
[37] I am grateful to Professor Michael Duffy for this observation.

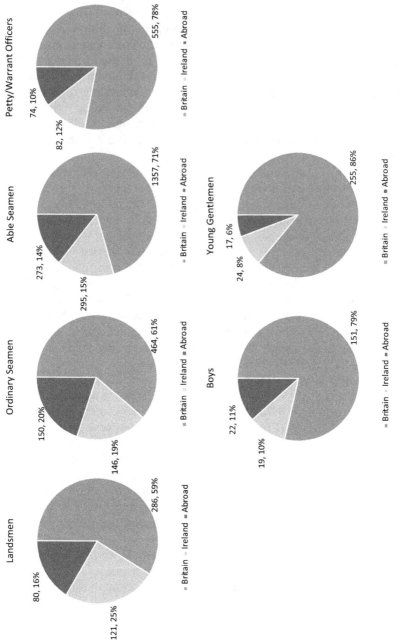

Figure 1.6 Origins of crews by rating.

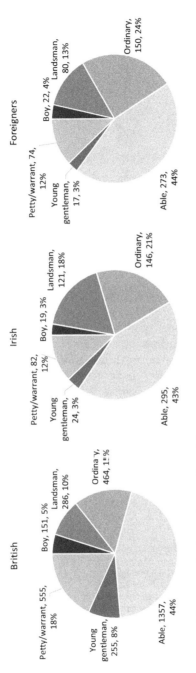

Figure 1.7 Ratings of crews by origin.

British

Petty/warrant, 555, 18%

Young gentleman, 255, 8%

Boy, 151, 5%

Landsman, 286, 10%

Ordinary, 464, 15%

Able, 1357, 44%

Irish

Petty/warrant, 82, 12%

Young gentleman, 24, 3%

Boy, 19, 3%

Landsman, 121, 18%

Ordinary, 146, 21%

Able, 295, 43%

Foreigners

Petty/warrant, 74, 12%

Young gentleman, 17, 3%

Boy, 22, 4%

Landsman, 80, 13%

Ordinary, 150, 24%

Able, 273, 44%

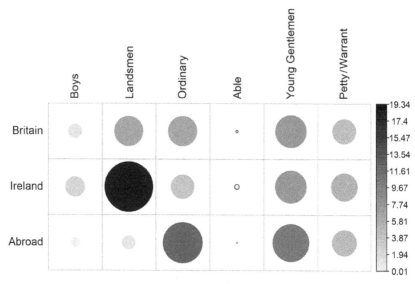

Figure 1.8 Post-hoc chi-square test, rank and rating by origin.

also relatively few among 'boys' and 'young gentlemen' (11% and 6%, respectively). This is entirely unsurprising, since most lower deck boys were poor orphans recruited in Britain through the efforts of the charitable Marine Society, whilst 'young gentlemen' were 'cadets' training to be commissioned officers – a career, as we saw, only open to Britons.[38]

Statistical analysis reveals that these differences are meaningful: there is a significant association between origin and rating, even though the effect size is small.[39] Further testing, however, can give indications as to *why* these differences were significant, or, in other words, how much of the significance depended on foreigners.[40] As can be seen in **Figure 1.8**, the only striking tendencies in their case were the rather high number of

---

[38] Roland Pietsch, 'Ships' Boys and Youth Culture in Eighteenth Century Britain: The Navy Recruits of the London Marine Society', *The Northern Mariner/Le marin du nord* 14:4 (2004), 11–24; Cavell, *Midshipmen*.

[39] $\chi^2(1) = 133.5369$, $p < .01$, $\varphi_c = 0.124$.

[40] The procedure used here and in the rest of this chapter is a post-hoc chi-square test, based on the standardised residuals method. See Appendix 2. The graphs in Figures 1.8, 1.9, and 1.11 were made using the 'corrplot' and 'ggplot2' packages in R: Taiyun Wei and Viliam Simko, *R Package 'corrplot': Visualization of a Correlation Matrix* (2021, Version 0.92) https://github.com/taiyun/corrplot; Hadley Wickham, *ggplot2: Elegant Graphics for Data Analysis* (New York: Springer-Verlag, 2016) https://ggplot2.tidyverse .org.

ordinary seamen and low number of young gentlemen. It was Irishmen, instead, who showed the most distinctive pattern, being disproportionately represented among the unskilled workforce. In a way, then, being born in Ireland would have been a stronger predictor of a man's situation in the Navy than being born abroad. We can also see this in **Figure 1**.7: the different ratings were generally represented in similar proportions among foreigners and Irishmen, except for the fact that 18% of Irishmen were landsmen, as opposed to 13% of foreigners. The results chime with the secondary literature on Irish recruitment in the 1790s: thousands of land labourers were pushed to join the Navy by a severe crisis in employment and food prices.[41]

It is very revealing that if the test is repeated on a sample excluding men born in North America or the West Indies (257 in total), whose legal and cultural difference from Britons is hazier, the remaining foreigners' tendency to be rated 'ordinary' increases (**Figure 1.9**). It is difficult to explain this phenomenon. Testing of respective length of service could help, but is made nearly impossible by the format of naval musters. Given the age similarities examined in Section 1.8, a high incidence of the 'ordinary' rating might hide a form of subtle discrimination, a glass ceiling stopping skilled foreigners from achieving the rating of able. Yet, there is another more plausible explanation: even among British recruits, those rated 'ordinary' instead of 'able' were men who, whilst having seafaring experience, tended to have served on smaller 'fore-and-aft' rig vessels on the coasting trades, rather than in the larger 'square-rigged' long-distance ships.[42] Many continental European seamen, as we shall see in Chapters 5 and 6, had exactly this type of experience. Therefore, their rating as 'ordinary' might have simply been a fair reflection of their skill.

Another possibility investigated was that cultural background may have affected these men's opportunities. We know from Admiralty correspondence that literacy, numeracy, and competence in the English language determined a man's chance of being employed as petty officer.[43] Did they also influence his progression to able seaman? Literacy, always a problematic metric, is extremely difficult to reconstruct for Royal Navy sailors, especially in the absence of signatures on musters.[44]

---

[41] Nicholas Rogers, 'British Impressment and Its Discontents', *The International Journal of Maritime History* 30:1 (2018), 52–73, at 71; Dancy, *Myth*, 50–1.

[42] Jeremiah Dancy, 'Sources and Methods in the British Impressment Debate', *The International Journal of Maritime History* 30:4 (2018), 733–46, at 735.

[43] See Section 3.1.3.

[44] On the use of signatures for estimating literacy, see Mark Hailwood, '"The Rabble That Cannot Read"? Ordinary People's Literacy in Seventeenth-Century England', *The*

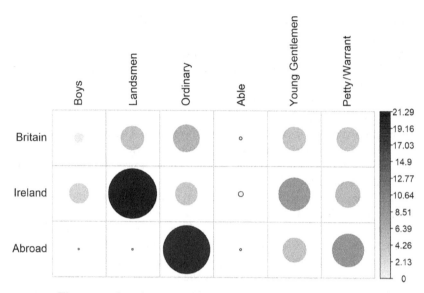

Figure 1.9 Post-hoc chi-square test, rank and rating by origin, excluding North Americans and West Indians.

For numeracy, however, it is possible to analyse our sample through the principle of age heaping: persons with lower levels of numeracy (in the Western European sense) tend to report their age rounded up or down to the nearest multiple of 5, and thus through figures ending in either 0 or 5.[45] This can be measured in a given population on a scale called the Whipple index (WI), which may, in turn, be converted to a value between 1 and 100, for ease of comparison (ABCC index).[46] Foreign-born seamen appear to have been less numerate (WI = 141.09 and

Many-Headed Monster, 13 October 2014 https://manyheadedmonster.wordpress.com/2014/10/13/the-rabble-that-cannot-read-ordinary-peoples-literacy-in-seventeenth-century-england/; R. S. Schofield, 'Dimensions of Illiteracy, 1750–1850', *Explorations in Economic History* 10:4 (1973), 437–54, esp. 440–4; David Cressy, 'Levels of Illiteracy in England, 1530–1730', *The Historical Journal* 20:1 (1977), 1–23, esp. 2–3, 7.

[45] Matthias Blum and Karl-Peter Krauss, 'Age Heaping and Numeracy: Looking behind the Curtain', *Economic History Review* 71:2 (2018), 464–79; Brian A'Hearn, Jörg Baten, and Dorothee Crayen, 'Quantifying Quantitative Literacy: Age Heaping and the History of Human Capital', *The Journal of Economic History* 69:3 (2009), 783–808. Military records tend to skew the results of age heaping tests, because of the high concentration of ages around 20 (A'Hearn, Baten, and Crayen, 'Quantifying Quantitative Literacy', 797). Yet, because seamen's age trends were similar across origin groups, this test is still valuable for comparing them.

[46] The WI can range in value between 100 (no age heaping, and, therefore, perfect numeracy) and 500 (all ages end in 0 or 5). The ABCC index is calculated as {1 − [(WI − 100)/400]} × 100. See Blum and Krauss, 'Age Heaping', 466.

Table 1.3. *Results of age heaping test by origin group*

	n	WI	ABCC index
Britain	3,038	105.28	**98.68**
Northern Europe	216	112.5	**96.88**
West Indies	61	115.38	**96.16**
Eastern Europe	7	125	**93.75**
Ireland	684	129.86	**92.54**
North America	186	145.39	**88.65**
Southern Europe	82	182.69	**79.33**
Africa	12	214.29	**71.43**
Indian Ocean and China	34	277.78	**55.56**

ABCC index = 89.728) than Irishmen, who, in turn, were less numerate than Britons. The results of further splitting by origin can be seen in **Table 1.3**.

These figures match the views of both contemporaries and historians on levels of formal education among eighteenth-century European sailors: northerners were generally seen as more literate and numerate.[47] In the sample, seamen from Scandinavia, Germany, and the Netherlands show higher numeracy than Irishmen and any other group apart from Britons. Instead, men coming from southern Europe, as well as Africa and the Indian Ocean, appear to display extremely low levels of numeracy, at least by the very Eurocentric standards assumed by the Whipple test and by the British method of reckoning age. One important consideration, indeed, is that the results of age heaping tests may be affected by cultural and linguistic incomprehension, leading officers and clerks to jot down rough estimates of a man's age. Whatever the reason, anyway, these findings show that there was a clear variation in cultural capital between different groups of 'foreign-born' seamen.

Yet, if we try to use these same groupings to observe patterns of employment in the Royal Navy, the results show that northern Europeans did not fare better than southerners (whose rating distribution was nearly

---

[47] Jelle van Lottum and Bo Poulsen, 'Estimating Levels of Numeracy and Literacy in the Maritime Sector of the North Atlantic in the Late Eighteenth Century', *Scandinavian Economic History Review* 59:1 (2011), 67–82; Jelle van Lottum, Jan Lucassen, and Lex Heerma van Voss, 'Sailors, National and International Labour Markets and National Identity, 1600–1850', in Richard W. Unger (ed.), *Shipping and Economic Growth 1350–1850* (Leiden and Boston, MA: Brill, 2011), 309–51, at 341–2; Jelle van Lottum and Jan Luiten van Zanden, 'Labour Productivity and Human Capital in the European Maritime Sector of the Eighteenth Century', *Explorations in Economic History* 53 (2014), 83–100, at 90–2.

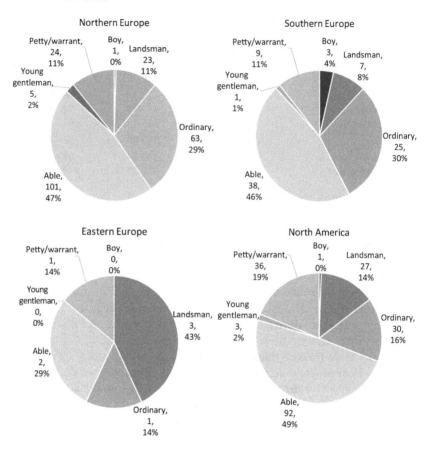

Figure 1.10 Ratings of crews by origin (foreign).

identical) or men from other continents (**Appendix 3** and **Figure 1.10**). Numeracy levels, then, or cultural and linguistic competency, seemingly had no impact on rating. It is worth mentioning that there is a significant statistical difference between the ratings of these different origin groups,[48] but, as can be seen in **Figure 1.11**, this is entirely due to young boys from Asia (or men perceived as 'boys') being enlisted in disproportionate numbers, possibly as officers' servants.

---

[48] As expected, cell frequency was often < 5; Fisher's Exact Test was used instead of a chi-square test, with simulated p-value based on 100,000 replicates: p < .01. See Appendix 3 for the contingency table. Figure 1.11 is built using the same procedure as Figures 1.8 and 1.9, but is to be considered for descriptive purposes only.

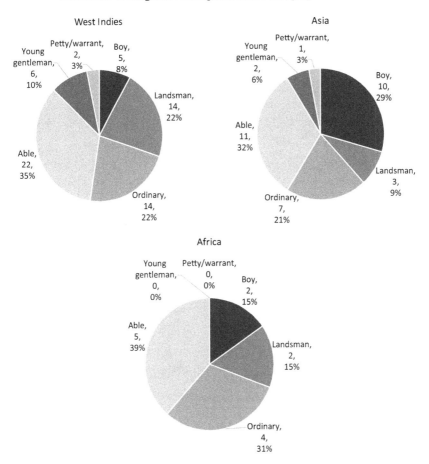

Figure 1.10 (*cont.*)

1.8   Ages

The final question for which the dataset was interrogated was whether foreigners would show significantly different age patterns from Britons and Irishmen. **Figure 1.12** indicates that the curves are very similar, although there is a difference in mean values, with Britons being the youngest, on average twenty-five years and two months old, foreigners slightly older, at twenty-six years and ten months, and Irishmen once again showing the largest deviation, with an average age of twenty-seven years and a half. The median ages were 23, 25, and 26, respectively, and the mode was 20 for Britons and 21 for foreigners and Irishmen.

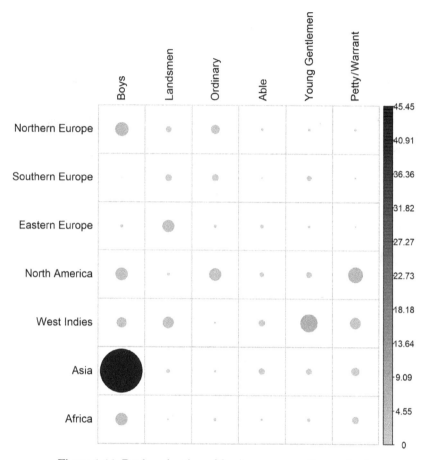

Figure 1.11 Rank and rating of foreign groups, cell contributions.

The fact that the average Irish sailor was older makes his disproportionate chances of being rated landsman even more striking: in a training-
intensive profession, in theory, age should reflect skill (and therefore
rating).[49]

Among foreigners, we saw that there was little variation in rating and
some in numeracy or language skill, but this does not seem to be
reflected in their age patterns: American and northern and southern
European sailors were very close to each other in age and very similar
to the Irish. Eastern Europeans were about two and a half years older, but

---

[49] Dancy, *Myth*, 49.

Ages

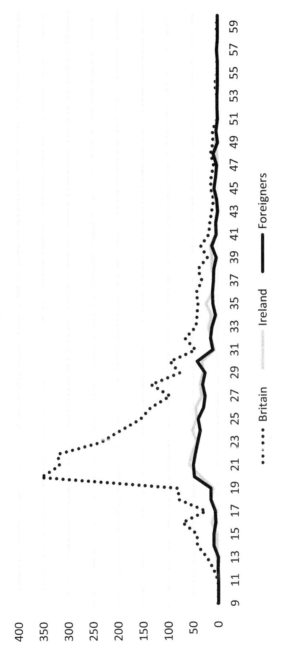

Figure 1.12 Age distribution by origin.

Table 1.4. *Age summary statistics by foreign-origin group*

	Mean age	Median age	Modal age
Britain	25.16	23	20
Ireland	27.49	26	21
Eastern Europe	29.43	23	N/A
Southern Europe	27.66	25	21
North America	27.58	26	21
Northern Europe	27.3	26	22
West Indies	24.77	22	20
Africa	24.67	23	20
Indian Ocean and China	21.44	20.5	20

their sample was very small, so it is difficult to draw conclusions from it. West Indians and Africans resembled the British more, and Asian seamen (as discussed, often rated 'Boys') were the only ones returned as significantly younger (**Table 1.4**). Overall, these were demographically rather similar men.

1.9   Conclusion

We can draw three main conclusions from this sample study. First, the ongoing war increased manpower pressure and, therefore, demand for foreign-born sailors to supplement the Navy's ranks. This will be a running theme in the book. Second, the largest group of foreign-born sailors did not come from the overseas empire, but from continental Europe – even in extra-European stations. We will look at some of them more carefully in Chapters 5 and 6.

Finally, and most importantly, a foreign birthplace did not translate into sharp rating differences below the level of petty officer. Some foreigners did tend to be rated as ordinary seamen more often than chance would dictate, but this may have reflected the fact that many of them were not 'blue water' (long distance) seamen. The prevalence of Asian 'boys' also needs further investigation. Ultimately, however, being born in Ireland mattered more, as a predictor of rating, than being born, generically, 'abroad'. This suggests that classifications based on birthplace and state boundaries had relatively limited meaning and impact, in terms of employment opportunities in the Navy and seafarers' basic demographic traits. If a possible flaw of quantitative analysis is relying on artificially constructed categories, it can also help to deconstruct them, demonstrating their lack of significance, and helping to identify which of them return the most meaningful patterns. The next few chapters tackle other types of category – foreignness as defined by the law, and then foreignness as defined by religion, language, or racialised physical difference.

2 'Sacred and Indestructible' Bonds
Alien Seamen, Subjecthood, and the Navy

Aboard HMS *Nightingale*, in September 1811, the fourteen-year-old volunteer first class Camillo Corri succeeded in irritating his Scottish messmate Robert Ritchie. 'He is a complete turncoat', Ritchie wrote in his journal only a day after meeting him: '– denies he was born in Scotland, which pleases the English, who seem grealty [*sic*] to despise the Scots: he also claims the honour of being born in Italy; But if I mistake not, he was born in Edin'.[1] Ritchie was not mistaken: the muster book confirms this fact, and we also know that Camillo Corri was the son of a famous Italian musician, Natale Corri, settled in Edinburgh with his family since at least 1792.[2] Whatever his assertions on the matter, then, Camillo was legally a Scot and a Briton, because he was born on British soil.

'Identity' is in many ways a muddy concept: in particular, self-identification in varying contexts should be distinguished from external identification imposed on the individual by others.[3] This chapter focuses on this tension, and on the role that the specific label of 'subjecthood' or lack thereof ('alienhood') might have played in naval seamen's lives. These men, both necessary and mobile, offer a privileged vantage point for assessing the power of the state that labelled them.

Belonging to a community, in the early modern period, chiefly meant being inserted in a local network of '*interconnaissance*': people moving outside this became unpredictable and uncontrollable, because they had

---

[1] The National Library of Scotland, Edinburgh [henceforth NLS], GB233/MS.9232, Robert Ritchie, Journal of Voyages, 1811–12, f. 10.

[2] TNA, ADM 37/3109, Muster Book of HMS *Nightingale*, September–October 1811, [f. 6]. Ritchie introduces him as 'son of the musician in Edin'. David J. Golby, 'Corri Family (*per. c.*1770–1860)', *Oxford Dictionary of National Biography*, online ed. [henceforth *ODNB*] (Oxford: Oxford University Press, 2014) www.oxforddnb.com/view/article/69602; James Grant, *Cassell's Old and New Edinburgh: Its History, Its People, and Its Places*, 6 vols. (London: Cassell, Petter, Galpin & Co., 1881–7?), II, 178–9; Edinburgh City Archive, SL115/2/1, Aliens Register, 1798–1803.

[3] Rogers Brubaker and Frederick Cooper, 'Beyond "Identity"', *Theory and Society* 29 (2000), 1–47, at 15–16.

no interests, property or family acting as warranty against their behaviour, and nothing to prevent their assuming a fake identity. This is where the identification labels of modern states came into play.[4] They remained, however, an imperfect tool: how far were these labels, clearly assigned to individuals in administrative documents, actually effective and meaningful in people's lives? This question takes us into a broader historiographical debate, surrounding the power of modern states over individuals and groups, and, in the face of that, the validity of transnational historical approaches.

Some kinds of transnational history have been accused of presenting an optimistic, 'romanticised' 'success story' of the transcending of state borders in favour of unity, movement, and exchange, which ignores the barriers and constraints of violence and power.[5] The state and its borders, functioning through 'categorical' and 'absolute' classifications, have a fixed physical and socio-political existence, which can often be underestimated in studies of culture and transnational fluidity of movement.[6] However, while transnationalism is easily overemphasised, equally, the movement of some specific groups of people may at times become functionally useful or indispensable and, therefore, be facilitated by the state system. The state itself is sometimes forced, in its search for resources, to act *against* the barrier to circulation that frontiers normally constitute. In such circumstances, the labels by which states officially classify, control, and reclaim or disclaim individuals can become all but meaningless. Age-of-sail seamen, during wartime, were a type of transnational migrant whose (inward) mobility it was in the interest of many countries' authorities to foster. Thus, they are an excellent case study to understand the category of legal 'foreignness' as it developed in modern 'nation states', and the tensions inherent to it.

Isaac Land, criticising Marcus Rediker's vision of eighteenth-century sailors as living rebelliously above and detached from official structures and 'authority', suggests that seamen, precisely owing to their mobility, tended to be especially aware of the legal implications of states.[7] Indeed,

---

[4] Gérard Noiriel, *État, nation et immigration : vers une histoire du pouvoir* (Paris: Belin, 2001), 313–14, 338–48; John C. Torpey, *The Invention of the Passport: Surveillance, Citizenship, and the State*, 2nd ed. (Cambridge: Cambridge University Press, 2018).

[5] Heinz-Gerhard Haupt, 'Une nouvelle sensibilité : la perspective "transnationale"', *Cahiers Jaurès* 200 (2011–12), 173–80, at 178–9; Morieux, *Channel*, 18.

[6] Thomas M. Wilson and Hastings Donnan, 'Nation, State and Identity at International Borders', in eidem (eds.), *Border Identities: Nation and State at International Frontiers* (Cambridge: Cambridge University Press, 1998), 1–30; David M. Potter, 'The Historian's Use of Nationalism and Vice Versa', *The American Historical Review* 67:4 (1962), 924–50, at 927–8.

[7] Rediker, *Between the Devil and the Deep Blue Sea*, 5, 7–8, 79–80; Land, *War*, 17–19.

according to Nathan Perl-Rosenthal, sailors were the first group of individuals who came to be identified through 'modern' systems of citizenship papers, as a result of the controversies surrounding their employment during the 'Age of Revolutions'.[8] The British state was especially effective in reclaiming jurisdiction over and ownership of its seafaring subjects; sailors, in turn, had learnt to make active use of the law and even contribute to its shape, using it as a 'weapon of choice' to obtain redress.[9] In many ways, then, the question of seamen's legal affiliations complicates the argument of modern historians who place the origins of non-elite individuals' 'coming to nationality', becoming aware of the concrete effects of this 'latent quality', only at the end of the nineteenth century.[10]

At the same time, however, in comparison to other social categories, non-British seamen in Britain had relatively little to gain or lose by national labels and constraints, particularly when under naval employment. This was not necessarily due to the rebellious proto-anarchic spirit identified by Rediker, as much as to some leeway left by the states themselves, striking a compromise for the preservation of their power. A strategic adoption, remoulding, or evasion of legal labels was performed not only by the sailors,[11] but by the British state itself. This sheds light on a fundamental contradiction, nested at the very core of modern states' existence: the supposedly fixed demarcations that define and justify their being may prove, if strictly observed, incompatible with their prosperity, leading them to rely instead on hybrid cultural and legal categories. Yet, cultural labels are intrinsically pliable, whereas legal boundaries in theory are not. Historians have observed the tension between 'uniformity' and 'privileges' in Ancien Régime subjecthood law,[12] but the status of sailors during the French Wars, the supposed harbingers of 'modern' state systems, alerts us to the fact that this tension has perhaps never been fully solved.

---

[8] Perl-Rosenthal, *Citizen Sailors*.

[9] Danilo Pedemonte, 'Deserters, Mutineers and Criminals: British Sailors and Problems of Port Jurisdiction in Genoa and Livorno during the Eighteenth Century', in Maria Fusaro, Bernard Allaire, Richard J. Blakemore, and Tijl Vanneste (eds.), *Law, Labour and Empire: Comparative Perspectives on Seafarers, c. 1500–1800* (Basingstoke: Palgrave Macmillan, 2015), 256–71; Richard J. Blakemore, 'The Legal World of English Sailors, c. 1575–1729', ibid., 100–20.

[10] Will Hanley, *Identifying with Nationality: Europeans, Ottomans, and Egyptians in Alexandria* (New York: Columbia University Press, 2017).

[11] Land, *War*, 27–8; Morieux, 'Diplomacy'.

[12] Peter Sahlins, *Unnaturally French: Foreign Citizens in the Old Regime and After* (Ithaca, NY and London: Cornell University Press, 2004), 6–7.

This chapter considers the legal status of aliens in eighteenth-century Britain and its specific implications for seamen, in both civil and criminal law, and most notably at the moment of transition from alienage to subjecthood through naturalisation. We will look, in turn, at disabilities (incapacities established by law), privileges and advantages, and finally the legal context of the naturalisation of seamen.

2.1   Seamen and the Disabilities of Aliens

In most European countries, throughout the eighteenth century, a legal divide separated 'natural-born subjects' and 'aliens'. In Britain, the rights of a native could derive equally from being born within British territory (*jus soli*) or of a British father or paternal grandfather (*jus sanguinis*).[13] It has been argued that 'institutional limitations on migration were particularly strong in England', certainly by comparison with Dutch legislation.[14] However, by the standards of many other contemporary countries, the degree of freedom granted to aliens in Britain was actually considerable.

Eighteenth-century mercantilist theories stressed the importance of population size for the prosperity of a country, and for this reason, at different times, several European states actively encouraged immigration: examples include the United Provinces, Prussia, and Russia.[15] Other Ancien Régime powers, however, strongly resisted the settlement of foreigners or imposed taxes and restrictions like the French *droit d'aubaine*, according to which, if aliens died without heirs who were natural-born French subjects, all their property would be confiscated

---

[13] William Blackstone, *Commentaries on the Laws of England, in Four Books*, 13th ed. (London: A. Strahan, 1800), 372–4; Alexander Cockburn, *Nationality: or the Law Relating to Subjects and Aliens, Considered with a View to Future Legislation* (London: William Ridgway, 1869), 7–25; Clive Parry, *British Nationality Law and the History of Naturalisation* (Milan: Giuffrè, 1954), 5–6, 10–14, 43–6, 50–2, 60–3, 74–82, 91–6, 107; Silvia Marzagalli, 'Négoce et politique des étrangers en France à l'époque moderne : discours et pratiques de rejet et d'intégration', in Mickaël Augeron and Pascal Éven (eds.), *Les Étrangers dans les villes-ports atlantiques : Expériences françaises et allemandes XVᵉ-XIXᵉ siècle* (Paris: Les Indes Savantes, 2011), 45–62, at 46–7; Andreas Fahrmeir, *Citizens and Aliens: Foreigners and the Law in Britain and the German States, 1789–1870* (New York and Oxford: Berghahn Books, 2000), 43–6.

[14] Van Lottum et al., 'Sailors', 329–35.

[15] Lucassen and Penninx, *Newcomers*; Roger P. Bartlett, *Human Capital: The Settlement of Foreigners in Russia, 1762–1804* (Cambridge: Cambridge University Press, 1979), 23–30. On populationism, see Daniel Statt, *Foreigners and Englishmen: The Controversy over Immigration and Population, 1660–1760* (Cranbury, NJ: Associated University Presses, 1995), 44–51, 74–90, 99–109.

by the crown.[16] In 1790s France, wartime measures escalated into persecution.[17] Even in France, the system allowed wide exceptions to discrimination, dictated by reciprocity agreements with other states, or by local policies.[18] These exceptions always depended on convenience: the crucial distinction was between *useful* and *useless* aliens, and the law bent to encourage the former.[19] Seamen were a particularly useful type of immigrant, especially in wartime. In Britain, however, the backdrop of an already very lax system deprived any special encouragement of most of its meaning.

Whilst perhaps not a match for the extraordinary openness of the Dutch Republic, the British state's legal discrimination towards aliens was minimal, even beyond considerations of utility.[20] The *droit d'aubaine* was extraneous to British tradition, and the Crown never had the prerogative to expel aliens, or bar them from entry: this could be done only through special legislation.[21] In peacetime at least, foreigners were free to come and go, trade (though with higher duty rates), marry, own movable property, and leave it to their heirs.[22] During wartime, more stringent controls were instituted, most notably in the Alien Acts of 1793, 1798,

---

[16] Paola Avallone, 'Il controllo dei "forestieri" a Napoli tra XVI e XVIII secolo. Prime note', *Mediterranea* 3 (2006), 169–78; Michael Rapport, *Nationality and Citizenship in Revolutionary France: The Treatment of Foreigners, 1789–1799* (Oxford: Clarendon Press, 2000), 33–4; Peter Sahlins, 'Sur la citoyenneté et le droit d'aubaine à l'époque moderne : réponse à Simona Cerutti', *Annales. Histoire, Sciences Sociales* 63:2 (2008), 385–98; Cerutti, *Étrangers*, 31–76.

[17] Renaud Morieux, 'Des règles aux pratiques juridiques : le droit des étrangers en France et en Angleterre pendant la Révolution (1792–1802)', in Ph. Chassaigne and J.-P. Genet (eds.), *Droit et société en France et en Grande-Bretagne (XIIᵉ-XXᵉ siècles). Fonctions, usages et représentations* (Paris: Publications de la Sorbonne, 2003), 127–47, at 129, 132, 134–5, 137–9; Rapport, *Nationality and Citizenship*, 88–90, 142–50, 186–7, 194–207; Morieux, *Channel*, 300–3; Tozzi, *Nationalizing France's Army*, esp. 122–7; Noiriel, *État*, 312.

[18] Peter Sahlins, 'The Eighteenth-Century Citizenship Revolution in France', in Andreas Fahrmeir, Olivier Faron, and Patrick Weil (eds.), *Migration Control in the North Atlantic World: The Evolution of State Practices in Europe and the United States from the French Revolution to the Inter-War Period* (New York and Oxford: Berghahn Books, 2003), 11–24, at 15–17.

[19] Rapport, *Nationality and Citizenship*, esp. 33–82, 194–208; Marzagalli, 'Négoce'. For the specific case of foreign troops in France, see Tozzi, *Nationalizing France's Army*, 44–5. For Britain, see Conway, *Britannia's Auxiliaries*, esp. ch. 5. Cf. the motivations for inclusive subjecthood in newly conquered imperial territories: Hannah Weiss Muller, 'Bonds of Belonging: Subjecthood and the British Empire', *Journal of British Studies* 53:1 (2014), 29–58, at 54–5.

[20] Fahrmeir, *Citizens and Aliens*, 152, 154, 163–73, 196–7, 209–22.

[21] Blackstone, *Commentaries*, 372; W. F. Craies, 'The Right of Aliens to Enter British Territory', *Law Quarterly Review* 6 (1890), 27–41; Fahrmeir, *Citizens and Aliens*, 193–4.

[22] Blackstone, *Commentaries*, 372; Fahrmeir, *Citizens and Aliens*, 163–73, 178.

and 1803.[23] Yet, these were in many respects only increases in passport and border policing, quite mild if compared to continental practice; they did deprive foreigners of the right of *habeas corpus*, but this was part of the general repressive twist of the Pitt administration, much condemned by contemporaries, more than the result of special discriminatory targeting.[24] In the Alien Acts, anyway, foreign mariners in employment were exempted from the requirements of registration upon arrival in a British port and passports to sail away.[25] Partial exception were, as can be imagined, *enemy* aliens.[26] The Admiralty regularly forbade sailors from enemy nations, and Frenchmen in particular, to serve under British colours. In practice, however, this attitude was often contradictory, as we shall see below.

Beyond emergency wartime measures, only three types of disabilities affected aliens in Britain. First, they could not fill 'positions of trust under the crown'.[27] This prohibition was indifferent to lower-deck seamen, who did not normally aspire to officers' commissions. Second, aliens could not possess land.[28] This, too, was an incapacity very unlikely to affect a Navy seaman, given his economic, professional, and cultural distance from the world of landed property. The jurist William Blackstone attributed this rule both to fears of foreign influence and to the conflicting allegiances into which an alien, according to feudal tradition, would enter by acquiring a new liege in the British monarch, in addition to his old sovereign.[29] Clearly, a man fighting in one of the king's ships had already committed to an even more explicit form of allegiance to the British Crown. Finally, the seventeenth-century Navigation Laws established that aliens could not own or be masters of English or Irish (and later Scottish) ships, trade with British colonies, or constitute more than a quarter of the crew of any English or Irish merchantman.[30] The former two rules were again mostly irrelevant to the ordinary sailor, for obvious socio-economic reasons; the crew regulations, by contrast, had more concrete repercussions. Instituted in 1660, they aimed both to prevent customs abuses by foreign ships, making English vessels readily identifiable, and to provide English sailors with more secure

---

[23] 33 Geo. III c. 4; 38 Geo. III c. 50; 43 Geo. III c. 155; Margrit Schulte Beerbühl, 'British Nationality Policy as a Counter-Revolutionary Strategy during the Napoleonic Wars: The Emergence of Modern Naturalisation Regulations', in Fahrmeir et al., *Migration Control*, 55–70, at 56–8; Morieux, *Channel*, 296–300, 303–6.

[24] Morieux, 'Des règles aux pratiques juridiques', 130–7.

[25] 33 Geo. III c. 4 § v; 38 Geo. III c. 50 § viii; 43 Geo. III c. 155 § xi, xxvii.

[26] Morieux, 'Des règles aux pratiques juridiques', 145–6.

[27] Fahrmeir, *Citizens and Aliens*, 163–4.   [28] Blackstone, *Commentaries*, 372.   [29] Ibid.

[30] Lawrence A. Harper, *The English Navigation Laws: A Seventeenth-Century Experiment in Social Engineering* (New York: Columbia University Press, 1939), 34–60.

employment, turning the merchant service into a 'nursery of seamen' for the Navy.[31] The effects of this legislation, repealed in 1849, subsisted until 1853, and from 1794, crews in the coasting trades had to be entirely British.[32]

The one-quarter limitation, nonetheless, was normally lifted in wartime, when the demand of the Navy absorbed much of British maritime manpower.[33] A statute of 1776, renewed annually during the American War, temporarily allowed three-quarter foreign crews, and the concession was repeated in 1793 and 1803.[34] Such statutes were, in fact, redundant: an Act of 1740 had already made provision for this to be authorised, via a simple royal proclamation, in any 'Future War'.[35] Other exceptions were also granted: on American and West Indian routes and east of the Cape of Good Hope, respectively, British-held Black enslaved men and Lascar sailors counted as British, even if born outside British territories.[36]

Most importantly, crew limitations imposed by the Navigation Acts did not affect foreigners' employment opportunities in the Navy. It is true that naval power was a crucial consideration underlying the Acts, whose function of preserving a reserve of national seamen loomed large in contemporary thinking.[37] However, the 1660 Act concerned not shipping as such, but 'Goods or Commodities' 'Imported into or Exported out of' the King's dominions, so it paradoxically ignored naval vessels.[38] In fact, crew capping in merchantmen might have, if anything, pushed alien mariners towards the Navy, when they found themselves stranded in Britain.

If general alien legislation only seemed to create marginal disadvantages for the non-native sailor, this does not mean that laws targeting certain groups were unknown. Black men bought by the Crown, for example, were declared in 1807 automatically free from enslavement from the time of their entry into the armed forces.[39] Yet, 'liberated Africans' who were (forcibly) absorbed into the Navy and military still suffered from unequal treatment enshrined in statute. As remarked in a clause of the Slave Trade Act of March 1807,

---

[31] Ibid., 53, 55; Perl-Rosenthal, *Citizen Sailors*, 27–8.

[32] Harper, *English Navigation Laws*, 390, 414.   [33] Ibid., 68, 349.

[34] 16 Geo. III c. 20. Renewed: 17 Geo. III c. 34; 18 Geo. III c. 6; 19 Geo. III c. 14; 20 Geo. III c. 20 § i; 21 Geo. III c. 11; 22 Geo. III c. 16. For the French Wars period, see 33 Geo III c. 26; 43 Geo. III c. 64. See also: 34 Geo. III c. 68.

[35] 13 Geo. II c. 3 § i, iii.   [36] 34 Geo. III c. 68 § viii.

[37] Stephen Conway, 'Another Look at the Navigation Acts and the Coming of the American Revolution', in McAleer and Petley, *Royal Navy and the British Atlantic*, 77–96.

[38] 12 Car. II c. 18.   [39] 47 Geo. III sess. 1 c. 32 § cii. But see Section 7.3.2.

none of the Provisions of any Act as to enlisting for any limited Period of Service, or as to any Rules or Regulations for the granting any Pensions or Allowances to any Soldiers discharged after certain Periods of Service, shall extend, or be deemed or construed in any Manner to extend, to any Negroes so enlisting and serving in any of His Majesty's Forces.[40]

In these cases, however, it could be argued that legal status as 'aliens' in the modern-state sense was not an important factor in determining these men's situation. It was not their hailing from abroad that defined their lives, but rather racist classifications and their enslaved past. Many of them were not even strictly speaking aliens: the question of subjecthood in the empire was highly contested throughout the eighteenth century, but by the time of the French Wars, it was generally accepted that being born on British colonial soil and being free were sufficient for a Black man to be deemed a subject.[41] This did not, as seen here, remove other disabilities, which not only put him on the same footing as non-British Black persons, but, in fact, ranked him behind non-British whites. Similar discriminatory practices could be seen, in commercial shipping, in the case of Lascar sailors from territories controlled by the East India Company.[42] Throughout the empire, and well into the twentieth century, legal British subjecthood often did not result in equal status for indigenous populations, in the face of ulterior racist legislation and practices.[43] We see here a clear example of Cerutti's category of 'étranger', which does not necessarily overlap with that of 'those born outside' the country, but is instead a much more complex notion, representing a marginality that can easily 'criss-cross' territorial framings of

---

[40] 47 Geo. III sess. 1 c. 36 § xvii. See also 47 Geo. III sess. 1 c. 32 § ciii.

[41] Brooke N. Newman, 'Contesting "Black" Liberty and Subjecthood in the Anglophone Caribbean, 1730s–1780s', *Slavery & Abolition* 32:2 (2011), 169–83; Morieux, 'Des règles aux pratiques juridiques', 144; Christopher L. Brown, 'From Slaves to Subjects: Envisioning an Empire without Slavery, 1772–1834', in Philip D. Morgan and Sean Hawkins (eds.), *Black Experience and the Empire* (Oxford: Oxford University Press, 2006), 111–40, at 117–20, 133–6; Weiss Muller, 'Bonds of Belonging', 32–51; Eliga H. Gould, 'Zones of Law, Zones of Violence: The Legal Geography of the British Atlantic, circa 1772', *The William and Mary Quarterly* 60:3 (2003), 471–510, at 505. On the inclusivity of subjecthood in different imperial contexts, see Hannah Weiss Muller, *Subjects and Sovereign: Bonds of Belonging in the Eighteenth-Century British Empire* (Oxford: Oxford University Press, 2017); Sudipta Sen, 'Imperial Subjects on Trial: On the Legal Identity of Britons in Late Eighteenth-Century India', *Journal of British Studies* 45:3 (2006), 532–55.

[42] Sherwood, 'Race'.

[43] John Chesterman, 'Natural-Born Subjects? Race and British Subjecthood in Australia', *Australian Journal of Politics and History* 51:1 (2005), 30–9, at 32–5, 38–9; Lauren Benton, *Law and Colonial Cultures: Legal Regimes in World History, 1400–1900* (Cambridge: Cambridge University Press, 2002), 167–209.

the legislation.[44] Again, these are, in some ways, residuals of Ancien Régime models, defining 'belonging' to national communities in terms of personal or group privileges.[45]

We shall return to the role of racial notions in the Navy, in Chapter 4. For now, we can say that the legal concept and status of 'alien' had negligible impact on the lives of seamen in the British service, at least as far as disabilities were concerned. A partially different case can be made regarding advantages. However, these will need to be qualified, too, bearing in mind the gap between theory and practice.

2.2   The Privileges of Alien Seamen

The main legal advantage that alien sailors enjoyed over most British colleagues was formal exemption from being impressed into the Royal Navy. This controversial form of forced recruitment was systematically used throughout the century. A 1740 Act listed as protected, next to men over fifty or under eighteen, or who had 'used the sea' for less than a set amount of time, 'every Foreigner, being a Mariner, Seaman or Landman', employed in British merchantmen or privateers.[46] Both consular authorities and the Admiralty released protection certificates, detailing name, age, physical description, and birthplace.[47] When in September 1800 the French Consulate decreed that 'all foreign seafaring men resident in the territory of the Republic, who have married French women, and sailed on board merchant vessels, are liable to serve in the vessels belonging to the State', some British papers reacted with indignation. 'This measure is the greatest outrage upon the general liberty of man, that ever took place', *The London Packet* railed, 'a measure which tramples upon Justice, Patriotism, and Nature'.[48] This outcry became, then, another opportunity to cast British liberties and rights against the shadow of the French tyrannical system: rhetorical attacks founded on

---

[44] Cerutti, *Étrangers*. See also Morieux, 'Des règles aux pratiques juridiques', 129, 138, 141.

[45] See the question of Black persons and subjecthood in Ancien Régime France: Rapport, *Nationality and Citizenship*, 18–20. An analogous example is the position of Jews in several Ancien Régime countries: Marzagalli, 'Négoce', 48–9.

[46] 13 Geo. II c. 17. Apprentices, seamen in the coal trade, and some fishermen were also exempt, seasonally, by trade or by skill: 13 Geo. II c. 28 § v; 2 Geo. III c. 15 § xxii–xxiv; 11 Geo. III c. 38 § xix; 48 Geo. III c. 110 § xxvii; 50 Geo. III c. 108; 51 Geo. III c. 34 § vi.

[47] See, for example, Caird Library, National Maritime Museum, Greenwich [henceforth NMM], ADL/J/9, Impressment exemption form for Reyer Torsen, 25 April 1807; TNA, ADM 7/398, Register of Protections from Being Pressed – Apprentices, Foreigners and Others, 1795–1801.

[48] *London Packet, or New Lloyd's Evening Post*, 8–10 September 1800.

'humanitarian patriotism' were a strategy which both countries reciprocally pursued in those decades, particularly with reference to the treatment of prisoners of war.[49] In practice, however, British behaviour was not different.

First, in Britain, marriage or settlement in the country also seemingly sufficed to make someone liable to impressment. In the correspondence relative to impressed foreigners, the recurrent formula to justify discharge requests was that a man 'never was either married or settled in England': having a British wife was enough to make an application fail.[50] This was a clear survival, right into the nineteenth century, of older, prestatal definitions of belonging, understood as having 'stakes' in a local community.[51] The state's convenient adoption of these definitions when they suited its interest, despite the existence, by then, of parallel, formally codified legislation on alienhood and protections of aliens, shows the weakness of such codified legislation. Importantly, as will be seen below, a British wife or residence were not enough for a man to be considered a naturalised subject. American authorities, in particular, pointed out the grating double standard that Britain applied in this matter towards foreigners settled in Britain on the one hand and Britons settled in the United States on the other: the Royal Navy deemed both categories compelled to serve.[52]

Second, even for aliens who were not settled, the rules were less strict and constant than they seemed, in both validity and enforcement. An Act of 1798, for instance, suspended for five months all exemptions from impressment.[53] Further, laws were not always followed in practice, as shown most clearly by the 1812 American War, which had impressment

[49] Renaud Morieux, 'Patriotisme humanitaire et prisonniers de guerre en France et en Grande-Bretagne pendant la Révolution française et l'Empire', in Laurent Bourquin et al. (eds.), *La politique par les armes. Conflits internationaux et politisation, XVe–XIXe siècles* (Rennes: Presses Universitaires de Rennes, 2014), 301–16. The parallel was also in contemporaries' minds: the *Sun* complained that, 'upon the same principle with which the French Government mean to compel all Foreign Seamen resident in the Republic to enter into their Navy, they may oblige all the Foreign Military whom they take prisoners, to enter into the French Army': *Sun*, 11 September 1800.

[50] See, for example, NMM, ADM/B/202, Board of Admiralty, In-Letters, August-November 1801, Navy Office, 10 September 1801; TNA, ADM 1/1052, Letters from Commanders-in-Chief, Portsmouth, 1802, nn. 201–400, 204, M. De Courcy to Admiral Milbanke, 26 February 1802; 236, William Bradley to Admiral Milbanke, 9 March 1802; ADM 1/736, Letters from Commanders-in-Chief, Nore, 1803, 266, B. S. Rowley to Evan Nepean, 23 August 1803.

[51] Noiriel, *État*, 313–14.

[52] See, for example, Rufus King to Lord Grenville, 30 November 1796, reported in *British and Foreign State Papers – 1812–1814, Volume I*, 170 vols. (London: James Ridgway and Sons, 1841), II, 1382–3.

[53] 38 Geo. III c. 46.

as a precipitating factor. The position of impressed Americans, admittedly, compared to that of subjects of other states, was very ambiguous. To begin with, Britain refused to recognise as American citizens Britons who had been granted naturalisation by the United States: the two countries thus disagreed on the very definition of 'who was an American'.[54] In 1797, the British Admiralty's law officer suggested that 'the Treaty of Peace with America' in 1783 could 'be considered as a renunciation on the part of the Crown to all rights over American Citizens', and because its text did not distinguish on the basis of birth, this ought to apply not only to those born in America, but also to those who were born in Europe yet were resident in America at the time of independence, and had continued to be so afterwards. However, he also decisively ruled that 'residence in America, clearly commenced' after the treaty, could 'give no better claim... against any right of the King of Great Britain' to someone's 'allegiance' or 'services', 'than a residence in any other foreign & independent Country'.[55] This created a conflicting claim in the case of those naturalised American after 1783.

Besides, American seamen, because of their language fluency and cultural similarity, could struggle to prove that they were not British, which afforded widespread malpractices on the Navy's part.[56] The historiography has perhaps overemphasised the difficulty in distinguishing Britons from Americans: 'among that class of People called Seamen', the American Secretary of State wrote in 1800,

we can readily distinguish between a native American and a Person raised to manhood in Great Britain or Ireland; and we do not perceive any reason why the capacity of making this distinction should not be possessed in the same degree by one Nation as by the other.[57]

An English source complaining about the number of British sailors hiding away in the US service, in 1812, also stated that 'there is little difficulty in pointing out an American Seaman amidst a thousand Englishman [sic]'.[58] Yet, Americans were clearly less 'different' from

---

[54] Zimmerman, *Impressment*, 21–6; Cockburn, *Nationality*, 70–8; Perl-Rosenthal, *Citizen Sailors*, 140–53, 183, 186–7.

[55] TNA, ADM 7/303, Law Officers' Opinions, 1796–7, n. 21, Impress Americans National Character, 10 February 1797.

[56] Zimmerman, *Impressment*, 18, 25, though see 86; Perl-Rosenthal, *Citizen Sailors*, 10–11, 48, 82–3, 129–39; Cockburn, *Nationality*, 71–2. See also: TNA, ADM 1/3850, Letters from Foreign Consuls, 1796–8, David Lenox to Evan Nepean, 4 October 1797.

[57] John Marshall to Rufus King, 20 September 1800, in *British and Foreign State Papers – 1812–14, Volume I*, II, 1402.

[58] The Huntington Library, San Marino [henceforth HL], Robert Saunders Dundas, Viscount Melville Papers, 1812–1814, mssHM 81135, 'Anonymous – Proposal for recovering the British seamen in the American service', 15 September 1812.

Britons than men from other countries, and this was conveniently exploited by all sides. In this context, even official identification papers could count for little.[59] One illustrative case is that of young Henry Geddes, 'a native of Charlestown S. Carolina', as recorded in 1805 by Thomas Simpson, surgeon of HMS *Arethusa*:

he was impressed from an american [*sic*] ship in the Thames, under circumstances that do no honour to the persons employed in that department as he has the most undeniable testimonials of his being an American. ... I apprehend from his simplicity that he will not get away from want of a knowledge of the proper steps to be taken for this purpose.[60]

Americans, however, were not the sole targets of unlawful impressment. The frequent violations of statute are proven by abundant circumstantial evidence, including hundreds of letters of complaint written by foreign consuls (not only American, but also Swedish, Danish, Prussian, Spanish, Genoese, and others) to the British Admiralty, requesting the release of their countries' subjects.[61] The Admiralty was extremely wary of granting discharges, meticulously checking individuals' birthplaces, and whether they had accepted a bounty at the time of joining, which would legally make the men volunteers and invalidate their application.[62] This concern reflected a commonly adopted ruse on the part of sailors: some aliens who volunteered explicitly promised that they would not later request a discharge, and the Admiralty itself instructed its officials to make a note of the seamen's mode of entry, to prevent such requests.[63] Yet, these consuls' letters also clearly show that a large number of aliens had genuinely been impressed. Many more cases of abuse may have never come to official attention: casual remarks in logs and journals show that the impressment of known foreigners, including some who could in no way be mistaken for British, was accepted as a common occurrence among Navy personnel. In November 1805, Thomas Simpson treated for scurvy William Rogers and William Noel, 'both... foreigners the first a Portuguese and the latter an American': 'they were both impressed from the homeward bound West India fleet',

[59] Zimmerman, *Impressment*, 28–9, 36, 41–2; Perl-Rosenthal, *Citizen Sailors*, 140–53.
[60] TNA, ADM 101/86/1, Thomas Simpson, Journal of HMS *Arethusa*, 14 May 1805–14 June 1806, f. 13.
[61] TNA, ADM 1/3849 to ADM 1/3858, Letters from Foreign Consuls, 1793–1820.
[62] The correspondence on this matter is incredibly vast. For some examples, see NMM, ADM/B/212, Board of Admiralty, In-Letters, November–December 1803, Navy Office, 6 December 1803.
[63] TNA, ADM 1/2066, Letters from Captains, Surnames L., 1800, nn. 1–200, 3, Charles Henry Lane, 2 January 1800.

he notices, in a matter-of-fact fashion.[64] In the musters of ships, sailors are often openly listed with their non-British birthplaces and surnames, and as pressed.[65] Not even the fiction of legality was maintained: the meticulous bureaucracy of the Admiralty meticulously, and indifferently, documented flagrant violations of the law.

Aliens were liberally pressed all over the globe: in a 1810 list containing two Danes, one German and one Norwegian, their original places of impressment are listed as 'Monte Video', Lisbon, 'Massina', and Madras, one of them out of a transport, one out of a British East India ship.[66] The press gangs ashore, presumably, would have also been aware of the foreignness of some of their victims. In a case tried at the Old Bailey in 1793, after a Swedish sailor had been murdered by a press gang, it emerged that this had raided a tavern where Swedish sailors habitually sojourned (the owner was a Swede) and tried to drag them away, being well aware of their origin. The cry 'Swanskey, come out' was reported by some witnesses.[67]

If neither legal status nor appearance as strangers were sufficient protection, however, it was often the latter, rather than the former, that simplified these men's liberation, as the consuls seem to have known well. It is very revealing, indeed, that the somewhat cautious formula almost invariably used by the American envoys in their requests for release was 'Seamen representing themselves to be', 'represented to be', or 'said to be' 'Citizens of the United States of America'.[68] Consuls of other countries, instead, confidently stated the fact of their alienage: 'x *are* subjects of y' [my emphasis], 'x being a subject of y', and 'x, a native of y'.[69] In 1796, the Danish consul requested the discharge of Christian Nielsen Ohl, an impressed Dane: Ohl was 'examined... in the Danish Language', after which a consul's employee swore that his being a Danish subject was 'ascertained beyond all doubt'. The Board of

---

[64] TNA, ADM 101/86/1, Simpson, HMS *Arethusa*, f. 14.

[65] See, for example, TNA, ADM 37/280, Muster Book of HMS *Arethusa*, November–December 1805, ff. 3, 12, 13, 15; McCranie, 'Recruitment of Seamen', 84–101, at 95.

[66] TNA, ADM 1/3760, Letters from the Transport Board, January–September 1810, 30 January 1810, ff. 22–4.

[67] Tim Hitchcock et al., *The Old Bailey Proceedings Online, 1674–1913*, version 7.0, www .oldbaileyonline.org [henceforth *OBP*], October 1793, trial of Richard Tuart (t17931030–66). See also examples in Berit Eide Johnsen, *Han sad i prisonen... Sjøfolk i engelsk fangenskap 1807–1814* (Oslo: Universitetsforlaget, 1993), 133.

[68] See, for example, TNA, ADM 1/3850, containing 19 examples between July 1797 and November 1798. There are occasional exceptions to this formula, especially when the papers were unmistakable: David Lenox to Evan Nepean, 5 February 1798; Joshua Johnson to Evan Nepean, 11 February 1796; David Lenox to Evan Nepan, 14 May 1798.

[69] TNA, ADM 1/3850 contains 27 examples (June 1796–November 1798).

Admiralty seemed to accept this rather weak form of 'cultural' evidence, as they ordered the man's discharge, 'if he should bona fide appear to be a Danish subject'.[70] In short, unlike Americans, for whom subjecthood or lack thereof was highly disputed, and often only demonstrable through official papers, aliens coming from another country often would have been undeniably recognisable as such. In an era of still dubious personal papers, legal subjecthood or citizenship mattered much less than ethnic or 'cultural' outlook, in identifying a man.[71]

As has been seen, then, the greatest legal privilege enjoyed by alien seamen in Britain, exemption from impressment, was often thwarted by practice, and potentially meaningless if not backed by other forms of evidence, such as diplomatic support and 'foreign' appearance. A second area where we can look for special treatment of aliens is criminal legislation and practice, in both civilian and naval courts.

2.3   'Persons That Cannot Discern between Their Right Hand and Their Left Hand': Alien Seamen and British Criminal Law

In 1795, the Italian sailor Lewis Bonnevento/Beneventa faced trial in the Old Bailey for stabbing a fellow seaman in a London lodging house. An interpreter was present, and 'half of the Jury were foreigners, because the prisoner was one'.[72] The privilege of a half-foreign jury derived from ancient customary practices, connected to a 'personal' rather than 'territorial' understanding of the law: jurors drawn from a certain local, religious, ethnic, or even institutional community (for instance Jews and universities) were deemed to have special competence in trying fellow members, their presence also ensuring 'fair dealing'.[73] This arrangement is another example of the group 'privileges' and 'legal pluralism' that globally preceded the rise of the modern centralised and supposedly uniform 'nation-states'.[74] Nineteenth-century Whiggish accounts used

---

[70] TNA, ADM 1/3850, Letters from Foreign Consuls, 1796–8, George Wolff to Evan Nepean, 2 May 1796.

[71] Perl-Rosenthal, *Citizen Sailors*, 27–44; Noiriel, *État*, 317–29, 339–40.

[72] *OBP*, April 1795, Lewis Bonnevento (t17950416-42); *Courier and Evening Gazette*, 18 April 1795; *The Register of the Times – Volume 4* (London, 1795), 352.

[73] Marianne Constable, *The Law of the Other: The Mixed Jury and Changing Conceptions of Citizenship, Law, and Knowledge* (Chicago, MI and London: The University of Chicago Press, 1994), 1–2, 96–111; James C. Oldham, 'The Origins of the Special Jury', *The University of Chicago Law Review* 50:1 (1983), 137–221, at 164–71; Matthew Lockwood, '"Love Ye Therefore the Strangers": Immigration and the Criminal Law in Early Modern England', *Continuity and Change* 29:3 (2014), 349–71.

[74] Benton, *Law*; Rapport, *Nationality and Citizenship*, 20–9.

the mixed jury allowance to highlight England's liberality towards foreigners, but this exceptionalist stance left contemporary continental
jurists somewhat sceptical.[75]

A half-jury, it has been argued, may have allowed foreigners higher
rates of acquittal or lesser charges, into the eighteenth century.[76]
However, even if alien mixed juries were called '*de medietate linguae*', by
then considerations of language and cultural competence were secondary: the 'alien half' was not even required to be from the same country as
the defendant, doubtlessly reducing its usefulness.[77] This was precisely
because, with the emergence of the levelling 'territorial' state, in the eyes
of British law, the artificial category of alien began to be assigned more
importance than cultural elements of foreignness, which were more
immediately relevant to people's personal lives.[78] The situation was even
less favourable when sailors embarked with the Royal Navy, where a jury
de medietate linguae was intrinsically impossible: courts martial had to be
composed of five to thirteen senior officers, and we know that normally
officers could not be aliens.[79] The only exception that I could find relates
to half-juries in the four Dutch ships commissioned into the Navy in
1800, which are discussed in Chapter 6.[80]

Did alien seamen, then, face the courts in exactly the same legal
position as their British colleagues? Perhaps not always. Positivist legal
historiography tends to disregard as non-legal anything not codified in
writing; yet, this is reductive.[81] Any significant example of alien sailors'
differential legal treatment, indeed, derived not from state legislation, but
from less formal practices – diplomatic negotiations and judicial mercy.

First, alien seamen facing courts martial had the advantage that their
country's diplomatic representatives could sometimes intervene. The
Dane Lorenz Hansen, in May 1798, tried to obtain the release of a
'Danish mariner' accused of taking part in an 'affray', and personally
vouched for him with the Admiralty ('I know this Man to be of a good
decent family in Norway'); the imperial consul Christopher Henry
Martens, a few months later, requested the release of an Austrian soldier
who, employed in a British ship, had got 'toxicated' while on leave, and

[75] J. D. Meyer, *Esprit, origine et progrès des institutions judiciaires des principaux pays de l'Europe*, 2 vols. (Paris: G. Dufour et Ed. D'Ocagne, 1823), II, 212–18.
[76] Lockwood, '"Love Ye"', 362–5.
[77] Constable, *Law of the Other*, 112–27; Oldham, 'Origins of the Special Jury', 169–71; Fahrmeir, *Citizens and Aliens*, 180–1.
[78] Constable, *Law of the Other*, 137–48.   [79] 22 Geo. II c. 33 § xii, xiv.
[80] 39 & 40 Geo. III c. 100 § v.
[81] Constable, *Law of the Other*, 4–5, 26–7, 67–95, 149–52.

was now in prison.[82] Unfortunately, the outcome of these pleas is often unknown. When it has survived, however, it shows that consular interference was not always effective, precisely because the boundaries between states' jurisdictions were contested and open to manipulation. In 1801, John Williams, an American sailor, was tried for mutiny; the American envoy attempted to obtain his discharge, arguing that Williams was an American subject, and that he had not entered the Royal Navy voluntarily.[83] While the former claim was accepted, the latter was proven highly dubious in the face of the evidence. According to Admiralty lawyers, this prevented an acquittal,

> because, it is perfectly clear that, whenever the Subject of one Prince or State enters voluntarily into the Service of another, and contracts certain positive Obligations in Consequence of the New Relation he has adopted, he is equally amenable to the Laws which relate to his Condition with the natural born Subjects of such Prince or State, and equally liable to punishment for the breach of them.[84]

The overall principle seems clear: once a man *voluntarily* put himself under the naval regulations of the British Crown, no power in the world could save him from being treated, in front of British martial law, exactly like his fellow British shipmates. Again, we see that, when convenient, the British state would readily ignore legal distinctions between aliens and subjects, or maintain a fluid interpretation of them, to its advantage.

Legal practice could result in a second, informal type of leniency towards foreigners. At Bonnevento's trial, one of the foreign jury members arrived late and then attempted to find a substitute; though this would have normally resulted in a 'heavy penalty', the judge told him that 'as he was a foreigner, and perhaps not well acquainted with the rules of our Courts of Justice, the Court would, on this occasion, overlook what had happened'.[85] Similar examples of tolerance are found in naval courts martial, as well.

In November 1806, at Barbados, three seamen faced judgement for their involvement with the mutineers who had taken HMS *Dominica* to an enemy port.[86] One of them, called Naiad Suare, was the ship's cook, a Black fugitive from enslavement and a 'native of Martinique'.[87] As he

---

[82] TNA, ADM 1/3850, Letters from Foreign Consuls, 1796–8, Lorenz Hansen to the Lords Commissioners of the Admiralty, 17 May 1798; Christopher Henry Martens to Evan Nepean, 13 November 1798.

[83] TNA, ADM 7/305, Law Officers' Opinions, 1800–2, nn. 28–9, John Williams.

[84] Ibid.   [85] *Courier and Evening Gazette*, 18 April 1795.

[86] John D. Byrn (ed.), *Naval Courts Martial, 1793–1815* (Farnham and Burlington, VT: Routledge, 2009), 427–36.

[87] Ibid., 435.

declared in his defence, he had acquiesced to cooperate only when threatened with a cutlass: he strongly opposed navigating the *Dominica* into Martinique, 'for if my master was to catch me in a French port, he would hang me'.[88] Even though his sentences in the recorded minutes appear perfectly correct, one of the witnesses related that on the day of the mutiny he had heard him 'speaking in broken English'. This statement was not questioned by the court, which suggests that either an unrecorded interpreter was present, or, as usual, trial minutes are heavily shaped by the transcriber.[89] Either way, it seems clear that Suare presented as a 'foreigner'. He was convicted and sentenced to death, but the court martial immediately wrote to Admiral Cochrane, Commander-in-Chief of the station, begging 'to recommend him for mercy', as he 'appears ignorant of the magnitude of the crime and to have acted under the influence of fear from the threats made him'.[90] On 17 December, Suare was accordingly pardoned.

Leniency based on specific circumstances of the accused, for example age, is frequently found in eighteenth-century naval courts martial, and even Britons could be shown mercy because they had been 'seduced' by someone else to commit a crime.[91] In most cases, however, the first half of the court's plea for Suare would have appeared nonsensical: ignorance of the gravity of that most heinous of crimes, mutiny, would not have been deemed a valid excuse. In theory, the Articles of War were to be 'hung up in some Public Places of the Ship, and read to the Ship's Company once a Month'; whether this was effectively done remains open to doubt, but it was clearly expected that all men in the service be acquainted with them.[92] Thus, only one other type of attenuating circumstance offers a parallel.

Courts martial tended to show tolerance even towards the worst crimes, if committed in a state of 'insanity'. In 1812, landsman William Kinder, who had – for the third time in four years – repeatedly struck a lieutenant with his fist, was acquitted, mainly after all witnesses unanimously confirmed that he frequently showed signs of 'madness'.[93] Likewise, in 1808, Marine Alexander Vannetta (or Vannett), presumably

---

[88] Ibid., 431–2, 435.
[89] Ibid., 432. On the problem of the transcriber's voice, see Raphael Samuel, 'Perils of the Transcript', *Oral History* 1:2 (1972), 19–22.
[90] Byrn, *Naval Courts Martial*, 435.
[91] Markus Eder, *Crime and Punishment in the Royal Navy of the Seven Years' War, 1755–1763* (Aldershot and Burlington, VT: Ashgate, 2004), 10, 81–5, 145–6.
[92] *Regulations and Instructions Relating to His Majesty's Service at Sea*, 13th ed. (London, 1790), 47.
[93] Byrn, *Naval Courts Martial*, 125–30. On the Navy's relative indifference towards mental disorders, see Catherine Beck, 'Patronage and Insanity: Tolerance, Reputation and

a foreigner himself, since during the trial the questions posed included 'what Countryman' he was and whether he understood English, went on a sudden rampage, stabbing fourteen shipmates. He was sentenced to death, but the court recommended a 'commutation of punishment', on the grounds of his 'derangement'.[94] In general, whenever a case warranted suspicion, courts martial tended to investigate carefully the possibility of defendants' insanity, repeatedly inquiring on the matter with all witnesses.[95] One cannot but be struck by the parallel between this and the procedure followed in the court martial of the Maltese seaman Francisco Falso, tried for sodomy in 1798: 'Do you know whether Francisco Falso has always understood the Orders, that have been given him?', 'Did you ever hear the Articles of War read on board?', 'Does Francisco Falso speak or understand English?', 'Did you ever hear the Maltese speak English?', the witnesses were asked.[96] We do not know whether his foreignness would have carried enough weight to affect the sentence, or subsequent recommendations for mercy, since both Falso and his lover were acquitted for lack of proof, but the repeated questions signify that it was a matter worth considering. This suggests that cultural and linguistic extraneousness were possibly deemed a form of disability analogous to insanity. A similar juridical analogy appears again and again in various historical contexts, put to different uses: white settlers in 1820s Australia drew it to argue that Aboriginal people should not be 'tried in colonial courts';[97] during the American Civil War, in military tribunals, 'ignorance' and 'madness' were both used by defendants as proof of the lack of '*mens rea*', or 'criminal intent', although especially the former plea was often unsuccessful.[98] In the British naval case, the analogy seemingly underlay the very procedure of some courts, and warranted special leniency towards men like Suare. The crucial difference between insanity and ignorance was that, whilst leniency towards 'lunatics' was explicitly

---

Mental Disorder in the British Navy 1740–1820', *Historical Research* 94:263 (2021), 73–95.

[94] TNA, ADM 7/307, Law Officers' Opinions, 1805–8, n. 68, Court Martial of Alexander Vannetta, 31 December 1808.

[95] See, for example, the cases of John Wheeler (1811), John Mose (1806), and James Seymonds alias Simmons (1808): Byrn, *Naval Courts Martial*, 288–93, 438, 450–1.

[96] TNA, ADM 1/5364, Courts Martial Papers, August–September 1798, Francisco Falso and John Lambert, 18 September 1798. I found this case thanks to a mention in Roy Adkins and Lesley Adkins, *Jack Tar: The Extraordinary Lives of Ordinary Seamen in Nelson's Navy* (London: Abacus, 2008), 12.

[97] Benton, *Law*, 189.

[98] R. Gregory Lande, *Madness, Malingering, and Malfeasance: The Transformation of Psychiatry and the Law in the Civil War Era* (Washington, DC: Brassey's, Inc., 2003), 14–15, 17–39, 157–63, 179–80, 200–1.

prescribed by statute, and a legal principle in civilian criminal law, leniency towards foreigners was likely not.[99]

The man thus pardoned or acquitted would benefit from this discretionary interpretation of written law, and arguably the British state benefited, too. Douglas Hay's view of pardons purely as deliberate instruments of power has been questioned,[100] but it is true that, whether saved by compassion or by economical calculations, an able-bodied alien had some value for the Navy. His legal condition as alien, on paper, did not entitle him to any significant favouritisms. Cultural 'otherness', however, potentially perceived as a structural deficiency not unlike mental confusion, prompted a merciful treatment. We should avoid slipping into an unduly rosy account, here: in other occasions, cultural prejudice or racism may well have swayed the courts in the opposite direction, resulting in special harshness. In either case, nonetheless, it was not documentary, legal difference, but – if anything – the wholly social and cultural *perception* of difference, which ultimately mattered in influencing a foreign defendant's fate.

One last reason why the legal category of 'alien' is unhelpful when studying seamen's lives is that, particularly in their case, the very boundaries between aliens and subjects could be rather blurred. It is precisely here that the dubious weight of official labels is thrown into relief most clearly.

2.4   The Naturalisation of Alien Seamen

A state's right of protection over foreign seamen serving under its flag has sometimes been recognised in international law, even if it runs contrary to all other established norms.[101] In early nineteenth-century Britain, it was reflected in the rather ambiguous concept of the 'character of a British Mariner', which, according to Sir William Scott, judge of the High Court of Admiralty, was invested on any foreign sailor domiciled in the country: this is the case seen above of seamen 'married or settled' in Britain.[102] Domicile (as opposed to mere residence), with its power to

---

[99] For some of the relevant legislation, see 39 & 40 Geo. III c. 94; 48 Geo. III c. 96 § xxvii.

[100] Douglas Hay, 'Property, Authority and the Criminal Law', in Douglas Hay et al., *Albion's Fatal Tree: Crime and Society in Eighteenth-Century England* (London: Allen Lane and New York: Pantheon, 1975), 17–63, at 22–6, 40–63; Peter King, 'Decision-Makers and Decision-Making in the English Criminal Law, 1750–1800', *The Historical Journal* 27:1 (1984), 25–58; John H. Langbein, 'Albion's Fatal Flaws', *Past & Present* 98 (1983), 96–120; Eder, *Crime and Punishment*, 5–6, 133–4.

[101] Watts, 'Protection'. For the case of US shipping, see Zimmerman, *Impressment*, 17, 19–21, 25, 49–51.

[102] Watts, 'Protection', 697; Perl-Rosenthal, *Citizen Sailors*, 121–2.

'impress' 'national character', was, in fact, as vaguely defined a category then as it is today.[103] In equally vague terms, nineteenth-century international jurists also mentioned the idea that, in wartime, seamen were 'to be characterised by the country in whose service they are employed'.[104] These general rather nebulous principles found some measure of formal expression in the legislation that, throughout the eighteenth century, offered British naturalisation to alien seafarers. The chaotic nature of this legislation is, arguably, the focal point where some crucial internal contradictions of the modern state became most clearly exposed.

Naturalisation was, in early modern Britain, a long and costly process, usually only pursued by wealthy merchants.[105] Some of these wealthy merchants, however, while embroiled in bureaucratic procedures, may have wished that they were seamen: a statute of the sixth of Anne (1707), aiming to promote trade, established that,

> for the better encouraging of foreign Mariners and Seamen to come and serve on board Ships belonging to the Kingdom of *Great Britain*... every such foreign Mariner or Seaman who shall... have faithfully served on board any of Her Majesty's Ships of War, or any Privateer or Merchant or trading Ship or Ships, Vessel or Vessels, which at the Time of such Service shall belong to any of Her Majesty's Subjects of *Great Britain*, for the Space of two Years, shall, to all Intents and Purposes, be deemed and taken to be a natural-born Subject of Her Majesty's Kingdom of *Great Britain*.[106]

The provision was repeated in an Act of 1740, this time with the additional specification that service had to take place 'during the time of War'.[107] Nothing in this second Act seems to indicate that the previous statute was still deemed in force: even if the wording is almost the same, Anne's Act is never cited in the text. The validity of the 1740 Act itself, then, after the end of the War of Jenkins's Ear, is also uncertain: did 'during the time of War' mean any war, or just the present one?[108] An Act of 1780 reconfirmed this statute's rulings on naturalisation, noting that 'Doubts have arisen' on their 'true Intent and Meaning'; yet, once again, the text spoke of 'the last War' and 'the present Hostilities', leaving its applicability to subsequent conflicts open to interpretation.[109] It is true that a statute not formally repealed retains its legal value. Indeed, we know that this was the case throughout the period of the French Wars,

---

[103] Richard Wildman, *Institutes of International Law – Volume Two: International Rights in Time of War* (London: William Benning & Co., 1850), 36–45.
[104] Ibid., 97–8; Perl-Rosenthal, *Citizen Sailors*, 121–2.
[105] Fahrmeir, *Citizens and Aliens*, 71, 84–6, 92; Statt, *Foreigners and Englishmen*, 34–7. For some figures, see Beerbühl, 'British Nationality Policy', 58–66.
[106] 6 Ann. c. 37 § xx.   [107] 13 Geo. II c. 3 § ii.   [108] 13 Geo. II c. 3 § i, iii.
[109] 20 Geo. III c. 20 § iii; Parry, *British Nationality Law*, 90–1.

because a parliamentary bill of 1818, proposing temporary limitations to naturalisations, explicitly excepted those that previous Acts 'made for encouraging Seamen to enter into His Majesty's service'.[110] Most modern historians report the two-year rule as valid into the nineteenth century, and so did the jurist Joseph Chitty in his 1820 treatise.[111] The legal reality, however, was more intricate.

Puzzlingly, indeed, in 1794, another Act allowed aliens to be masters of British ships (an 1802 statute extended this to Ireland), and deemed British mariners for the purposes of the Navigation Laws, if they had *three* years of wartime naval service, a certificate of good behaviour, and proof of having taken the Oath of Allegiance.[112] Why was this provision necessary, if after two years they were considered naturalised subjects anyway? Naturalisation did not allow access to civil or military offices under the Crown,[113] but commanding merchantmen – or working in them – clearly did not fall under either category. Even more curiously, the text of the Act listed the ways in which a man might be qualified a 'British' master or seaman as 'by Birth, Naturalisation, Denization, Conquest or Service', thus effectively differentiating naturalisation from rights acquired by service.[114] Whilst this bill underwent several amendments in both Houses before being passed, unfortunately no relevant details of the debates survive.[115]

Overall, it appears that the legislation on this matter was layered, in frequent need of re-establishment, and occasionally contradictory, leading us to suspect that the rule was not always known or followed. Even though the formulation in the 1707 Act, 'shall… be deemed and taken to be a natural-born Subject', seems to suggest an automatic transition, on which a seaman had no say, the sources show that eligibility to naturalisation did not mean that naturalisation was inevitable, or in fact particularly coveted by seamen. In 1808, Lars Jansby, a Swede, had served for 'about 9 years' in the British 'Merchant and Transport

---

[110] 'A proposed bill to prevent aliens, for a limited time, from becoming naturalised, or being made or becoming denizens; except in certain cases' (June 1818), *19th Century House of Commons Sessional Papers*, I, 579, ProQuest U.K. Parliamentary Papers https://parlipapers.proquest.com/parlipapers.

[111] Fahrmeir, *Citizens and Aliens*, 70; Zimmerman, *Impressment*, 82–3; Joseph Chitty, *A Treatise on the Law of the Prerogatives of the Crown* (London: Joseph Butterworth and Son and Dublin: John Cooke, 1820), 14.

[112] 34 Geo. III c. 68 § vii; 42 Geo. III c. 61 § viii.   [113] Cockburn, *Nationality*, 29–34.

[114] 34 Geo. III c. 68 § viii.

[115] *Journals of the House of Lords, Beginning Anno Tricesimo Quarto Georgii Tertii*, 1794, XL, 94a, 112b, 115b, 118b, 120a, 216a, 219a, 244a; London, Parliamentary Archives, HL/PO/JO/10/7/965, Records of the House of Lords: Main Papers, British Mariners Bill – Amendments and Clauses, 3 April 1794.

Service'. He survived shipwreck and, upon stepping on English soil, immediately went to the Commercial and Naval Register and Insurance Office, to request a protection from impressment. As he swore in his affidavit, he 'had not done any Act to become a Subject of his Britannic Majesty', presumably meaning the oath-taking process.[116] The protection was denied to him; two days later, a press gang caught him and, despite his protests, kept him imprisoned in poor conditions for several days, alleging irregularities in his papers.[117] This might simply be another example of impress service prevarication, since, according to Jansby, the regulating officer had no difficulties in accepting that he was a Swedish subject.[118] However, more was probably at stake. Jansby was, by his own declaration, culturally well assimilated: he had chosen to leave American shipping 'preferring the British Service not only from Treatment whilst on Board but the Manners & Constitution of the Country'; he had 'made himself acquainted with the Language Customs' and 'acted and performed the duty of Second Mate and Boatswain of several Ships of large dimensions'.[119] Very similar is the case of Wilhelm/William Schroeder, a Prussian sailor who for thirteen years had 'constantly' served in 'British Merchant Ships', but 'never committed any Act to become a Subject of his Britanic [sic] Majesty'.[120] He was nevertheless impressed, in 1809, and, in justifying this action, the lieutenant and surgeon subsequently observed that he 'did not answer the description in his protection', resided in London, and 'spoke good English'.[121] The law regulating who was a subject, who was not, and who became one was weak and open to interpretation and abuse: in this context, again, we find that a man who shed most of his appearance of foreignness possibly lost his most valuable bargaining card.

If men like Jansby and Schroeder were legally alien but culturally 'Briticised', the opposite case was also possible: seamen who were legally naturalised, but still culturally 'foreign'. This theme emerges most forcefully in xenophobic discourse. Already in 1693, during a heated parliamentary debate on the naturalisation of foreign protestants, the MP and Mayor of Bristol Sir John Knight had expressed the core of the question: 'foreign Merchants will naturalise foreign Seamen; and when the Press-Masters find them, they will *Dutchen spraken, ya min Heer,* and avoid the Service; but at the Custom-House, Exchange, and in all

---

[116] TNA, ADM 7/307, Law Officers' Opinions, 1805–8, n. 61, Lars Jansby, 8 March 1808, f. 2.
[117] Ibid., ff. 2–4.   [118] Ibid., f. 3.   [119] Ibid., f. 1.
[120] TNA, ADM 7/308, Law Officers' Opinions, 1809–10, n. 27, Wm. Schroeder, 6 February 1810.
[121] Ibid., ff. 2, 5.

Corporations, they will be found as good Englishmen as any of this House'.[122] It is probably true that seamen would have attempted, to some extent, to play the system to their advantage: a gap between legal and cultural identification can make one of the two irrelevant, at any given time, or create tension and displacement, but it can also offer considerable leeway to individual agency.[123] Lars Jansby, indicting the press gang officers in King's Bench, was living proof of this. The problem with arguments like that of Knight, however, was that the actual advantage that could be drawn from claiming legally British status was rather meagre.

Admittedly, naturalised seamen no longer counted as foreigners for the Navigation Laws, thereby gaining fuller access to British peacetime employment.[124] This, though, was the only tangible benefit, and it did not immediately affect a man already engaged in the naval service, until at least the end of the conflict. The highly hypothetical ability to possess his own plot of British land, buy an English ship, and save on customs duties would scarcely make any difference to his daily life. As argued by Cerutti, social integration is a process in which institutional recognition, per se, only plays a minor and indirect part, and over which the early modern state never exerted 'monopoly' of control.[125] Aside from few dubious economic advantages, naturalisation was at best rather meaningless, and often even problematic, as for Jansby and Schroeder.

More broadly, the main issue was that, as a poorly-thought-through political measure in conditions of national necessity, seamen's naturalisation was not only indifferent in practice to the lives of individuals, but also theoretically in contradiction with some of the pillars of the state's self-definition. Thus, once again, application proved very different from the letter of the statutes, especially when the complexities of international law came into play.

The relative levity with which the naturalisation of seamen was regarded is well enshrined in a speech that the Tory George Canning gave in the House of Commons, in 1813. Rejecting the assertions of the Whig MP Samuel Whitbread, who equated British practice to that of Americans, he specified that the 1707 Act, while allowing foreigners to 'participate in all the blessings of the British constitution', as 'a testimony

---

[122] Debate on Naturalising Foreign Protestants, 7 November 1693, in *The History and Proceedings of the House of Commons: Volume 2, 1680–1695* (London: Chandler, 1742), 415–45.

[123] On seafarers' strategic self-fashioning, see Land, *War*, 27–8; Morieux, 'Diplomacy'. For other examples of strategic use of, alternatively, belonging and extraneousness, see Cerutti, *Étrangers*, 167, 214–17; Benton, *Law*, 85, 99–100, 165–6.

[124] Harper, *English Navigation Laws*, 389.   [125] Cerutti, *Étrangers*, 17–20, 63–9, 292–9.

of national gratitude to brave men of whatever country who may lend their aid in fighting the battles of Great Britain', still left 'untouched and unimpaired their native allegiance'. The provision was not intended, he clarified amidst the 'hear, hear!'s of the House, as 'an encouragement to them to deny or to undervalue the sacred and indestructible duty which they owe to their own sovereign, and to their native soil'.[126] This must be placed in the rhetorical – and rather hypocritical – context of the War of 1812, and particularly within the debate on 'indelible' or 'indefeasible allegiance', which saw Britain and the United States accusing each other of stealing national seamen.[127] Nevertheless, a public stance of this kind still left the naturalised foreigner (American or otherwise), and most harshly the one who had fought for Britain against his old country, with little more than a worthless honorary title in his hands. The Napoleonic Code, for example, decreed the confiscation of property and expulsion from French territory of Frenchmen naturalised abroad without authorisation; if they fought against France, as was obviously the case with Royal Navy sailors, the penalty was death.[128] What use could then be the formal naturalisation granted by a government that afterwards refused to afford protection?[129]

In short, the naturalisation of a Navy seaman was, for him, a legally confused process, socially and culturally almost irrelevant, economically only marginally advantageous, and even, partly because of its legal flimsiness, potentially dangerous. The state itself that, pressed by need, offered naturalisation to attract seamen was intrinsically unable to guarantee the consistency and permanency of this measure, which contradicted its own essence. The final result was that official legal status came to matter little to either of the two parties involved, and a weak understanding of it proved convenient to both.

2.5   Conclusion

In eighteenth-century Britain, the political will and economic pressure to impose disabilities on aliens were relatively weak.[130] This holds particularly true for seafaring men, a crucially useful group for a state that largely

---

[126] Hansard, House of Commons, vol. 24, 'Address Respecting the War with America', 18 February 1813, cc. 593–649, at 630–2, 634–7 https://api.parliament.uk/historic-hansard/commons/1813/feb/18/address-respecting-the-war-with-america.

[127] Zimmerman, *Impressment*, 21–9, 81–4; Cockburn, *Nationality*, 70–8.

[128] Cockburn, *Nationality*, 54.

[129] For the subsequent history of contradictions inherent to naturalisation and indelible allegiance, see Fahrmeir, *Citizens and Aliens*, 46–51, 63–4, 86, 91–3.

[130] Ibid., 238.

drew its wealth and power from the sea. Hence, in times of need, even the residual barriers that interest ordinarily imposed on foreigners were specially lifted for seamen. The Navigation Laws were relaxed during wartime, and the Royal Navy was wide open to recruits. At the same time, alien mariners enjoyed no preferential treatment over British seamen. The few legal provisions that would have acted in this sense were either, like exemption from impressment, regularly transgressed in practice, being contrary to the national interest, or ultimately almost meaningless, as in the case of the half jury. Any benefits stemmed not from the letter of the law, but from the discretion of individual enforcers, moved not by a man's position as a non-subject, but by his situation as a cultural outsider, coupled with practical considerations. Both safety or release from impressment and post-verdict leniency were often granted on the basis of an appearance of foreignness, rather than pieces of paper, in the same way as the only severe disability, relating to pensions and discharges, targeted the racially and socially 'other' Black servicemen, regardless of their birthplace and subject status.

The limited significance of legal status to a naval seaman's life can be seen, finally, in the chaotic, contradictory, and uncertain shape of the legislation that sanctioned his transition from alien to subject: this legal transition was very often out of phase with his cultural and social transition,[131] and in practice, again, it was frequently the latter that had the most immediate effect on his identification in the eyes of others. Because his status as an alien had so little impact on his service in the British Navy, moreover, there was not much that the superficial gift of naturalisation could do for him, in material terms at least – and indeed, it could prove damaging.

Camillo Corri, a Scot in British law, grew up in an Italian household, surrounded by the artistic traditions of his parents' native land, and in these he found the source of his deepest personal pride. Lars Jansby, instead, moved by admiration and convenience, found in Britain his perfect new motherland; yet, he remained legally a Swede. It is important not to reduce the role of legal categories to nothing: for Corri, British subjecthood meant that one day, perhaps, he could have aspired to a commission as lieutenant;[132] for Jansby, the lack of British subjecthood meant that he could eventually escape the press gang. As we shall see, the end of the war would also brusquely remind everyone of the weight of

---

[131] Ibid., 93; Statt, *Foreigners and Englishmen*, 186–92.

[132] No officer named Camillo Corri ever passed the examination for lieutenant. See Bruno Pappalardo, *Royal Navy Lieutenants' Passing Certificates (1691–1902)*, 2 vols. (Kew: List and Index Society, 2001).

subjecthood. At the same time, however, beyond specific moments of personal or collective crisis, legal categories only accounted for a relatively minimal part of these men's life, and of the daily obstacles, privileges, and meaning with which it was invested – by them and by others. These categories and labels, much like patriotic claims, were deployed when strategically useful, but then immediately shelved again. This, most importantly, was not only done by the individuals themselves, but also by the very states that set the labels. Whilst by definition reliant on rigid categorisations, structures, and procedures, which it invented, the power of the modern state was also, for its survival, forced to ignore and undermine these same categorisations, structures, and procedures, caught in an existential blackmail that ultimately revealed its contradictions and conceptual weaknesses.

The compromises that Navy officials made when it came to legal boundaries help us to put into context a different type of compromise, which they also regularly practised: the accommodation of cultural difference. An institution that did not hesitate to ignore even 'hard' state-defined boundaries was, as can be imagined, relatively unconcerned with 'softer' forms of distinction, and particularly with prejudices and categorisations relating to cultural traits – several of which were then commonly defined in terms of national characters. Chapters 3–6 explore the ways in which these differences and preconceptions were tackled.

Part II

The Nation

3   A Babel and a Gehenna
Languages and Religions

A pragmatic, open-ended recruitment drive had to contend not only with the legal boundaries of states, but also with forms of cultural prejudice that were ingrained in popular attitudes and political discourse. This prejudice often rested on the identification of ethnically inferior antitheses to an idealised British nation. The disparaging attitude of elites and the general public alike could extend not only to extra-European peoples and inhabitants of imperial territories, but also to the 'uncivilised' Eastern European, the 'effeminate' Catholic, and even to certain categories of Briton.[1] At the same time, essentialist ideas of race and culture were not yet fully consolidated. Much debate occurred, among intellectuals, on the nature and origin of cultural difference and 'national characters'. These were understood as encompassing peculiarities in language, religion, 'manners', and forms of social organisation, as well as physical traits like skin colour or assumed fitness to a specific climate, and the effects of climate itself on human nature.[2] The 'cultural' and the 'biological' were, thus, inextricably entangled in common typologies of 'race'.[3] The main fault line, then, separated those who perceived supposed differences between peoples as fundamental, immutable, and irreconcilable from those who believed them to be contingent, historical,

---

[1] Larry Wolff, 'La géographie philosophique des Lumières : L'Europe de l'Est et les Tartares de Sibérie au regard de la civilisation', in Antoine Lilti and Céline Spector (eds.), *Penser l'Europe au XVIIIᵉ siècle : Commerce, civilisation, empire* (Oxford: Voltaire Foundation, 2014), 167–80; Kathleen Wilson, *The Sense of the People: Politics, Culture and Imperialism in England, 1715–1785* (Cambridge: Cambridge University Press, 1995), 185–6, 191–2, 202, 282–4; Paul Stock, '"Almost a Separate Race": Racial Thought and the Idea of Europe in British Encyclopaedias and Histories, 1771–1830', *Modern Intellectual History* 8:1 (2011), 3–29, esp. at 16–29. On the nineteenth-century evolution of intra-British racialisation, see Colin Kidd, 'Race, Empire, and the Limits of Nineteenth-Century Scottish Nationhood', *The Historical Journal* 46:4 (2003), 873–92.
[2] Kathleen Wilson, *The Island Race: Englishness, Empire and Gender in the Eighteenth Century* (London and New York: Routledge, 2003), 11–12.
[3] Stock, '"Almost a Separate Race"', 4–9, 26–9.

and 'accidental'.[4] Naval administration, I will show, mostly subscribed to the latter view: a belief in the ultimate malleability of men had to underlie any large-scale recruitment policy. Yet, this did not remove prejudices and preoccupations on the individual level. Racial and ethnic stereotypes and categorisations were often deeply intertwined with, and masked as, practical concerns.

Most of the men serving in the Navy were supposedly English speakers (with variations of accent), Church of England Protestants (by birth if not belief), and 'white British'. Were any deviations from this norm regarded as significant, and if so why? The aim of this part of the book is establishing how far the push of a strongly disciplined institution would have sufficed to sideline, suppress, or even utilise difference or perceived difference. In this chapter, we begin by looking at the two aspects of national characters that had the most immediate practical and political impact on naval life: language and religion. Both could be linked by Navy personnel to racial and essentialist understandings of human difference. However, they were also among the most changeable traits in a recruit.

3.1   Babel

How should we imagine the soundscape of a Navy deck? The answer is, Elin Jones has recently argued, as coordinated by precise traditions of labour and dissent, but also (often deliberately) 'ambiguous' to the ears of the non-initiated.[5] This ambiguity was amplified by the wide range of languages, dialects, and argots that mingled, or simply coexisted, within the dense community of a crew. The memoirs of the Scottish sailor Robert Hay, with which this book opened, described a Navy guardship as a 'Babel' and a 'hubbub', ringing with the 'discordant notes' of many different British and European tongues.[6] These were merely the ones of which he knew and which he could identify. As in any cosmopolitan context, in the eighteenth-century Navy, speech was one of the most prominent factors of differentiation and even a barrier to communication. Not only did sailors speak different languages, but they frequently did not understand English. Not fully mastering the language of a receiving community can often create serious disadvantage for an immigrant,

---

[4] On this tension, see Silvia Sebastiani, 'Nations, Nationalism and National Characters' in Aaron Garrett (ed.), *The Routledge Companion to Eighteenth Century Philosophy* (London and New York: Routledge, 2014), 593–617; Wilson, *Island Race*, 6–15; Stock, '"Almost a Separate Race"', 7–14.

[5] Elin Jones, 'Space, Sound and Sedition on the Royal Naval Ship, 1756–1815', *Journal of Historical Geography* 70 (2020), 65–73.

[6] Hay, *Landsman Hay*, 44–5.

becoming a 'deficiency'.[7] However, because the Navy needed these men, a lack of English language skills did not necessarily prejudice their recruitment. As a result, language was in many ways the Navy's problem, more than the individual's.

Much like at Babel, insufficient understanding between officers and men could create obstacles to the smooth functioning of the fleet. Additionally, the association of languages with national characters easily led to value judgements on individuals' qualities.[8] However, verbal linguistic difference, incomprehension, or difficulties in the Navy may not have been as logistically and politically problematic as might be initially assumed. Men from within the British Isles and Ireland could encounter equal or superior barriers to comprehension to those born abroad: 'English' speakers aboard a ship were a mosaic and a spectrum, rather than a uniform majority. At the same time, the Navy appeared relatively indifferent to a man's lack of understanding of English (of any sort), suggesting that it was not deemed, in practice, an overly important matter. Some historians have argued that linguistic uniformity and centralisation, including within and through institutions, was a trademark pursuit in the formation of modern nation-states.[9] Yet, predating these policies and frameworks, we find much more variegated systems, where functional multilingualism was the norm, and boundaries between languages blurry.[10] Paul Cohen has flagged up the risks of teleology and misrepresentation inherent to tracing back 'linguistic nationalism' and centralising efforts to the early modern period.[11] The late eighteenth-century Royal Navy sat on the cusp of change, but, I will demonstrate, was not yet acting systematically as a branch of a centralising modern state.

---

[7] For some in-depth case studies, see Anne J. Kershen (ed.), *Language, Labour and Migration* (Aldershot and Burlington, VT: Ashgate, 2000).

[8] Dean Kostantaras, 'Perfecting the Nation: Enlightenment Perspectives on the Coincidence of Linguistic and "National" Refinement', *European Review of History* 24:5 (2017), 659–82; Sebastiani, 'Nations'.

[9] Anderson, *Imagined Communities*; Peter Burke, *Languages and Communities in Early Modern Europe* (Cambridge: Cambridge University Press, 2004), 160–72; Rachel Leow, *Taming Babel: Language in the Making of Malaysia* (Cambridge: Cambridge University Press, 2016).

[10] Eric R. Dursteler, 'Speaking in Tongues: Language and Communication in the Early Modern Mediterranean', *Past & Present* 217 (2012), 47–77.

[11] Paul Cohen, 'Langues et pouvoirs politiques en France sous l'Ancien Régime : cinq anti-lieux de mémoire pour une contre-histoire de la langue française', in Serge Lusignan et al. (eds.), *L'introuvable unité du français. Contacts et variations linguistiques en Europe et en Amérique (XIIe- XVIIIe siècle)* (Quebec City: Presses de l'Université Laval, 2012), 109–43; Dursteler, 'Speaking in Tongues', 51, 53–4.

Due to the nature of the evidence, here I limit the discussion to verbal forms of language and communication; 'gesture' (or 'kinesics'), for example, which has been shown to vary widely across cultures and social groups, does not feature explicitly in this study.[12] Non-verbal interactions might well help to explain more fully how spoken English was bypassed. Early modern linguistic encounters also entailed a complex sphere of multisensorial cultural 'translation', which affected how speakers of a certain language were perceived.[13] What follows, however, will not centre on questions of social and cultural integration. Rather, I focus on the purely functional aspects of mutual intelligibility for safety, efficiency, and professional integration. How widespread was linguistic difference in the Navy? How well did sailors who were not native speakers speak and understand English? And, finally, what were the consequences of linguistic difference, and how far did they cause problems for the Navy?

3.1.1   The Limits of Monolingualism among British and Irish Seamen

Linguistic difference and incomprehension were not the sole purview of 'foreigners' intended as persons coming from abroad. First of all, we must remember that the English spoken aboard ships was infused with technical naval jargon and peculiar turns of phrase, which may have puzzled even the native English landsman. So, we can say that few people were 'native speakers' of 'Navy English' as such; it was a language which was learnt with the ropes.[14] Admittedly, Paul Gilje has qualified the cryptic nature of the maritime argot (real or performed), showing that much of it was, in fact, intelligible to shore-based contemporaries, in a society in which the boundaries between sea and land were fuzzy.[15] So, the debate on this point remains open. What is beyond doubt is that, aside from professional and class affiliation, geographical origin and accent also created linguistic boundaries. Men from all over the British

---

[12] Keith Thomas, 'Introduction', in Jan Bremmer and Herman Roodenburg (eds.), *A Cultural History of Gesture: From Antiquity to the Present Day* (Cambridge: Polity Press, 1991), 1–14; for a modern sociolinguistic perspective, see Max S. Kirch, 'Non-Verbal Communication across Cultures', *The Modern Language Journal* 63:8 (1979), 416–23.

[13] John Gallagher, 'The Italian London of John North: Cultural Contact and Linguistic Encounter in Early Modern England', *Renaissance Quarterly* 70 (2017), 88–131.

[14] Rediker, *Between the Devil and the Deep Blue Sea*, 162–5.

[15] Paul A. Gilje, *To Swear like a Sailor: Maritime Culture in America, 1750–1850* (Cambridge: Cambridge University Press, 2016), esp. ch. 2. See also Isaac Land, 'The Many-Tongued Hydra: Sea Talk, Maritime Culture, and Atlantic Identities, 1700–1850', *Journal of American & Comparative Cultures* 25:3–4 (2002), 412–17.

Isles and Ireland, suddenly faced with the 'southern English' standards of naval administration, could be cast as linguistic outsiders.

Many seamen were identifiable by their 'different' ways of speaking English. In January 1804, Captain Bertie of the *Windsor Castle* observed that John Connor, one of his sailors, did 'not appear a Citizen of the United States of America': 'in my opinion by his Language [he] appears to be one of Ireland'.[16] Scottish manners of speech were also distinctive: picturesque transcriptions of Scottish shipmates' accents make their appearance in sailors' memoirs, interspersed with Scots words, and straining intelligibility for the English reader.[17] Sociologists have studied patterns of 'racialisation by voice' of Irish-accent people in modern Britain, with differences in pronunciation and grammar, due to the superimposition of English over the native Gaelic, cast as 'wrong' and 'inferior'.[18] Similarly, in the eighteenth-century Navy, other accents could be perceived in a pejorative way by southern English speakers: Scottish midshipmen in particular were abundantly mocked and bullied by their English messmates, and even by some other, more integrated Scots, because of their accent and 'barbarous', often obscure vocabulary.[19]

Besides the almost 'foreign'-sounding accents, sometimes seamen from the 'Celtic Fringe', or from more remote regions of England, did genuinely speak a different language. Many were bilingual: letters written home by Welshmen used both English and Welsh phrases.[20] Others, however, were not bilingual at all. The surgeon of HMS *Shannon*, in 1813, noted in his journal that one of his patients, an Irishman, 'could not make himself understood readily being able to speak only his own native Irish'.[21] The man had only been in the service two days, but

---

[16] TNA, ADM 1/1065, Letters from Commanders-in-Chief, Portsmouth, 1804, 46, A. Bertie to George Montagu, 12 January 1804.

[17] John Nicol, *Life and Adventures 1776–1801*, ed. Tim Flannery (Melbourne: The Text Publishing Company, 1997 [Edinburgh, 1822]), 68.

[18] Bronwen Walter, '"Shamrocks Growing out of Their Mouths": Language and the Racialisation of the Irish in Britain', in Kershen, *Language*, 57–73.

[19] Caputo, 'Scotland, Scottishness, British Integration and the Royal Navy' (2018), 97–101; Basil Hall, *Fragments of Voyages and Travels: Chiefly for the Use of Young Persons*, 9 vols. (Edinburgh: R. Cadell and London: Whittaker & Co., 1831–3), I:I, 82. On perceptions of the Scots language, see James G. Basker, 'Scotticisms and the Problem of Cultural Identity in Eighteenth-Century Britain', in John Dwyer and Richard B. Sher (eds.), *Sociability and Society in Eighteenth-Century Scotland* (Edinburgh: Mercat Press, 1993), 81–95.

[20] See, for example, John Morris to his parents, 14 June 1794, and John Davis to his parents, 15 June 1794, both in Helen Watt and Anne Hawkins (eds.), *Letters of Seamen in the Wars with France 1793–1815* (Woodbridge: The Boydell Press, 2016), 88–94.

[21] TNA, ADM 101/120/3, Medical and Surgical Journal of HMS *Shannon* by Alexander Jack, 30 July 1812–29 July 1813, f. 21.

linguistic barriers could also persist after several years in the Navy, as in the case of Peter Fraser, a Scottish Marine aboard HMS *Gloucester* in 1812: despite being very experienced, he still only spoke Erse.[22]

As far as linguistic integration was concerned, then, a neat subdivision between men born in the British Isles and abroad, that is, a subdivision based on the principles of legal and political subjecthood, would be an artificial endeavour. This offers a first hint to the fact that, as a branch of a state that was still far from linguistic uniformity internally, naval administration would not have deemed multilingualism a paramount concern.

3.1.2   Speaking English and Speaking English Too Well

Country of origin often was as a reasonable predictor of variations in sailors' command of English. No doubt, Americans had fewer problems on that front. It has also been noted that early modern seamen from the North Sea and Baltic understood each other reasonably well: whilst English was on the periphery of this linguistic world, it could generally be learnt with facility by other northern Europeans.[23] This conclusion does clash with some modern studies, which have shown that mutual intelligibility between speakers of different European languages is low – even within the same linguistic family, and regardless of whether such intelligibility is inherent or acquired (i.e., existing before or after study or contact).[24] However, among Germanic languages, exposure has proven the strongest predictor of intelligibility.[25] Serving in the Navy, and in British shipping more generally, came with high levels of exposure to English.

Sometimes, although fluent or at least able to communicate in English, seamen retained enough of their original accent and forms of speech to

---

[22] Edward Mangin, 'Some Account of the Writer's Situation as Chaplain in the British Navy', in *Five Naval Journals 1789–1817*, ed. H. G. Thursfield (London: Navy Records Society, 1951), 31.

[23] L. Heerma van Voss, 'North Sea Culture, 1500–1800', in Roding and van Voss, *North Sea and Culture*, 21–40, at 25–8.

[24] Vincent J. van Heuven, Charlotte S. Gooskens, and Renée van Bezooijen, 'Introducing MICRELA: Predicting Mutual Intelligibility between Closely Related Languages in Europe', In J. Navracsics and S. Bátyi (eds.), *First and Second Language: Interdisciplinary Approaches – Studies in Psycholinguistics 6* (Budapest: Tinta könyvkiadó, 2015), 127–45.

[25] Charlotte Gooskens and Femke Swarte, 'Linguistic and Extra-Linguistic Predictors of Mutual Intelligibility between Germanic Languages', *Nordic Journal of Linguistics* 40:2 (2017), 123–47, at 138–42. On early modern uses of German across northern Europe, see, for example, Burke, *Languages*, 127.

be immediately identifiable as non-natives. In January 1814, a writ of habeas corpus to free him from the service was successfully served for Johan Henrick Berglagen, an impressed sailor from Manslow near Bremen, because 'from his dialect', there was 'no doubt of his being a native of Germany'.[26] The same exact formulation was used for the Swede Jonas Jonson.[27] Sailors clearly kept their distinctive accents frequently enough for the Admiralty to use them as a criterion to ascertain foreignness, as we saw in Chapter 2. In 1814, the Transport Board, asking for directions regarding five American sailors, who were claimed from prison by the Prussian consul, was instructed to 'report whether from accent manners or local knowledge these persons appear to be Americans british [*sic*] or [?] foreigners'.[28]

When literate sailors directly corresponded with the Admiralty, we can actually hear their accent. Beyond spelling variations attributable to weak standardisation, class, regional English, and level of literacy, some letters show the specific idiosyncrasies produced by the influence of another mother tongue. A Prussian sailor requesting to be sent home in 1814 deployed turns of phrase such as 'I ham a Prusian', 'Arbour duty', 'I ham a hold Man' (an old man), and the Germanism 'it is all Pace With this Cuntry and Mine'.[29]

At the same time, the documents often report stories of Scandinavian and German sailors, in particular, whose English had become virtually indistinguishable from that of native Britons. This did not always mean that they sounded English. Especially Scandinavians could develop a Scottish accent: in 1793, the Swede Lawrence Leymon was called a 'Scotch buggar' by a member of the press gang he was trying to oppose, and a few years later the Dane Christian Nielsen Ohl, impressed into HMS *Champion*, 'had been represented to the Lords Commissioners of the Admiralty as a North Briton'.[30] Geographical vicinity and common trading routes must have played a part, here. Moreover, Scandinavian languages and Scots share some similarities – not only lexical and syntactic, but also phonetic, especially in Orkney and Shetland, whose

---

[26] TNA, ADM 1/1230, Letters from Commanders-in-Chief, Portsmouth, 1814, nn. 101–200, 137a, George Fowke to Richard Bickerton, 22 January 1814.

[27] TNA, ADM 1/1229, Letters from Commanders-in-Chief, Portsmouth, 1814, nn. 1–99, 31, George Fowke to Richard Bickerton, 5 January 1814.

[28] TNA, ADM 1/3766, Letters from the Transport Board, January–August 1814, Transport Office to J. W. Croker, 27 July 1814.

[29] TNA, ADM 1/1230, Letters from Commanders-in-Chief, Portsmouth, 1814, nn. 101–200, 101, Freederick Huff to the Admiralty, 17 January 1814.

[30] *OBP*, October 1793, trial of Richard Tuart (t17931030–66); TNA, ADM 1/3850, Letters from Foreign Consuls 1796–8, George Wolff to Evan Nepean, 2 May 1796.

ancient Norn language was a variant of Norwegian.[31] Yet, the confusion between Scandinavians and Scots might also be connected to the rather blunt and generic way in which Englishmen often classed Scottish accents and dialects as 'other'.

More examples can be found, anyway, of foreign-born sailors sounding perfectly 'English'. In January 1804, aboard HMS *Leviathan*, a man called Charles Hendricksen declared himself a Swede, asking for discharge: 'his speaking the English Language with so much propriety', however, prompted his captain to retain him in the service until he could produce some reliable proof of his origin.[32] The following month, the same captain recommended caution in granting the discharge of another Swede, Andrew Pattison (Peterson), on identical grounds: 'the Man is so much like an English Man, and speaks the Language so well'.[33] Pattison, marked in the muster as coming from 'Gottenburgh', was eventually discharged at Portsmouth on 15 February, 'p[er] order being a Swede', but Hendrickson, curiously a Norwegian according to the muster, was not so lucky, and was still aboard in April. The two men, it should be noted, were both able seamen, thirty-seven and thirty years old, respectively, so likely to have many years of sea and potentially English-language employment behind them.[34] We know that these instances were not simply the result of the paranoia of a single officer, because the same patterns of suspicion recur elsewhere in Admiralty documents.[35]

An advanced level of fluency had implications, both for the sailors and for the naval administration. Paradoxically, it could have even more serious implications than a lack of knowledge of English. On the one hand, if language is officially assumed as a prime signifier of 'foreignness',[36] complete linguistic assimilation can be taken to mean complete cultural

---

[31] George Broderick, 'The Development of Insular Celtic', in Per Sture Ureland (ed.), *Entstehung von Sprachen und Völkern: Glotto- und ethnogenetische Aspekte europäischer Sprachen – Akten des 6. Symposions über Sprachkontakt in Europa, Mannheim 1984* (Tübingen: Max Niemeyer Verlag, 1985), 153–80, at 155; Alexander Pavlenko, 'On the Use of "Be" as a Perfective Auxiliary in Modern Shetland Dialect: Hybridization and Synctactic Change', in P. Sture Ureland and Iain Clarkson (eds.), *Language Contact across the North Atlantic: Proceedings of the Working Groups Held at University College, Galway (Ireland), August 29–September 3, 1992 and the University of Göteborg (Sweden), August 16–21, 1993* (Tübingen: Max Niemeyer Verlag, 1996), 75–82; J. C. Wells, *Accents of English 2: The British Isles* (Cambridge: Cambridge University Press, 1986), 398–9.

[32] TNA, ADM 1/1065, Letters from Commanders-in-Chief, Portsmouth, 1804, nn. 1–150, 84, H. W. Bayntun to George Montagu, 17 January 1804.

[33] TNA, ADM 1/1066, Letters from Commanders-in-Chief, Portsmouth, 1804, nn. 153–300, 158, H. W. Bayntun to George Montagu, 1 February 1804.

[34] TNA, ADM 36/15834, Muster Books of HMS *Leviathan*, January–April 1804.

[35] See, for example, the case of the Prussian Wilhelm Schroeder, in Section 2.4.

[36] Perl-Rosenthal, *Citizen Sailors*, esp. 32–44, 153, 164, 167–71.

and legal assimilation. Thus, the authorities responded with scepticism to the pleas of such seamen to be discharged as foreigners. On the other hand, men who spoke excellent English could also be perceived as a threat: their ability to escape common categorisations and 'camouflage' themselves as British, if they so chose, was a dangerous skill in wartime and within a military institution. In June 1806, the Lords of the Admiralty were greatly alarmed to discover that the Prussian Simon Bohag, pretending to be a Simon Hall from Marylebone, had been entered as a labourer at Woolwich Dockyard, 'the Officers' not perceiving 'any indication' of his 'being a Foreigner by his accent or otherwise', and then promoted to warden.[37] The Navy was rightfully wary: throughout the eighteenth century, industrial espionage in dockyards was the main technique through which France and Spain kept their ship designs up to date with British innovations.[38]

As will be seen below, linguistic miscommunication at sea could occasionally cause practical problems. Therefore, the obvious assumption is that a poor understanding of English would constitute a significant element of differentiation and perhaps be deemed troublesome by Navy officers. However, the opposite could also apply: for a seaman, *lacking* an appearance of foreignness, where it was expected, could be even more problematic, legally and bureaucratically. It was not language per se that singled out the experiences of some sailors, as much as the expectations connected to it. British authorities assumed a priori that the category of 'foreignness' was applicable to a certain individual, according to stereotypical outlines. Someone who was an immigrant and a foreigner in legal terms was expected to be a 'foreigner' in his manner of speech, as well, and vice versa. A British subject would ideally be a native English speaker and have an 'English' accent: when this equivalence failed, it was intrinsically striking, and such cases helped to reinforce narratives of otherness, extraneity, and even barbarism and remoteness from civilisation. At the same time, a man who was legally foreign only became an object worthy of notice, confusion, or even mistrust when he deviated from 'normal' patterns and learnt English to an extraordinary, 'native' level of competency. In both cases, expectations, rather than objective factors, dictated what was remarkable, as a target of mockery or concern.

---

[37] NMM, ADM/B/222, Board of Admiralty, In-Letters, April–June 1806, Navy Office to William Marsden, 25 June 1806.

[38] Larrie D. Ferreiro, 'Spies versus Prize: Technology Transfer between Navies in the Age of Trafalgar', *The Mariner's Mirror* 93:1 (2007), 16–27; Mariano Juan y Ferragut, 'Jorge Juan: su misión en Londres y la construcción naval española', in *Cuaderno n. 68 del Instituto de Historia y Cultura Naval – Jorge Juan y la ciencia ilustrada en España* (Madrid: Ministerio de Defensa, 2013), 91–107.

The question that remains to be answered is: if a 'foreigner' speaking perfect English could cause concern, what was the concern caused by someone not speaking English at all? If northern European seamen mostly appear to have faced little difficulty with English, it is less straightforward to assess how far sailors from other language areas were able to cope. In the case of Lascars, for example – a colonial category hiding huge cultural and linguistic diversity – problems of communication were removed, because orders were routinely filtered down to them through the medium of their special petty officers, the ship *sarangs* and *tindals*.[39] The situation of sailors from southern Europe is slightly more complicated.

3.1.3   Not Speaking English

Systematic information on sailors' knowledge of English is unfortunately lacking. Yet, a general impression can be gained from occasional documents. In August 1801, seventeen 'foreigners' who were serving in the armed tender *Charlotte* were to be tried by a court martial at Chatham; among them, it was noted, there was 'not a single individual who can read English, or that appears to understand sufficient English to comprehend the charge exhibited against him'.[40] A list was attached, indicating for each of them 'Where Born' and 'Languages they understand': it included one Swede, two Germans, and two Dutchmen, but most of the men were French, Italian, Spanish, or Portuguese, and the languages spoken reflected this. Only the Swede, an Azorean Portuguese, an Italian, and a Quebecois were marked as speaking at least 'a little English'.[41] The sample in this case is too small to draw distinctions by origin, but other, longer sources of this kind offer some insight. In December 1800, the Transport Board transmitted to the Admiralty two lists of foreign prisoners of war who were willing to enter the Navy, including 'remarks' on their seafaring experience, ability, and command of English.[42] Out of 123 names, 103 were reported with unambiguous details of their English proficiency: 22 men spoke English, one 'good' English, 29 'little' or 'a little', and a strikingly high 51 (50%) none at all (**Figure 3.1**). Most of this sample (58 men) was composed of southern

---

[39] Michael H. Fisher, 'Indian Ghat Sarangs as Maritime Labour Recruiting Intermediaries during the Age of Sail', *Journal for Maritime Research* 16:2 (2014), 153–66, at 155–6.

[40] TNA, ADM 1/733, Letters from Commanders-in-Chief, Nore, 1801, nn. 2–600, 579, Lachlan McLean to Bartholomew Samuel Rowley, 18 August 1801.

[41] Ibid.

[42] TNA, ADM 1/3740, Letters from the Transport Board, July 1800–March 1801, Transport Office to Evan Nepean, 17 December 1800, ff. 290–7.

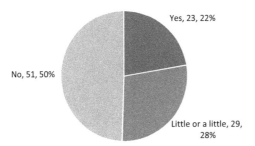

Figure 3.1 Declared English language competence among recruits.

Europeans, including Italians, Portuguese, and men from various Mediterranean islands. Among this group, as many as 69% spoke no English, whereas only 14% spoke it confidently. This is decidedly different from the situation in other groups: most of the Scandinavian sailors knew at least some English, with 41% speaking it and 42% speaking it a little. Among Germans and Dutchmen, by far the largest categories were those speaking a little English (54% and 55% respectively), but again only 15% and 9% among them spoke no English at all (**Figure 3.2**). While these groupings are rather crude, it seems clear that overall southern Europeans spoke 'less' English.

If northern European languages all enjoyed some mutual intelligibility, this was also the case for southern European ones, many of which have common Romance roots.[43] Moreover, frequent contacts between Mediterranean European and North African Arabic languages had produced the so-called *Lingua Franca*, a common patois spoken and understood, in its several variations, by seafarers and traders all over that sea basin.[44] None of these linguistic forms, however, had anything in common with English. An example surviving in Admiralty records well

---

[43] Charlotte Gooskens et al., 'Mutual Intelligibility between Closely Related Languages in Europe', *International Journal of Multilingualism* (2017), 1–25, at 5–6, 13–14, 18.

[44] Jocelyne Dakhlia, *Lingua Franca : Histoire d'une langue métisse en Méditerranée* (Arles: Actes Sud, 2008); Nora Lafi, 'La langue des marchands de Tripoli au XIXe siècle : Langue franque et langue arabe dans un port méditerranéen', in Jocelyne Dakhlia (ed.), *Trames de langues : Usages et métissages linguistiques dans l'histoire du Maghreb* (Paris: Maisonneuve & Larose, 2004), 215–22; Claude Liauzu, 'Mots et migrants méditerranéens', *Cahiers de la Méditerranée* 54:1 (1997), 1–14; John Gallagher, 'Language-Learning, Orality, and Multilingualism in Early Modern Anglophone Narratives of Mediterranean Captivity', *Renaissance Studies* 33:4 (2019), 639–61, at 649–54; Dursteler, 'Speaking in Tongues', 67–8, 73–4.

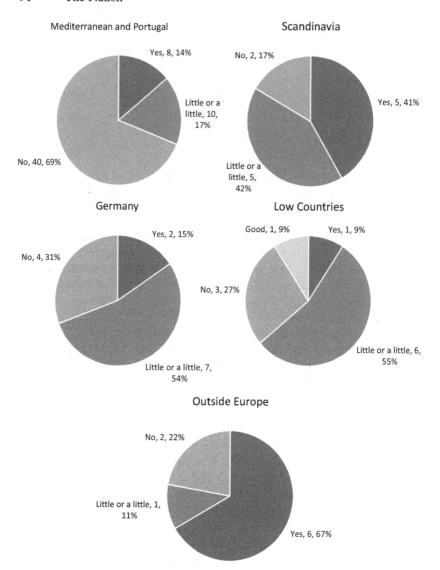

Figure 3.2 Provenance and declared competence in the English language.

illustrates this point. The court martial of the Maltese sailor Francisco Falso, taking place in the River Medway in 1798, had to be interrupted when it became clear that he was not understanding the proceedings, and an Italian was called to act as interpreter:

The Court conceiving Francisco Falso did not perfectly understand the Charge against him, nor what the Evidence adduced against him, sent for an Interpreter… Peter Colombo, a Native of Leghorn, and a Protestant was sworn to give an exact Interpretation of what Falso might say, & also of such Questions as he might wish to ask any Witness, like wise to state to him the Evidence brought forward with Exactness. The Evidence as far as gone through was then read & explained to Colombo, who repeated it to Falso.[45]

Despite originating from two different regions of the Mediterranean, these two men readily understood each other, presumably through Italian. English speakers were cut out from this system, unless they knew at least one of the languages upon which it relied. Mutual intelligibility was non-existent.

Falso, we saw in Chapter 2, may have violated the Articles of War simply because they had never been translated to him. How could the Navy function, then, when not all men understood the orders, or could make themselves understood? Why were interpreters only brought in when a sailor had to face a court martial, as in this case, or as in the case of the seventeen men from the *Charlotte* tender? The fact that foreigners from the Mediterranean and further afield were regularly enlisted, sometimes in considerable numbers, means that the problem must have been somehow overcome.

Language difference could no doubt create obstacles to the smooth running of a fleet. In 1797, the English consul in Malta reported that, because of the 'corruption' of some Maltese names in naval records, he was unable to track down their owners and 'discontinue' the payment of wages to their families. Sometimes, this was the result of a deliberate ploy on the part of the men, who gave the Navy not their surnames but their nicknames, with the intent to 'deceive' and ensure that their pay would not stop immediately if they deserted or died. However, using the nickname instead of the surname, the consul noted, was 'a general custom here among the low class', and, into the twentieth century, nicknames could be found in electoral registers on the island; one of the purposes of this tradition was indeed identifying people, in a society where many names and surnames were very common.[46] Therefore, it is also possible that some of these sailors were not manipulators, but victims, of language.

---

[45] TNA, ADM 1/5364, Courts Martial Papers, August–September 1798, Francisco Falso and John Lambert, 18 September 1798.

[46] TNA, ADM 30/63/6, Pay Lists of Maltese Seamen, 1793–8, William England to the Principal Officers and Commissioners of His Majesty's Navy, 4 August 1797. On Maltese nicknames, see J. Cassar Pullicino, 'Social Aspects of Maltese Nicknames', *Scientia* 12:2 (1956), 66–94; Stanley Fiorini, 'A Survey of Maltese Nicknames I: The Nicknames of Naxxar, 1832', *Journal of Maltese Studies* 16 (1986), 62–82.

In August 1802, the Navy Board found itself having to justify, to a rather displeased Board of Admiralty, why there had been such a delay in preparing the remittance bill for wages owed to a few Maltese: this was due to 'the difficulty of tracing these Men thro' the different Ships they have served in, and their Names being spelt so differently with several Ships'.[47] English clerks, when tackling foreign names, made mistakes that could have important repercussions. The consequences of linguistic diversity could be even more serious: at the end of the nineteenth century, in a climate of heightened xenophobia, the risks of incomprehension at sea would become the target of public preoccupation. During the Parliamentary debates over the 1896 Merchant Seamen (Employment and Rating) Bill, it was observed that all foreigners employed in British ships 'should be able to understand the common orders given on board the vessel', because, as proven by recent fatal accidents, 'it was absolutely dangerous to have a crew of foreigners... unable to understand' them.[48] French-Wars-era naval ships were never likely to have a majority of non-English speakers aboard, as could be the case in late nineteenth-century merchantmen. However, the concern may at first sight appear a valid one.

Military multinational institutions tend to find different solutions to the problem of linguistic comprehension. Ancien Régime French regiments used interpreters and standardised, translated sets of commands.[49] The Napoleonic Army adopted a combination of 'regionally based recruitment', which would reduce linguistic diversity within each regiment, and deliberate use of military service as an instrument of linguistic and national integration.[50] In general, a centralising and homogenising attitude has often been seen as the most efficient path. A prime example is the French Foreign Legion, founded in 1831, where a strong organisational culture tackles any deficiencies in understanding through a structured top-bottom approach, systematic language training and mentoring, and an expectation that all recruits will learn French, and use it among themselves as a 'lingua franca'.[51] One would expect a flat

---

[47] NMM, ADM/B/205, Board of Admiralty, In-Letters, June–September 1802, Navy Office, 7 August 1802. The spelling of Black sailors' names also varied: Rankin, 'Nineteenth-Century Royal Navy Sailors', 191.

[48] Hansard, House of Commons, vol. 37, 'Merchant Seamen (Employment and Rating) Bill', 28 February 1896, vol. 37, cc. 1433–47, at 1434–5 https://api.parliament.uk/historic-hansard/commons/1896/feb/28/merchant-seamen-employment-and-rating.

[49] Tozzi, Nationalizing France's Army, 34–7.

[50] Stewart McCain, The Language Question under Napoleon (Basingstoke: Palgrave Macmillan, 2017), 151–78.

[51] David B. Balkin and Leon Schjoedt, 'The Role of Organizational Cultural Values in Managing Diversity: Learning from the French Foreign Legion', Organizational Dynamics 41 (2012), 44–51, at 45, 47–8.

imposition of English to have been the case, even more so, in an institution like the British Navy, which, unlike the Legion, was not explicitly created as a foreign unit, but only hosted foreigners as a 'guest' minority and complementary manpower. Yet, paradoxically, the fact that the Navy was not explicitly designed to be multinational meant that no formal structure was in place for overcoming linguistic difficulties – which were, therefore, left to the management of individuals. It can be suggested, then, that cross-linguistic communication aboard naval ships happened according to some of the patterns automatically adopted, outside an institutional context, by speakers of different languages: communication in the 'higher status' or 'more widespread' of the two's native languages (in this case, obviously English); adoption of a common language as 'lingua franca' (depending on who interacted, English, French, the Mediterranean *Lingua Franca*, or some other pidgin); or, finally, 'receptive multilingualism', with each party using their own language, but understanding the other's.[52]

Institutional efforts on the Navy's part were sparse. Some captains believed that languages were necessary in the profession, and feeble attempts were made to teach languages to prospective officers: the Portsmouth Naval Academy, for example, had a French language teacher.[53] Yet, one of the main sources of pride for the British Navy was that its officers were mostly formed directly aboard ships, from a young age, rather than in shore-based schools: their formal instruction was, thus, rather haphazard and unsystematic.[54] Perhaps, growing up in cosmopolitan shipboard environments and travelling all over the world would benefit their basic spoken languages. This, however, was in no way a regulated process. When officers' linguistic skill did not suffice, mediators were hired, but the evidence seems to suggest that these were not used primarily for dealing with the men.

Lord Keith and Sir William Sidney Smith both employed interpreters in the Mediterranean: one of them, the Greek Thomas Amaxaris, received 5 shillings a day between 1798 and 1800 (£7 10s per month), until his pay was brought to the level of the Turkish Dragomen serving

---

[52] Anja Schüppert, Nanna Haug Hilton, and Charlotte Gooskens, 'Introduction: Communicating across Linguistic Borders', *Linguistics* 53:2 (2015), 211–17; Helka Riionheimo, Annekatrin Kaivapalu, and Hanna-Ilona Härmävaara, 'Introduction: Receptive Multilingualism', *Nordic Journal of Linguistics* 40:2 (2017), 117–21.

[53] William Henry Dillon, *A Narrative of My Professional Adventures (1790–1839)*, ed. Michael A. Lewis, 2 vols. (London: Navy Records Society, 1953–6), I, 20; Cavell, *Midshipmen*, 27.

[54] Cavell, *Midshipmen*, 21–30.

with the Army, on average £8 per month.[55] In 1808, George Moore was paid one dollar per day for his service as interpreter of Turkish and Arabic aboard HMS *Tigre*, in Egypt.[56] This wage level was almost twice as much as what a warrant officer like a boatswain or a purser would be paid on a first rate ship (£4 10s).[57] Text translators (often the same person as interpreters) were paid similar sums, up to £150 per annum, as shown by the precedents unearthed when, in 1807, the Lords of the Admiralty attempted to cap this at £50 for two translators of Dutch, Curaçoa, and French in the Jamaica station.[58] Overall, it can be seen from the level of their pay that these interpreters were of a wholly different social class from even the highest-ranking lower-deck seamen. Their linguistic skills were refined, extending to the written language, and their use was primarily for interacting with the elites ashore, local merchants and authorities, rather than with seamen in the daily running of the ship.

The hiring of these external figures as interpreters did not necessarily mean that, at any given time, naval ships lacked common seamen aboard able to hold complex conversations in both English and another language: a commander might simply choose not to trust a lower-deck sailor with sensitive transactions and information. Interpreters are a prime example of 'cultural brokers' or 'gatekeepers', and, as such, they are invested with considerable power.[59] For this reason, it might have been preferable to ensure that such brokers were not, at the same time, full (and subordinated) members of the institution on whose behalf they mediated. The question remains of how far bilingual sailors would be employed to help in the everyday routine of a ship. This must have happened, although I have found only one example. Francis Austriac, a French officer captured at Surinam, was kept aboard HMS *Cyane* for eighteen months, serving 'as Pilot and Interpreter', and being 'treated',

---

[55] NMM, ADM/B/219, Board of Admiralty, In-Letters, June–August 1805, Navy Office, 6 August 1805 and 9 August 1805.

[56] NMM, ADM/B/231, Board of Admiralty, In-Letters, April–May 1808, Navy Office, 26 April 1808.

[57] Rodger, *Command*, 626.

[58] NMM, ADM/B/225, Board of Admiralty, In-Letters, January–March 1807, Navy Office, 8 January 1807.

[59] Simon Schaffer, 'Introduction', in Simon Schaffer, Lissa Roberts, Kapil Raj, and James Delbourgo (eds.), *The Brokered World: Go-Betweens and Global Intelligence, 1770–1820* (Sagamore Beach, MA: Science History Publications, 2009), ix–xxxviii; Franziska Heimburger, 'Of Go-Betweens and Gatekeepers: Considering Disciplinary Biases in Interpreting History through Exemplary Metaphors. Military Interpreters in the Allied Coalition during the First World War', in Beatrice Fischer and Matilde Nisbeth Jensen (eds.), *Translation and the Reconfiguration of Power Relations. Revisiting Role and Context of Translation and Interpreting* (Zurich and Berlin: Lit Verlag, 2012), 21–34.

much to his chagrin, as a common 'foremast Man'.[60] Perhaps, anyway, shipboard interpreting was not as indispensable as we may imagine. In professional matters at least, language might not have been an exceedingly significant issue, after all.

'Mobility' in early modern Europe often went hand in hand with a form of 'pragmatic, oral, everyday language-learning' and multilingualism, which privileged effectiveness over fluency.[61] Additionally, the crews of sailing vessels (landsmen excepted) possessed specific and advanced training and experience. This was potentially less true by the time of the 1896 Merchant Seamen Bill: with the advent of steam, it has been argued, engineering competence became crucial, but the bulk of the maritime workforce was deskilled.[62] Thus, in the early nineteenth century, the crew of a ship would have shared a common professional background, which was not necessarily the case in later decades. High professionalisation was accompanied by technical language and understanding. The early modern armed forces in general, because of their internationalism, offered particularly fertile ground for technical lexical exchange.[63] In officer schools all over Europe, from Russia to Italy, navigation was often taught by British teachers, using British methods and translations of British textbooks; large numbers of British and Dutch officers were also employed in operational roles in the newly founded fleets of the northern powers.[64] Shipbuilding, too, was a form of knowledge that

[60] TNA, ADM 1/734, Letters from Commanders-in-Chief, Nore, 1801, nn. 615–909, 710, 30 September 1801 and enclosures.
[61] Gallagher, 'Language-Learning', quote at 661; Dursteler, 'Speaking in Tongues'.
[62] Jari Ojala and Jaakko Pehkonen, 'Technological Changes, Wage Inequality and Skill Premiums: Evidence over Three Centuries', *Government Institute for Economic Research – VATT Working Papers 5* (Helsinki, 2009); Aimee Chin, Chinhui Juhn, and Peter Thompson, 'Technical Change and the Demand for Skills during the Second Industrial Revolution: Evidence from the Merchant Marine, 1891–1912', *The Review of Economics and Statistics* 88:3 (2006), 572–8; Jari Ojala, Jaakko Pehkonen, and Jari Eloranta, 'Deskilling and Decline in Skill Premium during the Age of Sail: Swedish and Finnish Seamen, 1751–1913', *Explorations in Economic History* 61 (2016), 85–94.
[63] Burke, *Languages*, 129–30; Dursteler, 'Speaking in Tongues', 62–3.
[64] Ryan, 'Navigation'; Timothy McEvoy, 'Finding a Teacher of Navigation Abroad in Eighteenth-Century Venice: A Study of the Circulation of Useful Knowledge', *History of Science* 51 (2013), 100–23; Maria Rosaria Enea and Romano Gatto, *Matematica e marineria: Accademia e Scuole di Marina nel Regno di Napoli* (Naples: La Città del Sole, 2013?), 45–56; Martino Ferrari Bravo, 'The Nautical School of Venice of 1739 and the English Teachers. Navigation Training in Venice: Between Seamanship and Science', *Transactions of the Naval Dockyards Society* 5 (2009), 39–49; Fedosov, 'Under the Saltire'; Cross, 'Elphinstones'; Koziurenok, 'Голландскe офицеры'. The most extensive transnational study of the history of navigation teaching is Margaret E. Schotte, *Sailing School: Navigating Science and Skill, 1550–1800* (Baltimore, MD: Johns Hopkins University Press, 2019).

Figure 3.3 Compasses in the Museo Mario Maresca, Meta (Na).
By kind permission of Massimo Maresca; photograph by Sara Caputo

travelled transnationally.[65] Partly as a result, the technical terminology of navigation and vessel parts was often rather similar, for example, in English, Russian, and Germanic and Nordic languages.[66] Even in the Mediterranean, some level of familiarity with English nomenclature can be assumed: as shown by present-day museum collections, a good proportion of the navigational instruments used aboard eighteenth- and nineteenth-century southern Italian merchantmen was of British make and had the names of winds and cardinal points indicated with their English initials (**Figure 3.3**).[67] That the terminology was either shared or widely understood is crucial: according to some linguists, lexical

[65] N. A. M. Rodger, 'Form and Function in European Navies, 1660–1815', in Leo Akveld et al. (eds.), *In het kielzog: Maritiem-historische studies aangeboden aan Jaap R. Bruijn bij zijn vertrek als hoogleraar zeegeschiedenis aan de Universiteit Leiden* (Amsterdam: De Bataafsche Leeuw, 2003), 85–97, at 88–90; Bruijn, *Dutch Navy*, 150.

[66] See, for example, the glossary of terms in Ryan, 'Navigation', 91–5; John Harland, *Seamanship in the Age of Sail: An Account of the Shiphandling of the Sailing Man-of-War 1600–1860, Based on Contemporary Sources* (London: Conway, 2015), 10–18.

[67] See, for example, the catalogue of the 'Mario Maresca' naval museum in Meta (province of Naples): Massimo Maresca, *Il Museo navale Mario Maresca di Meta* (Castellammare di Stabia: Nicola Longobardi editore, 2008), 22–3, 59–63, 98–9. See also Massimo Maresca and Biagio Passaro, *La Marineria della Penisola Sorrentina e la cantieristica in legno da Marina d'Equa a Marina Grande: Shipowners, Shipping and Wooden Shipbuilding in the Sorrento Peninsula* (Sorrento: Con-fine edizioni, 2011), 36. I am grateful to Massimo Maresca for helpful information on this point.

similarities are the second most significant factor in predicting spoken mutual intelligibility across languages, after exposure.[68]

Ultimately, we can assume that training and professionalism could, to a large extent, compensate for linguistic incomprehension. The vast majority of British naval crews would understand some English: most of the seamen were from English-speaking areas of Britain and Ireland, Americans, northern Europeans, and natives of British colonies. Virtually all the warrant officers, and the majority of the petty officers, the men whose good command of English was most indispensable, were either British or Irish, or American.[69] The Navy would have ensured that those who *needed* full linguistic competence be able to prove it: when Franciso [*sic*] Natale, in June 1807, applied to be appointed as Assistant Surgeon, the Sick and Hurt Board, before recommending him for examination, verified his past conduct as well as the fact that 'he speaks English sufficiently well to be understood'.[70]

At the same time, this was not required of everyone aboard. Whilst an accurate understanding of orders could prove crucial during the dangers of manoeuvring, storms, and battles, these are intrinsically contexts where there is no space for elaborate linguistic expression, and gestures or simple commands can easily serve the purpose, especially if a crew is, on average, professionally competent. The Navy hired interpreters if and when it was necessary for a seaman to have detailed comprehension and an opportunity to speak, as in a court martial. The rest of a seafarer's routine hardly requires much verbal communication. Thus, for a common seaman, it would have been relatively easy to fulfil his daily duties, regardless of his level of English fluency, even simply by previous knowledge and imitation of his colleagues. In the 1800 Transport Board list of volunteer prisoners of war, whether a man was marked as 'able' and 'fit for service', or simply 'fit for the merchant service' rather than the Navy, bore no correlation with his English language abilities, but rather seemed to depend on physical conditions or weakness.[71] Peter Fraser, the Erse-speaking Marine seen above, who 'had acquired but a few words of English', was still described as 'a great while in the service, and one of the best'.[72]

---

[68] Gooskens and Swarte, 'Linguistic and Extra-Linguistic Predictors', 138–43.

[69] See Appendix 2: nearly 90% of the sampled petty officers were British or Irish. On the necessity to have linguistically competent non-commissioned officers, see also McCain, *Language Question*, 162–5.

[70] TNA, ADM 98/24, Sick and Hurt Board to the Admiralty, 1806–8, 8 June 1807, f. 65.

[71] TNA, ADM 1/3740, Letters from the Transport Board, July 1800–March 1801, Transport Office to Evan Nepean, 17 December 1800, ff. 290–7.

[72] Mangin, 'Some Account', 31.

Finally, we should note the obvious: linguistic skills are subject to constant improvement with exposure, and British sailors themselves would have often acquired other languages. When an Algerine vessel was wrecked on the Cornish coast, in 1760, a local man who had worked in the Levant trade was able to communicate with the survivors using a mixture of *Lingua Franca* and Italian.[73] At the end of his career in the Navy and in the merchant services of various countries, the sailor William Spavens, from Lincolnshire, spoke Dutch, was able to tell the difference between Norwegian and Danish, and even knew of the system of Chinese written characters.[74] In the seventeenth century, the English seaman Edward Coxere claimed to have learnt French, Dutch, Spanish, and the *Lingua Franca*.[75] Once again, a neat distinction between an 'English' Navy and the rest of the maritime world would cement seafarers' experiences into rigid boxes and force us to forget their fluidity.

3.1.4   Summary

A clear absence from our discussion here is social, as opposed to professional, integration. This remains an open and mostly unanswerable issue, mainly because it would have varied widely among ships and individuals: again, 'the Navy' was not a single community. It was, however, a single, rigidly structured institution. And on institutional patterns, we can well draw some conclusions.

Much like today, in the eighteenth century, speaking in a different accent or language was a clear marker of 'foreignness'. However, in a Navy in which men from many parts of the United Kingdom displayed linguistic distinctiveness, this kind of difference was not exceptional. There were also considerable variations among non-Britons in how much or how little English they were able to deploy and understand, with some of them, particularly from Nordic countries, mastering it to near-native levels. Linguistic diversity, overall, functioned in ways that could not easily be mapped onto 'national' barriers. Coming from a different country to Britain was not, per se, the major single predictor of linguistic difficulties, which depended, instead, on regional and local origin on the one hand and wider sea basins and language group areas on the other. Furthermore, aboard ships, the language required professionally would be very technical, standardised, repetitive, and often

[73] Dakhlia, *Lingua Franca*, 305–6.
[74] William Spavens, *Memoirs of a Seafaring Life*, ed. N. A. M. Rodger (London: The Folio Society, 2000 [1796]), 10, 156, 198.
[75] Gallagher, 'Language-Learning', 639–40, 648.

consisting of terms that underwent phonetic transposition across languages. Language, then, was not necessarily a barrier to service aboard, and no one had any interest in casting it as such.

However, language did become a problem when linguistic competence was implicitly adopted as an indicator of political and legal 'nativity', or 'foreignness'. A foreign-born sailor speaking with an accent, or not understanding English, was no novelty, and he fitted perfectly within both his peers' and the institution's assumptions and expectations. The real cause of wonder, instead, was a man *defying* expectations – a Briton still not sufficiently 'civilised' to speak English, or, even more disquietingly, a potentially very dangerous 'foreigner' who could readily exploit or camouflage his foreignness, and, in some sense, outwit the state itself. Thus, the clash between preconception and reality, and the failure of some men to fit into the system's boxes, perhaps caused more issues than effective differences and linguistic disabilities, which the cosmopolitan and manpower-hungry Navy had adapted to absorb and bypass in its daily workings.

In the next section, we move on to examine another type of difference in the fleet. Much like language, religion was a relatively modifiable personal trait. Yet, whilst religious diversity lacked the potential practical consequences of linguistic diversity, it was often deeply felt, and, at the end of the eighteenth century, it could still be seen as politically problematic. Again, like language, faith was also subject to racialisation and prejudice. The necessities of manning, I have argued so far, engendered something of a laissez-faire administrative attitude. Which form did this take in matters of religion?

3.2   Gehenna

Evidence of religious practices in the Navy is relatively limited. Religion in general is rarely mentioned in ship records and official correspondence. This is in itself significant, but perhaps not, contrary to what we might expect, as a symptom of spiritual indifference. Certainly, from the point of view of Evangelical reforming officers, the eighteenth-century Royal Navy was a pit of sin, blasphemy, and atheism.[76] Whilst the

---

[76] The key text on this matter is Blake, *Evangelicals*. See also Rediker, *Between the Devil and the Deep Blue Sea*, 167, 169–71; Roald Kverndal, *Seamen's Missions: Their Origin and Early Growth – A Contribution to the History of the Church Maritime* (Pasadena, CA: William Carey Library, 1986), 91–5. On the links between the Evangelicals and the Navy, see Gareth Atkins, 'Christian Heroes, Providence, and Patriotism in Wartime Britain, 1793–1815', *The Historical Journal* 58:2 (2015), 393–414; idem, 'Religion, Politics and Patronage in the Late Hanoverian Navy, c.1780–c.1820', *Historical Research* 88:240 (2015), 272–90.

Articles of War explicitly condemned cursing, and stated that every ship should hold regular services, in practice, relatively few did.[77] Moreover, Marcus Rediker and Alain Cabantous have argued that early modern long-distance seafarers tended to be rather detached from shore-based forms of cult, sharing instead a separate, transnational, and specifically maritime sense of faith, superstition, and the supernatural.[78] These factors might at first sight suggest that religious diversity would not have been a prominent concern in the Navy, because, for most officers and men, official religion itself was not.

This picture, however, has been complicated by historians like Christopher P. Magra and Richard Blake, who have shown that eighteenth-century British seafarers were often rather conventionally devout.[79] Furthermore, while anti-Catholic feeling had begun to subside by the French Wars, many British servicemen still held deep-seated prejudices towards Catholics, which emerged, for instance, in their Mediterranean encounters.[80] Religion was an important factor in the dichotomy that we shall explore in Chapters 5 and 6, between southern Europeans from Catholic countries, seen as 'backward' by Royal Navy officers and politicians, and northern Europeans, for example the Dutch, perceived instead as mostly similar to the British. Catholic seamen were themselves far from conforming to stereotypes of atheism, or Rediker's picture of detachment from land-based cults. All this raises major questions regarding their integration aboard Royal Navy ships.

The issue is, in fact, even more complex, if we move beyond this simplified tension between Protestantism and Catholicism and consider their internal nuances, and other denominations and religions. Even when Sunday services were held aboard, by a chaplain or captain, the text used would be the Church of England Prayer Book, which would have been problematic for many Nonconformists. And what of members

---

[77] N. A. M. Rodger (ed.), *Articles of War: The Statutes Which Governed Our Fighting Navies 1661, 1749 and 1886* (Havant: Kenneth Mason, 1982), 22, art. i–ii.

[78] Rediker, *Between the Devil and the Deep Blue Sea*, 153–4, 161, 169–86, 203; Alain Cabantous, *Le ciel dans la mer : Christianisme et civilisation maritime, XVIe-XIXe siècles* (Paris: Fayard, 1990).

[79] Christopher P. Magra, 'Faith at Sea: Exploring Maritime Religiosity in the Eighteenth Century', *International Journal of Maritime History* 19:1 (2007), 87–106. See also Blake, *Evangelicals*, 103, 225–67; Jesse Lemisch, 'Listening to the "Inarticulate": William Widger's Dream and the Loyalties of American Revolutionary Seamen in British Prisons', *Journal of Social History* 3:1 (1969), 1–29, at 21–2.

[80] Joseph Clarke, 'Encountering the Sacred: British and French Soldiers in the Revolutionary and Napoleonic Mediterranean', in Joseph Clarke and John Horne (eds.), *Militarized Cultural Encounters in the Long Nineteenth Century: Making War, Mapping Europe* (Basingstoke: Palgrave Macmillan, 2018), 49–73.

of faiths that entailed strict ritual, hygienic and food-related prescriptions, in a Navy that fed itself on salt beef and pork?

We can assume Church of England Protestantism as the standard of reference, both institutionally and roughly by background, for the majority of seamen in the Navy: likely around 88% of the English and Welsh population, it has been estimated, was nominally 'Anglican' in 1800, although this figure was set to decrease.[81] How far was religious difference from this standard, or 'religious foreignness', an important issue in the service? Once again, it is difficult to generalise on how sailors interacted with their peers – whether religious at all or of faiths other than theirs. However, we can examine the extent to which some seamen preserved or changed their original religious beliefs and practices once aboard Royal Navy ships, and the ways in which the Navy reacted to such behaviours.

3.2.1   Regulating Religion?

Multifaith chaplaincy raises complex problems in contemporary Western militaries, where state institutions strive for an explicitly non-confessional stance.[82] The eighteenth-century British Navy was in some ways simpler to manage, being structurally expected to conform to the doctrine of the Church of England. This institutional background, however, was not as rigidly enforced or deeply felt as in other fleets.

In some navies, services and devotion were a regular part of shipboard life. This was obviously the case in the vessels of the Order of St John of Malta, but also in other fleets across the Mediterranean, for example the Spanish (which explicitly invited the enlistment of non-subjects if they were Catholics) or the Neapolitan.[83] Russian men-of-war carried an Orthodox secular priest, a 'Papa', who celebrated services regularly with enthusiastic participation from the crews, and devotional images were publicly displayed aboard.[84] Ships in the Danish Navy also had a *skibspræst*, who officiated Lutheran services most Sundays, sailing duties

---

[81] Clive D. Field, 'Counting Religion in England and Wales: The Long Eighteenth Century, c. 1680–c. 1840', *Journal of Ecclesiastical History* 63:4 (2012), 693–720, esp. at 710–11.

[82] Kim Philip Hansen, *Military Chaplains and Religious Diversity* (New York and Basingstoke: Palgrave Macmillan, 2012).

[83] Joseph F. Grima, *The Fleet of the Knights of Malta: Its Organisation during the Eighteenth Century* (San Ġwann: BDL Publishing, 2016), 335–51; Carla Rahn Phillips, '"The Life Blood of the Navy": Recruiting Sailors in Eighteenth-Century Spain', *The Mariner's Mirror* 87:4 (2001), 420–45, at 423, 426. On southern Italy, see Chapter 5.

[84] *A Voyage to St. Petersburg in 1814, with Remarks on the Imperial Russian Navy. By a Surgeon in the British Navy* (London: Sir Richard Phillips & Co., 1822), 62–3.

and conditions permitting, held communion once a month, and even performed confirmations of young boys aboard; Muslims, Jews, and Hindus could not enter the service without being baptised.[85]

This quick overview offers a rather stark contrast with the Royal Navy. Until the end of the eighteenth century, chaplains in British men-of-war were sparse, frequently absentees holding sinecures; even when they were physically present, their services and sermons were few and far between, with the exception of individual ships and squadrons under 'Blue Light' Evangelical commanders.[86] Many chaplains occupied their time aboard with intelligence, diplomatic or secretarial duties, or scientific and literary pursuits.[87] Leaving aside their extra 'groats' deducted from the crew's wages, they were nominally paid only like able seamen until 1797, and even less thereafter, since their pay was not increased then.[88] Further proof of the Navy's indifference towards religion can be found in the very structure of its institutional records. Other eighteenth-century European forces sometimes registered the confession of individuals – the Ancien Régime French Army *Contrôles de troupe* are an example of this practice.[89] Royal Navy musters, instead, even when they started including birthplace, never had a column for reporting faith, which did not appear anywhere else in Admiralty documents, either.

There were, it must be said, at least two senses in which religion mattered in the fleet. First, it mattered to civilian religious organisations and individuals, who saw sailors and war prisoners as categories at spiritual risk, but also potentially very useful vessels to spread confessional messages abroad.[90] Missionary societies like the Anglican Society for Promoting Christian Knowledge (SPCK) (from 1698) and the non-denominational Naval and Military Bible Society (from 1779) and British and Foreign Bible Society (BFBS) (from 1804) worked with all seamen, distributing the Scriptures and tracts, and leading to what Roald Kverndal has termed 'Naval Awakening' at the beginning of the

---

[85] Joen Jakob Seerup, 'Søetaten i 1700-tallet: Organisation, personel og daglidag i 1700-tallets danske flåde' (unpublished PhD thesis, University of Copenhagen, 2010), 156, 339–43.

[86] N. A. M. Rodger, 'The Naval Chaplain in the Eighteenth Century', *British Journal for Eighteenth-Century Studies* 18 (1995), 33–45; Blake, *Evangelicals*, 70–81; Kverndal, *Seamen's Missions*, 94–9.

[87] Gordon Taylor, *The Sea Chaplains: A History of the Chaplains of the Royal Navy* (Oxford: Oxford Illustrated Press, 1978), 177–80, 198–215; Rodger, 'Naval Chaplain', 36–7; Blake, *Evangelicals*, 75–7.

[88] Taylor, *Sea Chaplains*, 169, 232–5.   [89] Tozzi, *Nationalizing France's Army*, 229.

[90] See, for example, Johnsen, *Han sad*, 90–113, 118–27.

nineteenth century.[91] They also specially catered for non-English speakers, servicemen and civilians alike, through translations of the Scriptures in Welsh, Irish, and Gaelic, besides a vast array of other languages.[92] In 1808, the SPCK was offering frequent contributions to furnish Swedish and Finnish sailors in the Navy with Bibles and Prayer Books in their language, via the Swedish Church in London.[93] The Religious Tract Society produced publications not only for French prisoners of war, but also for Dutch and German seamen and soldiers in the British service.[94] Navy and Army recruits of all origins were supplied abroad, as well, for example, by representatives of the BFBS operating in the very cosmopolitan waters of Gibraltar and Malta.[95] As can be seen, while often extensive in scope, these missionary activities were carried out independently of the naval institutional structures and in a broadly pluri-denominational spirit. As such, they were not imposing a unifying standard of faith: the service remained multi-confessional and largely unregulated from the point of view of religious belief.

Sailors' religion, however, did not only matter to civilian missionaries. By the end of the century, the Navy itself was becoming aware of the value of maintaining regular shipboard religious practice, to foster patriotism, unity, and especially discipline. Even otherwise non-devout officers, like the Earl of St Vincent, became active promoters of chaplains and services.[96] One of the main targets of this policy was, besides French revolutionary 'atheism',[97] the Catholic component in the fleet.

Catholic faith, in the specific case of Irishmen, could be associated by Navy officers with dubious loyalty, especially during the 1797 mutinies and the Irish rebellion the following year. Whilst the Irish contribution to unrest in the fleet has been much debated by historians, many

[91] Kverndal, *Seamen's Missions*, 71–90, 99–103; R. W. H. Miller, *One Firm Anchor: The Church and the Merchant Seafarer, an Introductory History* (Cambridge: The Lutterworth Press, 2012), 119–20, 122–4; Atkins, 'Christian Heroes', 407–9.

[92] See, for example, W. O. B. Allen and Edmund McClure, *Two Hundred Years: The History of the Society for Promoting Christian Knowledge, 1698–1898* (London: Society for Promoting Christian Knowledge, 1898), 202–4. I am grateful to Dr Nicholas Dixon for this reference.

[93] Allen and McClure, *Two Hundred Years*, 206.

[94] Samuel G. Green, *The Story of the Religious Tract Society for One Hundred Years* (London: The Religious Tract Society, 1899), 15–16.

[95] Cambridge University Library: British and Foreign Bible Society's Library, BSA/D1/5/4, Correspondence Books (Home and Foreign), vol. 4, June 1810–September 1812, ff. 52–6, Captain F. Reynolds, 13 July 1810. I owe this reference to Professor Renaud Morieux.

[96] Rodger, 'Naval Chaplain', 39–42; Blake, *Evangelicals*, 2, 82–104, 141, 151; Lincoln, *Representing*, 109–35.

[97] Blake, *Evangelicals*, 99.

contemporaries certainly thought that it was substantial.[98] For our purposes here, this mistrust matters more than the truth. Certain officers mentioned the 'Religious inducement of extirpating Hereticks' as a motive for the Irish mutineers.[99] Some loyal Irish seamen also believed that they ought to defend themselves publicly and reassert a model of allegiance to King and Constitution which held true 'disregarding any Thing that tends to Difference of Religion'. Thus, they openly condemned some of their compatriots' 'black and detestable Intentions... carried on under the false Mask of Religion': 'Was there ever so horrid a Deed sanction[ed] by any Religion, or religious Men?', they asked. 'On the contrary, all Religion or Laws, either Divine or Human, must shudder at the gross Insult offered by Men who deviate from the Principles of all good Men and Christians'.[100]

The main issue was that Catholics regularly joined the Navy, but the law in theory forbade it. A bill brought by Lord Howick (then Foreign Secretary) in March 1807 aimed, among other concessions, to let Catholics and Dissenters into the Army and Navy officially, with explicit freedom of worship; it was bluntly rejected by the King and led to the dismissal of the Ministry of All Talents.[101] The bill would have entailed, in practice, a relatively minor change for lower-deck seamen, given the overall ritual laxity of shipboard life, and the lack of checks on recruits' faith: it would simply be allowing 'that by right which was already allowed by connivance', as Howick put it, besides possibly encouraging more Catholics to volunteer or not choose foreign service.[102] The proposed concession was, however, of momentous importance in the case of officers. Both commissioned and warrant officers, indeed, unlike the common seamen, were required by the Test Acts to take the Oath of Supremacy and Allegiance upon entry. This rule was updated with new oaths under William and Mary and again repeatedly throughout the

---

[98] For arguments in favour and against Irish involvement, see respectively Marianne Elliott, *Partners in Revolution: The United Irishmen and France* (New Haven, CT and London: Yale University Press, 1982), 134–44; Rodger, *Command*, 448–52.

[99] Devon Archives and Local Studies, Devon Heritage Centre, Exeter [henceforth DA], 152M/C/1798/ON/3, Political and Personal Papers of Henry Addington, 1st Viscount Sidmouth, 1705–1824, J. P. Bastard to Henry Addington, 20 August 1798.

[100] National Museum of the Royal Navy, Portsmouth [henceforth NMRN], 1988/500, The Papers of the Penrose and Coode Families, 1772–*c*.1880, n. 292, 'Statement from the Irishmen serving on HMS *Sans Pariel* [sic] (1794) [sic] of their allegiance to the sovereign', 22 September 1798.

[101] Hansard, House of Commons, vol. 9, 'Roman Catholic's Army and Navy Service Bill', 5 March 1807, cc. 2–20 https://api.parliament.uk/historic-hansard/commons/1807/mar/05/roman-catholics-army-and-navy-service; Robert Scott, *The History of England; During the Reign of George III Designed as a Continuation of Hume and Smollett*, 4 vols. (London: J. Robins and Co., 1824), IV, 49–50.

[102] Hansard, HC, 'Roman Catholic's Army and Navy Service Bill', cc. 4, 16.

eighteenth century.[103] The text was adamant, leaving no leeway whatso-
ever: by the 1790s, officers had to declare that 'no Foreign Prince,
Person, Prelate, State or Potenta[t]e, hath or ought to have, any
Jurisdiction, power, Superiority Preeminence or Authority, ecclesiastical
or Spiritual within this Realm'; abjure the doctrine of transubstantiation;
affirm that the Roman cults of Mary and the saints and the mass were
'Superstitious and Idolatrous'; and finally 'profess, testify and declare
solemnly in the presence of God' that they did

> make this declaration and every part thereof in the plain and ordinary sense of the
> Words now read unto me, as they are commonly understood by English
> Protestants without any evasion equivocation or mental reservation whatsoever,
> or without any dispensation already granted me for that purpose by the Pope.

They also had to forswear any 'hope' for later annulment.[104]

Some Jewish or Nonconformist officers could perhaps find work-
arounds in this formula, but they were still required to receive the sacra-
ment in public; it is unclear how often this obligation was enforced in
practice, but it could clearly engender moral dilemmas.[105] For a devout
Catholic, in any case, the oath itself constituted an insurmountable hurdle,
effectively barring him from service. Acts of Indemnity were passed
throughout the period to allow more latitude to persons in office who
had not yet taken the oaths, but this did not alter the practical require-
ment.[106] In 1808, for example, Mr Levisse, who had been chosen as
French master at the Portsmouth Royal Naval College, saw his appoint-
ment 'cancelled' because, 'being a Catholic', he 'could not take the Oaths'
necessary for the warrant.[107] The result was the paradoxical situation that
Henry Grattan highlighted in the Commons in 1805: Navy Catholics
'contribute one-third to its numbers, and have not a commission'.[108]

---

[103] The crucial acts were: 25 Car. II. c. 2; 1 W. & M. c. 8; 1 Geo. I Stat. 2 c. 13. For the
regulations specific to the Navy, and their changes over time, see TNA, ADM 7/313,
Law Officers' Opinions, 1816–19, n. 28, 'Extract from the Statutes on the subject of
Oaths of Allegiance &c. so far as relates to Officers in the Navy', 25 February 1817, and
n. 32, 12 May 1817.

[104] TNA, ADM 1/493, Letters from Commanders-in-Chief, North America, 1795–6, ff.
298–9, Captain Wemyss Oath of Supremacy and Allegiance, 26 October 1795. See
also: ADM 1/392, Letters from Commanders-in-Chief, Mediterranean, 1794, 3, Lord
Hood to Philip Stephens, 5 January 1794, and enclosures.

[105] Geoffrey L. Green, *The Royal Navy and Anglo-Jewry 1740–1820: Traders and Those Who
Served* (London: Geoffrey Green [The Self Publishing Association], 1989), 16.

[106] TNA, ADM 7/313, Law Officers' Opinions, 1816–19, n. 28.

[107] NMM, ADM/B/232, Board of Admiralty, In-Letters, June–July 1808, Navy Office,
2 July 1808.

[108] Hansard, House of Commons, vol. 4, 'Roman Catholic Petition', 13 May 1805, cc.
833–950, at 927 https://api.parliament.uk/historic-hansard/commons/1805/may/13/
roman-catholic-petition#S1V0004P0_18050513_HOC_10.

What terrified the politicians who opposed the 1807 bill was not the idea that freedom of worship would bring divisions within the crews. An MP warned against a scenario in which 'the priests disseminate their popish doctrines through the ship: some are converted, some not; disunion is thus bred among the seamen; and, instead of preparing to beat the common enemy they turn against one another, and fall to controversial preaching'. He was laughed down by the House.[109] 'Sailors will hardly debate on board a ship, upon the question of, whether the Thirty Nine Articles ought to be agreed to or not', quipped Samuel Whitbread the following year.[110] Perhaps, as we shall see, he was being unfair to the men. Yet, overall, the real concern behind the religious requirements was not with shipboard spiritual harmony, but with institutional structures and political dangers. A Catholic captain would choose a Catholic chaplain, Spencer Perceval pointed out, and the whole ship's allegiance would be in doubt in case of a French invasion of Ireland.[111] Clearly, the times were not ripe for the British establishment to accept having a Catholic, and especially an Irish Catholic, in a position of power outside Ireland.[112] These fears, however, did not impact substantially on what was permitted among the ratings.

As we have seen, then, the institutional structures of religious practice in the Navy were weak. Non-institutional organisations actively attempted to proselytise among seamen, disciplinary concerns came to encourage worship provision, and, most importantly, political fears policed Catholics' access to positions of authority. However, the lack of a strong framework of devotions and belief left considerable freedom of expression to individuals. How did they use it?

3.2.2   Diversity, Accommodation, and Conversion

When discussing the Navy's relative tolerance of all faiths, it is important to avoid a romanticised portrayal of their coexistence aboard. The very patriotic and Francophobic rhetoric of which the service was imbued still partly relied on anti-Catholic sentiment. A 1790s recruitment poster, for

---

[109] Hansard, HC, 'Roman Catholic's Army and Navy Service Bill', c. 15.

[110] Hansard, House of Commons, vol. 11, 'Roman Catholic Petition', 25 May 1808, cc. 549–638, at 633 https://api.parliament.uk/historic-hansard/commons/1808/may/25/roman-catholic-petition.

[111] Hansard, HC, 'Roman Catholic's Army and Navy Service Bill', c. 11.

[112] Catholic officers in Ireland could hold commissions from 1793; in 1813, a new statute clarified that these remained valid even when their service took them to other British territories. However, these Acts mostly related to the Army, as Ireland did not have its own Navy establishment: 53 Geo. III c. 128.

example, launched an appeal to the 'Royal Tars of Old England': 'All who have good Hearts, who love their KING, their COUNTRY, and RELIGION, who hate the FRENCH, and damn the POPE' should join the Navy.[113] Unless this was completely misguided advertising, we can assume that the constituency to whom it was addressed, and who joined as a result, would broadly share in these antipathies. Surviving naval memoirs, whatever their reliability, also report the odd tale of desecrating humour at the expense of Catholic shipmates. In 1799, at Plymouth Hospital, the funeral of an Irish seaman, a 'zealous Roman Catholic', was disrupted by another sailor who had been hidden by some friends into a replacement coffin and jumped out of it, terrorising the deceased's 'countrymen' and their priest. 'Two or three of the poor Irishmen', the narrator recounts with some gusto, 'were so frightened that they fainted, while others uttered horrible shrieks, and exclaiming, "the Lord Jasus have mercy on us poor sinners."'.[114] We can distinguish here more than a hint to the classic slurs with which Catholics were tarred: superstitious fear and effeminate weakness. The governor of the hospital offered a 'considerable reward' for whoever would deliver the culprits, but they were never found: the joke was presumably too popular.

On the Navy's part, too, tolerance without special, consistent accommodation was not sufficient to amount to freedom of worship in practice and for everyone. In the United Provinces, for example, where the Navy was administered and fed in a very similar way to the British, the Amsterdam Admiralty could not make provisions for Jewish ritual and alimentary rules, so no Jew ever entered, despite their substantial numbers in the city.[115] Using names, town or country of origin, and a few other sparse pieces of information, Geoffrey L. Green has tracked down about 70 Jews who served in the British Navy between 1750 and 1820, on both the lower deck and quarterdeck: his preliminary estimate is that Jewish sailors may have been around 0.25% of the fleet.[116] Similarly, we know that at least some Muslim men entered the Navy: for instance, the muster book of HMS *Santa Dorotea*, stationed in the Mediterranean, lists two ordinary seamen called 'Mahomet' and 'Harrohomet' (Ahmed?), twenty and twenty-nine years of age, who were both born in Algiers and who both deserted in Tripoli on 1 April 1801,

---

[113] NMM, 659.133.1:355.216:094, Item PBB7084, *Volunteers… Let Us, Who Are Englishmen, Protect and Defend Our Good King and Country against the Attempts of All Republicans and Levellers, and against the Designs of Our Natural Enemies…* ([Lewes]: W. & A. Lee, c.1797).

[114] *Narrative of the Travels and Voyages of Davis Bill* (Brattleborough, VT: William Fessenden, [1810]), 101–2.

[115] Bruijn, *Dutch Navy*, 179.

[116] Green, *Royal Navy and Anglo-Jewry*, 43–59, 220–7, 229–36.

after seven months of service. The same muster contains another 'Mahomet', in fact, a twenty-five-year-old ordinary seaman from Bengal who remained in the ship for nine months in 1798–9.[117] By necessity, these men would have had to relinquish their observance, whatever their preference: service aboard would have prevented them from properly keeping the prescribed festivities, the Sabbath or *Jumu'ah*, and a kosher or halal diet, among other things.[118] Discharge 'for being a Jew' was possible, but not universally granted.[119] Religious toleration then meant something different for different people. However, these were relatively specific cases. Non-Anglican Christians, including Catholics, could still thrive on the lower deck, and the Navy itself, in a pragmatic spirit, sometimes came to cater for this.

A small oil painting survives in the underground Sanctuary of tal-Mensija, in San Ġwann, Malta. It depicts a catastrophic event that occurred in March 1800, the burning and shipwreck of HMS *Queen Charlotte*, Lord Keith's flagship, near the island of Capraia (by Leghorn). This painting is an ex voto, probably dedicated by a surviving sailor, or his relatives. The caption, in Italian, thanks Christ for the fact that 175 people escaped alive (**Figure 3.4**).[120] Here, we have tangible evidence of a Maltese man who kept his private faith whilst in the Navy. Catholic devotion was strong among southern European seafarers, and this had to be borne in mind even in diplomatic agreements. In February 1795, a Maltese Knight of the Order of St John proposed, among the terms for recruitment of Maltese seamen into the Royal Navy, that they be granted their own Catholic chaplain in each ship. A religious Order undoubtedly had a political interest in ensuring that its subjects retained their faith, but the sailors' perspective was considered, too: 'Would not the Maltese', the

---

[117] TNA, ADM 36/14389, Muster Book of HMS *Santa Dorotea*, March–May 1802, ff. 5 and 19, nn. 83, 374, 375.

[118] Green, *Royal Navy and Anglo-Jewry*, 52.   [119] Ibid., 51–2.

[120] The text of the caption, in Italian, reads: '*LA NAVE CAROLET COMANDATO* [*sic*] *DAL AMMIRAGLIO LORCIF COL SUO EQUIPAGIO* [*sic*] *DI N:° 965 PERSONE CORSE LA DISGRAZIA DEL INCENDIO SOTTO LAQUE* [*sic*] *DI GORGONA VICINO DI LIVORNO E PER GRAZIA DEI SS: CHRISTO CONFORTO DE TRIBULATI SI SALVORONO* [*sic*] *N.° 175 PERSONE SU LI 2. MARZO. 1800.*' ('The ship Carolet commanded by Admiral Lorcif with its crew of 965 people had the disgrace of the fire in the waters of Gorgona near Leghorn and by the grace of the Holy Christ comfort of the afflicted 175 people were saved on 2 March 1800'). The ex voto is also briefly discussed and reproduced in A. H. J. Prins, *In Peril on the Sea: Marine Votive Paintings in the Maltese Islands* (Valletta: Said, 1989), 46–8. I owe this source to the exquisite kindness of Dr Liam Gauci of the National Maritime Museum of Malta, who showed me Prins's volume and gave me directions to the church. I would also like to thank the priest and congregation of the Santwarju Tal-Madonna Tal-Mensija for allowing me to take photographs of the tablet.

Figure 3.4 Ex voto, [1800], *Sanctuary of Tal-Mensija*, San Ġwann, Malta.
Photograph and editing by Sara Caputo

Knight observed, 'infinitely attached to their cult, loathe enlisting to serve for a long time on vessels which do not offer them but a foreign cult, and where they will not find these consolations which become so sweet and so necessary?'.[121]

The arrangement above never came into being, because the negotiations for an alliance failed. However, the Navy itself did offer some institutional shortcuts. In 1777, the discovery of a Catholic priest covertly catering for Irishmen in Haslar Hospital ruffled feathers among the Presbyterian hospital councillors, forcing the more tolerant First Lord of the Admiralty to take action.[122] Yet, by the French Wars, the climate had changed: in 1794, the resident Commissioner at the same place freely

---

[121] TNA, FO 49/2, Foreign Office and Predecessor, Malta, Consul William England, Captain Alexander John Ball, and the Grand Master, April 1789–1800, f. 88, Chevalier de Thuisy via Mons. Saladin to Lord Grenville, 27 February 1795: '*Les Maltois infiniment attachés à leur culte ne pourroient* [sic] *ils pas repugner* [sic] *à s'engager pour servir longtems* [sic] *sur des vaisseaux qui ne leur offriroient* [sic] *qu'un culte étranger et où ils ne trouveroient* [sic] *pas ces consolations qui deviennent Si douces et si necessaires* [sic]*?*'.

[122] Rodger, 'Naval Chaplain', 40.

'permitted a Roman Catholic Priest, to pray with, confess and perform other duties of his Office to the Irish Catholic Sailors', and the Sick and Hurt Board only sought formal approval from the Admiralty Board afterwards.[123] Catholic ministers were also allowed to officiate for Catholic Marines at Chatham and men sentenced to death in 1798–9.[124] In courts martial, Catholic witnesses were 'sworn upon the cross' or 'according to the Romish mode'.[125]

This kind of allowance and overall laxity, and the cultural melting pot that they created aboard warships, could even foster conversions, especially when the Navy sailed to Catholic waters like the western Mediterranean. In this sense, Samuel Whitbread and the other MPs who laughed at the idea of seamen debating doctrine were mistaken. Richard Blake has explored the ways in which devout sailors spread the Word amidst the irreligiosity of the naval lower decks.[126] In the same way, different faiths could also interact and affect each other. The records of the ecclesiastical authorities in Malta, for example, contain the minutes of the examination of several British sailors, who appeared in front of the tribunal seeking conversion to Catholicism. Some, like the Irishman 'Ricardo Walsc' (Richard Walsh) and the Englishman 'Gio[vann]i Mor' (John Moore), had been persuaded to do so during their permanence in shore-based Venetian and Maltese hospitals, and were not very knowledgeable as to the details of the Protestant faith that they were reneging ('I suppose to be a Calvinist', Moore declared).[127] Other depositions, however, are precious evidence of the sometimes extensive theological discussions that sailors could have aboard ships, and of the influence that they exerted on each other. A good example is that of 'Giovanni Anson' (John Anson), a twenty-year-old English seaman who in 1793 sailed aboard an English merchantman, from Leghorn to Malta. During this trip, he had conversations on matters of religion with two shipmates, a Portuguese and a Maltese, and was 'instructed by them on the errors' of the Protestant 'sect', and on the 'Sanctity, and truth of the Roman Catholic Religion', thus resolving to 'embrace it and abjure' his previous faith.[128] Service in

---

[123] TNA, ADM 98/16, Sick and Hurt Board to the Admiralty, 1793–4, 1 September 1794, f. 365.

[124] Taylor, *Sea Chaplains*, 226–7.   [125] Byrn, *Naval Courts Martial*, 164, 315, 366, 576.

[126] Blake, *Evangelicals*, 225–67.

[127] Archives of the Metropolitan Cathedral, Mdina [henceforth AMC], AIM Processi criminali 137, Spontanea de Heresi Jo'is Mor, 12 July 1793, ff. 145–52; Spontanea de Heresi Ricardi Walsc, 7 April 1794, ff. 153–60. Again, I am extremely grateful to Liam Gauci for pointing me in the direction of these records.

[128] AMC, AIM Processi criminali 137, Spontanea de Haeresi Johannis Anson, 12 March 1793, ff. 137–44: '*in occasione di questo mio ultimo viaggio avendo avuto discorso in punto di Religione con un Maltese, ed un Portughese imbarcati sù la Nave med[esi]ma sono stato da*

the British Navy could also facilitate similar religious crises, as shown by the case of 'Giacomo Gins' (James Jenks?), a twelve-year-old Irish boy who was questioned by the tribunal in May 1795. He had reached Malta a month before aboard a British '*corvetta*' (presumably the interpreter's rendering of a sloop or a frigate, since the Royal Navy did not have corvettes at the time), on which he was a lower-deck boy. He was from a Protestant family, had always lived in Protestant countries, and cockily declared that he could not explain the errors of his sect, 'owing to my childhood, tender age, and changing of countries', but all he knew was that he now wanted to be a Catholic.[129]

3.2.3 Summary

In conclusion, much as with language or legal status, the Navy was concerned with religious difference only when it came to senior positions. Unlike in other contemporary military and naval institutions, religious considerations had little or no impact on institutional practice and provision, recruitment criteria, and muster-keeping. Missionary societies were very active in Christianising the sailors, but mostly in a private and multi-confessional, very generic capacity. Some officers adopted religion as a moral and disciplinary tool, and the oath requirements meant that commissions and warrants were still unavailable to devout non-Anglicans. However, Catholics, who were one of the main targets of such policies, were, in practice, freely allowed onto the lower decks, and even, at times, specifically catered for. Without special accommodations, there were limits to the extent to which various types of devotion were possible aboard. Yet, from the few surviving sources, the impression is that of an overall very colourful environment, in which all types and gradations of faith, or no faith at all, mingled and shaped each other, as the Navy turned its eye to what it deemed more important matters.

Where does this all leave us, then? Not only were linguistic and religious diversity targets of xenophobia and cultural prejudice, but they both had the potential to create disorder in the fleet. Communication barriers between officers and men could raise practical concerns, and some religious confessions were closely associated with political disloyalty.

---

questi istruito sulli *Errori della Setta, che prima professavo, e su la Santità, e verità della Religione Cattolica Romana, cosichè mi sono risoluto di abbracciar questa e di abiurare tutti gli errori, nei quali fin'ora sono vissuto.*'

[129] AMC, AIM Processi criminali 137, Spontanea de Haeresi Jacobi Gins, 6 May 1795, ff. 189–92: '*Non sò esprimere l'Errori di mia Setta attesa la mia Fanciullezza* [sic]*, tenera età e mutazione de' Paesi*'.

Additionally, language and religion were both recognised as especially unstable aspects of national characters: English could be learnt to native levels and faith be hidden or undergo conversion. This created issues of control for a state that often identified a man's legal status by the language he spoke or the religion he practised. Why, then, did the Navy ultimately show little concern for these kinds of diversity and transformations in its ships and fail to impose systematic uniformity and regulation? The answer is strictly practical. The risks and disadvantages of hiring non-English speaking or non-Protestant recruits mattered relatively little when compared to the manning needs that these seamen fulfilled. In Chapter 4, we shall see how this reasoning worked when other, even more complex forms of cultural prejudice were at play.

4 'Complexions of Every Varied Hue'
Racial Beliefs, Biopower, and Acclimatisation

> Travelling besides affording opportunities to judge of foreign manners, frequently causes a disinterested traveller to look at home, where he will often find that ignorance, and its offspring, prejudice, can turn white black, or the contrary.[1]

This casual observation appears in the account of the voyages of Francis V. Vernon, an Irish midshipman. During the peace after the American War, he went travelling around the Mediterranean, and observed some discrepancies between what he had expected of other peoples and reality. Lieutenant William Bowers, from the generation after Vernon, also stated in his memoirs that, his 'English notions of men and things having been more than once revised by early travel and experience, any false ideas I might have formed of our neighbours [here the French, in 1816] were easily corrected'. He condemned his 'unbending countrymen''s 'deep-rooted prejudices springing from ignorance and conceit', their 'imagined superiority, and the contempt in which they held every other nation'.[2] These two young officers, whose remarks nicely bookend our period, were simply echoing a well-established intellectual trope.

Some Enlightenment thinkers dismissed the apparent dichotomy between national characters and the universal, common traits of humanity: national characters, clearly, were only superficial myths, and people were at bottom the same everywhere. This, they pointed out, was especially clear to travellers.[3] Even when they considered national character, and sometimes in the same breath as deeply racist remarks, famous philosophers like David Hume tended to emphasise the pre-eminence of 'moral' causes of distinctiveness, such as forms of government,

---

[1] Francis V. Vernon, *Voyages and Travels of a Sea Officer* (London, 1792), 208.

[2] William Bowers, *Naval Adventures during Thirty-Five Years' Service*, 2 vols. (London: Richard Bentley, 1833), I, 298–300.

[3] John G. Hayman, 'Notions on National Characters in the Eighteenth Century', *Huntington Library Quarterly* 35:1 (1971), 1–17, at 2. For an overview of the topic, see Sebastiani, 'Nations'.

economy, and religion, over 'physical' ones like climate.[4] Hume argued that 'the human mind is of a very imitative nature', and spending time together, for example under a shared 'political body', would make individuals become similar to each other, 'communicating... their vices as well as virtues'.[5] 'Progress' was seen by many, most notably Adam Ferguson, as a shared ability of all humanity and always existing at least in potential among all peoples, no matter how 'barbarous'.[6] These theories are reflected in some contemporary naval practices.

The eighteenth-century British Navy was an institution both intrinsically composed of (and led by) travellers, like Francis Vernon and William Bowers, and gathering people in very tight quarters, under the same regulations. For many officers, views acquired through travel and faith in the reforming power of strict discipline tempered tropes of national character, and its perceived physical, racial, and climatic aspects in particular. Some factors operated against this. Practical considerations of efficiency and safety induced naval commanders to take into account physical differences, particularly as related to the state of health of the seamen, and give credence to the most authoritative medical theories of the day. Moreover, because the Navy was an integral part of an expansive overseas empire, and served as its defender and enforcer, both officers and seamen partook in mindsets that were structurally steeped in racist beliefs. Thus, sailors' characteristics, such as better or worse tolerance to certain climates and diseases, physical shape and attitude for different types of work, or even simply phenotypical traits like skin colour, were easily racialised, which often resulted in forms of social closure and discrimination.[7] Almost paradoxically, however, the Navy's constant and urgent need for workforce led to a general weakness of racialised distinctions in its recruitment policies – which, in turn, resulted, for many officers, in the realisation that a man's suitability to being forged

---

[4] Hayman, 'Notions', 12–14; David Hume, 'Of National Characters', in *Essays Moral, Political, and Literary*, ed. Eugene F. Miller (Indianapolis, IN: Liberty Fund, 1987 [1777]). On Hume's infamously racist footnote n. 10, see, for example, Aaron Garrett and Silvia Sebastiani, 'David Hume on Race', in Naomi Zack (ed.), *The Oxford Handbook of Philosophy and Race* (Oxford: Oxford University Press, 2017); John Immerwahr, 'Hume's Revised Racism', *Journal of the History of Ideas* 53:3 (1992), 481–6; Silvia Sebastiani, 'Race and National Characters in Eighteenth-Century Scotland: The Polygenic Discourses of Kames and Pinkerton', *Cromohs* 8 (2003), 1–14, at 6. For a different declension of these theories, lending slightly more weight to physical causes, see also Montesquieu, *De l'esprit des lois, par Montesquieu. Précédé de l'analyse de cet ouvrage par D'Alembert*, 2 vols. (Paris: P. Pourrat F^res, 1831), I, 419–43.

[5] Hume, *Essays*, 202; Hayman, 'Notions', 13–14.   [6] Sebastiani, 'Race', 3.

[7] On social closure, and how 'races' become 'categories of practice', my thinking has been much informed by Mara Loveman, 'Is "Race" Essential?', *American Sociological Review* 64:6 (1999), 891–8.

into a useful hand criss-crossed the boundaries assigned by racial prejudice. Deployment choices, too, were not yet necessarily predicated on the inferiority and expendability of men construed as racially non-British. Erica Charters has suggested that medical practices relative to the military were a crucial element of the 'sinews of power' of the eighteenth-century British state.[8] In the case of the Navy, biopower principles and utilitarianism in the allocation of resources did not always sit easily with racist manpower selections, not least because many surgeons understood immunity or susceptibility to disease as acquired, more than innate. Acclimatisation, physical and cultural, partial or complete, remained on the table. The Navy of the French Wars, then, sits at a significant juncture before the substantial development of systematically racialised employment in nineteenth-century British shipping.

In the first section of this chapter, I examine the extent to which phenotypical differences could result in a man's discriminatory treatment within the Navy, independently of considerations of military utility. Black seamen of African ancestry, in particular, had to navigate very specific forms of racism and oppression. Subsequently, we focus on the instrumental aspects of biological categorisations: theories of 'racial immunity' or unsuitability to certain climates, and their influence on the strategic allocation of manpower; and the blending of cultural prejudice and racism in perceptions of discipline and hygiene.

4.1   Black Seamen

Black men in the Navy, historians now agree, probably constituted a relatively small percentage of crews.[9] Still, contemporary illustrations of naval life often depict Black sailors, acting as servants, or giving spectacle as they box white shipmates, but also dining as regular members of a mess, or consorting with white prostitutes in English port towns (see **Figures 4.1–4.3**). In this latter case, an alternatively coloured version of the print exists, portraying the seaman in question as white (**Figure 4.4**). Were the two men interchangeable? What was the difference between a white and a Black Jack Tar?

Many studies have now appeared on Black seamen and their position in the eighteenth-century Atlantic seafaring industry. They tend to posit

---

[8] Erica Charters, *Disease, War, and the Imperial State: The Welfare of the British Armed Forces during the Seven Years' War* (Chicago, IL and London: The University of Chicago Press, 2014).

[9] Nicholas Rogers, *The Press Gang: Naval Impressment and Its Opponents in Georgian Britain* (London and New York: Continuum, 2007), 93–4.

Figure 4.1 *A Milling Match between Decks* (1812).
Image: Library of Congress, Prints and Photographs Division, Cartoon Prints,
British (Reproduction Number: LC-USZ62–112877 (b&w film copy neg.); Call
Number: PC 1 – 11981 (A size) [P&P]) https://www.loc.gov/item/95507458/

that maritime employment, where racialised considerations were often
transcended by an interest in 'skill', offered both free and enslaved Black
men opportunities to gain a relative level of emancipation unknown
ashore, and even reinforce a shared sense of identity.[10] This is further
confirmed by the reluctance of colonial elites, perpetually afraid of rebel-
lions and escapes, to allow the participation of enslaved men especially in
longer-distance seafaring, in merchantmen, privateers, or naval ships.[11]
However, the situation in the Navy specifically has been the object
of debate.

[10] Bolster, *Black Jacks*; Philip D. Morgan, 'Black Experiences in Britain's Maritime
World', in David Cannadine (ed.), *Empire, the Sea and Global History: Britain's
Maritime World, c.1760–c.1840* (Basingstoke and New York: Palgrave Macmillan,
2007), 105–33; Kevin Dawson, *Undercurrents of Power: Aquatic Culture in the African
Diaspora* (Philadelphia: University of Pennsylvania Press, 2018); Perl-Rosenthal, *Citizen
Sailors*.
[11] Rogers, *Press Gang*, 91–3; Bolster, *Black Jacks*, 17–24.

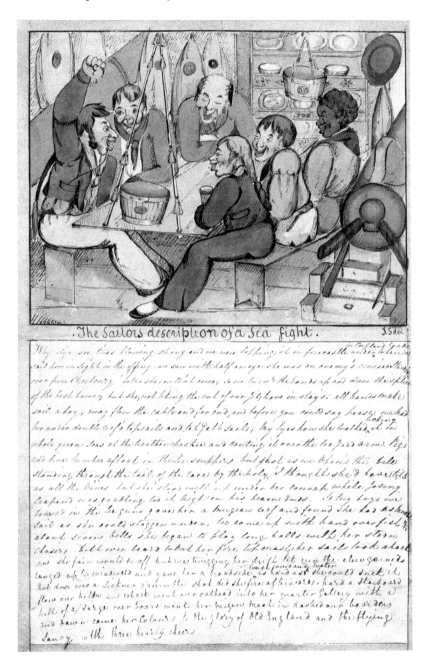

Figure 4.2 Lt John Sheringham, *The Sailors Description of a Sea Fight*
(1819–1825).

Figure 4.3 Thomas Rowlandson, *Accommodation. Or Lodgings to Let at Portsmouth!!* (1808) – Black seaman.
Image: © The Trustees of the British Museum (object n. 1872,1012.4940)
https://www.britishmuseum.org/collection/object/P_1872-1012-4940

Figure 4.4 Thomas Rowlandson, *Accommodation, or Lodgings to Let at Portsmouth!!* (1808) – white seaman.
Image: Metropolitan Museum of Art, New York, The Elisha Whittelsey Collection, The Elisha Whittelsey Fund, 1959 (accession n. 59.533.1983), Public Domain https://www.metmuseum.org/art/collection/search/811977

According to Vincent Carretta, 'the Royal Navy was free of institutional racism', and in it, since 'competence mattered more than colour', everyone was treated equally.[12] In contrast, Charles Foy has argued that, whatever the official policy and intentions, in practice, the system worked 'inequitably', being 'fair in form, but discriminatory in operation'.[13] Whilst Black sailors were needed to maintain a sufficient supply of workforce in Britain's maritime empire, and this did guarantee them some 'leverage' – often including freedom from enslavement – the Navy's priority remained efficiency, which sometimes meant acquiescing to discriminatory 'local practices'.[14]

Foy points out that, in a database he constructed, containing 1,300 eighteenth-century Black naval sailors, only very few ever held officer rank (midshipmen, lieutenants, and a post-captain).[15] This, we should note, is not only the result of racist discrimination: we know that not being born a British subject automatically disqualified a man from holding or hoping for a commission, and many Black seamen would have been born in non-British colonies or in Africa. Moreover, while only a negligible percentage of old or wounded seamen in receipt of a pension could be identified as Black, this might also have been affected by other factors, as Foy himself points out: for example, residence on the wrong side of the Atlantic, which resulted in all American (and indeed non-London-based British) seamen facing the same disadvantage.[16] In the first half of the eighteenth century, a sample study has shown, only 3% of Greenwich Hospital pensioners were born abroad.[17] Therefore, when attempting to measure the impact of racialised prejudice on a man's experience, it is important to control for other factors.

All this, in any case, does not negate the fact that government policies and legislation, or the racism of naval personnel and harbour communities, could significantly affect the opportunities available to a Black sailor. For example, we saw how the Act of Parliament that abolished the slave trade also introduced restrictions on freed Black servicemen's pension and discharge rights.[18] In the Indian Ocean, the British and French governments agreed in 1805 that non-white prisoners could only be exchanged against each other.[19] The Navy, however detached and different from the land, did not move in a social, cultural, and political

---

[12] Vincent Carretta, 'Naval Records and Eighteenth-Century Black Biography', *Journal for Maritime Research* 5:1 (2003), 143–58, at 145–6.
[13] Foy, 'Royal Navy's Employment', esp. 6–7, 31–4.   [14] Ibid., 8–11, 20.
[15] Ibid., 15–16, 32.   [16] Ibid., 17–18. See also Section 7.2.3.
[17] Martin Wilcox, 'The "Poor Decayed Seamen" of Greenwich Hospital, 1705–1763', *International Journal of Maritime History* 25:1 (2013), 65–90, at 71–3.
[18] Section 2.1.   [19] Morieux, 'Indigenous Comparisons', 69.

void. Whilst historians such as Marcus Rediker and Peter Linebaugh famously suggested the existence, in the eighteenth-century maritime Atlantic, of widespread, cross-racial working class solidarity, this thesis has been questioned by recent historiography, even including scholars who would compare the situation of impressed naval seamen to that of the enslaved.[20] For Nicholas Rogers, for example, the eighteenth-century Atlantic was more similar to a 'dog-eat-dog' world, where white seamen, however oppressed, were not immune from racism and often colluded in slavery.[21] According to Isaac Land, British seamen actually based their claims to Britishness and freebirth rights on a racial contraposition between the white 'true British seaman' and Black slaves and 'unmanly' 'mongrel' seamen from the imperial peripheries.[22] These racial tensions emerge very clearly in various sources relating to shipboard power dynamics. In 1780, for example, Barlow Fielding, a Black man, had reached the position of boatswain, but he had to be transferred to a different ship because the crew had 'taken a dislike to the man's colour' and failed to respect him.[23]

Most importantly, we should remember that, as a tool of imperial dominion, the Navy was institutionally on the frontlines of the very same repressive and exploitative practices that fuelled eighteenth- and nineteenth-century racism. In the colonies, it partly served the function of protecting the white planter classes from insurrections of the enslaved.[24] Even when, after 1807, Navy ships were engaged in patrols against slave traders, these operations remained fully embedded in racialised understandings of humanity and humanitarianism (not to mention international power struggles and financial considerations).[25] Throughout the war, naval officers, influenced by the interests of Caribbean and North American elites, were often wary of recruiting enslaved Black persons in the fleet, tending to segregate them as shore auxiliaries; Black seamen could be treated with contempt or denied

---

[20] Rediker, *Between the Devil and the Deep Blue Sea*; Linebaugh and Rediker, *Many-Headed Hydra*.

[21] Rogers, *Press Gang*, 93, 99–100; Morgan, 'Black Experiences', 127.

[22] Isaac Land, 'Customs of the Sea: Flogging, Empire, and the "True British Seaman" 1770 to 1870', *Interventions* 3:2 (2001), 169–85.

[23] Rodger, *Command*, 394.

[24] Siân Williams, 'The Royal Navy and Caribbean Colonial Society during the Eighteenth Century', in McAleer and Petley, *Royal Navy and the British Atlantic*, 27–50.

[25] Robert Burroughs and Richard Huzzey (eds.), *The Suppression of the Atlantic Slave Trade: British Policies, Practices and Representations of Naval Coercion* (Manchester: Manchester University Press, 2017); Mary Wills, *Envoys of Abolition: British Naval Officers and the Campaign Against the Slave Trade in West Africa* (Liverpool: Liverpool University Press, 2019), esp. chs. 3 and 5. See also Section 7.3.2.

the status of prisoners of war and sold as part of prizes, even when they had not been enslaved before.[26] Whatever his rank and status, the colour of a man's skin always made him liable to be seen as a slave by prejudiced peers, superiors, and even inferiors.

This evidence casts very problematic light on Carretta's thesis that the Navy was 'free of institutional racism'. The Navy was part and parcel, and in fact one of the principal upholders, of a structurally racist society. Yet, beyond external pressures and individual prejudices, there are some important ways in which the Navy, unlike other parts of that society, did not impose systematic, official, or specific barriers and limitations to non-white seamen's rights, opportunities, and status. The fleet could then become a 'refuge' from oppression, however flawed.[27] 'Fairness' of treatment, whether in theory or in practice, is too positive a term, only valid in a limited and relative sense. The Navy was *not* 'colour blind', because no eighteenth-century institution could be. However, its open-ended regulations, originally designed under the assumption that seamen would be white British men, forgot to say anything about anyone else – a state of affairs which could, in this case, favour all parties.

First of all, official naval documents display little interest in the identification and classification of a man by 'race'. Indeed, historians attempting to track down 'non-white' naval sailors struggle, because musters and pay lists did not systematically report any indications on the matter, and standardised 'description books' of crews only became common well into the nineteenth century.[28] When it comes to the Navy, Foy's *Black Mariner Database* of seamen in Atlantic shipping has to rely on occasional snippets of information, collated through long, patient work, background knowledge, and insight.[29] Sometimes, the colour of a man's skin can be deduced from nicknames, which does signify special attention paid to it by shipmates: seamen racialised as Black were often assigned diminutives, names of objects or of 'royalty', but their appella-tives could also be explicitly linked to appearance (for example, 'Tom Coffee').[30] In these cases, phenotype was construed as an individual's most distinctive, and in fact identifying, trait. Most of the time, however,

---

[26] Rogers, *Press Gang*, 81–2, 92–5; Charles R. Foy, '"Unkle Sommerset's" Freedom: Liberty in England for Black Sailors', *Journal for Maritime Research* 13:1 (2011), 21–36, at 23–4.

[27] Bolster, *Black Jacks*, 31–2; Rodger, *Wooden World*, 159–61.

[28] Carretta, 'Naval Records', 147. On nineteenth-century racial classifications in the Navy, see Rankin, 'Nineteenth-Century Royal Navy Sailors'.

[29] Charles R. Foy, 'Uncovering Hidden Lives: Developing a Database of Mariners in the Black Atlantic', *Common-place* 9:1 (2009) www.common-place-archives.org/vol-09/no-02/tales/.

[30] Rankin, 'Nineteenth-Century Royal Navy Sailors', 187–8.

the way someone looked only became administratively important when the Navy needed to keep track (and hold) of its hands: naval authorities provided detailed descriptions of skin colour ('ruddy', 'sallow', 'fresh', 'fair', 'dark', 'brown', etc.) in lists of deserters, together with any other – not necessarily racialised – distinctive traits: hair and eye colour, scars, a limp, regional accents, or body shape and stature.[31]

Occasionally, correspondence and courts martial records did explicitly report the fact that a defendant or witness was 'a black man', or a 'negro', something that would clearly not have happened in the case of other physical traits. In December 1800, George Hynes, identified by the main witness, out of the two defendants, as 'the black man', was tried for committing sodomy with another seaman ('the young man').[32] An explicitly racist note emerged in the testimony of another witness, the ship's corporal: when asked by the court if he remembered 'what dress' Hynes had on at the time of the event, he replied that he did not: the man 'was very black and dirty'.[33] In other cases, however, trial transcripts barely even revealed whether a man was Black: the minutes of the court martial of Isaac Wilson, accused of committing sodomy with a ship goat in 1809, go on for several pages before one of the witnesses very casually mentions, at the end of his deposition, that 'the prisoner was in the habit of looking after the goat. He is an American Negro'.[34] The comment probably reflects the speaker's disparaging association of Black seamen with a specific task: many eighteenth-century ship cooks and stewards were Black, as those were relatively low-skilled roles in which an enslaved past ashore could offer some expertise.[35] Whatever the reason for this reference, the fact that racial categories almost went unmentioned makes us wonder how many other records actually concern Black defendants or witnesses, without making it explicit.

Lack of mention in the records does not mean that racialised distinctions were deemed unimportant. Yet, anecdotally, the outcomes and procedures of the trials that we know for sure concerned Black men do

---

[31] See several examples in TNA, ADM 1/1043, Letters from Commanders-in-Chief, Portsmouth, 1800, nn. 801–999; ADM 1/1041, Letters from Commanders-in-Chief, Portsmouth, 1800, nn. 401–600, 478, Mark Milbanke to Evan Nepean, 6 June 1800.

[32] John D. Byrn, *Naval Courts Martial*, 328.   [33] Ibid., 331.   [34] Ibid., 339.

[35] Charles Foy, 'Seamen "Love Their Bellies": How Blacks Became Ship Cooks', 10 August 2014, *Uncovering Hidden Lives: Eighteenth Century Black Mariners* https:// uncoveringhiddenlives.com/; Harold D. Langley, 'The Negro in the Navy and Merchant Service – 1789–1860, 1798', *The Journal of Negro History* 52:4 (1967), 273–86, at 277–8; Bolster, *Black Jacks*, 32–3, 81–2; Alan Cobley, 'Black West Indian Seamen in the British Merchant Marine in the Mid Nineteenth Century', *History Workshop Journal* 58 (2004), 259–74, at 262–3.

not seem to show very distinctive patterns. The seaman accused of sodomy with a goat was freely allowed to cross-examine witnesses, including one of his lieutenants, and eventually acquitted for lack of proof.[36] Similarly, during his 1803 court martial, Quamin, a Black pilot accused of deliberately running aground a Navy sloop in Port Royal, cross-questioned the witnesses at length, including the master and the purser, and even the sloop's captain himself (who was the prosecutor).[37] In his sodomy trial, in 1796, Captain Charles Sawyer was outraged that 'the mere ipse dicit of a black man, who would possibly sell his father and mother for half a bit', was accepted as valid evidence against him; outraged or not, however, he was still found guilty.[38] The way in which courts martial established the trustworthiness of witnesses, beyond any initial racist prejudice, is well illustrated by the case of sailor Charles Ferret, earlier in the century. In 1761, towards the end of the Seven Years' War, his testimony resulted in two of his white shipmates being hanged for sodomy. At first, 'it was objected, that being a black, he could not be admitted to swear against a Christian'. However, the court asked Ferret 'whether he had been baptized' and found out that he had – in fact 'Commodore Keppel was one of his godfathers'; Ferret was illiterate, but a free man, 'receiving his own pay'. Most importantly, 'he knew the nature of an oath, and believed he would incur God's highest displeasure, if he gave a false evidence'.[39] On the basis of these declarations, Ferret was allowed to testify. White boys deemed too young to understand the import of an oath were not, as we can see from an example in 1805.[40] Ultimately crucial to ensuring a witness's credentials, then, was not his being Black or white, but his knowing about and partaking in the cultural and religious system of values on which the judicial procedure was predicated. If prejudice assumed a link between appearance and cultural belonging, any essentialism was still sufficiently weak to allow for their decoupling.

The fact that in the Royal Navy Black men were permitted to testify against whites seems hardly an extraordinary concession, until we remember that this was not the case, for example, in the American Navy.[41] When it became a permanent body, in 1798, the US Navy did

---

[36] Byrn, *Naval Courts Martial*, 338.   [37] Ibid., 500–7.

[38] This case is described in Burg, *Boys at Sea*, 93–4.

[39] TNA, ADM 12/26, Analysis and digest of court martial convictions, arranged by offence: SI-W, 1755–1806, G. Newton & c., 2 July 1761, ff. 21–2. This case is also mentioned in Rodger, *Wooden World*, 159.

[40] Ibid., Mr Bartlet Ambler, 22 April 1805, ff. 65–6. The reader wishing to pursue this reference should be aware that these testimonies concern extremely distressing cases of child rape.

[41] Foy, 'Royal Navy's Employment', 34.

not even officially allow the enlistment of Black or mixed-race seamen.[42] In the Royal Navy, by contrast, John Perkins, a Jamaican 'mulatto', managed to rise to the rank of post-captain. He is often cited by historians to show the theoretical openness to 'talent' of the British naval career, even though his case was a one-off, and perhaps the exception that confirms the rule.[43] The idea of a Black commissioned officer might have felt outlandish to many contemporaries, and indeed, some evidence suggests that, as in the case of the boatswain Barlow Fielding, Perkins had to face racialised insubordination in at least one of his ships.[44] Still, there was no formal prohibition against his promotion, making it possible in the first place.

Men racialised as Black still suffered aboard ships from everyday discrimination. Views of their appearance as peculiar and 'deviant' often resulted in their being put at the centre of the carnivalesque rituals of Line-Crossing, to enhance the ridicule of the occasion.[45] They also faced more serious forms of injury.[46] At the beginning of 1807, the Admiralty learned that Admiral Russell, aboard HMS *Dictator*, had been brutally flogging Peter Salagara, a Cuban Spanish prisoner who refused to enter the Navy: Russell had 'administered some wholesome chastisement,... he being a Negro and speaking the English language'. Salagara even resorted to self-harm in an attempt to make himself ineligible for the service. Having heard his story, however, the Lords Commissioners of the Admiralty immediately ordered to take him back to the West Indies and discharge him; the man refused to step back on a ship, being now afraid and mistrustful, and insisted to be put in prison instead, to be regularly exchanged in future: this was granted.[47] The Admiralty's response does not annul his sufferings, nor the fact that less desperate and less lucky men would not have escaped the situation. The lack of regulations authorising the flogging of Black potential recruits, however, meant that there was a way out for him, even against the racism of a powerful Admiral.

---

[42] Langley, 'Negro in the Navy', 275–6.

[43] Douglas Hamilton, '"A Most Active, Enterprising Officer": Captain John Perkins, the Royal Navy and the Boundaries of Slavery and Liberty in the Caribbean', *Slavery & Abolition* 39:1 (2018), 80–100; N. A. M. Rodger, 'Perkins, John [*nicknamed* Jack Punch] (c.1745–1812)', *ODNB* (2008) www.oxforddnb.com/view/10.1093/ref:odnb/9780198614128.001.0001/odnb-9780198614128-e-50232; Morgan, 'Black Experiences', 118–19; Rodger, *Wooden World*, 272; Wilson, *Social History*, 123–4.

[44] Hamilton, '"Most Active, Enterprising Officer"', 89.

[45] For one example, see Frederick Hoffman, *A Sailor of King George*, ed. A. Beckford Bevan and H. B. Wolryche-Whitmore (London: John Murray, 1901), 14.

[46] Morgan, 'Black Experiences', 127.

[47] TNA, ADM 12/129, Admiralty Digest 1807 – Part 3, 79.17, summary of letters from Admiral Douglas, 29 March, 1 April, 6 April 1807 (quote from the summary).

One last example well illustrates the mixture of on-the-ground discrimination and official equalisation, and the constant tension between practice and theory. In 1808, Britain captured the Island of Marie-Galante, a dependency of Guadeloupe. As the 'European troops' succumbed to disease in large numbers, they were replaced by some of the local Black men who had been enslaved in French estates. Eventually, Admiral Cochrane had these soldiers reassigned to the naval ships on the Leeward Islands station: on the muster books, they appeared as supernumeraries 'for Victuals only' (i.e., not entitled to pay), with the made-up rating of 'Colonial Marines'. In March 1815, the Admiralty received a query from the captain of HM Sloop *Arachne*, at Portsmouth. Two of these privates, Nicholas Saville and Gadeo St. Kits, had served in his sloop since June 1811 and October 1812, respectively. How were they to be disposed of now? More importantly, were they allowed wages, 'as the Pay Books are now making up'?[48] The Admiralty consulted the Colonial Office. The reply came a week later, and as it happened from a politically sympathetic source – the Liverpoolite Lord Bathurst, then Secretary of State for War and the Colonies, who was a moderate ally of emancipationism:

as the Men in question appear to have been enlisted, and to have been thereby rendered in every respect free Persons, Lord Bathurst cannot acquiesce in their being treated in any other manner than as white Men would be treated in a similar situation.[49]

Admittedly, individual inclinations may have played a role in these instructions, but Bathurst was following an official line: by law, enlistment would serve as a (quasi-, we have seen) levelling factor between white and Black recruits. The two Marines, who were 'unprovided with Uniform Cloathing Arms or Accoutrements', were then 'discharged to Head Quarters, with Pay Lists for the time they have served in the Arachne, as is usual in regard to white Men in a similar situation'.[50]

---

[48] TNA, ADM 1/1248, Letters from Commanders-in-Chief, Portsmouth, 1815, nn. 153–300, 282, Sir Richard Bickerton to John Wilson Croker, 11 March 1802, and enclosure (Captain Godfrey to Sir Richard Bickerton, same date).

[49] TNA, ADM 1/4232, Admiralty, Letters from Secretaries of State, January–March 1815, Henry Goulburn to John Barrow, 18 March 1815. Bathurst was a supporter of improvement in the conditions of the enslaved, and personally and politically close to William Wilberforce: Neville Thompson, *Earl Bathurst and the British Empire 1762–1834* (Barnsley: Leo Cooper, 1999), 170–82; N. D. McLachlan, 'Bathurst at the Colonial Office, 1812–27: A Reconnaissance', *Australian Historical Studies* 13:52 (1969), 477–502, at 485–8.

[50] TNA, ADM 1/1249, Letters from Commanders-in-Chief, Portsmouth, 1815, nn. 301–450, 313, Sir Richard Bickerton to John Wilson Croker, 22 March 1815.

After years of exploitation, reference to the centralised machine of military bureaucracy re-established fair employment terms, decoupling racist considerations from legal status, and assigning more weight to the latter. The war was ending, and Saville and St. Kits were told that they could not continue as Marines, but could become seamen; 'if they do not wish to do this', the instructions to the Admiral stated, 'he is to enquire what they would desire to do'. The two men wanted 'to be sent to the West Indies to serve as soldiers in a Black Regiment', which was granted.[51]

Overall, we can see that racial discrimination strongly shaped individuals' lives. Yet, from above, the Navy's administrative silence on matters of 'race' meant that Black men stood at least a chance of enjoying comparable treatment. Liberal egalitarianism had little to do with this: the utilitarian reduction of people to pairs of 'hands' is intrinsically levelling. Whatever their ethnicity, skilled seamen were all useful and precious manpower.

4.2   'Feeble Natives of a Warmer Climate': Constitution, Health, and Biopower

Beyond their impact on the everyday lives of individuals, contemporary beliefs in racial differences had important implications for what was deemed to be the efficient running of the Navy. Medical theories associating particular immunities or vulnerabilities to disease to different 'races' and 'constitutions', and the military and colonial applications of such theories in the eighteenth, nineteenth, and early twentieth centuries, are well-studied subjects.[52] Scholars building on Michel Foucault's work identify these processes as part of mechanisms of 'biopower' or

---

[51] TNA, ADM 12/174, Admiralty Digest 1815 – Part 3, 83.15, summary of letters from General Williams, Horse Guards, and Admiralty, 27 March, 27 April, 1 May 1815.

[52] Warwick Anderson, 'Disease, Race, and Empire', *Bulletin of the History of Medicine* 70:1 (1996), 62–7; idem, 'Immunities of Empire: Race, Disease, and the New Tropical Medicine, 1900–1920', *Bulletin of the History of Medicine* 70:1 (1996), 94–118; Mark Harrison, '"The Tender Frame of Man": Disease, Climate, and Racial Difference in India and the West Indies, 1760–1860', *Bulletin of the History of Medicine* 70:1 (1996), 68–93; Wendy D. Churchill, 'Efficient, Efficacious and Humane Responses to Non-European Bodies in British Military Medicine, 1780–1815', *The Journal of Imperial and Commonwealth History* 40:2 (2012), 137–158; Charters, *Disease*; Rana A. Hogarth, *Medicalizing Blackness: Making Racial Difference in the Atlantic World, 1780–1840* (Chapel Hill, NC: University of North Carolina Press, 2017); Suman Seth, *Difference and Disease: Medicine, Race, and the Eighteenth-Century British Empire* (Cambridge: Cambridge University Press, 2018), esp. 18–21, 167–276, 280–9.

'bio-politics' – the modern state's strategic use and control of human bodies and health as a 'resource'.[53]

Overall, medical theories related to resistance to climate, coupled with a drive towards military efficiency, led the British state to allocate foreign troops and personnel to their native countries, in preference to Britons, who were deemed to have considerably lower chances of survival.[54] Throughout the eighteenth and nineteenth centuries, the Royal Navy squadrons serving off West Africa made extensive use of local hands, particularly for shore watering and supplying, owing to their alleged greater tolerance to the temperature and fevers.[55] That coast, indeed, had long been known as the 'grave' of Europeans. The mortality rate in certain localities may have been up to 66.8% per annum (Cape Coast Command, 1823–26).[56] Similar circumstances influenced the employment of Black men for dockyard work in another insalubrious location, the Caribbean.[57] Some research has questioned the extent to which, in the West Indies at least, European Navy seamen would be effectively prone to disease.[58] Moreover, while the overall mortality rate for Europeans in West Africa, in the period 1787–1850, has been estimated as 43.3% by Philip Curtin, other scholars have since qualified these figures.[59] Yet it is clear that foreign stations, and tropical and near-tropical climates in particular, were often unforgiving to the health of the British sailor. The men certainly fell victim, if not of the temperature, of lethal pathogens, most notably those causing yellow fever and malaria. This was aggravated by the lack of childhood-acquired immunity, genetic resistance, and adequate medical understanding or treatments.[60] All of

[53] 'Biopower' in Ian Buchanan (ed.), *A Dictionary of Critical Theory*, 2nd ed. (Oxford: Oxford University Press, 2018). For a systematic study applying these concepts to a British colonial context, see James S. Duncan, *In the Shadows of the Tropics: Climate, Race and Biopower in Nineteenth Century Ceylon* (Aldershot: Ashgate, 2007).

[54] Churchill, 'Efficient, Efficacious and Humane Responses', 138–41; Charters, *Disease*, 12–14, 17, 18, 41–2, 53–85.

[55] Rankin, 'Nineteenth-Century Royal Navy Sailors', 183; Foy, 'Royal Navy's Employment', 28–32.

[56] H. M. Feinberg, 'New Data on European Mortality in West Africa: The Dutch on the Gold Coast, 1719–1760', *Journal of African History* 15:3 (1974), 357–71, at 359.

[57] Foy, 'Royal Navy's Employment', 25.

[58] Coriann Convertito, '*The Health of British Seamen in the West Indies, 1770–1806*' (unpublished PhD thesis, University of Exeter, 2011).

[59] Feinberg, 'New Data'.

[60] P. D. Curtin, '"The White Man's Grave:" Image and Reality, 1780–1850', *Journal of British Studies* 1:1 (1961), 94–110. For a historical argument in favour of innate resistance (though not immunity) to yellow fever, see Kenneth F. Kiple and Virginia H. Kiple, 'Black Yellow Fever Immunities, Innate and Acquired, as Revealed in the American South', *Social Science History* 1:4 (1977), 419–36; Lauren E. Blake and Mariano A. Garcia-Blanco, 'Human Genetic Variation and Yellow Fever Mortality

this likely constituted a disadvantage of Europeans against some local populations – although the latter's total immunity was itself a racialised myth.

Whatever the medical reality, in any case, there is no doubt that contemporary Britons firmly believed in the dangers of 'exotic climates', and their ideas of efficiency and sensible practice were inevitably shaped by such beliefs. In 1807, the Sick and Hurt Board pointed out the problematic nature of an Order in Council of two years earlier, which required a set length of service before naval surgeons could retire at 10s per day, but made 'no distinction' 'between Surgeons who have never been out of the European Seas' and those who had 'ruined their Constitution' in tropical climates.[61] British seamen who had been wounded or had proved unable to bear warmer weather and its relative diseases were regularly declared unfit for duty at those latitudes, or sent home being of 'no use to the service in this climate'.[62] James Dalziel, surgeon of HMS *Swiftsure* when it was stationed in the Gulf of Naples, in 1798–1800, reported that the 'flux' was striking significant numbers of the men who had been sent ashore. He was convinced that those of a 'fair complexion' with 'sandy hair', a 'very white skin', and freckles would 'generally suffer most from a dysentery in a warm climate' and be more likely to be affected by it than those with darker skins.[63] Even whilst implying that the northerners' bodies were stronger, medical reports readily acknowledged their disadvantage in warmer climes: 'The Robust vigorous Constitution', according to an 1812 memorandum, 'is more obnoxious to Fever in Sicily than a spare puny [?] Habit: and British or German Soldiers often suffer severely, in Situations where Spaniards, Italians, or the Natives of Countries bordering on the Mediterranean, either escape entirely; or are affected in a milder

during Nineteenth Century U.S. Epidemics', *mBio* 5:3 (2014), 1–6. See also J. R. McNeill, *Mosquito Empires: Ecology and War in the Greater Caribbean, 1620–1914* (Cambridge: Cambridge University Press, 2010), 44–6. On genetic resistance to malaria, see, for example, Carolina López et al., 'Mechanisms of Genetically-Based Resistance to Malaria', *Gene* 467 (2010), 1–12.

61 TNA, ADM 98/24, Sick and Hurt Board to the Admiralty, 1806–8, 15 May 1807, ff. 57–8.

62 See, for example, TNA, ADM 101/93/1, Medical and surgical journal of HMS *Canopus* for 17 June 1806–16 June 1807 by A Martin, Surgeon, f. 60; ADM 101/123/1, Medical journal of HMS *Theban* for 16 November 1813 to 16 November 1814 by William Ure, surgeon, f. 4.

63 TNA, ADM 101/121/3B, Medical journal of HMS *Swiftsure* for 8 July 1798 to 9 July 1799 by James Dalziel, f. 40; ADM 101/121/3C, Medical journal of HMS *Swiftsure* for 9 July 1799 to 9 July 1800 by James Dalziel, f. 7. On the racialisation of dysentery, see also Hogarth, *Medicalizing Blackness*, 187–9.

degree'.[64] In some places, therefore, men coming from areas beyond Britain and northern Europe, once racialised as climate-resistant, could become particularly precious.

In the summer of 1799, Sir Sidney Smith recruited thirty-six volunteers from Constantinople to replenish the complement of his ship at Cyprus,

being in absolute want of a number of Seamen used to Boat Service in this Climate to carry on the Current and necessary Service without exposing Englishmen to the Sun by day, and heavy dews by night which exposure has been found to occasion Sickness and death among them.[65]

This might be read as a desire to spare Britons and deploy expendable foreigners in the most wearing tasks – a practice that was to become very common in nineteenth-century shipping, with the supposedly 'heat resistant' non-white seafarers underpaid and systematically assigned to the most unforgiving work in stokeholds.[66] In the French Wars, too, the line between practical justifications and moral judgements on which men were most disposable could be rather fine. This can be seen, for example, in the language deployed by naval surgeon James Lind, earlier in the century: he saw the likely sacrifice of '"unseasoned Europeans"', '"gallant soldiers"' or '"brave seamen"', as inconsistent with '"British humanity"'.[67] Often, however, the considerations were genuinely practical: where the conditions dictated it, foreigners were spared, and Britons deployed.

Recruits coming from warmer latitudes suffered considerably when exposed to the dismal weather of northern European and Atlantic waters; some Navy officials tried to take this into account. Discharged men from foreign corps in the Mediterranean were classed into categories including 'Men Capable of Garrison duty in the Mediterranean' and 'Men Capable of Garrison duty in a Colder Climate', and redeployed accordingly.[68] In November 1805, HMS *Arethusa*'s surgeon noted of George Leviscomte, 'a man of colour', that 'this poor creature has never been in Europe

---

[64] University of Nottingham, Manuscripts and Special Collections [henceforth NMS], Pw Jd 751/1, '*Memorie* relative to the Health of the Army in Sicily, submitted to His Excellency Lt. General Lord William Bentinck', 1812, f. 2.

[65] NMM, ADM/B/202, Board of Admiralty, In-Letters, August–November 1801, Sir William Sidney Smith to Spencer Smith, 1 June 1799; Navy Office to Evan Nepean, 19 November 1801.

[66] Tony Lane, 'The Political Imperatives of Bureaucracy and Empire: The Case of the Coloured Alien Seamen Order, 1925', in Diane Frost (ed.), *Ethnic Labour and British Imperial Trade: A History of Ethnic Seafarers in the UK* (London: Frank Cass, 1995), 104–29, at 109–10.

[67] Cited in Seth, *Difference and Disease*, 109, 284.

[68] NMS, Pw Jd 4028, Plan for Discharged Men from Foreign Corps, n.d.

before and is not yet inured to a northern climate': 'I do believe if we were to winter here that the mere rigor of the winter would kill him and several others of the same description that we have on board'. The surgeon discharged them to duty when the ship arrived 'in a warm climate near Madeira'.[69] Perhaps, the Admiralty Board had similar considerations in mind when, in December 1807, after allowing eight 'Black Men and Men of Colour', prisoners of war in Britain, to enter the Navy, it directed the Commander-in-Chief at Plymouth to 'put them on board Ships going Southward'.[70] Lascar sailors' lack of resistance to cold climates was well known (and in commercial shipping used to argue for proportionately lower wages).[71] 'The great change of climate, and manner of life' provoked by travelling to Europe from India would, according to contemporary surgeons, 'naturally' cause these 'feeble natives of a warmer climate' to fall prey of illnesses like fever and pneumonia: as such, they had to be taken care of in a special way, with 'a more stimulating diet', not too far from that of their homeland, warm clothing, encouragement to take care of their bodies, and the right balance between activity and rest.[72] This condescending attitude, it should be noted, was the same that naval commanders and the medical establishment applied towards British sailors: the eminent East India Company surgeon William Hunter explicitly drew the parallel between specific provisions necessary for Lascars in Europe and for Europeans in tropical climates.[73]

On the whole, it seems that a differential deployment of men was not necessarily discriminatory in nature. An increasingly refined sense of efficiency in allocating resources, the result of a long and costly war, ensured that often the Navy as an institution operated in a flexible and strictly practical mindset: the seamen available simply had to be used where they had the best chances of being serviceable the longest. Racial vilification and blanket negative stereotypes of inferiority could only fit this system up to a point.

There is one further consideration. A definite shift in European medical views of immunity from innate and 'racial' to acquired probably happened

---

[69] TNA, ADM 101/86/1, Journal of HMS *Arethusa* by Thomas Simpson, Surgeon, 14 May 1805–14 June 1806, f. 13.

[70] ADM 12/129, Admiralty Digest 1807 – Part 3, 83.6, summary of letter from Captain Barker, 30 December 1807.

[71] Fisher, 'Indian Ghat Sarangs', 157.

[72] William Hunter, *An Essay on the Diseases Incident to Indian Seamen, or Lascars, on Long Voyages* (Calcutta: The Honorable Company Press, 1804), 1–18.

[73] Hunter, *Essay*, 10.

only around the end of the nineteenth century, with microbiology.[74] However, rigid connections between 'race' and susceptibility or immunity to diseases were themselves a product of the first half of the nineteenth century: previous theories had allowed for more flexibility, and conceded that 'acclimatisation' and 'seasoning' could mitigate the effects of one's native constitution.[75] Admittedly, this chronology is not neat. Some Enlightenment polygenist thinkers already painted humanity as divided into species, each 'fitted' by Providence to a specific climate: people, Lord Kames claimed, end up unavoidably 'degenerating in a climate to which they are not fitted by nature'.[76] This went even further than climatic determinism: 'race' came to be seen as intrinsic and a 'cause', rather than an 'effect' of climate.[77] According to Erica Charters, military colonial experience itself, and the realisation that, instead of 'acclimatizing', British soldiers in the Indies almost inevitably fell sick, was a crucial contributing factor in this shift, from the Seven Years' War onwards.[78] However, possibly owing to greater mobility, perceptions prevalent in the Navy seem to have been more nuanced than a flat innatism.[79]

Suman Seth has shown that even if John Atkins, naval surgeon in the first half of the eighteenth century, was one of the earliest polygenists, he racialised physical appearance, but not disease.[80] Two other Navy surgeons, Charles Bisset and James Lind, made no medical distinction between seasoned white and Black men: a '"sudden change of Climate"' was the cause of sickness, rather than intrinsic bodily differences.[81] By the French Wars, these views were in transition. However, with some partial exceptions, such as Dalziel's complexion theories, naval surgeons' remarks on a seaman's suitability or unsuitability to a certain climate were not intrinsically tied to racial beliefs, as much as to an appreciation

---

[74] Anderson, 'Immunities of Empire', 105–10.

[75] Anderson, 'Disease, Race, and Empire', 64–5; Harrison, '"The Tender Frame of Man"', 70, 73–93; Seth, *Difference and Disease*.

[76] Henry Home, Lord Kames, *Sketches of the History of Man*, 4 vols., 2nd ed. (London: W. Strahan and T. Cadell and Edinburgh: W. Creech, 1778), I, 8–10, 20–30; Sebastiani, 'Race', 5. On the arguments surrounding polygenism and monogenism, see Curtin, '"White Man's Grave"', 103–4; Stock, '"Almost a Separate Race"', 7–14. On the role of religion in preserving monogenism, see Colin Kidd, *The Forging of Races: Race and Scripture in the Protestant Atlantic World, 1600–2000* (Cambridge: Cambridge University Press, 2006).

[77] Kames, *Sketches*, 21–2, 50–63, 72–8; Hudson, 'From "Nation" to "Race"'. For an in-depth discussion of eighteenth-century debates, see Seth, *Difference and Disease*, 167–276.

[78] Charters, *Disease*, 14, 17, 142–71, 192–4.

[79] On the implications of this mobility from the point of view of surgeons' observations, see Seth, *Difference and Disease*, 288–9.

[80] Ibid., 196–207.   [81] Ibid., 261–2, 106–11.

of circumstances. It was not only African and South Asian people who were signalled as particularly liable to sickness in northern waters, but also white Europeans who had served for long periods in tropical climates, upon their return.[82] This was the case aboard HMS *Bombay*, in the summer of 1808. The ship had received into its complement a large number of men who had spent 'several years in warm climates', so the surgeon braced himself to face an epidemic of the 'inflammatory and other complaints which men are liable to who are exposed to cold weather after a long residence in tropical climate'; the sailors were all, for example, 'obliged to wear flannel'. The result after a few months was, in his view, satisfactory: although their poor acclimatisation made them 'less able to bear the winters cold of England', these men nearly all survived to see the spring.[83] Of James Brown, a Marine caught ill with 'cold, catarrhal complaints with hoarseness' in November 1804, the hospital surgeon noted that he had 'been several years in a hot Climate'; similarly, Armourer Thomas Knight's cough, chest pains, and other complaints, in the winter of 1800–1, had started upon his return to England and were partly attributed to his 'having lived the last four years intemperately, in a hot climate'.[84]

Similar situational variations in a man's liability to disease were also considered in the case of non-white sailors. In June 1813, Abraham Methodist, a Black man, was discharged to Plymouth Hospital with pneumonia. Whilst part of the failure to recover was blamed on 'his own indolent dirty disposition', the surgeon noted that Methodist had 'not been lately accustomed to the winter weather in England: & consequently never easy but when before the galley fire'.[85] The use of the adverb 'lately' is extremely revealing, here: Methodist was not deemed unsuited to the climate because of his assumed racial traits, but because of his most recent experiences. Sidney Smith's Constantinople recruits were '*used to* Boat Service in this Climate', not naturally fit for it; George Leviscomte was '*not yet* inured to a northern climate'.[86] Lascar seamen's susceptibility to disease was also seen as oscillating, being higher on their return journeys from Britain, where they would have become used to a

---

[82] Ibid., 111.
[83] TNA, ADM 101/91/4, Journal of HMS *Bombay* by John Knox, Surgeon, 14 May 1808–13 May 1809, ff. 49–50.
[84] TNA, ADM 101/112/5, Medical journal of His Majesty's Prison Hospital ship *Le Pegaze* [*Le Pegase*] from the 25 January 1804 to 14 January 1805 by [William Bickley Smith?], Surgeon, f. 5; ADM 101/84/6A, Medical journal HMS *Ambuscade* for 26 August 1800 to 27 August 1801 by Thomas Hendry, f. 10.
[85] TNA, ADM 101/125/3, Medical and surgical journal of HMS *Ville de Paris* for 25 March 1813 to 24 March 1814 by William Warner, Surgeon, f. 8.
[86] See footnotes 65 and 69 above.

'more nourishing, stimulating diet'.[87] In all these cases, lack of acclimatisation was treated as contingent, rather than intrinsic. What about the 'indolent dirty disposition'?

4.3   'Naturally Filthy in Their Cloathes and Indolent in Their Habits': Disease and Discipline

By the end of the eighteenth century, British naval medicine was solidly grounded on the joint pursuit of efficiency and discipline. Older paternalistic principles, stressing both the officers' duty of care towards the men and the latter's irresponsibility towards their own body, were beginning to shade into new theories of strict and uniform social, moral, hygienic, and medical control.[88] The Navy's role in 'healing and cleansing' British society at large, through recruitment, reformation, and useful employment of the lowest classes, had become a staple of national political rhetoric.[89]

In general, British naval officers had a poor opinion of the health and cleanliness standards of most other European navies. In December 1800, the Swedish fleet was described to the British Secretary of State as being 'in the most deplorable and despicable situation imaginable'.[90] In 1795, a British surgeon visited a ship belonging to the Russian squadron anchored at Sheerness, to assist in stopping a fever epidemic. Among the causes, next to the 'sand' and 'wet earth' 'shingle ballast' – which, as the captain himself recognised, made the lower decks perpetually damp – he noted the 'putrid stench' coming from the Russian sailors' '*shubs* or sheep-skin great coats'. The men wore 'the woolly side next their body', and these coats contributed to 'nourish the seeds of contagion, and

---

[87] Hunter, *Essay*, 9–10.

[88] The key work on the oeconomy of British naval and military medicine is Charters, *Disease*. On paternalism and discipline, see, for example, Christopher Lawrence, 'Disciplining Disease: Scurvy, the Navy, and Imperial Expansion, 1750–1825', in David Philip Miller and Peter Hanns Reill (eds.), *Visions of Empire: Voyages, Botany, and Representations of Nature* (Cambridge: Cambridge University Press, 1996), 80–106, esp. at 82–3, 95; J. D. Alsop, 'Warfare and the Creation of British Imperial Medicine, 1600–1800', in Geoffrey L. Hudson (ed.), *British Military and Naval Medicine, 1600–1830* (Amsterdam and New York: Rodopi, 2007), 23–50, at 37–9; Lincoln, *Representing*, esp. 172, 176–8. I question the notion that these theories of medical control could be effectively applied in practice in Sara Caputo, 'Treating, Preventing, Feigning, Concealing: Sickness, Agency, and the Medical Culture of the British Naval Seaman at the End of the Long Eighteenth Century', *Social History of Medicine* (advance article, 2021).

[89] Rodger, *Command*, 397.

[90] TNA, ADM 1/4185, Admiralty, Letters from Secretaries of State, September–December 1800, Mr Talbot to Mr Fisher, 16 December 1800.

increase its virulence'. Therefore, he insisted with multiple Russian commanders that the garments be destroyed: they might have been useful in the 'dry, cold, frosty' Russian weather, but they were very harmful in the British 'chilly wet weather'.[91] During a voyage aboard a Russian ship, in 1814, another British naval surgeon recorded some less than flattering observations on the medical and hygienic conditions prevalent in that fleet. He pointed out

not merely the general neglect of personal cleanliness common to most foreigners, but a peculiar characteristic of it, namely, the presence of certain *creeping things*, which with us are considered to be confined to the lowest and idlest objects of the most squalid poverty.[92]

This passage refers to his observation of officers' own personal cleanliness, which was of course reflected in the rest of the crew: 'among the seamen this nuisance prevails to an extent surprising and disgusting in the extreme, arising from the utter disregard of the officers to their comforts and cleanliness'.[93] He went on to describe the poor quality of medical provision and competence, and the high incidence of sickness, caused by a general 'neglect of personal cleanliness, damp air, and want of exercise', even when the ships themselves were clean.[94]

As long as these seamen remained aboard their countries' respective vessels, such commentaries from British officers could be taken merely as pitiful, self-complacent observations on the poor state of the less organised allies. Constant military cooperation and exchange, however, blurred the dividing lines between one fleet and the other. In 1809, '37 Italian Troops' who had volunteered for the Army of the King of Naples embarked aboard HMS *Comus*: they were 'so much in want of Cloathing' that the captain 'found it necessary for the health and cleanliness of the Crew' to have each of them freely issued with a shirt and 'Duck trowsers', out of the purser's stock.[95] When in 1795 hundreds of sick Russian sailors had to be accommodated in British naval hospitals, the Sick and Hurt Board repeatedly insisted on the 'necessity of keeping' them 'as separate as possible from the other Patients'.[96] The potential spreading of diseases into the British fleet had to be considered. The phenomenon

---

[91] James Carmichael Smyth, *An Account of the Experiment Made at the Desire of the Lords Commissioners of the Admiralty, on Board the Union Hospital Ship, to Determine the Effect of the Nitrous Acid in Destroying Contagion, and the Safety with Which It May Be Employed* (London: J. Johnson, 1796), 39–40, 42–3.

[92] *Voyage to St. Petersburg*, 9.   [93] Ibid.   [94] Ibid., 10–15, 20–3.

[95] NMM, ADM/B/235, Board of Admiralty, In-Letters, January–February 1809, Navy Office, 12 January 1809.

[96] TNA, ADM 98/17, Sick and Hurt Board to the Admiralty, 1795–6, 13 August 1795, 2 September 1795, 15 December 1795, ff. 211–14, 228–9, 318–19.

would have been far from unprecedented: for example, the typhus epidemic that had ravished the Dutch fleet in the 1730s was attributed to the input of foreigners, with their unusual clothing and diet.[97]

Royal Navy officers were very alert to the risk of disease introduced by any new hands, especially if ill-equipped with bedding and clothing.[98] Yet 'foreigners', similarly to other categories of displaced outsiders like vagrants and paupers, were an obvious target of suspicion. In this context, cultural prejudice and material reality often become indistinguishable. In June 1800, the *Royal William*'s surgeon, at Spithead, reported to the Commander-in-Chief that the fever epidemics that had caused several casualties might have been brought 'in the cloaths' of the 'foreigners' taken from prison to serve 'as disposeables [*sic*] for the Fleet'. 'They are Men of different Countrys, naturally filthy in their Cloathes and indolent in their habits and understanding very little English the most unremitting attention fails to keep them Clean'. The surgeon then 'was under the necessity of issuing again to them more Cloathes than the Regulations of the Service allows'.[99] In late eighteenth-century Britain, elite reformers were beginning to conceptualise the spreading of 'moral' and 'physical' disease, indiscipline and illness, as inextricably linked.[100] In this case, foreigners' limited linguistic skills, which we saw were usually not deemed too problematic, could come to be seen as further aggravating lazy habits and vice.

In such circumstances, racial prejudices crept their way in, as administrative inefficiencies and different cultural practices happened to align with a British sense of superiority.[101] Indiscipline and uncleanliness, Norbert Elias has argued, are characteristic of the 'anomie' that powerful groups scathingly attribute to 'outsiders'.[102] Nonetheless, this prejudice did not take an immutable shape. Because seamen, British and not, were deemed an intrinsically irresponsible category, a lack of cleanliness was not always blamed on them, but on the weak discipline and poor leadership in their navies and countries. The British surgeon describing the Russian fleet in 1814 in such disparaging terms had a very high opinion of the Russian seamen themselves, despite their defect of being slightly

---

[97] Bruijn, *Dutch Navy*, 172.

[98] See, for example, TNA, ADM 1/1065, Letters from Commanders-in-Chief, Portsmouth, 1804, 75, J. Wainwright to George Montagu, 16 January 1804.

[99] TNA, ADM 1/1041, Letters from Commanders-in-Chief, Portsmouth, 1800, nn. 401–600, 468, Thomas Pickmore to Admiral Mark Milbanke, 4 June 1800.

[100] Lawrence, 'Disciplining Disease', 95–8; Robin Evans, *The Fabrication of Virtue: English Prison Architecture, 1750–1840* (Cambridge: Cambridge University Press, 1982), 115–16.

[101] Cf. Charters, *Disease*, 49–50.   [102] Elias, *Established*, xxv–viii.

passive: 'the Russian sailors possess all the requisites for becoming the first among their profession – courage, fortitude, patience, obedience, hardihood, and activity'.[103] 'The chief defect in Russian discipline', he explained, was 'the want of proper superintendence by the officers', who, committing a 'fatal, but seemingly a fixed error', neglected to combat the men's natural 'idleness', refused to muster them regularly, and maintained that 'the health of the men was their affair alone and no other person's', besides showing very poor hygienic habits themselves.[104] 'The virtues of the Russian, are all his own', he concluded; 'his faults those of his officers, or at least of their mode of discipline.'[105]

This manner of thinking, we shall see, was quite common, and it had important implications. If the issue lay in cultural and administrative structures, rather than an intrinsic inferiority of individuals, then integration into the allegedly well-functioning culture and administration of the British Navy could no doubt solve it. Medical problems resulting from climate were overcome through both calculated manpower deployment choices and individuals' adaptation and acclimatisation. In an analogous way, medical problems resulting from 'bad' cultural habits could be solved by the very fact of enlistment in the British Navy, and by the 'acclimatisation' of the individual to new social and disciplinary practices.

4.4   Conclusion

Officers and Admiralty Lords, surgeons, and shipmates could be imbued with racist prejudice, and so was, of course, much of the legislation. Racial classifications, however, were not a prime guiding principle by which naval personnel was accounted for. All the Navy needed was hands to function – 'manpower', more than men. This is not to say that there was a uniformity of use: assumed differential tolerance to specific climates, for example, was put to work in the fleet's global reach. For many surgeons, however, immunity and susceptibility to disease were personal characteristics, apt to being slowly remoulded, if necessary. Similarly, poor medical conditions and the idea of 'filthiness' were clearly linked to national prejudice, but this prejudice targeted the administrative and leadership structures of foreign countries and navies, above and beyond individuals. Dirt and disease could be swept away by dressing a man in the clean clothes of a British sailor, whilst the Navy's iron discipline would stamp down and keep in check any bad habits or tendencies to relapse.

---

[103] *Voyage to St. Petersburg*, 19–20.   [104] Ibid., 9–22.   [105] Ibid., 21.

It is important to note that, if the Navy saw the assimilation of most men as possible, the methods and level of effort that, in the views of naval officials, had to be exerted in each case could vary, often depending on the assumed differences between peoples. Even while asserting that moral causes of national character could trump physical and climatic ones, some eighteenth-century thinkers believed that the degree of control needed to manage a people would depend on the extent of the climate-induced defects that had to be compensated.[106] As will be seen in the next two chapters, echoes of this way of thinking also informed the attitude of naval officers. Mediterranean and northern European sailors, both groups represented aboard British warships, were often integrated by different means. Greater cultural and material distance from 'British' standards resulted in more complex and fraught paths to acceptance.

---

[106] Montesquieu, *De l'esprit des lois*, 426, 428–31, 442–3; Melissa Calaresu, 'Looking for Virgil's Tomb: The End of the Grand Tour and the Cosmopolitan Ideal in Europe', in Jaś Elsner and Joan-Pau Rubiés (eds.), *Voyages and Visions: Towards a Cultural History of Travel* (London: Reaktion Books, 1999), 138–61, at 146–7.

5   'They Cannot Keep the Sea beyond a Passage'

The Royal Navy and Recruitment in the Two Sicilies

For most of the French Wars, the British Navy maintained a fleet in the Mediterranean. Like many others, this sea basin had been for centuries a rich space of encounter, connection, and interdependent 'redistribution', where cultures interacted and brewed distinctively across shared environments.[1] However, the Mediterranean's several 'narrow-sea orbits' formed often inward-looking commercial and cultural clusters.[2] British merchants had established solid local networks, and especially through the system of protection passes, sheltering traders from the assaults of North African corsairs, Britain had become an important player in Mediterranean power dynamics.[3] During these wars, the groundwork was laid for the country's deep imperial engagement in the area throughout the nineteenth century. Yet, from a cultural point of view, Royal Navy ships still found themselves surrounded by a maritime 'world' in which they were most clearly newcomers and outsiders.[4] Physical distance from Britain, differing seafaring traditions, language barriers, and religious contrasts all contributed to creating a mutual sense of extraneousness. Countries from this region, then, offer a useful case study to

---

[1] The literature is vast, but see, for example, Peregrine Horden and Nicholas Purcell, 'The Mediterranean and "the New Thalassology"', *The American Historical Review* 111:3 (2006), 722–40; Fernand Braudel, *The Mediterranean and the Mediterranean World in the Age of Philip II*, 2 vols., 2nd ed., trans. Siân Reynolds (London: Collins, 1972); Peregrine Horden and Nicholas Purcell, *The Corrupting Sea: A Study of Mediterranean History* (Oxford: Blackwell Publishing, 2000), esp. 22–5, 485–523; Molly Greene, 'The Mediterranean Sea', in David Armitage, Alison Bashford, and Sujit Sivasundaram (eds.), *Oceanic Histories* (Cambridge: Cambridge University Press, 2017), 134–55.

[2] John Chircop, 'The Narrow-Sea Complex: A Hidden Dimension in Mediterranean Maritime History', in Gordon Boyce and Richard Gorski (eds.), *Resources and Infrastructures in the Maritime Economy, 1500–2000* (St. John's, Newfoundland: International Maritime Economic History Association, 2002), 43–61.

[3] Tristan Stein, 'Passes and Protection in the Making of a British Mediterranean', *Journal of British Studies* 54 (2015), 602–31.

[4] This 'cultural alienation' had an impact even on merchants: Katerina Galani, *British Shipping in the Mediterranean during the Napoleonic Wars: The Untold Story of a Successful Adaptation* (Leiden and Boston, MA: Brill, 2017), esp. 34–5.

oppose to that of the North Sea basin, explored in the next chapter, of which Britain was itself a part. By the end of the eighteenth century, northwestern European thinkers and travellers had begun to exhibit substantial political, cultural, and even racial prejudices towards southern European populations, casting the South as a backward counterpoint to the developing trajectory of the rest of Europe.[5] These prejudices were clearly present in the minds of British naval officers, when they considered their options for recruitment and joint operations.

A mindset of this kind, however, was not static. The round trip from England took on average two to three months, forcing British commanders and diplomats to act and react in relative independence from their homeland.[6] Obliged to rely on local supplies and manpower, they could stubbornly persist in their received negative views, but also find that recruits were more amenable to be shaped into effective naval sailors than cultural and racial stereotypes would allow. Key to this process of reframing, I argue, was the ambivalent position occupied by naval officers from the Mediterranean in their relations with British colleagues.

This chapter focuses on the specific case of men from the Kingdom of the Two Sicilies, for two reasons.[7] First, Britain cultivated extremely close diplomatic relations with this country. Second, Neapolitan and Sicilian seamen had relatively little experience of foreign contacts and travel outside the Mediterranean, which set them apart even more starkly from the global outlook of the British fleet. This was not the case, for example, for Maltese sailors: the crews of the galleys of the Order of Malta, a cosmopolitan crucible, included men from every corner of Europe and North Africa, and their chaplains were warned that they would have to deal with 'people of all nations, and diverse condition, too'.[8] Neapolitan ships were very different. After briefly sketching the international diplomatic context, and its effects on manpower exchanges,

---

[5] See, for example, Roberto M. Dainotto, 'Does Europe Have a South? An Essay on Borders', *The Global South* 5:1 (2011), 37–50; Maria Clara Paulino, 'The "Alien" European: British Accounts of Portugal and the Portuguese, 1780–1850', in Martin Farr and Xavier Guégan (eds.), *The British Abroad since the Eighteenth Century, Volume 1: Travellers and Tourists* (Basingstoke: Palgrave Macmillan, 2013), 101–16.

[6] Michael Duffy, 'British Naval Intelligence and Bonaparte's Egyptian Expedition of 1798', *The Mariner's Mirror* 84:3 (1998), 278–90, at 278.

[7] 'Kingdom of the Two Sicilies' is a post-Restoration official designation, since Naples and Sicily were not constitutionally united before then, but the term was informally in use in the eighteenth century. Unless otherwise clear, I use 'Neapolitan' and 'Sicilian' interchangeably for the period up to 1806. After 1806, 'Neapolitan' pertains to the Kingdom of Naples, under French control, and 'Sicilian' to the Kingdom of Sicily, still ruled by the exiled Bourbon King Ferdinand, with British support.

[8] National Library of Malta, Valletta [henceforth NLM], AOM 1931, '[Ruolo dell'equipaggio della] "S. Giovanni"', 1712–35; AOM 1927, [Comm. Manso],

we shall look in turn at the experiences of officers and of lower-deck hands in the Royal Navy.

5.1   Diplomacy, Power, and Manpower

5.1.1   Unequal Partners

The relationship between Britain and the Two Sicilies was based, throughout the eighteenth century, on a very unequal balance of power. Southern Italy exported raw materials to Britain and purchased finished products, in what has been described as a quasi-colonial situation; occasionally, British traders even made use of smuggling, market-flooding, and political blackmail to keep Neapolitan and Sicilian manufactures in a depressed state.[9] As the Neapolitan Francophile intellectual Vincenzo Cuoco put it in 1806, in Italy, 'the English... exerted a commercial despotism little inferior to that which they exert in the Indies'.[10]

This situation had two contradictory results. On the one hand, the forceful influx of British products, travellers, fashion, and culture powerfully influenced many aspects of life.[11] 'Anglomania' and admiration towards Britain's culture, constitution, and 'freedom', coupled with practical and commercial concerns, led to imitation in various sectors.[12] The maritime context was one of the most affected: traditional Mediterranean shipbuilding techniques and typologies of sailing vessels (the small *polacche*, *pinchi*, and *tartane*, for example) were gradually replaced by square-sail larger vessels modelled on French and British examples.[13] Well into the nineteenth century, Neapolitan merchant captains sailed relying on sextants, octants, and telescopes of British make.[14]

'Instruzione [*sic*] per il Cappellano di Galera', n.d., f. 10: '*gente di varie nazioni, e di condizioni anche diverse*'.

[9] Eugenio Lo Sardo, *Napoli e Londra nel XVIII secolo: Le relazioni economiche* (Naples: Jovene, 1991), esp. 33–43, 139–56, 181–200, 245–311; Gigliola Pagano de Divitiis, *Il commercio inglese nel Mediterraneo dal '500 al '700: Corrispondenza consolare e documentazione britannica tra Napoli e Londra* (Naples: Guida Editori, 1984), 6–30.

[10] Vincenzo Cuoco, 'La politica inglese e l'Italia', in *Scritti vari – Parte prima: Periodo milanese (1801–1806)*, ed. Nino Cortese and Fausto Nicolini (Bari: Gius. Laterza e figli, 1924), 201–13, at 211 [*Giornale Italiano*, 5–8 January 1806]: '... *esercitavano un dispotismo commerciale poco minore di quello che esercitano nelle Indie*'.

[11] Dieter Richter, *Napoli cosmopolita: Viaggiatori e comunità straniere nell'Ottocento* (Naples: Electa Napoli, 2002); Arturo Graf, *L'anglomania e l'influsso inglese in Italia nel secolo XVIII* (Turin: Ermanno Loescher, 1911), 106–39, 400–12.

[12] Graf, *Anglomania*, esp. 120–1, 140–55, 405–12.

[13] Maresca and Passaro, *Marineria*, 9–10.

[14] Maresca, *Museo navale*, 22–3, 59–63, 98–9; Maresca and Passaro, *Marineria*, 36. See Chapter 3, Figure 3.3.

On the other hand, strong Anglophobia arose among Enlightened reformist intellectuals, culminating in the revolution of 1799.[15] This kind of feeling was not prevalent at the Bourbon court, especially during the time when John Acton (born in France but from an English family) was '*de facto* prime minister' and Queen Maria Carolina was close to Admiral Nelson, Sir William Hamilton, British Minister Plenipotentiary in Naples, and his wife Emma.[16] However, antipathy towards the British simmered among naval and port officers, with what consequences we shall see in a minute.

Trade, with its cultural and social implications, was not the only factor skewing the balance of power in favour of Britain: during the French Wars, the Two Sicilies came to depend on the British Navy for their very survival. After entering the war on the British side in 1793, Naples temporarily withdrew, signing a separate peace with France in October 1796; even during this phase of neutrality, it retained good relations with Britain, and eventually it renewed its alliance, once the Italian peninsula became threatened by the French armies.[17] The kingdom's reliance on the Royal Navy reached a new high in 1798–9 and is well expressed in the panicked tone of several letters sent to Hamilton by Acton: 'What should we do if we remain without an English Fleet?', he was asking in August 1798.[18] As he put it most elaborately at the end of January 1799,

We must depend hope and confide in the British help and protection to have it res[?] the same hopes we have, and have only in the British Flag for the preservation of Sicily. No Treaty was ever so happily signed, and in such a critical time for us, as the last which you have performed and concluded. All our prospects of safety and political assistance rely in that very Treaty.[19]

Queen Maria Carolina also begged Nelson not to leave Sicily with his ships.[20] Such an imbalance of power, openly acknowledged, allowed

---

[15] Lo Sardo, *Napoli e Londra*, 335–57.

[16] Stuart Reid, 'Acton, Sir John Francis Edward, Sixth Baronet (1736–1811)', *ODNB* (2008) www.oxforddnb.com/view/article/76; Lamberto Radogna, *Storia della marina militare delle Due Sicilie (1734–1860)* (Milan: Mursia, 1978), 27–9; Brian Fothergill, *Sir William Hamilton: Envoy Extraordinary* (London: Faber and Faber, 1969).

[17] Giuseppe Bianco, *La Sicilia durante l'occupazione inglese (1806–1815)* (Palermo: Alberto Reber, 1902), 9–12; Fothergill, *Sir William Hamilton*, 284–90, 294–6, 301–8.

[18] British Library, London [henceforth BL], Egerton MS 2640, General Sir John Francis Edward Acton Neapolitan Prime Minister: Correspondence with Sir W. Hamilton, vol. ii., 1797–1800, Acton to Hamilton, 7 August 1798. See also 18 June 1798, 18 August 1798, 15 January 1799.

[19] Ibid., Acton to Hamilton, 29 January 1799.

[20] On criticisms of Nelson's attachment to the Sicilian court, leading him to openly disobey orders, see, for example, A. T. Mahan, *The Life of Nelson: The Embodiment of the Sea Power of Great Britain*, 2nd ed. (Boston, MA: Little, Brown, and Company, 1899), 395–403; Roger Knight, *The Pursuit of Victory: The Life and Achievement of Horatio*

Britain to wrestle whatever concessions it deemed useful. This included the de facto takeover of the island of Malta, which, before falling into French hands, had been ruled by the Order of the Knights of St. John, but as a Sicilian fief.[21] After the end of the Peace of Amiens, in 1803, and especially from 1806, when the Bourbon court was once again exiled in Palermo, the defence of Sicily came to depend entirely on the British occupying troops, financial subsidies, and Royal Navy.[22]

5.1.2   Seamen on Loan

The dynamics of power, and the consequent anxiety of the Neapolitan court to please its British ally, meant that the Royal Navy had access to any workers it needed. The local dockyard personnel, to begin with, was regularly employed aboard British ships for repairs. After the Battle of the Nile, for example, the British squadron needed substantial refits: men hired (for a total of hundreds of workdays) included carpenters, caulkers, joiners, sawyers, and divers, from the Neapolitan arsenal of Castellammare.[23]

More permanent employment was also arranged. In the treaty signed on 1 December 1798, the Two Sicilies pledged to provide not only any material and supplies that the British squadron in the Mediterranean might need, but also 'such a number of sailors as it shall require, to the amount of three thousand'. The conditions were, at least on paper, rather strict:

[They will] be put upon the same footing as English sailors on board the said squadron of his Britannic majesty, both as to bounty money on their entering, and to pay, during their continuance in his service; and also as to all other advantages and profits enjoyed by the English sailors on board the said squadron. The sailors furnished by his Sicilian majesty shall not be employed

---

Nelson (London: Penguin Books, 2006), 311–27, 332–41; Alexander Allardyce, *Memoir of the Honourable George Keith Elphinstone K. B. Viscount Keith, Admiral of the Red* (Edinburgh and London: William Blackwood and Sons, 1882), 221.

[21] Desmond Gregory, *Malta, Britain, and the European Powers, 1793–1815* (Cranbury, NJ: Associated University Presses, 1996); Piero Pieri, 'L'origine della dominazione inglese a Malta', *Archivio storico di Malta* 19:4 (1938), 377–410.

[22] Bianco, *Sicilia*, 20–1, 38–45.

[23] Archivio di Stato, Naples [henceforth ASN], Affari Esteri, 4333, Generi Somministrati agli Inglesi dai Regj Arsenali 1800–1813, 'An Account of the Repairs of His Majesty's Ship Culloden _ with an Account of Boatswains and Carpenters Stores Suppled [*sic*] the Ships of the Squadron under the Command of Rear Admiral Sir Horatio Nelson K: B: from the Arsenal at Naples, as also an Account of the Number of Artificers and Caulkers &c. employed from the same Arsenal betwen [*sic*] the 22nd September and the 15th October 1798', 2 June 1800.

out of the Mediterranean sea, nor engaged for a longer period than that of the continuance of the present war.[24]

The fact that Italian sailors were to be treated exactly like Britons distinguishes them from colonial troops used by Britain in the nineteenth century. Yet, the skilled maritime workforce was jealously monitored by contemporary states, because, in mercantilist terms, it constituted a precious resource.[25] The very lending of these men, therefore, was a rather desperate measure on the part of Naples. It is unclear whether the treaty clause was ever fully used after 1798. The 1808 'Treaty of Alliance and Subsidy' and its 1809 renewed version made no reference to transfers of seamen, while the 1812 'Supplementary Treaty' only stipulated the lending of a Sicilian division to the British Army.[26] Nothing similar was mentioned, either, in the original Convention signed by the two powers in July 1793.[27] It seems likely, however, that the 1798 treaty was simply making official something that so far had been practised informally.

In January 1794, with his crews badly depleted by casualties, Lord Hood, British Commander-in-Chief in the Mediterranean, applied to the Grand Master of Malta for a 'Loan' of 1,000 men

to serve in His Majesty's Fleet, engaging not to carry them out of the Mediterranean and to return them with what pay may be due to them when their Services were no longer wanted, and also to give them a months [sic] Pay in Advance after they were embarked.[28]

---

[24] *The Parliamentary History of England, from the Earliest Period to the Year 1803*, 36 vols. (London: T. C. Hansard, 1819), XXXIV, 1179. For the Italian/French text, see ASN, Affari Esteri, Raccolta di trattati diplomatici estratti dall'Archivio del Ministero degli affari esteri, Volume 5: Trattati diplomatici dal 1791 al 1799, n. 32, *Traité d'Alliance entre S. M. le Roi des Deux Siciles et S. M. le Roi de la Grande Brétagne.*/*Trattato di alleanza fra S. M. il Re delle Due Sicilie e S. M. il Re della Gran Bretagna.* (Palermo: Stamperia Reale, [1798]), art. vii.

[25] Perl-Rosenthal, *Citizen Sailors*, 24–7. See also Conway, *Britannia's Auxiliaries*, esp. 164–75.

[26] *The Parliamentary Debates from the Year 1803 to the Present Time*, ed. T. C. Hansard (London: Longman et al., 1812), XI, 845–8; *Treaty of Alliance and Subsidy between His Majesty the King of the United Kingdom of Great Britain and Ireland, and His Majesty the King of the Two Sicilies; Signed at Palermo, the 13th May 1809* (London: A. Strahan, 1811); *Supplementary Treaty between His Majesty and the King of the Two Sicilies; Signed at Palermo the 12th of September 1812* (London: R. G. Clarke, 1812), arts ii–xii.

[27] *Convention between His Britannick Majesty and His Sicilian Majesty. Signed at Naples, the 12th of July, 1793.* (London: Edward Johnston, 1793).

[28] TNA, ADM 1/392, Letters from Commanders-in-Chief, Mediterranean, 1794, 8, Lord Hood to Philip Stephens, 21 January 1794. See also Lord Hood to Henry Dundas, [?] January 1794, reported in J. Holland Rose, *Lord Hood and the Defence of Toulon* (Cambridge: Cambridge University Press, 1922), 161; A. Mifsud, *Knights Hospitallers of the Ven. Tongue of England in Malta* (Valletta: Herald Print. Off., 1914), 285–6.

The arrangements, and particularly the promise to deploy the seamen only in home waters, prefigure those of the formal 1798 treaty with Naples. Britain did not, at the time, have any agreement with the Order of Malta, either, which, in fact, was a neutral power, and thus in providing seamen violated international conventions; however, recruitment allowances on the island had been part of a proposal for alliance vented and then abandoned in November.[29] In March 1794, having received only 400 of the expected hands, Hood also turned to Sir William Hamilton, the British envoy in Naples. Could he obtain from the King of the Two Sicilies, 'instead of a <u>fourth</u> Line of Battle Ship', 700 seamen to refill the complement of the British vessels? Within one month, King Ferdinand had agreed.[30] Hood then communicated this decision to the Secretary of the Admiralty, expressing 'hope and trust' that the 'step' he had taken out of necessity would be 'approved'.[31] This shows that, while the provision of ships for joint operations was formally stipulated in the 1793 Convention,[32] no allowance had been initially made by the Admiralty for borrowing clusters of men. The practice developed on the ground, answering the necessities of the campaign, and having as its stepping stone the increased familiarity brought about by local cooperation.

These diplomatic agreements do not appear to have worked as binding rules, on either side. On the one hand, to his astonishment, by mid-September Hood had not yet seen a single man of the 700 requested, and even worse, not even a single ship, which led him to wonder what had become of the convention between the two countries.[33] As Hamilton reminded both the British government and Hood himself, the Kingdom of Naples was then struggling with internal conspiracies, of which the short-tempered British admiral had been repeatedly informed, and which required the presence of the Neapolitan squadron in the harbour.[34]

[29] Gregory, *Malta*, 60–1.

[30] Rose, *Lord Hood*, 161; TNA, ADM 1/392, Letters from Commanders-in-Chief, Mediterranean, 1794, 16, Lord Hood to Philip Stephens, 14 March 1794; NMM, CRK/7/57, Lord Hood to Sir William Hamilton, 19 February 1794; CRK/7/60, Hood to Hamilton, 15 March 1794; TNA, FO 70/7, General correspondence before 1906: Sicily and Naples – Sir William Hamilton, and Consuls, 1794, Hamilton to Lord Grenville, 5 March 1794; Hamilton to Grenville, 1 April 1794.

[31] TNA, ADM 1/392, Letters from Commanders-in-Chief, Mediterranean, 1794, 16, Hood to Stephens, 14 March 1794.

[32] *Convention between His* Britannick *Majesty and His* Sicilian *Majesty…, 1793*, art. iii.

[33] TNA, FO 70/7, Sicily and Naples – Sir William Hamilton 1794, Hood to Hamilton, 17 September 1794.

[34] Ibid., Hamilton to Grenville, 30 September 1794; Hamilton to Hood, 30 September 1794.

Moreover, while the recruitment of seamen had eventually been completed, no British ship had ever come to claim and collect them.[35] Whatever the excuses, the internal weakness of the Neapolitan state had effectively worsened its already subordinate position within the alliance: not conveying the ships and men at the established time gave the British admiral the higher moral ground.

On the other hand, some evidence suggests that the British Navy itself did not comply with the agreements, and nobody could call it to account for that. While the terms of the 1798 treaty tried to protect Naples's reservoir of seamen, it is clear that several men did follow the Royal Navy outside the Mediterranean. In 1830, the ex-sailor Michele Ajello, from Vico Equense ('Vicoquinza', near Naples), was resident in Paris and wrote a supplication to the Sicilian court, giving a brief account of his career. He had joined the British Navy at Naples in 1804, aged nineteen, 'seeing that the Kingdom was threatened', and 'yearning' – or so he claimed – 'to make himself useful to the King his Lord, allied with England'.[36] In the letter, he declared to have fought at Trafalgar aboard HMS *Phoebe*, although the muster books of the latter show no trace of him.[37] His story is not entirely implausible, however, because in 1807 he does appear in the crew lists of the second ship he names, HMS *Nassau*, as a twenty-three-year-old landsman ('Michael Allioes', from Naples).[38] The *Nassau* was then engaged in the seizure of the Danish fleet at Copenhagen: the Italian youth with no seafaring experience had fallen quite far from the tree, and there was very little that his king could or would do about it.

Overall, Neapolitans and Sicilians came to find themselves aboard Royal Navy ships on the backdrop of very asymmetrical economic and political relations, with the power differential between the two states exacerbated by an ongoing wasteful conflict. In this context, seamen were turned into diplomatic and military commodities, part of the contributions that the weaker party was eager to make to the efforts of the stronger ally. However, there was no lack of voices with something to say about it.

---

[35] Ibid., Hamilton to Hood, 30 September 1794; Acton to Hamilton, 6 October 1794.

[36] ASN, Affari Esteri, 4377, Viaggio del re Francesco I in Spagna, 1829–1830 – Suppliche, Michele Ajello, 7 June 1830. '*Vedendo che il Regno era minacciato… e bramando di rendersi utile al Rè suo Signore alleato dell'Inghilterra*'. I am very grateful to Gaetano Damiano for pointing me towards this source.

[37] TNA, ADM 36/16809, Muster Book of HMS *Phoebe*, September–October 1805.

[38] TNA, ADM 37/32, Muster Book of HMS *Nassau*, 1–20 September 1807, n. 402; ADM 35/2948, Pay Book of HMS *Nassau*, 1 May 1807–24 November 1809.

5.2   Between Admiration and Antipathy: The Officer Class

5.2.1   'Forces Sold into Prostitution': Joint Operations and Clashes of Authority

In 1800, during the Anglo–Neapolitan blockade of Genoa, the Neapolitan Admiral Carlo Vicuña seemed overly honoured to see that Lord Keith had placed the British sloop *Speedy* under his orders. 'This is the first time', he wrote to Acton,

> that an English vessel falls under a Neapolitan Commander; and since I am the most senior, so I see myself honoured to see under my orders a Captain of His British Majesty: and I hope that this Combination should bring the highest satisfaction to our Beloved Sovereigns, demonstrating the Esteem that the English have of our scarce talents.[39]

Naturally, whilst Vicuña was so proud to be commanding a British vessel, he was, in fact, himself under the general orders of a British admiral. Service under British command could, overall, be personally advantageous, because of the Anglophilia reigning at the Sicilian court. After Lord Keith praised the Neapolitan captains who had fought under his orders in the blockade, King Ferdinand granted a lifelong stipend to those who had been wounded and the right to wear a uniform to all the crews.[40] Captain Robert Hall, commanding the Royal Flotilla in Messina towards the end of the Napoleonic War, also helped the careers of several Sicilian midshipmen who had been serving under him. He successfully recommended them at Palermo and procured them employment in the Sicilian Navy over the heads of colleagues of superior seniority.[41] The pilot Pietro Anthawer, who had taken part in the blockade of Malta, was promoted to Brig Commander after being warmly commended by General Graham and the other British officers – again jumping ahead of more senior colleagues and attracting a storm of complaints.[42]

---

[39] ASN, Affari Esteri, 3664, Marina Real Ministero – Giugno 1800, Carlo Vicuña to Acton, 12 June 1800. '*Questa è la prima volta che un Bastimento Inglese dipende da un Comandante Napolitano; e siccome io sono il più anziano, così mi vedo onorato di vedere sotto i miei ordini un Capitano di S. M. Britannica: e spero che questa Combinazione debba portare la massima soddisfazione a' nostri Amabili Sovrani, dimostrando il Concetto, che gl'Inglesi fanno de' nostri scarsi talenti.*'

[40] ASN, Affari Esteri, 3666, Marina Real Ministero – Agosto 1800, Acton to Thurn, Vicuña, Espluga, and Fardella, 7 August 1800.

[41] See Section 5.2.2.

[42] ASN, 3664, Marina Real Ministero – Giugno 1800, Graham to Acton, 22 September 1800; Giovanni Guillichini to Acton, 22 September 1800; Affari Esteri, 3668, Marina Real Ministero – Novembre e Dicembre 1800, Acton to Thurn, 7 November 1800.

If some officers were happy to serve under the ally, and even reaped personal rewards, others showed a very different attitude. Most significant is the case of Commodore Bartolomeo Forteguerri. In 1793–4, during the siege of Toulon, he fell out with Admiral Hood, then acting as Commander-in-Chief of the joint Anglo–Spanish–Neapolitan–Sardinian operations. This clash, when observed from both sides, reveals some discrepancies in the participants' points of view: even an apparently 'objective' matter, like being employed in the British Navy, was in fact entirely dependent on interpretation.

Hood saw Forteguerri as 'undoubtedly, the proudest, most empty, and self sufficient man, I ever had anything to do with and totally ignorant of the common rudiments of Service', full of childishness, vanity, 'ignorance and folly': 'Commodore Forteguerri is no more fitt [*sic*] to command a squadron, than I am to make an archbishop', he was writing to Hamilton within a couple of months.[43] 'He is at the head of their Marine', Nelson observed of Forteguerri in April 1796, in a letter to Admiral Jervis, 'and fancies himself equal to any Officer in Europe', so 'he would not like the interference of a foreigner'.[44] The truth about Forteguerri's professionalism is now difficult to establish, and it is beyond doubt, judging from his correspondence, that he was not necessarily an accommodating man. Hood was himself imposing and uncompromising, and, a few months later, he alienated even British Army officers by claiming supreme command in joint operations.[45] However, Forteguerri's clash with the British had deeper roots.

His correspondence shows an ongoing concern for the physical position of the Sicilian flag in relation to those of the allies.[46] The worst argument with Hood took place when the latter tried to take direct control of the Sicilian ships. In a series of furious letters, Forteguerri complained that this breached the convention between the two powers and signalled an 'indecent dependency' on Britain, besides creating a dangerous confusion in loyalties and obedience: 'passing similar orders, any subordination and influence, so necessary for the decorum of the

---

[43] NMM, CRK/7/43, Hood to Hamilton, 20 November 1793; CRK/7/45, Hood to Hamilton, 3 December 1793.

[44] Nicholas Harris Nicolas (ed.), *The Dispatches and Letters of Vice Admiral Lord Viscount Nelson*, 2 vols. (London: Henry Colburn, 1845), II, 163. This sentence is also quoted in Francesco Lemmi, *Nelson e Caracciolo e la Repubblica Napoletana (1799)* (Florence: G. Carnesecchi e figli, 1898), 85.

[45] Rodger, *Command*, 430–1.

[46] ASN, Affari Esteri, 4339, Tolone. Spedizione delle truppe di Sua Maestà Siciliana. Carteggio fra Acton e il generale Bartolomeo Forteguerri, capo della squadra napoletana e carteggio di lord Hamilton, 1793–4, Bartolomeo Forteguerri to Giovanni Acton, 28 September 1793; 1 October 1793; 13 October 1793.

very nation, and flag, of the King my Lord, is dissolved'.[47] As he very bluntly put it, 'the will of the King of Naples is to join his forces, not to prostitute them'. According to Hood, the request to take control was perfectly legitimate, since Vice-Admirals and Rear-Admirals were similarly subordinated to him: the implications of this were, Forteguerri bitterly noticed, that 'a General Officer of an allied King must be regarded as one more name on the list of the British Navy'.[48] We see here that much of the clash seems to have originated from a very fundamental problem: determining who was in the British service. Contrasts over this point stemmed from perceptions of the power and position of each officer's respective country. It should be noted, incidentally, that Forteguerri's sense of identification with the Two Sicilies was entirely tied to the service of his king, rather than any form of ethnic national identity: originally from Siena, in the Duchy of Tuscany, he had only moved to Naples in 1783, aged thirty-two, when Acton had invited him into his new navy.[49]

We find a similar tension between submissiveness and pride among naval officers ashore. Throughout the 1790s and early 1800s, given that the survival of the kingdom depended on the allies, ministers and port commanders in Naples and Sicily showed great solicitude in providing British and Russian ships with all they might have needed, even at the cost of physically dismembering Neapolitan warships. In September 1798, since the kingdom's arsenals were drained of stores, but the British HMS *Vanguard* and *Alexander* needed new masts and spars, these were taken from royal ships: 'it is however very well that what is in our power should be and most usefully given and offerd [sic] to the Brave British men of war', Acton wrote to Hamilton on 24 November, in almost sycophantic tones.[50] The following day, workers in the harbour were intent on fitting a rudder dismantled from the Neapolitan *Partenope*

---

[47] ASN, Affari Esteri, 4339, Tolone, Forteguerri to Acton, 12 October 1793; Forteguerri to Hood, 11 October 1793; Forteguerri, Dettaglio di condotta dall'Arrivo della Squadra Napolitana fino al dì 12 di Ottobre 1793: '...*passando simili ordini resta sciolta qualunque subordinazione e influenza tanto necessaria per il decoro dell'istessa nazione, e bandiera, del Re mio Signore*'.

[48] ASN, Affari Esteri, 4339, Tolone, Forteguerri to Acton, 12 October 1793: '...*la volontà del Re di Napoli è di riunire, e non di prostituire le sue forze*'; '*i Vice Ammiragli, e i Retro Ammiragli ricevendo i medesimi ordini tutto è in regola secondo il suo parere, dunque un Uffiziale Generale di un Re alleato deve essere riguardato come un nome di piu* [sic] *nella lista della Marina Brittannica*'.

[49] Toni Iermano, 'Forteguerri, Bartolomeo', *Dizionario Biografico degli Italiani – Volume 49, Treccani*, 1997 www.treccani.it/enciclopedia/bartolomeo-forteguerri_(Dizionario-Biografico)/.

[50] BL, Egerton MS 2640, Acton to Hamilton, 24 September 1798.

onto HMS *Culloden*.[51] In April 1800, at Messina, orders arrived to provide British ships with ropes and anchors taken from the warship *Sannite*, but the port commander was forced to reply that only one anchor and one rope could be found, as all the others had already been given; in the meantime, the foremast of the *Sannite* had been sawed off to be refitted onto a Russian ship, but the Russian admiral, finding it rotten, demanded the mainmast of another ship, the *Archimede*. The Sicilian officers were prepared to comply.[52] The Neapolitan Navy, in short, two decades earlier the new jewel and pride of the kingdom, had become a reservoir that powerful allies could freely scavenge for spare parts. Again, however, the attitudes of Neapolitan and Sicilian officials towards the British were not always entirely subservient.

In January 1800, the captain of HMS *Lion* sent a written request, in English, to Giovanni Lettieri, the commander of Syracuse station. Lettieri responded praying him to write in either Italian or French, but the captain simply sent along his secretary, who also only spoke English. Finally enlightened by an interpreter, Lettieri replied that the matter was not his business, but had to be negotiated directly with the private merchant concerned. He would offer some mediation, but, he repeated, the British commander would have to communicate 'in an idiom understood by myself, as here the English language is universally unknown'.[53] This spirit of toleration, rather than enthusiastic cooperation, emerges occasionally in other transactions, as in a telling exchange between Giovanni Guillichini, port governor at Palermo, and Acton. In the autumn of 1800, the British bomb vessel *Stromboli* had violated the quarantine embargo at Palermo, and Guillichini had handled the situation with diplomacy, trying to bury the matter; Acton praised his conduct, but warned him to observe caution, owing to the constant risk of epidemics, and 'the little attention, paid by the English on the matter of public health'.[54] Acton's view was not entirely accurate: while historians such as John Booker emphasise British support for 'anticontagionist' theories in the name of free trade, more recent scholarship has also shown that Britons in the Mediterranean regularly acquiesced to local

---

[51] BL, Egerton MS 2640, Acton to Hamilton, 25 September 1798.

[52] ASN, Affari Esteri, 3663, Marina Real Ministero – Gennaio-Maggio 1800, Guillichini to Acton, 1 April 1800, 10 April 1800, 15 April 1800; Tommaso Vicuña to Acton, 2 April 1800.

[53] ASN, Affari Esteri, 4333, Generi Somministrati agli Inglesi dai Regj Arsenali 1800 al 1813, Giovanni Lettieri to Giovanni Acton, 14 January 1800: '...che frattanto si servisse il Comand.*te* del Vascello dichiarar questa ricerca in un'inteso [sic] da me Idioma, mentre qui s'ignora universalmente l'Inglese linguaggio'.

[54] ASN, Affari Esteri, 3668, Marina Real Ministero – Novembre e Dicembre 1800, Acton to Guillichini, 9 December 1800.

quarantine practices, in order to participate in commercial activities.[55] On the whole, however, British naval officers were outsiders to this geo-cultural system, and many of them, bent on pursuing military efficiency, reiterated their extraneity through behaviours that the locals had to tolerate, but could not but perceive as arrogant. In the same letter, Acton also replied regarding the issue of supplies that the British requested even if they were not intent on defending the kingdom, but rather on their own mission to Egypt: these were to be granted, for the sake of the alliance, but not if they were goods of prime necessity.[56] From the British point of view, Neapolitan and Sicilian officers worked for the Royal Navy, but the reality was more nuanced. The same subtleties were at play even when southern Italian officers came to find themselves directly embarked in British men-of-war.

5.2.2 'The Miserable Caracciolo': Transnational Patronage and 'Exchange Programmes'

While the Two Sicilies arguably had much to lose from indefinite-term lending of manpower to the British, they had everything to gain from having their young officers learn their ropes – or find some form of temporary employment, when the Sicilian fleet could not guarantee it – in the ships of the ally. As the clergyman Don Vincenzo Lena observed in 1806, trying to be awarded a regular wage after years of voluntary English teaching at the Palermo naval academy, the English language

---

[55] John Booker, *Maritime Quarantine: The British Experience, c.1650–1900* (Aldershot and Burlington, VT: Ashgate, 2007). Cf. instead Alex Chase-Levenson, *The Yellow Flag: Quarantine and the British Mediterranean World, 1780–1860* (Cambridge: Cambridge University Press, 2020); Costas Tsiamis, Eleni Thalassinou, Effie Poulakou Rebelakou, and Angelos Hatzakis, 'Quarantine and British "Protection" of the Ionian Islands, 1815–1864', in John Chircop and Francisco Javier Martínez (eds.), *Mediterranean Quarantines, 1750–1915: Space, Identity and Power* (Manchester: Manchester University Press, 2018), 256–79. On the characteristic, long-standing roots of quarantine practices in the Two Sicilies and in the Mediterranean more generally, see Raffaella Salvemini, 'A tutela della salute e del commercio nel Mediterraneo: La sanità marittima nel Mezzogiorno pre-unitario', in Raffaella Salvemini (ed.), *Istituzioni e traffici nel Mediterraneo tra età antica e crescita moderna* ([Rome]: Consiglio Nazionale delle Ricerche, Istituto di Studi sulle Società del Mediterraneo, 2009), 259–96; Silvia Marzagalli, 'Maritimity: How the Sea Affected Early Modern Life in the Mediterranean World', in Mihran Dabag, Dieter Haller, Nikolas Jaspert, and Achim Lichtenberger (eds.), *New Horizons: Mediterranean Research in the Twenty-first Century* (Paderborn: Ferdinand Schöningh, 2016), 309–31, at 313–14. On the fortunes of anticontagionism in Western and Northern Europe, particularly later in the nineteenth century, see Erwin H. Ackerknecht, 'Anticontagionism between 1821 and 1867', *Bulletin of the History of Medicine* 22 (1948), 562–93.

[56] ASN, Affari Esteri, 3668, Marina Real Ministero – Novembre e Dicembre 1800, Acton to Guillichini, 9 December 1800.

was 'more difficult, and more necessary for navigation, than the French', 'owing to the attachment that is had with England, absolutely maritime Nation in which at any time there is need to trade'.[57] Naval cadets in the pre-1799 Neapolitan *Accademia di Marina* studied on textbooks translated from French, on locally produced volumes, but also on an Italian edition (1778) of John Robertson's *The Elements of Navigation*, which was the standard manual for British trainee officers.[58] Some of these cadets also ended up physically serving in the Royal Navy. We can sketch a microhistory of the British service of a few of these Italian gentlemen.

We have seen how some officers benefited from British patronage. This was particularly true of young men at the start of their careers. When the naval academy in Palermo was closed in 1812, several cadets found themselves unemployed. Some sent applications to join the gunboats of the Royal Flotilla at Messina, but the Sicilian court redirected the requests to Commodore Robert Hall, its commander, since the boats were not 'maintained at the Sicilian Government's expense'.[59] The combined Anglo–Sicilian Flotilla depended on British subsidies, and some of its officers belonged to the British Navy.[60] Robert Hall himself was a British post-captain, appointed to the Flotilla in April 1811 with the pay and allowances of a fifth-rate commanding officer; in the autumn of that year, he had accepted the temporary rank of '*Brigadiere*' in the Sicilian armed forces, to facilitate operations, but he remained first and foremost a Royal Navy officer, answering to the British Admiralty.[61] The hybrid Flotilla was a valid option for young Sicilians, but not a permanent one: in 1814, fourteen-year-old Cristoforo Cafiero, who had been selected by Hall as 'sufficiently instructed in the nautical art, and English

[57] ASN Sezione Militare, Segreteria antica, 337, Accademia di Marina (Sicilia) 1809–12, 'Merito del Sac^e. D. Vincenzo Lena Interprete Inglese per la Deputazione di Piazza', attached to letter from Diego Naselli to the King of the Two Sicilies, 1 December 1806; Letter from Lombardo, Consiglio di Real Marina, 22 June 1808: '*la più necessaria per l'attaccamento che si ha con l'Inghilterra, Nazione assolutamente marittima in cui in ogni tempo vi è necessità di commerciare*'.

[58] Enea and Gatto, *Matematica e marineria*, 45–56.

[59] ASN Sezione Militare, 377, Accademia di Marina 1809–12, Palazzo to Mario Espluga, 17 December 1812. See also Palazzo to Francesco Pulzella, 19 June 1812.

[60] *Supplementary Treaty 1812*, art. xi; J. K. Laughton and R. O. Morris, 'Smyth, William Henry (1788–1865)', *ODNB* (2015) www.oxforddnb.com/view/article/25961. See also NMS, Pw Jd 5564, Papers relating to the Sicilian flotilla; Pw Jd 5660, Instructions to Brig. Genl. Hall commanding the combined flotilla, 1812; Pw Jd 5940, State of the royal flotilla, 1814.

[61] TNA, ADM 1/1945, Letters from Captains, Surnames H., 1812, 61, Richard Bickerton, William Domett, Frederick John Robinson and John Barrow to Robert Hall, 4 April 1811; 78, Robert Hall to Sir Wilson Croker, 1 December 1811.

Language', and had become a protégé of his, found himself stranded ashore when the Flotilla was dissolved.[62] Other midshipmen who had served in the gunboats, or aboard British warships, were left in the same position, and Hall successfully recommended a few of them for promotion to '*alfieri di vascello*' in King Ferdinand's Navy. As a British officer, he made for an excellent patron.[63]

Beyond the Flotilla, southern Italian midshipmen also appear elsewhere in the musters of the British Mediterranean squadron. For example, the twenty-one-year-old Neapolitan Philip Thovez (or Thovaz) was a midshipman aboard HMS *Victory* at Trafalgar, and another Neapolitan midshipman, twenty-year-old Joseph Dell Carretto [*sic*], was in HMS *Royal Sovereign* in May 1805.[64] In most cases, their foreign birth would have eventually barred them from a career as commissioned officers in the Royal Navy.[65] However, they could still retain some ties with Britain. After volunteering in Naples, Thovez had been in HMS *Camelion* and then a supernumerary for victuals in HMS *Termagant*, before being transferred to the *Victory* in October 1804; he served in other Royal Navy ships after Trafalgar and on 23 January 1809 became a purser.[66] His lasting connection with the Nelson family is shown by the fact that, from 1820, he was chosen as the agent in charge of the administration of the Duchy of Bronte, in Sicily. After his death, in October 1839, he was buried in the neighbouring church of Maniace.[67] At the same time, a translation of his will, originally redacted in Italian, was also proved in London by his widow

---

[62] ASN Sezione Militare, Segreteria antica 378, Accademia di Marina (Sicilia) 1813–15, Ignazio Staiti to the King of Sicily, 22 August 1814. Cafiero was '*istruito sufficientemente nell'arte nautica, e Lingua Inglese*'.

[63] See ASN Sezione Militare, Segreteria antica 378, Accademia di Marina 1813–15, Antonio Schreiber to the King of Sicily, August? 1814; Staiti to the King of Sicily, 5 April 1814; Palazzo to Staiti, Hall, Micheroux and the Giunta di Anzianità, 8 January 1814; Hall to Ruggiero Settimo, 30 December 1813; Hall to Settimo, 15 March 1814; Staiti to the King of Sicily, 14 July 1814; supplication from Camillo Manganaro; Ignazio Cafiero to Diego Naselli, 15 August 1814; Ignazio Staiti to the King of Sicily, 9 September 1814.

[64] Bruno Pappalardo, 'Trafalgar Ancestors', The National Archives www.nationalarchives .gov.uk/trafalgarancestors/advanced_search.asp.

[65] See Section 2.1.

[66] TNA, ADM 36/16370, Muster Book of HMS *Termagant*, October–November 1804; *The Navy List, Corrected to the End of December, 1819* (London: John Murray, [1820]), 116.

[67] Lucy Riall, *Under the Volcano: Revolution in a Sicilian Town* (Oxford: Oxford University Press, 2013), 61–2; Daniele Palermo, *Dal feudo alla proprietà: Il caso della Ducea di Bronte*, electronic ed. (Palermo: Mediterranea – Ricerche Storiche, 2012), 19; Mario Carastro, 'E dopo Graefer? Gli amministratori della Ducea sino al 1873', Bronte Insieme – La ducea inglese ai piedi dell'Etna (1799–1981), 2005 www.bronteinsieme.it/2st/nelson_graefer1.htm.

Elizabeth and deposited in the registers of the Prerogative Court of Canterbury, final evidence of a life led across two countries.[68]

British service did not only serve to cultivate transnational networks, however. In June 1799, in the aftermath of the Neapolitan Revolution, Nelson ordered the court martial and execution of the Neapolitan Admiral Francesco Caracciolo. The officer was hanged from a yardarm, and his body tossed into the sea. Less than twenty years earlier, Caracciolo had been a young officer seconded into the British Navy. His story is worth reconstructing in some detail, because it casts light on the tensions between the two services that we have been discussing so far.

In 1779, towards the beginning of Acton's reforms of the Sicilian Navy, twenty-nine cadets and pilots were sent into foreign navies for training: ten went to France, ten to Spain, one to Sweden, and at least eight (in the first instance, at least), led by the young nobleman Francesco Caracciolo, joined the British Navy.[69] The Sicilian King 'was very desirous of profiting of the present moment [the American War] to form officers for the little marine intended to be established here for the protection of the Commerce of this Country against the Barbaresques'.[70] Britain was, on the surface, cordially happy to assist, even though William Hamilton, in classified letters, expressed mistrust, suspecting that the Habsburg House was the true power behind the rise of this new navy.[71] Everyone's main concerns were the import of naval stores and the building of warships: the training of a handful of young midshipmen must have seemed, by comparison, a relatively insignificant matter, easily requested and granted.

This episode is frequently mentioned in Italian secondary literature, because the future Admiral Caracciolo was to become an important and much-loved figure in Neapolitan history.[72] Some texts even report that,

---

[68] TNA, PROB 11/1933/71, Will of Philip otherwise Filippo Thovez of Bronte, Sicily, 4 August 1840.

[69] ASN, Affari Esteri, 3668, Marina Real Ministero – Novembre e Dicembre 1800, 'Notamento degli ufficiali, che furono destinati nelle spedizioni di Francia, Spagna, Inghilterra, e Svezia'. Their names, according to this list, were Francesco Caracciolo, Giovanni Bausan, Ignazio Tranfi, Luigi Quattromani, Giuseppe Rodriguez, Agostino Melber, Mario Ricciardelli, and Benedetto Ianni (pilot).

[70] TNA, FO 70/1, General correspondence before 1906: Sicily and Naples – Sir William Hamilton and Consuls, 1780–1781, William Hamilton to the Earl of Hillsborough, 7 March 1780, ff. 42–3. See also Caputo, 'Mercenary Gentlemen', 817.

[71] TNA, FO 70/1, Sicily and Naples – Sir William Hamilton 1780–1, Hamilton to Hillsborough, 17 May 1780, 3 April 1781, ff. 87–9, 196–8.

[72] Lo Sardo, Napoli e Londra, 329; Giuseppe Porcaro, Francesco Caracciolo (Naples: Arturo Berisio editore, 1967), 14–23; Radogna, Storia della marina militare, 29–30; [Benedetto Maresca], 'I marinai napoletani nella spedizione del 1784 contro Algieri (da un diario contemporaneo)', Archivio storico per le province napoletane 17:1 (1892), 808–50, at 816–17.

in January 1780, he distinguished himself at the Battle of Cape St Vincent, under Admiral Rodney, earning the praise of British superior officers.[73] A mid-nineteenth-century source also notes that another of the young men, the pilot Fileti, was well respected by the British and died of yellow fever whilst in the Royal Navy.[74] Aside from these brief mentions, however, no historian ever stops to examine these officers' experience. Even contemporary sources just stated that Caracciolo's 'skill… in handling ships' was 'acquired in England', although this seems a gross exaggeration, since in 1779 the man was already twenty-seven years old and had previously commanded a ship.[75] Indeed, seamanship was not the main focus of the mission: Caracciolo had been instructed by Acton to pay particular attention to British artillery and arsenal technology, and especially to techniques to copper the hulls of vessels.[76] Very little material seems to survive, but a combination of diplomatic correspondence and ships' logs and musters helps to uncover some details.

The Neapolitan volunteers were split into two divisions, assigned to HMS *Marlborough* and HMS *Ardent*, respectively. Those who were aboard the latter – four midshipmen, one pilot, and two sailors – were captured by the French early in 1780, and promptly joined the French fleet.[77] The Two Sicilies were formally neutral in the war, so this was not considered betrayal. King Ferdinand allegedly felt 'uneasiness' at this change of sides,[78] but his main concern seemed to be that the four midshipmen be promptly replaced in the Royal Navy by four more young Neapolitan gentlemen, a wish that was granted '*avec grand Plaisir*' by the British government.[79] These men were simply tools, deployed without regard to loyalties, sides, or their own personal destinies, to help to channel expertise towards the nascent Sicilian Fleet, as rapidly as possible.

---

[73] Lemmi, *Nelson e Caracciolo*, 52; Mario Battaglini, *Francesco Caracciolo: La misteriosa tragica avventura del grande ammiraglio di Napoli* (Naples: Generoso Procaccini, 1998), 10–11; Porcaro, *Francesco Caracciolo*, 17–20; Radogna, *Storia della marina militare*, 30.

[74] Mariano D'Ayala, *Le vite de' più celebri capitani e soldati napoletani dalla giornata di Bitonto fino a' di nostri* (Naples: Stamperia dell'Iride, 1843), 144–5.

[75] De Nicola, 'Diario Napoletano dal 1799 al 1825', translated excerpt in H. C. Gutteridge (ed.), *Nelson and the Neapolitan Jacobins: Documents Relating to the Suppression of the Jacobin Revolution at Naples June 1799* (London: Navy Records Society, 1903), 193.

[76] Acton to Caracciolo, 26 November 1780, reported in Battaglini, *Francesco Caracciolo*, 51–2; see also Porcaro, *Francesco Caracciolo*, 21–2.

[77] TNA, FO 70/1, Sicily and Naples – Sir William Hamilton 1780–1, Comte Pignatelli to the Earl of Hillsborough, 11 March 1780, f. 51.

[78] Ibid., Hamilton to Hillsborough, 7 March 1780, ff. 42–3.

[79] Ibid., Hamilton to Hillsborough, 7 March 1780; Hillsborough to Pignatelli, 16 March 1780; Hamilton to Hillsborough, 11 April 1780; Hillsborough to Hamilton, 16 May 1780, ff. 42–3, 55, 67, 85–6.

Eight more of the Neapolitans (Caracciolo, 'Jean Baptiste Bausan', 'Augustin Melber', 'Giarep/Giassapi [Giuseppe] Rodriguez', 'Benedetto Janni', and 'Ignace Tranfi', together with 'Fransisco Barbera' and 'Tomaso Liardo', who do not appear in the list preserved in the Neapolitan archive) can be found listed among the complement of HMS *Marlborough*.[80] According to the master's log, between June 1779, when it started its commission, and the end of that year, the *Marlborough* only went on short cruises in home waters, and the men were always mustered in an English port.[81] Frequent exercises with the 'Great Guns' were reported, however, which must have been very useful for the purposes of Caracciolo's mission. Eventually, the ship took part in the Battle of Cape St Vincent, on 16 January 1780, against the Spanish.[82] As noted in the historiography, Caracciolo did somewhat distinguish himself, though the primary evidence that could be uncovered does not describe exceptional feats, suggesting that perhaps the Neapolitan interpretation of events may tend to overestimate them. The King of Naples, Hamilton simply reported, 'seem'd much pleased that the captain of the said Ship shou'd have placed so great a confidence in the Neapolitan as to have given him the command of some Guns during the action'.[83] In fact, the twenty-eight-year-old Caracciolo was probably more experienced than most British midshipmen, so the choice was not extraordinary. More noteworthy is the fact that the three Neapolitans who were aboard the *Phoenix*, the Spanish flagship, hence fighting *against* Britain and their colleagues, also received praise for their valour. As Admiral Don Juan De Langara wrote in the aftermath, the whole crew, Sicilian cadets included, showed 'courage', 'intrepidity', 'coolness' and 'perseverance', and 'gave the strongest testimonies of the most undoubted bravery, and zeal', 'eager to acquire, and participate in new glories'.[84] Again, the young Sicilians' bravery or competence evidently had nothing

[80] TNA, ADM 36/8616, Muster Book of HMS *Marlborough*, June 1779–August 1780.

[81] TNA, ADM 52/1858, Master's Log HMS *Marlborough*, 18 June 1779–30 June 1781. The muster tables are in TNA, ADM 36/8616, Muster Book of HMS *Marlborough*, June 1779–August 1780. According to Lemmi, Caracciolo 'on 22 March 1779 left on the Marlborough to fight, together with the English, in the American war' [my translation]: Lemmi, *Nelson e Caracciolo*, 52. In fact, the muster of the *Marlborough* reports Caracciolo and his companions as having joined on 28 July.

[82] TNA, ADM 52/1858, Master's Log HMS *Marlborough*.

[83] TNA, FO 70/1, Sicily and Naples – Sir William Hamilton 1780–1, Hamilton to Hillsborough, 4 April 1780, f. 64. The letter does not mention Caracciolo by name, but it seems legitimate to conclude that he was the Neapolitan 'Volunteer' being discussed.

[84] Letter from Don Juan De Langara to Don Andre [*sic*] Regio, Lieutenant-General of the Navy and Commander of the Cadiz department, 21 January 1780, reported in translation in the *Morning Post and Daily Advertiser*, 17 March 1780.

to do with the specific cause or side they happened to be fighting for; those battles were pure training, and their honour did not rest on allegiance to the Spanish or British colours.

After a cruise into the Mediterranean, almost as far as Algiers, HMS *Marlborough* was back in Spithead by early March, and there it remained until the end of June, when it left for a two-month voyage around Cape Finisterre and Ushant.[85] After St Vincent, the Sicilian midshipmen become completely invisible in the diplomatic correspondence, but the musters reveal some further data, and a less than exciting picture. Month after month, throughout their service, the guests are listed among the crew, as Able Seamen (a practice quite common even in the case of British young gentlemen). Caracciolo's name became progressively more and more misspelt, from 'Carraccio' to 'Casaccilo' to 'Carracilo', culminating in 'Consciollo' in March–June 1780 (hence immediately after the 'glorious' victory), and then back to 'Carracillo'/'Carracilo'. Because the ship was so often in port, all the mustering appears to have been done by the clerk of the cheque, a dockyard official, so the mistakes are less significant, but they certainly do not seem to signal increasing integration. The 'Carracilo' form, indeed, remained even when the shipboard officers took over again in the summer, only to turn into 'Carroccilo' for the Neapolitan's last few months aboard.[86] The environment of the Royal Navy, and possibly the British climate, were also proving hostile to the young strangers: before the year was out, Barbera had to be discharged to sick quarters (Haslar Hospital, 17 April), and Bausan as 'unserviceable' (26 August 1780).[87] The ship left again at the end of August, moving between hardly exotic locations, like Spithead, Torbay, and the Downs, and spending the vast majority of time moored there; by 25 September, Liardo had joined Barbera at Haslar, and on 24 February 1781, it was Ianni's turn to be transferred to Deal Hospital.[88] By the end of the period (the remaining men are all marked as discharged on 13 March 1781), only Caracciolo, Melber, Rodriguez, and Tranfi had avoided sickness.[89]

While the historiography only insists on Caracciolo's glorious behaviour, Hamilton's correspondence reveals some surprising facts, apparently

[85] TNA, ADM 52/1858, Master's Log HMS *Marlborough*.

[86] TNA, ADM 36/8616, Muster Book of HMS *Marlborough*, June 1779–August 1780; ADM 36/8615, Muster Book of HMS *Marlborough*, April 1780–January 1781; ADM 36/8962, Muster Book of HMS *Marlborough*, February–November 1781.

[87] TNA, ADM 36/8616, Muster Book of HMS *Marlborough*, June 1779–August 1780; ADM 36/8615, Muster Book of HMS *Marlborough*, April 1780–January 1781.

[88] TNA, ADM 51/577, Captains' Logs, Including MARLBOROUGH (18 June 1779–22 July 1783); ADM 36/8615, Muster Book of HMS *Marlborough*, April 1780–January 1781; ADM 36/8962, Muster Book of HMS *Marlborough*, February–November 1781.

[89] TNA, ADM 36/8962, Muster Book of HMS *Marlborough*, February–November 1781.

unknown to all the Italian biographers. Upon their return home, late in the summer of 1781, Caracciolo and two other unnamed young gentlemen were examined on their 'conduct', and their papers revealed 'some misconduct and various tracasseries': King Ferdinand 'expressed great displeasure, and ordered them to be confined separately in different Castles'.[90] In short, while for over two hundred years official accounts have tried to paint these cadets' experience as a smooth, honourable, gentlemanly exchange of expertise between two friendly (albeit unequal) nations, the reality might have also included quarrels and rowdy youthful behaviour, at best, or less than diplomatic interactions, at worst. Regardless of that, less than a week later, the Neapolitan ambassador in London was writing to the British government, expressing His Sicilian Majesty's gratitude for the *'bons traitemens'* and *'Egards'* received by the midshipmen, and promptly obtaining to send another contingent.[91]

Caracciolo went on to serve again under the British at Toulon in 1793 and in the Corsican and Genoese campaigns two years later, always commanding his own Sicilian ship.[92] Whilst there seem to be no ardent praises, Lord Hood mentioned in positive terms that he ('Chev'. Caracuolo') and another Neapolitan officer 'appear to be prudent well informed men, respecting Service'.[93] In his biography of Caracciolo, the Italian historian Giuseppe Porcaro, whose work is informed by a strong nationalistic interpretation of the events, cites some complaints that the Neapolitan admiral allegedly raised regarding the British behaviour at Toulon: the Neapolitan troops were being treated like 'subordinate auxiliaries' and 'Swiss sold for speculation'.[94] While unfortunately these quotes are reported without a source, they seem plausible, as they decidedly remind us of Forteguerri's contemporary protests.

In 1799, anyway, after siding with the Neapolitan Republic and becoming the commander of its navy, Caracciolo issued harsh proclamations against British intrigues and personally fought against the Royal Navy in the waters in front of Procida.[95] It was, eventually, aboard a

[90] TNA, FO 70/1, Sicily and Naples – Sir William Hamilton 1780–1, Hamilton to Hillsborough, 4 September 1781, ff. 267–8.

[91] Ibid., Prince of Caramanico to Hillsborough, 17 September 1781; Hillsborough to Caramanico, 29 September 1781; Caramanico to Hillsborough, 1 October 1781; Hillsborough to Hamilton, 5 October 1781, ff. 272, 278, 280, 288–9.

[92] Lemmi, *Nelson e Caracciolo*, 54; Battaglini, *Francesco Caracciolo*, 14–15; Radogna, *Storia della marina militare*, 43–6.

[93] NMM, CRK/7/44, Hood to Hamilton, 22 November 1793.

[94] Porcaro, *Francesco Caracciolo*, 59–60.

[95] Lemmi, *Nelson e Caracciolo*, 58–60, 70, 73–4; Battaglini, *Francesco Caracciolo*, 31–2, 70–7, 81–6; Porcaro, *Francesco Caracciolo*, 120–6.

British vessel that Nelson had him court martialled for his role in the Jacobin revolution; in very controversial circumstances, he was quickly hanged, on 29 June 1799.[96] Nelson called him 'the miserable Caracciolo', and Hamilton, in particular, was firm on the necessity of making an example of him: while the admiral wished to be tried by British officers, he was instead consigned to a hostile jury of Neapolitan and Sicilian commanders.[97] For Ferdinand and Maria Carolina, he was to be a high-profile example to discourage the Jacobinism in the fleet; moreover, owing to his detailed knowledge of the coasts of the kingdom, it was simply too dangerous to let him live.[98]

Giovanni Battista Bausan (1757–1825), the other exchange cadet who had a significant career, including collaboration with the Royal Navy at Toulon, also sided with the Neapolitan Republic in 1799. This cost him, in February 1800, the loss of all his properties and lifelong exile to France, but he later returned: in 1809, he distinguished himself as the commander of Murat's French and Neapolitan flotilla, which success-fully pushed back the British and Sicilian invasion forces.[99] Again, very little trace was left in him of his two years in the Royal Navy, except perhaps an increased professional competence which he eventually deployed against it.

The individual experiences of young naval gentlemen, then, could oscillate between the extremes of a Caracciolo and a Thovez, and the significance of service in the British Navy fell on a spectrum between temporary contact, with few long-term effects, and the seeds of a lifelong association with Britain. Midshipmen sent out in bulk by their own government, with a purely utilitarian target in mind, unsurprisingly seemed to develop fewer ties with their hosting institution and nation. More generally, the cooperation of southern Italian officers with the British Navy was rife with contradictions. Often, indeed, it was precisely what British and Sicilian officers had in common – a transnational sense of gentlemanly honour, refusing subordination, and similar loyalties to one or the other monarch – which prevented them from overcoming the fact that they came from different countries. Even mutual respect may

---

[96] Lemmi, *Nelson e Caracciolo*, 61–5; Battaglini, *Francesco Caracciolo*, 34–8; F. P. Badham, 'Nelson and the Neapolitan Republicans', *The English Historical Review* 13:50 (1898), 261–82, at 278–82; Mahan, *Life of Nelson*, 389–95.

[97] Nelson to Acton, 29 June 1799, in Gutteridge, *Nelson and the Neapolitan Jacobins*, 278–9; Hamilton to Acton, 27 June 1799, ibid., 251; Hamilton to Acton, 29 June 1799, ibid., 276–7.

[98] Battaglini, *Francesco Caracciolo*, 34–5, 95, 101; Badham, 'Nelson', 264.

[99] Nino Cortese, 'Bausan, Giovanni', *Dizionario Biografico degli Italiani – Volume 7, Treccani*, 1970 www.treccani.it/enciclopedia/giovanni-bausan_(Dizionario-Biografico)/; D'Ayala, *Vite*, 143–59; Bianco, *Sicilia*, 55; Radogna, *Storia della marina militare*, 58, 61–7.

have been made more difficult by the strong inequality between the two states, constantly present to the minds of all parties. This tense undercurrent, we shall see, offered British officers a chance of separating the seamen whom they were reclaiming as perfectly good recruits from the stereotypes of corruption and unreliability that they associated with those seamen's country.

5.3   Difference and Stereotype: The Lower Deck

The situation of Neapolitan and Sicilian seafarers, and general British attitudes in their regard, inherently drew local seamen and the British Navy apart. Pragmatic considerations and enforced cooperation, however, could turn the tide, especially as political goals became aligned. How did this process work?

Liberal historians, sympathising with the Jacobin Revolution, have tended to portray the popular classes in the Two Sicilies as superstitious, reactionary, deeply royalist, easily shepherded and fooled, impervious to revolutionary doctrines, yet violent and at times unpredictable.[100] Recently, scholars have tempered this judgement, seeking to dispel the derogatory stereotypes of exceptionality that plague the history of Naples.[101] However, there is little doubt that much of the population was detached from the essentially elite intellectual Jacobin leadership, either out of support for the Bourbon dynasty, or because engaged in a separate 'class war'. The Republic faced ongoing anti-French and anti-Jacobin violence in the city, and royalist bands in the countryside.[102] Writing from the reconquered Naples, in July 1799, Hamilton stated that, whilst the nobility changed sides depending on convenience, and the bourgeoisie was mostly Jacobin, 'the Lower Class' were 'Loyal to their Sovereigns almost to a man & detest french & more still [?] Jacobins'.[103] Broadly, this also applied to seafarers.

---

[100] John A. Davis, 'The Neapolitan Revolution of 1799', *Journal of Modern Italian Studies* 4:3 (1999), 350–8, at 350–3; idem, *Naples and Napoleon: Southern Italy and the European Revolutions (1780–1860)* (Oxford: Oxford University Press, 2006), 95–8; Richter, *Napoli cosmopolita*, 12–14.

[101] Anna Maria Rao, '"Missed Opportunities" in the History of Naples', in Melissa Calaresu and Helen Hills (eds.), *New Approaches to Naples c.1500 – c.1800: The Power of Place* (Farnham and Burlington, VT: Ashgate, 2013), 203–23, esp. 211–12, 223.

[102] Davis, *Naples and Napoleon*, 79–82, 88–126; Atanasio Mozzillo, *La frontiera del Grand Tour: Viaggi e viaggiatori nel Mezzogiorno borbonico* (Naples: Liguori Editore, 1992), 79–115; Marion S. Miller, 'Italian Jacobinism', *Eighteenth-Century Studies* 11:2 (1977–8), 246–52, at 247–8, 251–2; Filippo Ambrosini, *L'albero della libertà: Le Repubbliche Giacobine in Italia 1796–1799* (Turin: Edizioni del Capricorno, 2013), 186–203, 230–42.

[103] BL, Egerton MS 2640, Hamilton to Acton, 8 July 1799.

It is true that in Naples most fishermen sided with the Republic, enticed by fiscal concessions, and when the royal family fled to Palermo, at the end of 1798, substantial portions of Neapolitan naval crews immediately deserted.[104] Generally speaking, however, maritime communities remained staunchly royalist. In December 1798, some French émigrés were threatened by the Sicilian population, 'as the fury in the people is carried against that Nation to even madness': 'the people on the Coast', Acton wrote, 'in small places are wilder than that of Palermo'.[105] Though their motives are not fully clear, the Sicilian crews of all the corvettes that had to escort these French nobles to Trieste deserted en masse.[106] In theory, such deep anti-French feeling should have facilitated positive attitudes towards the British. The situation, however, was not as straightforward.

There is some evidence that the Bourbon court did its best to shield its populace from foreigners and potentially dangerous ideas. During the 1793 Toulon expedition, Brigadier Pignatelli, commander of the land troops, received categorical instructions to prevent the 'corruption' of 'sectarians' from infiltrating the Neapolitan rank and file: he was to keep the men 'isolated', rejecting any French, Savoyard, or Piedmontese recruits, and 'adopting the maximum circumspection' with other foreigners.[107] Even the British Navy could become a target of suspicion: in July 1800, the British consul in Palermo wrote an annoyed letter to Admiral Keith, stating that Emma Hamilton had 'persuaded' Queen Maria Carolina 'that the crew of the *Alexander* were all Jacobins, and that it was not safe for them to remain in that ship'.[108] Government policies and royal paranoia, however, were not the only factor limiting Neapolitan and Sicilian sailors' experience of transnational employment.

[104] Alida Clemente, *Il mestiere dell'incertezza. La pesca nel Golfo di Napoli tra XVIII e XX secolo* (Napoli: Alfredo Guida, 2005), 50; Radogna, *Storia della marina militare*, 48.

[105] BL, Egerton MS 2640, Acton to Hamilton, 28, 31 December 1798.

[106] Ibid., Acton to Hamilton, 21 January 1799.

[107] ASN, Affari Esteri, 3662, Marina Real Ministero – 1793–1799, 'Istruzioni p[er] agire unitam. alle forze Inglesi nella p[rese]nte Guerra contro la Francia', 16 September 1793: '...*dovrà tenersi isolata la Truppa il più che sia possibile. Questo assunto è raccomandato al Brigadiere Pignatelli, come il più delicato, urgente, ed indispensabile nell'attuale momento: Di qui è che non ammetterà Egli mai Reclute Francesi, nè tampoco Savojardi, nè Piemontesi, perché quelle Truppe servono unite; ma riceverà solo Italiani di altre Parti, Svizzeri, o Tedeschi, usando però la massima Circospezione pure con questi Stranieri, perchè non siano fatti introdurre da quei Settarj per Sedurre, e corrompere la Truppa, come pur troppo si è osservato essere accaduto in altri Servizj, per disseminarvi una Corruttela uguale a quella che ha disonorato la Truppa Francese.*'

[108] Arthur Paget to Lord Keith, 31 July 1800, in Christopher Lloyd (ed.), *The Keith Papers*, 2 vols. (London: Navy Records Society, 1950), II, 179. The muster for that month shows only one Neapolitan, but substantial numbers of both Maltese and Irishmen: TNA, ADM 36/14336, Muster of HMS *Alexander*, July–August 1800.

If trade and cultural exchanges with Britain exerted a constant influence on the lives of the bourgeoisie and aristocracy, the poor, especially outside the cosmopolitan bubbles of the two capitals, seem to have had limited familiarity with the British, at least before the Sicilian occupation. Southern Italian seafarers, while well acquainted with the Mediterranean shores and their peoples, had scanty chances to travel to Atlantic routes; despite some growth in the sector, by the end of the century, these still only attracted 5% or slightly more of Neapolitan ships' journeys.[109] Most of the trade between Britain and the Two Sicilies was carried out by British merchantmen, and local vessels were usually, until a few decades into the nineteenth century, not equipped for that kind of long-distance trade. Even when this developed, ship owners and captains from the Gulf of Naples had an explicit 'policy' of recruiting only among the local workforce, including when abroad.[110] Thus, whilst British, Dutch, Scandinavian, and even American and Hanseatic vessels were a familiar presence in the Mediterranean, and ships from other ports such as Marseille or Genoa had their own well-developed Atlantic networks,[111] many seamen from the Two Sicilies were not used to transnational service. The fishing communities, the historiography suggests, were even more conservative, isolated, and solidly rooted in their localities.[112]

Within the Sicilian Navy, where it is easiest to reconstruct birthplaces, the origins of crews were also hardly heterogeneous. Of the two frigates still in the service in 1810, the *Sirena* was entirely manned by Italians: over 97% of them were from the Two Sicilies, with 'foreigners' only represented by three Genoese, a man from Leghorn and one from Trieste (see **Table 5.1**). A significant majority originated from the Gulf of Naples (85.4%), and almost half of those from Naples specifically. The other frigate, the *Minerva*, showed similar patterns: it only carried sailors

[109] Lo Sardo, *Napoli e Londra*, 167–75; Biagio Passaro, 'Polacche, tartane e feluche. Navi e navigazione mercantile napoletane nel Settecento', in *Navis: Rassegna di studi di archeologia, etnologia e storia navale. Atti del II convegno nazionale, Cesenatico – Museo della Marineria (13–14 aprile 2012)* (Padua: libreriauniversitaria.it edizioni, 2014), 219–25, at 220, 224; idem, 'La navigazione mercantile napoletana nel Settecento attraverso il *Giornale del porto di Napoli*', in Biagio Passaro, Maria Sirago, and Pasquale Bruno Trizio, *Al servizio della Capitale e della Corte: La marineria napoletana nel Settecento* (Naples: Edizioni Scientifiche Italiane, 2019), 5–34; idem, 'Ruolo e consistenza della flotta mercantile napoletana nel XVIII secolo', ibid., 35–62.
[110] Maresca and Passaro, *Marineria*, 34.   [111] Marzagalli, 'Maritimity', 322–7.
[112] Clemente, *Mestiere dell'incertezza*, 13–19.

Table 5.1. *Origins of crew members of HSM Frigate* Sirena *(1810)*[1]

Origin			Number	Percentage of total
Kingdom of the			173	97.19
Two Sicilies				
	Gulf of Naples		*152*	*85.39*
		Naples	63	
		Ischia	25	
		Castellammare	15	
		Vico	14	
		Procida	9	
		Capri	8	
		Sorrento	8	
		Meta	6	
		Massa	2	
		Baja	1	
		Torre del Greco	1	
	Sicily		*15*	*8.43*
		Lipari	6	
		Pantelleria	3	
		Ustica	3	
		Messina	2	
		Alicuri (Alicudi)	1	
	Gulf of Gaeta		*4*	*2.25*
		Gaeta	3	
		Ponza	1	
	Amalfi Coast		*2*	*1.13*
		Conca	1	
		Positano	1	
Genoa			3	1.69
Leghorn			1	0.56
Trieste			1	0.56
TOTAL			178	

[1] ASN Sezione Militare, Ruoli Regie Navi Registri di Marina, Busta 3, n. 6, Frag.[a] Sirena, 1810. Counted here are only the crew members for whom birthplaces were reported: this excludes most officers, the '*marinai di pianta fissa*', and several other men for whom the space was left blank. One toponym was illegible. All surnames in the muster are of Italian origin.

from the Gulfs of Naples, Salerno, and Gaeta, Sicily and its islands, and Calabria, with the most 'exotic' origins being those of two Venetians.[113] It is unclear whether this depended on deliberate policy or natural

[113] ASN Sezione Militare, Ruoli Regie Navi Registri di Marina, Busta 3, n. 5, Frag.[a] Minerva, January 1810.

employment patterns, but the result was probably that sailors from the kingdom were not very familiar with shipmates from faraway lands.

Stemming from, and at the same time compounding, this lack of familiarity with northern European colleagues, cultural differences also set southern Italian seamen apart. Most importantly, they were passionately Catholic. Churches and sanctuaries in villages all over the coast are still full of ex votos dedicated by seafarers to the Virgin Mary and various local saints.[114] Sorrentine merchant vessels bore astern devotional painted screens ('*specchi di poppa*'), to which prayers could be addressed in difficult moments; masses were regularly held aboard ships, and the men carried in their personal chests figures of saints ('*santini*'), rosaries, and other religious objects.[115] Names of saints were extremely common in merchant shipping, and even in the Bourbon Navy: while the 1790s saw a prevalence of mythological and topographical choices, still by the middle of the 1780s four out of five of the largest naval vessels bore such names (*San Giovanni, San Gioacchino, Santa Dorotea,* and *Santa Teresa*).[116]

Limited experience of the extra-Mediterranean world, and a deep attachment to a form of religion that was broadly despised, once combined with generally limited English language skills, sealed the outsider status of southern Italians finding themselves in the Royal Navy. On top of this, British preconceptions of Mediterranean (and particularly South-Mediterranean) culture were far from positive. Neapolitan society was depicted by travellers, throughout the eighteenth century, according to the principles of climatic determinism: the heat of the environment stimulated irrational passions, and the bountiful nature produced laziness, an unfortunate combination resulting in an untrustworthy, enervated, and

---

[114] Maresca and Passaro, *Marineria*, 44–7; Maresca, *Museo navale*, 22, 55–7, 95. On the religiosity of eighteenth-century Sorrentine mariners, see Pasquale Bruno Trizio, 'Sulla rotta dell'olio: Monopoli e l'iniziativa marittima sorrentina tra il XVII e il XVIII secolo', in Passaro et al., *Al servizio della Capitale e della Corte*, 111–41, at 133, 136–41. For a collection of nineteenth and twentieth-century ex votos, preserved in Meta, see Basilica Pontificia Santa Maria del Lauro, *Storie di tempeste e di fede: Gli ex voto nel Santuario Santa Maria del Lauro* (Castellammare di Stabia: Eidos, 1998). I am very grateful to Professor Biagio Passaro for directing me to this volume, and accompanying me to visit this little-known collection. For some sixteenth-century examples, see Antonio Ermanno Giardino and Michele Rak, *Per grazia ricevuta: Le tavolette dipinte ex voto per la Madonna dell'Arco – Il Cinquecento* (Naples: Ci.esse.ti cooperativa editrice, 1983), 279–343. Whilst ship models can also be found in British churches, some research has rejected their interpretation as ex votos: Meredith Greiling, 'Sacred Vessels: British Church Ship Models', *The International Journal of Maritime History* 27:4 (2015), 793–7.

[115] Maresca, *Museo navale*, 21–2, 42–6; idem and Passaro, *Marineria*, 42–3.

[116] Radogna, *Storia della marina militare*, 31. A list of about thirty fishing boats that left Pozzuoli in 1846 only contains religious names: Clemente, *Mestiere dell'incertezza*, 75–6.

yet bestially violent population.[117] Some observers had a more nuanced view, questioning the idea of intrinsic laziness, but ultimately the 'picturesque' stereotypes proved hard to shed.[118] After the revolution, Naples came to be seen as not only noisy and chaotic, but also positively dangerous.[119] Such received notions, as contemporary Neapolitan intellectuals complained, were so powerful that they were blindly repeated and believed, regardless of the reality that a traveller witnessed.[120] Officers and diplomats were not immune from this. Even to Britons like William Hamilton, long settled in the country and deeply familiar with it, some local traditions, especially when connected to religious cults, appeared ridiculous, irrational, and backward. In 1780, in order to make the rain stop so that the Carnival processions could take place, the Neapolitan court paid a convent of friars to say some masses. 'I thought this fact too curious to pass unnoticed, considering the enlighten'd age in which we live', Hamilton wrote, incredulous.[121] The truth was that, at bottom, Britons were not equipped to understand Neapolitan and Sicilian society and could hardly fail to perceive it as poor, decadent, benighted, and inferior. This had an impact on their decisions regarding the recruitment of locals.

British officers could have a very poor received opinion of Neapolitan and Sicilian sailors. In the newly reconquered Naples, in the summer of 1799, Captain Thomas Foley, of HMS *Goliath*, was pleased that police duties ashore had been assigned to British seamen: 'bad as they are they are more to be depended on then [*sic*] native Napoliatans [*sic*]'.[122] Considering the notion that the British upper classes had of sailors' discipline once in port, this is quite an extraordinary statement. Technical competence was also questioned: 'I have no idea we shall get much good from them', Nelson observed in 1795, having been informed that some Neapolitan vessels were to join his squadron: 'they are not seamen, and cannot keep the sea beyond a passage'.[123] Similar perceptions could help to explain the relatively low numbers of southern Italian

[117] Mozzillo, *Frontiera del Grand Tour*, 9–54, 122–3.
[118] Melissa Calaresu, 'From the Street to Stereotype: Urban Space, Travel and the Picturesque in Late Eighteenth-Century Naples', *Italian Studies* 62:2 (2007), 189–203.
[119] Richter, *Napoli cosmopolita*, 14–20; Mozzillo, *Frontiera del Grand Tour*, 118–21.
[120] Calaresu, 'Looking for Virgil's Tomb'.
[121] TNA, FO 70/1, Sicily and Naples – Sir William Hamilton 1780–1, Hamilton to the Earl of Hillsborough, 8 February 1780, ff. 19–20.
[122] NLS, GB233/MS.3599, Lynedoch Papers, Thomas Foley to Sir Thomas Graham, 11 August 1799.
[123] Nelson to the Duke of Clarence, 19 January 1795, reported in Nicolas, *Dispatches and Letters*, II, 2. See also Porcaro, *Francesco Caracciolo*, 50.

recruits, even in the Mediterranean Fleet: while at least 115 confirmed Italians (thirty-six of whom were Neapolitans), plus unknown numbers of supernumeraries, served in the ships that eventually fought at Trafalgar, they are but 0.63% of the total, which was around 18,360 men.[124] In 1794, when the 700 recruits requested by Hood had been gathered, and Captain Montgomery, commanding a British ship, stopped in Naples 'in [sic] his way to the Levant', he was offered some of them, but 'declined taking any'.[125]

If British naval personnel could have strong prejudices towards Italian seamen, the opposite was also true. In March 1794, Acton was forced to write to Hamilton, apologising for the delay in procuring the 700 men requested by Hood: the recruitment operations, which had been entrusted to none other than Caracciolo, were proceeding slowly, despite offers of pay rise, benefits to the families, and other enticements. This was partly due to the season, given that most of the seamen in the kingdom were by then employed in the corn trade. However, despite King Ferdinand's wishes, 'no small opposition' was also caused by 'the inclination, the custom, the principles of Religion, and the Prejudices of this People of his'.[126] Around 14% of the men who served between 1798 and 1801 in the British Frigate *Santa Dorotea* came from various parts of Italy, but many of them rapidly deserted – most notably, fourteen out of seventeen Neapolitans.[127] The Royal Navy disliked Neapolitans, but Neapolitans also disliked the Royal Navy.

If the initial situation was unpromising, however, some men were still recruited, and the attitudes and prejudices of British officers could be shaped by this. To begin with, Italian seamen had unique, often irreplaceable skills, which could make them more valuable than ordinary Jack Tars. They spoke the language and knew the coasts, but their usefulness did not end there. British seamen were notoriously bad swimmers and, it has been suggested, deliberately kept so to avoid desertions.[128] Young men who had grown up in the warm Mediterranean, instead, would not have this problem. Sicilian warships, in fact, carried

[124] These data have been extracted from Pappalardo, 'Trafalgar Ancestors'.

[125] TNA, FO 70/7, Sicily and Naples – Sir William Hamilton 1780–1, Hamilton to Hood, 30 September 1794; Acton to Hamilton, 6 October 1794.

[126] BL, Egerton MS 2639, General Sir John Francis Edward Acton, 6th Baronet Neapolitan Prime Minister: Correspondence with Sir W. Hamilton, vol. i., 1781–98, n. 162, Acton to Hamilton, 4 March 1794: '...non picciola opposizione fa alla sollecitudine, con cui vorrebbe S. M. vederlo adempito, l'indole, il costume, i principj di Religione, ed i Pregiudizj di questo suo Popolo'.

[127] TNA, ADM 36/14389, Muster Book of HMS *Santa Dorotea*, January–February 1801.

[128] Rodger, *Wooden World*, 53; Brian Lavery, *Nelson's Navy: The Ships, Men and Organisation 1793–1815* (London: Conway Maritime Press, 1989), 144, 189.

among their complement '*sommozzatori*' (divers), a rating utterly unknown to the British Navy.[129] When, during refitting operations in the Gulf of Naples, a gudgeon fell overboard from HMS *Culloden* (a 74-gun third-rate,[130] hence with a crew of a few hundred), the expense records show that local divers had to be hired to recover it, for the relatively substantial sum of one ducat and twenty grains (about fifty-three pence, i.e., over four days' worth of wages for a British able seaman, and akin to what qualified shipwrights were paid in Britain).[131]

Despite all the stereotypes, Neapolitan men could also earn the respect of British officers even simply through brave conduct, once they were removed from the structures of their own Army and Navy. While Admiral Hood had nothing but contempt for Forteguerri and the other Neapolitan officers at Toulon, he explicitly exempted ordinary soldiers from blame. 'I hope and trust I shall never see the face of either again', he wrote, referring to Forteguerri and another Sicilian captain who had allegedly fled without helping to complete the evacuation of the port, 'for I am really sick of Neapolitan discipline. The strange and unaccountable panic that had seized His Sicilian majesty's officers *for I have a high opinion of the men* [emphasis added] made the retreat unavoidable'.[132] 'No one has a higher opinion of the Sicilian Troops than I have', he wrote a month later, 'and am very confident, had they had good officers to command them, none would have more distinguished themselves'.[133] Statements related to the Toulon defeat must always be taken with a degree of caution, since all the allies were eager to lay the responsibility at each other's doors. Forteguerri had, predictably, a very different version of the events surrounding the evacuation, explaining his retreat in rather convincing terms.[134] However, Hood's observation on the Neapolitan

---

[129] See the musters of Sicilian ships: ASN Sezione Militare, Ruoli Regie Navi Regisui di Marina, Busta 3.

[130] J. J. Colledge and Ben Warlow, *Ships of the Royal Navy: The Complete Record of All Fighting Ships of the Royal Navy* (Philadelphia, PA and Newbury: Casemate, 2010), 97.

[131] ASN, Affari Esteri, 4333, Generi Somministrati agli Inglesi dai Regj Arsenali 1800 al 1813, 'An Account of the Repairs of His Majesty's Ship Culloden'. The wage of an AB was £1 9s 6d twenty-eight-day month, that is, 354 pence per month, or 12.64 pence (just over one shilling) per day. See Rodger, *Command*, 625. For further details, and the conversion rate from ducats to pounds, see Section 7.2.2 and Appendix 4. British shipwrights in naval dockyards were paid 2s 1d a day plus overtime during most of the eighteenth century, between 4s 2d and 6s 3d during the French Wars (Portsmouth values), and 4s 6d or 5s (depending on the season) from 1812: J. M. Haas, *A Management Odyssey: The Royal Dockyards, 1714–1914* (Lanham, MD: University Press of America, 1994), 26, 31–2, 54; Roger Morriss, *The Royal Dockyards during the Revolutionary and Napoleonic Wars* (Leicester: Leicester University Press, 1983), 100–5.

[132] NMM, CRK/7/49, Hood to Hamilton, 24 December 1793.

[133] NMM, CRK/7/55, Hood to Hamilton, 30 January 1794.

[134] ASN, Affari Esteri, 4339, Tolone, Forteguerri to Acton, 5 February 1794.

rank and file sounds genuine in any case, since it does not serve any political purpose. In fact, already during the siege, and even as he wrote poisonous words against Forteguerri, he had been forced to defend himself from accusations of favouritism towards the Neapolitans: 'I do not hesitate to say', he confessed, 'that I have a far better opinion of the Sicilian Troops than I have of the Spanish'.[135] Most telling is a letter that he wrote to Hamilton, in March, when his diplomatic sense had somewhat subdued his anger, and he coolly declared himself 'satisfied', for the sake of 'Harmony, and good understanding' between their two countries, that Forteguerri had been fully acquitted by the King of Sicily:

Different nations Sir, have a different mode of enforcing subordination and discipline and what may be right and proper in one, may not suit the constitution and nature of the Government of another; for if an English squadron had not followed the commander in chief, but gone to another place, the officer commanding it, would not have been permitted to have done so a second time.[136]

The problem, then, was not with the Neapolitans and Sicilians themselves, but with their culture and institutions. An intelligent officer could avoid letting disdain towards a different system turn into cultural or racial spite, and incorporate good men in his own ranks, wherever they might be found.

Hood's praise of southern Italians was not an isolated case. At the end of November 1811, the Sicilian gunboat Flotilla, commanded by Robert Hall, fought a skirmish against the enemy, just off Messina. 'Nothing could exceed the Zeal and animation manifested by the Sicilian Seamen', Hall wrote in the aftermath, 'two of whom were killed, and eight wounded':

Accustomed to command British Seamen in this species of warfare, I must do the Sicilians the justice to declare that I never witnessed a better, or cooler fire. These Brave Men seek all opportunities of shewing their attachment to the British Service, and the Army Officers employed in the flotilla give the best impulse to their exertions.[137]

Almost incredulous, he was forced to acknowledge that these seamen were equal in valour even to the British. He probably interpreted as attachment to the 'British Service' what was, in fact, a determination to defend their own homes. During the 'Decennio Inglese' in Sicily, the local population developed an enthusiasm towards the British that was largely based on the

---

[135] NMM, CRK/7/43, Hood to Hamilton, 20 November 1793.
[136] NMM, CRK/7/60, Hood to Hamilton, 15 March 1794.
[137] TNA, ADM 1/1945, Letters from Captains, Surnames H., 1812, 78, Robert Hall to Sir Wilson Croker, 1 December 1811.

latter's role in staving off the French invasion.[138] Whatever their motives, anyway, these men had shown themselves well worthy of a place in the British Navy. Sicilian land troops earned equal praise from British Army officers for their zeal in defending the island.[139] A similar pattern can be seen in the case of British dealings with other 'foreign' workforce: in North America, during the War of 1812, Rear-Admiral Cockburn initially deemed Black recruits 'naturally neither very valorous nor very active'. After seeing them in action, however, he admitted that they had been 'getting on astonishingly, and are really very fine Fellows... they have induced me to alter the bad opinion I had of the whole of their Race'.[140] Stereotypes were pliable and could fail to withstand the trial by fire.

One final point needs to be considered. Leaving aside any cultural, linguistic, and religious factors, ultimately southern Italian and British sailors also had some important characteristics in common. Not only were they, obviously, engaged in the same profession, but also, as revealed by some initial statistical analysis carried out on two samples, they seem to have been remarkably similar demographically. I have compared the crew of the Sicilian frigate *Sirena* analysed above to that of a British frigate of similar size, HMS *Circe*, during its service in the North Sea at the end of the 1790s.[141] Detracting from the sample all seamen for whom ages were not reported, the sizes of the two cohorts were roughly equivalent (173 men aboard HMS *Circe* and 176 aboard the *Sirena*), and the mean ages were almost identical, 23.78 and 23.22 years, respectively. The age distribution of the two crews was, as can be seen in the two graphs below, rather similar, but with a noticeable difference in spread: the Sicilian ship seemed to carry younger boys, down to the age of seven (the youngest members of the *Circe*'s crew were thirteen), and older men (three of them were above fifty, with one aged sixty-three, aboard the *Sirena*, whilst the oldest in

---

[138] Michela D'Angelo, 'Oltre lo stretto. "Viva lu 'ngrisi, mannaja la Franza!"', in Renata De Lorenzo (ed.), *Ordine e disordine. Amministrazione e mondo militare nel Decennio francese – Atti del sesto seminario di studi "Decennio francese (1806–1815)"* (Napoli: Giannini Editore, 2012), 309–32.

[139] Bianco, *Sicilia*, 63–6; D'Angelo, 'Oltre lo stretto', 309–11, 330.

[140] The quotes are reported in Thomas Malcomson, 'Freedom by Reaching the Wooden World: American Slaves and the British Navy during the War of 1812', *The Northern Mariner / Le marin du nord* 22:4 (2012), 361–92, at 378–9. On a similar sense of 'surprise', and naval officers' reassessment of prejudices after direct contact with West Africans, see also Wills, *Envoys of Abolition*, 139–43.

[141] Data extracted from the musters: ASN Sezione Militare, Ruoli Regie Navi Registri di Marina, Busta 3, n. 6, Frag.ᵃ Sirena, 1810; TNA, ADM 36/12279, Muster Book of HMS *Circe*, September–October 1797. For a detailed breakdown of the origins of HMS *Circe*'s crew, see Caputo, '*Scotland, Scottishness and the British Navy*' (2015), 63, 76. This was entirely composed of British and Irish seamen, except for four Americans, two Danes, two Dutchmen, and one German.

HMS *Circe* were only forty-eight) (**Figures 5.1** and **5.2**). It may be that a career in the warmer Mediterranean climates could last longer. However, the bulk of the seamen were exactly in the same age group across the two navies. The median ages on the two frigates, indeed, were identical

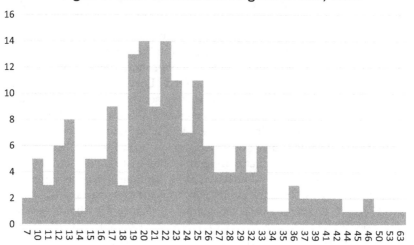

Figure 5.1 Ages of the crew of the Sicilian Frigate *Sirena*, 1810.

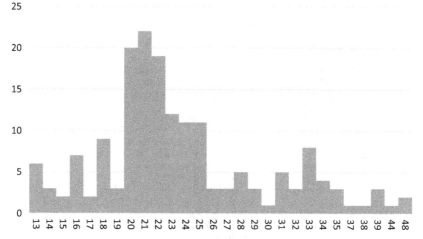

Figure 5.2 Ages of the crew of HM Frigate *Circe*, 1797.

(26.5 years), and the mode was also nearly the same, 21 for the *Circe* dataset, and 20 and 22 (bimodal distribution) for the *Sirena*. In short, and without falling into demographic determinism, it seems significant that most of these sailors were young men of approximately the same age. Perhaps, they had more in common, as a workforce, than a prejudiced officer may have initially thought.

5.4   Conclusion

Relations between Britain and the Two Sicilies were shaped, throughout the French Wars, by a heavy imbalance of power. Neapolitan seamen became a military commodity supplied upon request to the more powerful ally, nominally only for use within the framework of shared objectives, but in fact without ultimate control over this outcome. The unequal interaction between the two states affected individual and collective attitudes. Whilst some men chose the easier (and often profitable) route of compliance and cooperation, in many cases, the forced subordination to Britain brought more vividly to the surface some form of national pride – tied to gentlemanly honour for officers, local concerns for seamen, and loyalty to their own king for both groups. The weaker position of the Two Sicilies also influenced general British perceptions of Sicilian and Neapolitan seamen. Combined with cultural differences, it fostered broad negative stereotypes, which, in this void made of mutual unfamiliarity, had abundant scope to flourish.

Yet, despite all these systemic factors pulling them apart, British and Sicilian seamen could find themselves cooperating, with success and, eventually, mutual respect. For the seamen and some midshipmen, close-quarters, hard, and dangerous work towards a shared objective, combined with basic demographic and professional similarities, sufficed to create a new familiarity. Once again, this process was made easier by the utilitarian attitude that, beneath the prejudices of individual officers, underlay British naval recruitment policies. As we saw in the case of legal, linguistic, and religious barriers, integrating 'foreign' commissioned officers in the service proved more problematic. Status and professional dignity added the stressor of a fight for retaining command, and differing notions of discipline created insoluble rifts. This, however, meant that foreign officers could become a convenient scapegoat to solve the contradiction between xenophobic prejudice and the employability of non-British hands: foreign Jack Tars could almost shed their foreignness, if only they were removed from their corrupt and inept masters.

6 'From among the Northern Nations Alone'
Dutchmen, Danes, and Norwegians in the Fleet

The interactions of Britain and its fleet with other North Sea countries offer an effective counterpoint to the situation in southern Italy. Because of a combination of social, cultural, and political factors, the absorption of northerners into the British Navy was smoother and less contentious than that of men of other origins. At the same time, these very factors created a different set of problems.

Historians have depicted the early modern 'North Sea Region' as a Braudelian Mediterranean, emphasising its unity as a zone of cultural and migratory exchange.[1] Britain and the Netherlands were two crucial poles of this shared space; although Denmark and Norway lay geographically on its margins, migration, not least of seafarers, tightly linked them to it. The Royal Navy deemed Danish and Norwegian seamen excellent recruits. British officers also had an overall positive – if slightly less enthusiastic – view of Dutchmen's capabilities. This stemmed, I will argue, from strong similarities between the British and the Dutch seafaring traditions. As such, the idea of a northern European seaman, usually deemed skilled and worthy, seems to have been a contemporary 'category of practice' in evaluating foreign recruits.[2] How did the process operate on the ground?

This chapter begins by exploring the cultural and professional background of northern European sailors, their most common attitudes towards Britain, and the circumstances that made them attractive to the British Navy. I then present a case study, examining how similarity between the structure and professional ethos of the pre-1795 Dutch and British navies allowed a bold experiment: the wholesale absorption of entirely Dutch ships, manned and officered by Dutchmen, into the Royal Navy. Finally, I will discuss some of the concerns that the employment of northern European seamen raised among the British public.

---

[1] Van Lottum, *Across the North Sea*, 15–17. For a nuanced discussion, see the essays in Roding and van Voss, *North Sea and Culture*.
[2] For this use of the concept of 'categories of practice', see Brubaker and Cooper, 'Beyond "Identity"', 4–6.

6.1   'Half Englishmen'

Economists studying the 'non-monetary costs of migration' have argued that cultural differences or similarities significantly affect these costs, resulting in larger 'gross migration' (total of immigrant and emigrant flow) between places that are more 'alike', notably in terms of language intelligibility.[3] Geographical and travel distance is also an important factor, because it increases what are termed 'psychic' costs (the effects of removal from family and networks), as well as leaving potential migrants less informed about opportunities available.[4] All being equal, people unsurprisingly are more likely to migrate to places with language and culture similar to theirs, and which are more easily reachable. Admittedly, migration into a foreign naval service was less affected by distance than other forms of labour migration: it concerned both an intrinsically mobile population, seafarers, and a recruiter that was mobile itself, and often actually came to the 'migrant', when deployed in his home waters. Yet cultural and geographical proximity between other countries and Britain seems to have facilitated naval recruitment. Several factors favoured northern Europeans, when it came to service in the Royal Navy.

First, sailors from the North Sea and Baltic were generally quite used to working in a cosmopolitan environment, with some potential exceptions, like Swedes (the Swedish fleet was mostly manned through a peculiar 'allotment' system, by part-time peasant seamen).[5] The Dutch Republic was far too small to provide sufficient manpower for both its Navy and its extensive merchant and fishing trade. The Dutch maritime labour market, therefore, was increasingly and exceptionally multinational throughout the eighteenth century, and this formed a stark contrast particularly with southern European countries like France and Spain, or the Two Sicilies.[6] The Dutch Navy relied heavily on immigrants,

---

[3] Oliver Falck, Alfred Lameli, and Jens Ruhose, 'Cultural Biases in Migration: Estimating Non-Monetary Migration Costs', *Papers in Regional Science* 97:2 (2018), 411–38; Oliver Falck, Stephan Heblich, Alfred Lameli, and Jens Südekum, 'Dialects, Cultural Identity, and Economic Exchange', *Journal of Urban Economics* 72 (2012), 225–39.

[4] Aba Schwartz, 'Interpreting the Effect of Distance on Migration', *Journal of Political Economy* 81:5 (1973), 1153–69; Michael J. Greenwood, 'Research on Internal Migration in the United States: A Survey', *Journal of Economic Literature* 13:2 (1975), 397–433, at 398–9, 404–5, 410–11; Falck et al., 'Cultural Biases', esp. 412–13, 424–6.

[5] AnnaSara Hammar, 'How to Transform Peasants into Seamen: The Manning of the Swedish Navy and a Double-Faced Maritime Culture', *The International Journal of Maritime History* 27:4 (2015), 696–707.

[6] Jelle van Lottum, 'Some Thoughts about Migration of Maritime Workers in the Eighteenth-Century North Sea Region', *The International Journal of Maritime History* 27:4 (2015), 647–61, at 651–3; Paul C. van Royen, 'Mariners and Markets in the Age

well into the nineteenth century: an analysis of Amsterdam Admiralty musters from 1765 revealed that just 43% of men were natives of the United Provinces, and this had only risen to 59% in 1821. Of the 'Buitenlanders' ('foreigners'), 17% and 22%, respectively, came from Scandinavia.[7] The late eighteenth-century Dano–Norwegian Navy, it seems, had a lower proportion of foreigners, except among officers, but some Germans and Dutchmen could be found on its lower decks, too.[8] Moreover, it was very common for young Norwegians and Danes to move to Holland, and to a lesser extent Britain, to serve in their respective merchant marines and navies.[9] Often the migration was only temporary, but many also settled locally, forming immigrant communities; when they eventually returned home, some displayed 'somewhat foreign manners of speaking', wore English clothes or multiple breeches and golden buttons in the Dutch fashion, and had even changed, it was said, in their 'morals' and attention to 'cleanliness'.[10]

In this way, both Dutch and Scandinavian seamen gained considerable experience of cosmopolitan interactions, especially among each other and with Britain. Furthermore, the ships aboard which these sailors served were often large and, like the British, rigged for long-distance voyages. Dutch merchantmen, Vereenigde Oostindische Compagnie ships, and whalers sailed to the East Indies and all over the Atlantic and European seas.[11] The reach of Danish shipping was more limited, but trading activities still stretched to the Mediterranean and to Denmark's colonies in the West and East Indies, benefiting from

---

of Sail: The Case of the Netherlands', in Lewis R. Fischer (ed.), *The Market for Seamen in the Age of Sail* (St John's, Newfoundland: International Maritime Economic History Association, 1994), 47–57, at 51–6; van Rossum et al., 'National and International Labour Markets', 50–61; Karel Davids, 'Maritime Labour in the Netherlands, 1570–1870', in van Royen et al., *'Those Emblems of Hell'?*, 41–71, at 49–56, 62; Van Lottum et al., 'Sailors', 312–13, 316–27, 336–9.

[7] Jaap Bruijn, 'Zeevarenden', in G. Asaert et al. (eds.), *Maritieme Geschiedenis der Nederlanden – Deel 3: Achttiende eeuw en eerste helft negentiende eeuw, van ca. 1680 tot 1850–1860* (Bussum: Uitgeverij De Boer Maritiem, 1976–8), 146–90 at 153–4.

[8] Gustav Sætra, 'The International Labour Market for Seamen, 1600–1900: Norway and Norwegian Participation', in van Royen et al., *'Those Emblems of Hell'?*, 173–210, at 181, 184–5, 190–1; Hans Chr. Johansen, 'Danish Sailors, 1570–1870', ibid., 233–52, at 244–50.

[9] Sætra, 'International Labour Market', 191–210; Johansen, 'Danish Sailors', 250–1.

[10] Sætra, 'International Labour Market', 197–9, 203, 205–6; Ludvig Daae, *Nordmænds udvandringer til Holland of England i nyere tid* (Christiania: Alb. Cammermeyer, 1880), 120–1.

[11] For an overview of the various branches of eighteenth-century Dutch shipping, see Jaap R. Bruijn, *Zeegang: Zeevarend Nederland in de achttiende eeuw* (Zutphen: WalburgPers, 2016), esp. 49–54.

neutrality for as long as they could.[12] A familiarity with other cultures and countries was likely an advantage for a man joining a foreign and far-travelling service like the Royal Navy.

Next to this cosmopolitan outlook, northerners shared a second asset when it came to British recruitment. We saw that Scandinavian sailors, and to some extent Dutchmen and Germans, seemingly displayed higher levels of numeracy and/or English language skill than their southern European colleagues. Lack of fluency in English, I have argued, did not necessarily prejudice recruitment, and higher numeracy skills may not have substantially affected a man's rating in the British Navy. However, as some examples below will show, a good command of English could be construed as a bonus by recruiters. Literacy, numeracy, and language competence, some historians have suggested, may have been linked to higher 'productivity' (i.e. tons per man ratio) in the early modern shipping sector.[13] Given that the separation of the Navy from the maritime labour market more generally is largely artificial, it is possible that similar considerations of efficiency, implicitly or explicitly, would infuse Admiralty and commanders' manning preferences. Thus, a man who understood and perhaps read English might have fitted in better.

No doubt, traditional patterns of xenophobia could persist among sailors, especially given that the United Provinces, Denmark, and Sweden were all, at different stages of the war, among Britain's enemies. For example, rather unsurprisingly, a strong anti-Dutch sentiment existed in the British North Sea fleet around the time of the Battle of Camperdown. During the 1797 mutiny court martials at the Nore, John De Ruyter, Dutch seaman, proved to the court that the British Marine Jacob Parker had only sworn against him 'as I was a Dutchman and a Foreigner', and 'that if I had been English Irish or Scotch he would not swear against me'. Parker had stated this himself, and added that De Ruyter 'being a Dutch bugger he would hang him if he could'.[14]

[12] Hans Chr. Johansen, 'Scandinavian Shipping in the Late Eighteenth Century in a European Perspective', *The Economic History Review* 45:3 (1992), 479–93. There is a vast literature on eighteenth-century neutrality and the Nordic nations. See, for example, Silvia Marzagalli and Leos Müller, '"In Apparent Disagreement with All Law of Nations in the World": Negotiating Neutrality for Shipping and Trade during the French Revolutionary and Napoleonic Wars', *The International Journal of Maritime History* 28:1 (2016), 108–17; Dan H. Andersen and Hans-Joachim Voth, 'The Grapes of War: Neutrality and Mediterranean Shipping under the Danish Flag, 1747–1807', *Scandinavian Economic History Review* 48:1 (2000), 5–27.

[13] Van Lottum et al., 'Sailors', 341–4.

[14] TNA, ADM 1/5486, Courts Martial Papers: Nore Mutiny, 1797, n. 29, ff. 58–60. I am extremely grateful to Dr Callum Easton for signalling this case to me.

The dislike was often mutual. After the Royal Navy, pre-emptively breaking the peace, suddenly bombed Copenhagen in 1807, and dragged away the entire Danish fleet, many Danes developed a deep hatred towards Britain.[15] In their violent condemnation of the raid, the Whig Members of Parliament Richard Sharp and Samuel Whitbread pointed out to the Commons that all the expedition had accomplished was conquering the 'carcasses' and 'hulks' of some ships. In so doing, it had provoked the hostility of the truly important component of the Danish fleet, the seamen: Danes had until then been the largest foreign group in British merchant shipping, 'half Englishmen' by sympathies, 'almost as much attached to this country as to their own' in the case of Zealanders, Holsteiners, and Norwegians.[16]

Everything considered, however, these tensions did not prevent all seamen from serving in the British Navy. Many Dutchmen were part of the British squadron in the North Sea and fought in it at the battle of Camperdown, in October 1797, where the Dutch fleet was crushed. Eighty of them, mostly volunteers from among the prisoners taken at Saldanha Bay two years earlier, were aboard Rear Admiral Onslow's HMS *Monarch* and 'behaved during the action remarkably well'.[17] Others were scattered across the other ships, for example twenty in HMS *Montagu*.[18] In 1795, at the Nore, Admiral Dalrymple noted that 'an encouragement, at this time to Dutch Seamen, might be the cause of engaging many of the same Country to follow their Example' in joining the British service.[19] This was partly because political divides internal to the United Provinces cut powerfully across purely 'national' allegiances.[20]

It is also estimated that about 30% of Norwegian prisoners of war post-1807 entered British service. The majority chose the merchant fleet,

---

[15] For the context and aftermath of the bombardment, see Thomas Munch-Petersen, 'The Causes of the British Attack on Denmark in 1807 and the Danish Alliance with France', in Knut Arstad (ed.), *Krig på sjø og land: Norden i Napoleonskrigene* ([Oslo]: Forsvarsmuseet, 2014), 43–71; Kjeld Hald Galster, 'Den Britiske invasion i Danmark, terrorbombardementet af København og Flådens ran', ibid., 73–95; James Davey, 'The Royal Navy and the War with Denmark, 1808–1814', ibid., 97–124; Rasmus Glenthøj and Morten Nordhagen Ottosen, *Experiences of War and Nationality in Denmark and Norway, 1807–1815* (Basingstoke: Palgrave Macmillan, 2014), 28–58; Helge Gamrath et al. (eds.), *Nordjylland under Englandskrigen 1807–1814* (Aalborg: Aalborg Universitetsforlag, 2009).

[16] Hansard, House of Commons, vol. 10, 'Expedition to Copenhagen', 21 March 1808, cc. 1185–1235, at 1193, 1205, 1232 https://hansard.parliament.uk/Commons/1808-03-21/debates/c63b13c5-2462-4945-b68e-1005f3a313ad/ExpeditionToCopenhagen. These were all deemed parts of Denmark at the time.

[17] *The Edinburgh Advertiser*, 5–8 December 1797, 361.

[18] TNA, ADM 36/12756, Muster Book of HMS *Montagu*, September–October 1797.

[19] TNA, ADM 1/725, Letters from Commanders-in-Chief, Nore, 1795, 75, John Dalrymple to Philip Stephens, 2 March 1795.

[20] On the political situation, see Section 6.3.

but at least 5% of the combined Dano–Norwegian cohort, or around 300, opted for the Navy.[21] At the time Norwegians were often confused with Danes, given that Norway was a dependency of Denmark. Therefore, many of the men listed as coming from 'Denmark' in British musters may have been, in fact, Norwegians: in official correspondence, one encounters mentions of 'Danish' sailors 'native of Christian Sand in Norway'.[22] The two groups could differ in their attachment to the Danish cause. The choice to defect to the British service in order to avoid the hardships of captivity was frequently frowned upon by fellow prisoners, even among Norwegians.[23] However, Berit Eide Johnsen has argued that, especially for them, professional identity and traditional economic and cultural connections with Britain could trump pro-Danish loyalties.[24] During the course of the war, a tolerant British policy towards foodstuff imports into Norway drove a further wedge between Norwegian and Danish interests.[25]

Overall, despite some nuances of allegiance, a broadly cosmopolitan habit and long-standing connections eased the integration of Dutch, Norwegian, and Danish seamen into the British Navy. These factors also engendered an explicit preference on the part of the Admiralty.

6.2   'Very Serviceable in HM Fleet': The British Admiralty and Northern Seamen

In general, the British Admiralty and politicians had a much better opinion of northern European sailors, and especially of Scandinavians, than they did of other foreigners.[26] In 1814, when the Navy needed 'good seamen' to continue the American War, a proposal sent to the Home Office suggested applying to allied powers for some, but taking them 'from among the Northern nations alone'. Even in the case of Russian seamen, the proposal stated, 'it may be questioned whether' they 'would be found equal to the Americans'. Danish sailors were described as 'certainly the best among the nations of the North', but in

---

[21] Johnsen, *Han sad*, 129–31; eadem, 'Norske sjøfolk i prisonen', in Gamrath, *Nordjylland*, 285–96, at 287.

[22] TNA, ADM 1/3851, Letters from Foreign Consuls 1799–1800, Count Wedel Jarlsberg to Evan Nepean, 9 February 1799, f. 293.

[23] Johnsen, *Han sad*, 134–7; Ian MacDougall, *All Men Are Brethren: French, Scandinavian, Italian, German, Dutch, Belgian, Spanish, Polish, West Indian, American, and Other Prisoners of War in Scotland during the Napoleonic Wars, 1803–1814* (Edinburgh: Birlinn, 2008), 470; Glenthøj and Ottosen, *Experiences of War*, 104–5.

[24] Johnsen, *Han sad*, 52–77, 200–1, 137–8.

[25] Davey, 'Royal Navy and the War with Denmark', 118–20, 123–4.

[26] On Nordic sailors' respected skills: Johnsen, *Han sad*, 131, 133.

their case, as in that of Swedes, it was feared that matters of diplomacy and neutrality might interfere with recruitment. Norwegians were the solution: the ambiguous status of their country solved the diplomatic concerns, and they were 'a brave hardy race of men & a trifling advantage held out to them would tempt them into our Service'. The only caveat was the need to use 'more caution than if we had to do with Germans': 'the Danes and Norwegians', the report pointed out, 'are distinguished for an extraordinary attachment to their Country, & for the most implicit obedience to the will of their Sovereign'.[27] In short, the image presented was that of able, brave, proud, and loyal men, quite the opposite of the spiteful stereotype reserved to Mediterranean sailors. These notions were echoed in contemporary civilian travel accounts, even beyond Britain: for example, Swedes were described by one French author as taking 'the lead in point of morals' in Europe, characterised by 'strict honesty', and 'sober', except with drinking;[28] another traveller, a Dutchman, saw them as 'lively' and 'laborious', and the Danes as less hard-working but 'serious', 'phlegmatic', and 'constant' in their 'friendships'.[29]

Such was the enthusiasm of naval officers for these men that in 1811 young Danes who arrived in British ports aboard licensed vessels were enticed to enlist, even though Denmark was at war with Britain: the hope was that they 'might by a well drawn up address alluding to the late order for their countrymen to serve in the French & Dutch fleets be induced to prefer ours'. Far from being a last-resort 'foreign' manning option, these 'fine young seamen who speak English fluently from the long intercourse with this country', and 'would be very serviceable in HM Fleet', were in a position of substantial contractual strength: Royal Navy officers liked and needed them probably more than vice versa.[30] In the same year, when he assumed command of HMS *Venerable*, Sir Home Popham found its crew 'deficient in practical experience as it was exuberant in vice'. The solution he devised was recruiting some Danes from prisons of war, even by promising them that they would be sent back to prison if

---

[27] TNA, HO 44/47/37, Home Office: Domestic Correspondence, 1814–38, [signature cut], proposal for recruiting Danish and Norwegian seamen for service against America, 1814, ff. 73–6. On the British preference for Norwegians over Danes, see also Johnsen, *Han sad*, 138.

[28] Louis de Boisgelin, *Travels through Denmark and Sweden*, 2 vols. (London: Wilkie and Robinson, 1810), II, 166–7.

[29] 'Comparison between the Inhabitants of Denmark and Sweden', *The Universal Magazine of Knowledge and Pleasure* 85 (London: W. Bent, 1789), 150–1. This is an extract translated from a publication entitled 'Travel through Sweden, by a Dutch Officer' (see the same issue, at 148).

[30] TNA, ADM 1/1660, Letters from Captains, Surnames C., 1811, nn. 579–800, 586, William Croft to John Barrow, 14 January 1811.

the ship was deployed to the Baltic. 'I should humbly submit to their Lordships the propriety of indulging them', he wrote, 'as they are in general the most effective men in the Venerable, and will materially assist her equipment, though little can be expected from them afterwards'.[31] Not only were Scandinavian sailors seen as valid hands for the fleet, then, but they were sometimes deemed better even than Britons.

A certain preference for other northern Europeans, above southerners, can also be detected. Matters of diplomacy may have intervened, but in 1811, when twenty-five prisoners at Dartmoor volunteered for the service, the Admiralty directed to take all the Germans, but send the Spaniards to a Spanish ship, and the Portuguese back to Portugal.[32] Similarly, when some prisoners protested that they had volunteered for the Marines, rather than the Navy, the orders were to send the Sicilians back to prison, and 'the Dutch if they please, but if not' to let them become Marines.[33] The fact that the services of the Italians were declined even in a moment of need is a clear indicator that the Navy used different measures for men from different places. Dutch prisoners of war who wanted to enter seem to have enjoyed some negotiating leeway: some of them in the *Hero* prison ship in January 1796 were willing to serve, 'provided that they can get Bounty'. This was granted to them, at a time when many prisoners, Dutch and otherwise, were denied it.[34] This was presumably because the prison officer stated that in his 'oppinion [*sic*] they would be a great benefit to the Service, a more orderly quiet set of Men I never knew'.[35]

The relative appreciation, or even appetite, of the British Navy for these men impacted on the recruitment of individuals. In one instance, however, a unique, large-scale incorporation took place, which owed more to systemic attitudes and similarities.

6.3   'Crews of Different Nations, Acting Never So Cordially Together in the Same Cause': Integrating a Fleet within the Fleet

Throughout the late seventeenth and eighteenth centuries, the relationship between Great Britain and the United Provinces was marked by

---

[31] TNA, ADM 1/2338, Letters from Captains, Surnames P., 1811, nn. 349–500, 376, Home Popham to J. W. Croker, 2 February 1811.

[32] TNA, ADM 12/147, Admiralty Digest 1810–11 – Part 3, 79.16, summary of letters from the Transport Board, 11 and 16 July 1811.

[33] TNA, ADM 12/147, Admiralty Digest 1810–11 – Part 3, 79.16, summary of letters from Admiral Young, 21 July, and from the Transport Board, 31 July 1811.

[34] See Section 7.3.1.

[35] ADM 1/3167, Letters from Lieutenants, Surnames T., 1793–6, 15, John Thomson to Evan Nepean, 30 January 1796.

contradictions: fierce commercial rivalry, and disputes over the neutrality of Dutch shipping, culminated in the four Anglo–Dutch wars, the last one in 1780–4. The two countries were also, however, 'natural allies', and for some time even joined together under William III of Orange.[36] If British relations with other states like the Two Sicilies were markedly unequal, military and commercial superiority over the United Provinces soon became clear, but was never blatant. Whilst the naval agreement of 1689 gave Britain the bulk of the commitment as well as the overall command of any joint naval force, the Dutch always contributed effectively in the Nine Years' War, even when British politicians obstructed operations.[37] Additionally, the diplomatic link between the two countries was cemented, in the seventeenth century, by shared religion.[38] A hundred years later this had long ceased to be such an important matter, yet it did survive as an element of the British political rhetoric of alliance.[39]

By the 1790s, British stereotypes and portrayals of the Dutch were mixed, but overall positive.[40] Graeme Callister has convincingly shown that a solid, almost blind faith in the Netherlands' ultimate strength and European importance persisted among British ministers, from Pitt and Grenville to Castlereagh, shaping foreign policy until the end of the Napoleonic Wars.[41] In particular, the Dutch naval 'potential', regardless of the situation of the United Provinces' and later Batavian fleet, was still respected and feared by the British public and politicians.[42] Moreover, despite the Netherlands' siding with the French, 'long-standing latent British opinion' held onto the idea of 'natural allies', and construed the Dutch as ultimately 'unwilling allies of France'.[43] One of the strongest links between Britain and the United Provinces was their 'tradition of joint operations' at sea, and cordial collaboration between the officers of the two navies.[44] This British respect towards Dutch naval capabilities and personnel played out in a very peculiar fashion.

---

[36] E. S. van Eyck van Heslinga, 'A Competitive Ally. The Delicate Balance of Naval Alliance and Maritime Competition between Great Britain and the Dutch Republic, 1674–1795', in G. J. A. Raven and N. A. M. Rodger (eds.), *Navies and Armies: The Anglo–Dutch Relationship in War and Peace 1688–1988* (Edinburgh: John Donald Publishers Ltd, 1990), 1–11; N. A. M. Rodger, 'The British View of the Functioning of the Anglo–Dutch Alliance, 1688–1795', ibid., 12–32; Graeme Callister, *War, Public Opinion and Policy in Britain, France and the Netherlands, 1785–1815* (Cham: Palgrave Macmillan, 2017), 231–6.

[37] Rodger, 'British View', 12–13.   [38] Ibid., 12.

[39] Callister, *War*, 220–1, 226, 247, 272–3.   [40] Ibid., 223–36.

[41] Ibid., 252–62, 275–7; Rodger, 'British View', 23–7.

[42] Callister, *War*, 228–30, 236, 259–61.   [43] Ibid., 231–6, 263–81.

[44] Rodger, 'British View', 27.

In 1795, after the United Provinces had been overtaken by the French and had become the Batavian Republic, the *stadhouder*, Prince Willem V of Orange, had gone into exile in Britain.[45] In the summer of 1799, a joint Anglo–Russian expedition sought to retake the Netherlands: on 30 August, the Dutch squadron in the Vlieter mutinied in favour of the Prince, with the complicity of several officers, and surrendered to the British Vice-Admiral Mitchell and the Hereditary Prince, Willem V's son.[46] Ultimately, the British invasion as a whole failed, and the Dutch soldiers who in the meantime had joined the Orangist side were organised into a 'Dutch Brigade' on the Isle of Wight, under the orders of the Hereditary Prince.[47] Little studied, however, is what occurred on the naval side, to the prizes taken at the Vlieter.[48] They were brought back to England, and on 11 March 1800, a convention was signed between the British government and the Prince of Orange, containing provisions for four of them to be taken into the British service, entirely manned and officered by loyalist Dutchmen.[49] The final layout of the squadron can be seen in **Table 6.1**.

This solution had not been straightforward to achieve. In September 1799, under pressure from the Prince of Orange, British and Dutch

---

[45] G. J. Schutte, 'Willem IV en Willem V', in C. A. Tamse (ed.), *Nassau en Oranje in de Nederlandse geschiedenis* (Alphen aan den Rijn: A. W. Sijthoff, 1979), 187–228, at 203–5; 'Willem V', in P. C. Molhuysen and P. J. Blok (eds.), *Nieuw Nederlandsch biografisch woordenboek*, 10 vols. (Leiden: A. W. Sijthoff, 1911), I, 1556–60, at 1558–9.

[46] See, for example, E. Walsh, *A Narrative of the Expedition to Holland, in the Autumn of the Year 1799* (London: G. G. and J. Robinson, 1800), 32–5, 95–106; Simon Schama, *Patriots and Liberators: Revolution in the Netherlands 1780–1813*, 2nd ed. (London: Fontana Press, 1992), 393–4; Piers Mackesy, *Statesmen at War: The Strategy of Overthrow 1798–1799* (London and New York: Longman, 1974), 201–2; Philip Ball, *A Waste of Blood and Treasure. The 1799 Anglo-Russian Invasion of the Netherlands* (Barnsley: Pen & Sword, 2017), 49–55; Historical Manuscripts Commission, *Report on the Manuscripts of J. B. Fortescue, Esq., Preserved at Dropmore*, 10 vols. (London: His Majesty's Stationery Office, 1892–1927), V, 338–41, 344–5, 347.

[47] J. G. Kikkert, *Geld, macht & eer: Willem I, Koning der Nederlanders en Belgen 1772–1843* (Utrecht: Scheffers, 1995), 43.

[48] The sole, brief exception that I could find is a summary in Dorothea Josephine Antoinette van Breda Vriesman, *In woelig vaarwater: Marineofficieren in de jaren 1779–1802* (Amsterdam: De Bataafsche Leeuw, 1998), 169–71. Since I wrote this chapter, a short note has also appeared, presenting a copy of one of van Lelyveld's reports that is preserved in the UK National Archives: Nicholas Blake, 'The Complements of Four Dutch Ships Taken at the Texel in 1799', *The Mariner's Mirror* 106:3 (2020), 349–55.

[49] 39 & 40 Geo. III c. 100. For the various drafts of the Convention, see Koninklijk Huisarchief, The Hague [henceforth KH], Willem V A 31 Inv.nr. 2267, Stukken betreffende Nederlandse troepen en marineschepen in Engelse dienst, 1799–1800; TNA, ADM 1/4183, Admiralty, Letters from Secretaries of State, January–April 1800; George Hammond to Evan Nepean, 17 February 1800 and enclosures; 13 March 1800 and enclosures.

Table 6.1. *Dutch ships in the British service, 1800–1803*[1]

Ship name	Guns	Captain	Intended complement
Gelderland	68 (ship of the line)	Ian Tulleken (2nd Johan Christian Hellemann, *until 5 June 1801*)	450
Amphitrite	44 (frigate)	Job. Seaburne May	350
Ambuscade	36 (frigate)	Willem Van Voss	250
Galathé	18 (sloop)	Frans. Thomas Van Braam *From 19 February 1801:* Willem August van Spengler	100

[1] Source: KH, Willem V A 31 Inv.nr. 2271, Stukken betreffende de Nederlandse marineschepen en hun bemanningen in Engeland en de daarbij behorende briefwisseling tussen Willem V en B.P. van Lelyveld, commissaris van de prins voor het contact met de Engelse overheid, 1796, 1800–2, B. P. van Lelyveld to Evan Nepean, 29 April 1800; B. P. van Lelyveld to the Prince of Orange, 8 December 1800, 25 February 1801; Willem V A 31 Inv.nr. 2272, Stukken betreffende de Nederlandse marineschepen en hun bemanningen in Engeland en de daarbij behorende briefwisseling tussen Willem V en B.P. van Lelyveld, commissaris van de prins voor het contact met de Engelse overheid, 1803–4, J. C. Hellemann to B. P. van Lelyveld, 5 June 1801.

politicians recognised that immediately and openly incorporating the surrendered fleet into the British service would have alienated Orangist supporters in the Batavian Republic. Hendrik Fagel, ex-Greffier (secretary) of the Dutch States General, wrote to Lord Grenville, then British Foreign Secretary, urging that 'the appearance' be 'kept up' of the squadron 'being really at the Prince of Orange's disposition, and ready to be restored, in its present state, to the old and lawful government of the United Provinces as soon as it will be re-established' – an event that was then supposed to be in the near future.[50] As Fagel clarified, Willem was led to this demand more 'from the fear he really entertained of the impression the thing would produce in Holland, than from any desire of seeing these ships at his disposal'.[51] Indeed, when the following year it seemed that the Dutch Brigade would be deployed in Portugal, serving purely British interests, this attracted sneering remarks in the Batavian press.[52] Whilst Pitt wanted to use the ships as transports, both Lord Spencer and Henry Dundas, the First Lord of the Admiralty and the War Secretary, argued that the most

[50] H. Fagel to Lord Grenville, 6 September 1799, in *Manuscripts of J. B. Fortescue*, V, 362–3.
[51] H. Fagel to Lord Grenville, 7 September 1799, in *Manuscripts of J. B. Fortescue*, V, 372–3.
[52] Kikkert, *Geld*, 43.

feasible plan was to simply put them in ordinary, out of service. As Dundas pointed out, any use made of them by Britain could have been misconstrued, damaging the Orangist cause.[53] The men indispensable for upkeep could be kept aboard, and the others 'mixed in our ships... and thereby rendered useful to the public service'.[54] After long negotiations, however, the plan finally deemed to appease all sides was the compromise of a nominally Dutch but practically British squadron.

This arrangement was the product of diplomacy rather than military thinking, as both parties recognised: 'surely', as the Dutch administrator wrote, 'the exalted and gigantic Navy of great-Britain could stand in nò [sic] need of any subsidiary Ships of War'.[55] It was as hybrid and cumbersome a settlement as foreign regiments in the Army, but rather unusual for the senior service. The four ships sailed not under the Royal Navy's flag, but under that of the Prince of Orange.[56] This was immediately hoisted upon their surrender at the Vlieter.[57] They carried no British pennant aboard: to celebrate George III's birthday, in June 1800, Captain van Braam decided to fly the British colours, but, in order to do so, he had to borrow some Union Jacks from Vice-Admiral Graeme's squadron, requesting at least one per ship.[58] The Dutch squadron was also to be deployed under fairly restricted terms: 'in the European seas only, and for the Advantage of the common cause', as long as the war lasted or until the House of Orange was reinstated in the United Provinces.[59] Willem, pointing out that some places in the Mediterranean, like Venice, Trieste, Constantinople, and Crimea [sic], were still 'European' waters, but actually further than the American islands in terms of navigation time, even tried to prevent Dutch service beyond Gibraltar.[60] Yet these vessels were under the orders of the British

---

[53] Earl Spencer to Lord Grenville, 7 September 1799, and Henry Dundas to Lord Grenville, 10 September 1799, in *Manuscripts of J. B. Fortescue*, V, 376, 383.

[54] Henry Dundas to Lord Grenville, 10 September 1799, in *Manuscripts of J. B. Fortescue*, V, 383.

[55] KH, 2272, Nederlandse marineschepen en hun bemanningen, B. P. van Lelyveld to Evan Nepean, 16 April 1802, enclosed Pro Memoria, f. 4.

[56] [J. de Vaandrig Brauw], *Mijne emigratie in Duitschland, Engeland en Ierland, in de jaren 1799–1802* (Utrecht: N. van der Monde, 1837), 96.

[57] Vice-Admiral Mitchell to Evan Nepean, 31 August 1799 and enclosures, *Manuscripts of J. B. Fortescue*, V, 339–40.

[58] KH, 2271, Nederlandse marineschepen en hun bemanningen, F. T. van Braam to B. P. van Lelyveld, 9 June 1800, including copy of F. T. van Braam to Vice Admiral Graeme, 3 June 1800.

[59] TNA, ADM 1/4183, Admiralty, Letters from Secretaries of State, January–April 1800, George Hammond to Evan Nepean, 17 February 1800 and enclosures.

[60] KH, 2267, Nederlandse troepen en marineschepen, 'Considerations sur le projet de Capitulation', Prince of Orange, 19 December 1799.

Admiralty. In breach of the rules relative to aliens, all Dutch officers received commissions both from the Prince of Orange, nominally Admiral-General of the United Provinces, and from the British Crown.[61] The four ships were subject to the British Articles of War, which were specially translated and printed in Dutch to be displayed aboard.[62]

This is emblematic of the whole operation, which was an administrative and cultural translation, and an unprecedented experiment in the Royal Navy. The exiled Dutch officials were faced with the daunting task of creating from scratch a new hybrid system, in a foreign country, and with a chronic absence of resources. As remarked by B. P. van Lelyveld, the Prince of Orange's main advisor on the matter, it was nearly impossible to improvise a central organisation and authority such as those once provided by the Amsterdam Admiralty: the lack of personnel, expertise, and structure would cause endless 'difficulties and disagreements', so the best solution was for the British government to take these ships under its administrative wing.[63] A 'middle way' was suggested between the two systems: the crews' 'Wages and Allowances were to be computed according to the Ancient Dutch regulations', but paid by the British government, periodically, via a representative of the Prince of Orange.[64] This required setting a conversion rate between the Dutch and British currencies, eleven guilders (Dutch florins) to the pound.[65] Calculating even an average 'Dutch' wage was not straightforward, as each of the five pre-1795 Admiralties had maintained slightly different practices.[66] Victualling, it was eventually decided, was also to be administered directly by the British, as with any other ship in the Royal Navy.[67] All this was achieved through the mediation of the London 'House of Commerce' Donaldson, Glenny and May: in a 'peculiarly fortunate' turn of events, May happened to have spent many years working for the Amsterdam Board of Admiralty, so he knew both navies in depth. This resulted in a

---

[61] KH, 2271, Nederlandse marineschepen en hun bemanningen, B. P. van Lelyveld to Evan Nepean, 13 June 1800; 39 & 40 Geo. III c. 100. See also Sections 2.1 and 2.3.

[62] 39 & 40 Geo. III c. 100 § iv.

[63] KH, 2271, Nederlandse marineschepen en hun bemanningen, B. P. van Lelyveld to the Prince of Orange, 23 March 1800.

[64] Ibid., B. P. van Lelyveld to Evan Nepean, 28 May 1800.

[65] KH, 2272, Nederlandse marineschepen en hun bemanningen, B. P. van Lelyveld to Sir Andrew Snape Hammond, 18 June 1801, enclosed Pro Memoria, f. 13.

[66] Ibid., B. P. van Lelyveld to Sir Andrew Snape Hammond, 18 June 1801, enclosed Pro Memoria, ff. 4–5.

[67] KH, 2271, Nederlandse marineschepen en hun bemanningen, B. P. van Lelyveld to Evan Nepean, 28 May 1800.

serendipitous 'combination of Interest, knowledge, Information and good-will'.[68]

Both intermediaries and up-to-date information were indispensable ingredients if the project was to succeed. Among the correspondence of Willem V for the year 1799, there survives an extremely detailed memorandum on the organisation of the British Navy, including minute particulars on rates of pay, allowances, rules, and procedures.[69] This thorough research likely formed the basis for the very insightful and well-informed remarks which, after consultation with the Prince, van Lelyveld posed to the British Admiralty in April 1800. He requested that the Dutch ships be put 'upon the Same footing' as the British on matters such as exemptions from excise on spirits and tobacco, and asked what the provisions would be for Dutch sailors 'maimed' in the service, or deserting to Royal Navy ships and vice versa.[70] His work was impressively thorough, but he still felt the need to justify himself for potential omissions: 'in a course of business so novel to me', he wrote to the Comptroller of the Navy in 1801, 'and in circumstances so singular, I beg leave to claim the privilege of a Stranger'.[71]

Certain elements, inevitably, required adjustment. For example, unlike their British colleagues, Dutch officers in the four ships were not entitled to half pay; they were also dispensed from the requirements of the Test Acts, and as such free to profess the 'Popish Religion'.[72] The Prince of Orange, in issuing them commissions for service in the British Navy, had to ensure that their true level of seniority would not be misrepresented: the Royal Navy lacked the rank of '*Captain luijtenant* [*sic*]', or the concept of 'second captain' aboard a ship of the line.[73] A system of 'working equivalences' then had to be introduced, and, as is often the case, its political and administrative stakes failed to satisfy all

---

[68] TNA, ADM 1/4183, Admiralty, Letters from Secretaries of State, January–April 1800, B. P. van Lelyveld to the Prince of Orange, 21 April 1800; KH, 2267, Nederlandse troepen en marineschepen, Prince of Orange to [Evan Nepean?], 30 May 1800.

[69] KH, Willem V A 31 Inv.nr. 2241, Notities over de organisatie en de staat van de Engelse marine, 1799.

[70] KH, 2271, Nederlandse marineschepen en hun bemanningen, B. P. van Lelyveld to Evan Nepean, 29 April 1800, enclosed Pro Memoria, f. 2.

[71] KH, 2272, Nederlandse marineschepen en hun bemanningen, B. P. van Lelyveld to Sir Andrew Snape Hammond, 18 June 1801.

[72] 39 & 40 Geo. III c. 100 § i.

[73] KH, 2271, Nederlandse marineschepen en hun bemanningen, Prince of Orange to B. P. van Lelyveld, 6 December 1800; B. P. van Lelyveld to the Prince of Orange, 8 December 1800; B. P. van Lelyveld to Evan Nepean, 3 January 1801; 2272, Nederlandse marineschepen en hun bemanningen, B. P. van Lelyveld to Evan Nepean, 11 April 1801.

parties.[74] Because the British Admiralty was unable to officialise his position as second captain aboard the *Gelderland*, J. C. Hellemann found himself in what he deemed an unfair situation, and bluntly resigned.[75] Captains in the Dutch Navy had drawn profits from their being responsible for their own ship's victualling: this perk was no longer possible under the British system. Captains and lieutenants under the Dutch Admiralties also had a victualling allowance on top of their pay, drawn from said victualling profits; surgeons charged an extra to crews for their service. Neither of these perks was available in the British Navy, so this required further wage adaptations.[76] Overall, the Dutch captains in particular were now much worse off than they had been in their country's pre-revolutionary service, but their situation was carefully assessed and negotiated to be at least equivalent to that of British colleagues.[77]

The most complicated case was perhaps that of the purser (the shipboard warrant officer in charge of supplies): he was 'a Person, unknown under the Dutch Regulations', so he was introduced and rated the British way.[78] Van Lelyveld and the Prince of Orange worried that the entrepreneurial nature of the role, with profits often delayed by years, made it difficult to manage for any of the Dutch émigrés. Albeit unsuccessfully, they asked for the purser to be replaced by a simple distributor of victuals, to free the Dutch officers from 'too complex and vast a responsibility for people in their position'.[79] This illustrates well how some of the most important adjustments required were connected to the forms of refugee and immigrant displacement that we will explore in Part III of this book. On 27 June 1800, discussing the arrear daily allowances that the government was to pay to the Dutch officers, despite the absence of vouchers, van Lelyveld requested the British

[74] For a discussion of these processes of state-driven categorisation and comparison, see Morieux, 'Indigenous Comparisons', 55, 59–60, 64–74.

[75] KH, 2272, Nederlandse marineschepen en hun bemanningen, Prince of Orange to B. P. van Lelyveld, 27 May 1801 and enclosures; 9 June 1801 and enclosures; van Lelyveld to the Prince of Orange, 29 May 1801; 18 June 1801 and enclosures; 22 June 1801 and enclosures.

[76] KH, 2271, Nederlandse marineschepen en hun bemanningen, B. P. van Lelyveld to Evan Nepean, 'Pro Memoria about the Enclosed Pay Lists', 13 June 1800.

[77] Ibid., B. P. van Lelyveld to Evan Nepean, 28 May 1800; TNA, ADM 1/4183, Admiralty, Letters from Secretaries of State, January–April 1800, B. P. van Lelyveld to the Prince of Orange, 21 April 1800.

[78] KH, 2271, Nederlandse marineschepen en hun bemanningen, B. P. van Lelyveld to Nepean, 13 June 1800.

[79] Ibid., B. P. van Lelyveld to the Prince of Orange, 1 August 1800: '*une responsabilité trop compliquée et trop étendue, pour des gens situes* [sic] *comme Eux*'.

to take into consideration, that foreign Officers, situated as those Gentlemen were; having come over in a hurry; destitute of every thing from the nature of the circumstances that brought them here; – unacquainted with the Country, unknown; – and from the uncertainty of their destination, unable to make any arrangements otherwise than from one day to another, can not well, it is presumed, be assimilated to Gentlemen in His Majesty's Service, called up and remaining under orders.[80]

Summoned by the Prince of Orange, they had all travelled across various parts of Europe to come to serve (and later, in some cases, fetch their families from Holland), and they often had no written orders or receipts for these expenses.[81] They were 'Strangers', and 'no particular regulation can apply to a case, out of the common Course', van Lelyveld insisted with the British Admiralty almost ten months later, when the accounts still remained unsettled.[82]

Next to these adjustments, there were occasional difficulties pertaining to social interactions. One problem was the language of communications: van Lelyveld wrote fluently in Dutch, French, and English, and other Dutch officers used French, too, but not so the British: Admiral Graeme had to request Captain van Braam to translate Dutch documents into English for him.[83] We saw that linguistic difference was likely easily bridged when it came to the practical management of a ship, and seamen's oral day-to-day interactions; however, this was not the case for complex written texts, especially requiring diplomatic finesse.[84] Different traditions and expectations in the two services were also a potential source of discontent, which had to be carefully prevented. The reason why Dutch captains' wages had been reduced to align with those of their British peers was that they were all 'on the same Service', and any such difference 'might perhaps create some dissatisfaction' on the part of British colleagues.[85] The Dutch officers understood the situation and accepted the pay cut, although it was a heavy one for exiled and impoverished family men.[86] On the other hand, Dutch lower-deck seamen saw their conditions improved, again for diplomatic reasons: given that the

---

[80] Ibid., B. P. van Lelyveld to Sir Andrew Snape Hammond, Navy Office, 27 June 1800. See also: B. P. van Lelyveld to Sir Andrew Snape Hammond, 18 June 1801, enclosed Pro Memoria, f. 6.

[81] Ibid., B. P. van Lelyveld to Sir Andrew Snape Hammond, Navy Office, 27 June 1800, and enclosures.

[82] Ibid., B. P. van Lelyveld to Evan Nepean, 11 April 1801.

[83] Ibid., Vice Admiral Graeme to Captain van Braam, 3 June 1800.

[84] On this distinction, see Dursteler, 'Speaking in Tongues', 75–6.

[85] KH, 2271, Nederlandse marineschepen en hun bemanningen, B. P. van Lelyveld to Evan Nepean, 28 May 1800.

[86] TNA, ADM 1/4183, Admiralty, Letters from Secretaries of State, January–April 1800, B. P. van Lelyveld to the Prince of Orange, 21 April 1800.

ships were 'to have a constant intercourse with those of His Majesty', van Lelyveld pointed out,

it will be hardly possible to restrain the Common Sailor in his Victuals and Beverage to the old Dutch fare; which is scantier than the fare of an English Seaman, – but it may be expedient to indulge him sometimes, in order to prevent jealousies and animosities betwixt Crews of different Nations, tho' acting never so cordially together in the same Cause.[87]

As will be discussed in Chapter 7, differentials in salary and conditions of service could influence the men's perception of each navy as an employer. These differentials were never more apparent than when two navies were joined together.

The point causing most difficulties, in any case, was manning. There were some problems with deserters and stragglers: in February 1800, previous to the signing of the convention, some men from the captured ships, Dutch and of other origins, were reported as 'strolling about the coast' without documents; they had to be 'apprehended' and returned to their vessels.[88] However, the overall perception of Dutch recruits among British politicians was still positive. In October 1800, William Huskisson, Under-Secretary of State for War, found that the Hereditary Prince's soldiers on the Isle of Wight were 'almost the finest troops he ever saw, and exceedingly correct and exemplary in their behaviour'.[89] Also owing to the officers' work, Dutch seamen aboard all captured ships remained loyal, despite their pay and provisions being delayed for over six months after their surrender, which left them in miserable conditions.[90] The main problem was not the reliability but the scarcity of men.

The ships were manned with Dutchmen, some of them from the original Vlieter crews, some from prisons of war, 'as far as their loyal dispositions for the Common Cause would be known', and others, the plan initially stated, to be recruited on the continent.[91] A bounty was deemed

---

[87] TNA, ADM 1/4183, Admiralty, Letters from Secretaries of State, January–April 1800, B. P. van Lelyveld to the Prince of Orange, 21 April 1800.

[88] Ibid., Alien Office to Evan Nepean, 26 February 1800.

[89] Henry Dundas to Lord Grenville, 25 October 1800, in *Manuscripts of J. B. Fortescue*, VI, 361.

[90] KH, 2271, Nederlandse marineschepen en hun bemanningen, B. P. van Lelyveld to Evan Nepean, 29 April 1800, enclosed Pro Memoria, ff. 10–11; 2 September 1800, enclosure B and Pro Memoria; TNA, ADM 1/4183, Admiralty, Letters from Secretaries of State, January–April 1800, Grenville to the Lords Commissioners of the Admiralty, 1 March 1800, and attachments.

[91] TNA, ADM 1/815, Letters from Commanders-in-Chief, Plymouth, 1800, 608, Thomas Pasley to Evan Nepean, 9 October 1800; ADM 1/4183, Admiralty, Letters from Secretaries of State, January–April 1800, B. P. van Lelyveld to the Prince of Orange, 21 April 1800.

indispensable and provisionally set at a maximum of £15: van Lelyveld (wrongly, according to a marginal comment) believed that British bounties were then over twenty guineas, and emphasised that 'no competition can, nor ought, to take place' with the Royal Navy's own recruitment.[92] Ultimately, the idea of recruiting abroad was dismissed as too costly and uncertain, and the men who were in the captured ships were a 'Motley Crew', 'a great many... unfit, totally unfit for the Service', so prisoners became a significant resource, as a last resort.[93] The men thus procured proved loyal, even if van Lelyveld had initially seen their recruitment as an 'experiment', and the Dutch officers had opposed it.[94] However, the ships still needed solid Marine contingents, and the only way in which this could be achieved, despite the Prince's initial reluctance, was by transferring aboard 177 soldiers and officers taken from his army regiments on the Isle of Wight.[95] Accepting British men, van Lelyveld noted, was out of the question, because it would mean that the Prince was unable to hold up his part of the agreement with Britain.[96]

This concern with what the British officials would think reflected a more general problem: several glitches affected the operation, mainly because the British service remained the clear priority in the eyes of the Admiralty, and the Dutch were most obviously the junior partner. Van Lelyveld was repeatedly frustrated by Evan Nepean and the Board of Admiralty's delay in replying to his messages and fulfilling their side of the agreement.[97] In turn, he had to be very careful not to compromise the goodwill of the British government, on which the Prince had to rely. In October 1800, the instructions given to the Dutch officer in charge of recruitment were not to take any British subjects, even if they volunteered, and in general not to 'interfere in the least with any thing relating to His Majesty's more immediate Service'.[98] Van Lelyveld repeated multiple times that the ships were in need of repairs before they could go to sea, in particular the *Ambuscade*, 'which, if longer neglected, will be

---

[92] TNA, ADM 1/4183, Admiralty, Letters from Secretaries of State, January–April 1800, B. P. van Lelyveld to the Prince of Orange, 21 April 1800.

[93] KH, 2272, Nederlandse marineschepen en hun bemanningen, B. P. van Lelyveld to Sir Andrew Snape Hammond, 17 July 1802, enclosed Pro Memoria, ff. 14–16.

[94] Ibid., ff. 15–18.

[95] KH, 2272, Nederlandse marineschepen en hun bemanningen, B. P. van Lelyveld to the Prince of Orange, 22 June 1800, 22 July 1800 and enclosures, 30 July 1800; B. P. van Lelyveld to Donaldson, Glenny and May, 27 August 1800.

[96] Ibid., B. P. van Lelyveld to the Prince of Orange, 6 and 22 June 1800.

[97] Ibid., B. P. van Lelyveld to the Prince of Orange, 27 July 1800; KH, 2272, Nederlandse marineschepen en hun bemanningen, B. P. van Lelyveld to the Prince of Orange, 3 August 1801.

[98] KH, 2271, Nederlandse marineschepen en hun bemanningen, B. P. van Lelyveld to Capt. Lt. Mackay, 20 October 1800.

lost for the Service', and the *Gelderland*.[99] On 9 July 1801, the *Ambuscade* suddenly sank, just after leaving Sheerness.[100] Subsequent surveys revealed that the likely cause was the fact that the anchor hawse holes were placed too low: the Dutch Captain Van Voss, in fact supported by the Navy Board, had repeatedly insisted on their modification, but the Admiralty had refused.[101] Only after the disaster, when the ship was raised again, were the adjustments eventually authorised.[102] In short, the formal separation of these ships within the Navy resulted in a phenomenon that normally did not occur in the case of non-British men assimilated individually: the Dutch ships were sidelined and treated as a low priority by comparison with the rest of the fleet.

Despite all these difficulties, however, the incorporation of Dutch vessels into the Royal Navy, an incredibly complex operation, was completed relatively smoothly. Arguably, this demonstrates the overall similarity of the two systems, in terms of administrative principles, hierarchies, and values, and the mutual understanding among British and Dutch personnel. By way of comparison, we can notice how a similar attempt by the French fleet to employ two fully Dano–Norwegian crews, in 1808, ended in disastrous disagreement.[103] In May 1801, van Lelyveld thanked Nepean for the 'readiness', 'kindness', and 'most liberal manner' with which all the Dutch commanders had been treated 'throughout' by British Admiralty personnel and officers.[104] The squadron was eventually disbanded with the Peace of Amiens, and looking back van Lelyveld's assessment of the operation was positive. Considering the 'unfortunate auspices' under which it had begun, including the prolonged state of abandonment of the ships, the total lack of regulations, 'and a thousand small troubles of all kinds', he concluded that 'there are grounds to congratulate ourselves that this business was concluded so happily – without dissatisfaction, without the least smudge, without the smallest scandal'.[105] He was of course selectively forgetting the interminable

---

[99] See, for example, ibid., B. P. van Lelyveld to Evan Nepean, Pro Memoria, 20 October 1800.

[100] KH, 2272, Nederlandse marineschepen en hun bemanningen, Prince of Orange to B. P. van Lelyveld, 11 July 1801; van Lelyveld to the Prince of Orange, 13 July 1801; Evan Nepean to van Lelyveld, 10 July 1801 and enclosure; [Brauw], *Mijne emigratie*, 96.

[101] KH, 2272, Nederlandse marineschepen en hun bemanningen, B. P. van Lelyveld to the Prince of Orange, 3 August 1801, and enclosures.

[102] Ibid., B. P. van Lelyveld to the Prince of Orange, 11 August 1801.

[103] Glenthøj and Ottosen, *Experiences of War*, 103–4.

[104] KH, 2272, Nederlandse marineschepen en hun bemanningen, B. P. van Lelyveld to Evan Nepean, 25 May 1801.

[105] Ibid., B. P. van Lelyveld to the Prince of Orange, 24 May 1802: '*Quand je considére* [sic], *Monsigneur, sous quels auspices malheureux ce petit armement a commencé, – l'abandon complet où il a été tenu pendant un temps considérable, – le manque absolu de touts*

bureaucratic conundrums, British resistance, and officers' complaints, including the death threats he had received in the winter of 1802 from a disgruntled and turbulent lieutenant.[106] His general feeling, however, was one of achievement. The initial Act of Parliament specified that the Dutch officers were not entitled to half pay, but he had absolutely no difficulties in obtaining pensions for them from the Admiralty and the Prime Minister, as a 'favour'.[107] When the peace was signed, the situation in the Batavian Republic was not as was originally hoped, and it was now impossible to restore the government of the Prince with his ships.[108] These pensions thus became the last of 'an uninterrupted Series of kind and indulgent offices' the Dutch had received 'from the very day they arrived in this Country', as van Lelyveld told Nepean, conveying to him the Princess of Orange's 'Personal thanks'.[109]

Typically, the bureaucracy of the British Admiralty, disapproving of the 'mode' of payment that had been agreed, meant that these pensions could only be first issued over a year later.[110] The Admiralty also refused to reimburse expenses related to recruitment and unserviceable men, and van Lelyveld eventually had to go directly to the government, above the Board's heads, to obtain them.[111] Thus, the business was concluded, almost two years after the ships had been paid off. It had required rivers of ink, information-gathering, good communication, and accommodations and flexibility on both sides. Yet it had, somehow, succeeded. Even when contingent political will was not lacking, age-old administrative barriers stood in the way of the merger of two different states' departments. Long-standing traditions and 'ways of doing' were deeply engrained at the heart of each Navy and state and, therefore, in the minds of their members. The only thing that could help in overcoming these obstacles was a pre-existing, if imperfect, similarity in mindset and organisation, which minimised the need for translation and compromise. Van Lelyveld's middle way was just about close enough to either side to work.

---

règlements, – et mille petits embarras de tout genre : il y a lieu de se féliciter que cette affaire s'est terminée si heureusement, – sans mécontentement, sans la moindre éclaboussure, sans le plus petit scandale.'

[106] Ibid., B. P. van Lelyveld to the Prince of Orange, 9 April 1802 and enclosures.
[107] Ibid., B. P. van Lelyveld to the Prince of Orange, 24 May, 4 June 1802; to Evan Nepean, 16 April 1802 and enclosures, 23 April 1802, 2 June 1802 and enclosures; to the Earl of St. Vincent, 2 June 1802.
[108] Ibid., B. P. van Lelyveld to Evan Nepean, 16 April 1802 and enclosed Pro Memoria, ff. 9–11.
[109] Ibid., B. P. van Lelyveld to Evan Nepean, 23 April 1802.
[110] Ibid., B. P. van Lelyveld to the Princess of Orange, 23 December 1803.
[111] Ibid., B. P. van Lelyveld to the Prince of Orange, 28 March 1804 and enclosures.

6.4   Training a Rival 'Hardy Race'

One further nuance needs to be considered. Beyond the Admiralty, and in British public opinion at large, the recruitment of northern European seamen was not necessarily uncontroversial. We have seen the anxieties that could be caused by a supposed 'foreigner' being able to pass as 'British', camouflaging himself through his English fluency. This skill was particularly common among Nordic sailors, and, I have argued, one of the factors making them recruits of choice for the British Navy. Yet the very qualities that made a man a desirable entry – cultural similarity, professional competence, hard-working ethos, and loyalty – could turn him into a danger, and paradoxically provoke fears and jealousies which other more despised groups, like Mediterranean men or Lascars, did not.

Mercantile interests in the British Parliament campaigned incessantly, throughout the wars, against the liberal use of foreign shipping and seamen. This increased towards the end of the period, with the introduction of the license trade. Northerners were a specific target. In 1811, a petition from the traders of Kingston upon Hull reminded the Commons that 'Naval Superiority' was crucial to Britain's survival, and employing foreigners compromised it: 'the almost entire destruction of the Maritime Trade of France', it noted,

and the effeminate character of the Mediterranean Seamen, have hitherto disabled that Government from meeting our Navies on the Ocean with any chance of success; but in the North, and on the Coasts of the Baltic, a hardy race is trained, whose increasing numbers, in the present state of Europe, we cannot contemplate with indifference. (…) this country chiefly furnishes the means of their support, and enables them to pursue an avocation, which familiarizes them with toil and danger; an accurate knowledge of our Coasts, and of all the principal Ports of the Kingdom, thence becomes an object of easy attainment.[112]

A very similar note was struck the following year by Scarborough ship-owners. They noted the predominance of flags of 'Danes, Swedes, Russians, and other northern states' in British ports, accompanied by 'the rapid improvement in the appearance and skill of foreign seamen': 'a hardy and able race of mariners is thus reared'.[113] They were echoed, in

---

[112] 'Copy of the MEMORIAL against the LICENCE TRADE, presented by the Merchants and Ship Owners of the Town of *Kingston upon Hull*, to the Board of Trade', 4 April 1811, p. 2, in *Papers Relating to the Licence Trade, House of Commons Papers* n. 83, 1812 https://parlipapers.proquest.com/parlipapers.

[113] Hansard, House of Commons, vol. 22, 'Petitions from Scarborough – and Aberdeen, respecting Commercial Licences', 4 May 1812, cc. 1152–5 https://api.parliament.uk/historic-hansard/commons/1812/may/04/petitions-from-scarborough-and-aberdeen.

almost identical words, by the shipping interest of South Shields.[114] This ominous warning was only made plausible by the very respect that British elites had for northern European seamen – culturally, professionally, and, the choice of wording shows, even in gendered racial terms. The condemnation of 'effeminacy' manifested itself in British public discourse, throughout the century, not only in negative depictions of other countries (chiefly Catholic), but also as self-criticism, and a deep fear of national insufficiency and failure.[115] Mediterranean sailors could be seen as weaker, inferior, and thus less desirable recruits; however, on the stage of international competition, it was also imperative not to become like them, being overpowered by other more virile races.

6.5   Conclusion

From the point of view of the wartime Navy, seamen from northern Europe were, more so than their southern European colleagues, an intrinsically valuable commodity. They often hailed from a maritime ecosystem sharing multiple similarities and neighbourly ties with the British and were, in general, a highly skilled and reliable workforce. Scandinavians were particularly appreciated for their individual qualities, but joint operational traditions and administrative affinity also facilitated the employment of Dutchmen, as shown by the case of the Vlieter squadron.

High esteem could definitely turn into rivalry, or even fear, especially in the eyes of civilian interests, concerned about commercial and national competition, rather than immediate military utility. The paradox that immigrant labourers perceived as low-skilled and lazy are despised, and those perceived as highly skilled and industrious cause anxieties – both forms of 'moral panic' –[118] applied to British society's perceptions of foreign sailors during the French Wars. The Navy, however, had little time for either attitude, at least as long as the war

---

[114] Hansard, House of Commons, vol. 23, 'Petitions from the Merchants of Dunfermline and Paisley, and the Ship Owners of South Shields, respecting the Orders in Council', 20 May 1812, cc. 232–9, at 236–8 https://parlipapers.proquest.com/parlipapers.

[115] Wilson, *Sense of the People*, 185–205.

[116] For an application of the theory of moral panics to immigration, see Ian Fitzgerald and Rafal Smoczynski, 'Anti-Polish Migrant Moral Panic in the UK: Rethinking Employment Insecurities and Moral Regulation', *Sociologický Časopis / Czech Sociological Review* 51:3 (2015), 339–61. On moral panics in eighteenth-century England, see David Lemmings, 'Introduction: Law and Order, Moral Panics, and Early Modern England', in David Lemmings and Claire Walker (eds.), *Moral Panics, the Media and the Law in Early Modern England* (Basingstoke: Palgrave Macmillan, 2009), 1–21.

raged: making the most of the manpower available required both finding usefulness where stereotypes would have none, and seeking out the
very best sailors, regardless of future consequences. We shall explore
some of those consequences in the conclusion of the book, but before
then Chapter 7 will temporarily leave aside the Navy's perspective, to
turn instead to that of the sailors.

Part III

Displacement

7   Mercenaries, Migrants, and Refugees
Navy Crews as 'Motley Crews'

We can return, now, to that most general definition of a foreigner with which we started – a man 'of another country' – and in doing so consider *his* view. Why would a man 'of another country' come to find himself in the British Navy?

That is, we shall see, a badly formulated question. If anything, we should ask why he would not, given the conditions of the international employment market, and the convenient and coerced mobilities of wartime. Migrant workers and 'mercenaries' were a large group in the eighteenth-century maritime world, which also overflowed with refugees and displaced persons – ranging from political émigrés to war prisoners, from military and labour 'deserters' to individuals who had been dragged into, or had escaped, enslavement.[1] Yet we cannot say that our 'foreigner' here dissolves into a meaningless abstraction, fully jumbled into motley naval crews. There were specific opportunities and challenges that stemmed from migration and displacement, and they highlight the material core of what being 'of another country' meant – once the slippery legal and cultural layers of meaning that were superimposed on that are finally stripped away. If we define a 'foreigner' socially and through mobility, as a 'stranger', an 'outsider', and a 'migrant', rather than simply by original birthplace, state classifications, or cultural categories, we find, at last, a substantial practical difference between 'foreigners' and 'British' seamen. I stress here not only extraneousness, as Simona Cerutti does in her study of early modern continental contexts, but also, explicitly, geographical provenance.[2] 'Foreignness by provenance' was contingent, situational,

---

[1] See, for example, van Lottum, 'Some Thoughts'; idem, *Across the North Sea*; Kirsty Carpenter and Philip Mansel (eds.), *The French Émigrés in Europe and the Struggle against Revolution, 1789–1814* (Basingstoke: Macmillan Press Ltd, 1999); Renaud Morieux, *The Society of Prisoners: Anglo–French Wars and Incarceration in the Eighteenth Century* (Oxford: Oxford University Press, 2019); Matthias Van Rossum and Jeannette Kamp (eds.), *Desertion in the Early Modern World a Comparative History* (New York: Bloomsbury Academic, 2016).
[2] Cerutti, *Étrangers*.

and positional. It was provoked not simply or primarily by labels or perceptions, but by the physical travel distance from 'home' and domicile – a situation of *dis*-placement, which had social, bureaucratic, and economic effects of its own.

As with other forms of difference, the efficient machinery of the Navy often actively tried to minimise the impact of displacement, but in this case it met with greater, sometimes insoluble, difficulties. This is because the parameters and implications of geographical distance and displacement were not set by the state, like legal classifications, or intrinsically malleable, like cultural typologies and preconceptions: they were a concrete, physical reality, over which even the state had limited power and control. Mobility and displacement characterised, to some extent, the experience of each and every naval sailor. However, the Navy's direct institutional links to the British state, territory, and recruitment market engendered practical (if not yet legal) discrepancies in the *character* of its personnel's mobility.

It is in this sense, then, that looking at the how and why of enlistment becomes analytically useful. Perceptions of the 'quality' of naval life and employment, modes of entry into the service, and sailors' personal allegiances represent fundamental respects in which a man coming from afar could differ substantially from someone based in Britain. However, they are also crucial points of debate in British naval historiography. Consequently, considering the perspective of these migrants, refugees, and 'mercenaries', and broadening the definition of what we assume was a 'standard' British sailor, also affect our understanding of the Navy as a whole.

7.1   A Good Employer?

In the past few decades, a heated debate on the quality of living conditions aboard ships, and, connected to that, the true ratio of impressed men to volunteers, has been a core preoccupation of British naval historians. On the one hand, some, like Jesse Lemisch, Nicholas Rogers, Niklas Frykman, and Isaac Land, following both traditional popular understandings and an academic tradition of concern with working-class resistance, have painted a bleak portrait of eighteenth-century naval life.[3] For them, this was characterised by either 'never-ending labor' or 'mind-numbing boredom', the shocking violence of

---

[3] Jesse Lemisch, 'Jack Tar in the Streets: Merchant Seamen in the Politics of Revolutionary America', *The William and Mary Quarterly* 25:3 (1968), 371–407, esp. 381–2; Rogers, *Press Gang*; Frykman, 'Seamen'; Land, *War*.

battles, and 'a terroristic justice system' of cruel punishments.[4] Wages in the merchant marine were, especially in wartime, twice or three times higher than those in the Navy; whilst the latter also offered bounties and prize money, Rogers argues that this was offset by the relative freedom and shortness of employment in merchant vessels, and the availability of shore leave.[5] Privateers, too, were a convenient option in some parts of the world, less dangerous, more comfortable, and more profitable (if prizes were taken) than the Navy, and sometimes also offering bounties and benefits.[6]

On the other hand, a different set of historians, N. A. M. Rodger the most prominent among them, have been offering a largely positive portrayal of life in the service throughout the second half of the century. Naval sailors, they stress, benefited from free healthcare, opportunities for promotion, widows' pensions and invalidity compensations, bounties, prize money, and a disciplinary system that was harsh but less arbitrary than in merchantmen.[7] The ratio of tonnage per man was much lower in the Navy than in merchant shipping, with the result that work was less 'arduous', and life 'relatively easy'.[8] Recent studies have also posited that naval seamen's diet was abundant, nutritious, and rarely inedible as the Navy's critics would have it, and naval surgeons were competent professionals rather than the alcoholic quacks of Smollettian lore.[9] Such provision, it is argued, contrasted sharply with the treatment that sailors received in the merchant service, deregulated and thus more open to abuse and exploitation.[10] The nature of the advantages and disadvantages of naval service is thus highly contested, despite the

---

[4] Frykman, 'Seamen', 76–83.
[5] Rogers, *Press Gang*, 6, 83–4, 117, David J. Starkey, 'War and the Market for Seafarers in Britain, 1736–1792', in Lewis R. Fischer and Helge W. Nordvik (eds.), *Shipping and Trade, 1750–1950: Essays in International Maritime Economic History* (Pontefract: Lofthouse Publications, 1990), 25–42, at 35–6.
[6] Rogers, *Press Gang*, 97–8; Faye Margaret Kert, *Prize and Prejudice: Privateering and Naval Prize in Atlantic Canada in the War of 1812* (St John's, Newfoundland: International Maritime Economic History Association, 1997), 8, 77–108, 121, 156–7; David J. Starkey, *British Privateering Enterprise in the Eighteenth Century* (Exeter: University of Exeter Press, 1990), 59–78, 280–2.
[7] Rodger, *Wooden World*, 116–44; Dancy, *Myth*, 94–105, 187–8.
[8] Rodger, *Wooden World*, 40–1, 116.
[9] Janet Macdonald, *Feeding Nelson's Navy: The True Story of Food at Sea in the Georgian Era* (London and Mechanicsberg, PA: Chatham Publishing and Stackpole Books, 2004); 'Sustaining the Empire: War, the Navy and the Contractor State', University of Greenwich, 2006–9, www.gre.ac.uk/ach/gmc/research/projects/sustaining-the-empire; Rodger, *Wooden World*, 86–7; M. John Cardwell, 'Royal Navy Surgeons, 1793–1815: A Collective Biography', in David Boyd Haycock and Sally Archer (eds.), *Health and Medicine at Sea, 1700–1900* (Woodbridge: The Boydell Press, 2009), 38–62.
[10] Macdonald, *Feeding Nelson's Navy*, 11–12.

conciliatory stance of some recent historiography.[11] The extent to which life in the Royal Navy would have appealed to or repelled specific groups of men will be the object of the first part of this chapter, suggesting a new angle through which this debate can be continued. Material attractions fall under the umbrella of 'pull' factors of migration. Yet sailors often enlisted out of necessity, or even coercion, in a myriad of nuances – what demographers term 'push' factors.[12] It is to these that we turn next.

Finally, we look at the fraught question of 'allegiance', intended as both loyalties and duties (in the plural). It is important not to assume a mechanic correlation between individual sailors' choices and economic advantages or disadvantages. As argued by Kevin Linch, the 'branding' of recruits from abroad as simple 'mercenaries' is crude and potentially reductive: in nationalist narratives, it conveniently functions to obscure outsiders' contribution to the glory of 'British' arms.[13] Naval historians also tend to agree, if anything, on the fact that only focusing on material conditions and opportunities offered by the Navy would fail to explain seamen's enlistment fully. N. A. M. Rodger, on the one hand, argues that 'seamen were genuinely a peculiar class', characterised by 'imprudence', hence 'no analysis can do justice to them which attributes their actions simply to rational calculation'.[14] On the other hand, as observed by Isaac Land from a polarly opposite standpoint, reducing the debate on seamen's motivations for enlisting to the debate on living conditions in the Navy 'risks infantilizing' these men, denying them personal views not informed by immediate material needs.[15]

7.2   Migrants and Economic Calculations

7.2.1   Employment Markets

As a theoretical premise, first of all, we need to explode the purely national terms in which the position of the British Navy on the employment market is usually analysed. All parties to the debate on the quality of life in the Navy agree that, rather than being absolutely 'good' or 'bad', conditions of service can only be assessed in relation to the alternative options open to a man. This normally results in discussions of whether

---

[11] See, for example, Brunsman, *Evil Necessity*.
[12] On 'demand-pull' versus 'supply-push' factors of migration, which are often reciprocal and complementary, see, for example, Philip Martin and Gottfried Zürcher, 'Managing Migration: The Global Challenge', *Population Bulletin* 63:1 (2008), 3–20, at 4–5.
[13] Linch, 'Politics of Foreign Recruitment', 63.   [14] Rodger, *Wooden World*, 118.
[15] Isaac Land, 'New Scholarship on the Press Gang – Part 2 of 2', *Port Towns & Urban Cultures*, 3 August 2015 http://porttowns.port.ac.uk/press-gang2/.

naval employment was better or worse than life ashore *in Britain* or in the *British* merchant marine. Yet ignoring the existence of alternatives, and the fact that these alternatives assumed different configurations for different men, leaves our conclusions incomplete.

Seamen who were legally British encountered significant barriers to employment abroad, as the Royal Navy was relatively efficient in reclaiming subject (or alleged subject) sailors during wartime, even regardless of jurisdictions.[16] There is also a sense in which the labour market for seafarers in Britain tended to remain broadly national, unlike for example the Dutch: the British Isles constituted in themselves a sufficiently large 'catchment area'.[17] However, this does not mean that these islands formed a self-contained bubble. Even British seamen were perfectly aware of international options. In the late 1780s and early 1790s, substantial numbers were lured into the Russian merchant and naval service.[18] Throughout the French Wars, British sailors flocked to US merchantmen, privateers, and naval ships, as critics of impressment deplored.[19] Royal Navy commanders were worried by the attraction that the higher wages offered in American shipping could exert on their sailors: in 1819, in peacetime, American seamen were paid 12 dollars a month and British seamen only 7, leading British officers in Jamaica to suggest that 'the less intercourse they have with each other the better'.[20] In turn, as we shall discuss here, thousands of men came into the Navy from international markets. This shows that it is not possible to weigh the British Navy only against other contemporary British employers.

Optimistic and pessimistic views of the Navy, similar to those polarising modern historiography, also polarised contemporary opinion. The difference is that the latter often did consider the question on an international comparative scale. Critics sometimes noted that the Navy offered a poor deal to seamen, compared not only to British merchant ships, but also to the 30–40 dollars of American vessels.[21] The opposite

---

[16] Pedemonte, 'Deserters', esp. 263–5. For proclamations and regulations on the matter, see, for example, *British and Foreign State Papers – 1812–1814, Volume I*, II, 1356–7, 1367–8; *Regulations and Instructions* (1790), 34.

[17] Van Lottum et al., 'Sailors'; van Rossum et al., 'National and International Labour Markets', 53–4.

[18] TNA, ADM 106/1569, Navy Board In-Letters Promiscuous Letters M., 1790–1801, John Mitchell, 16 July 1791.

[19] *The Impress, Considered as the Cause Why British Seamen Desert from Our Service to the Americans* (London, 1810).

[20] NMRN, 1977/301, Officers' Letters, 1688–1900, 66, Home Popham, 11 July 1819.

[21] NMRN, 1988/500, The Papers of the Penrose and Coode Families, 1772–*c.*1880, 298, 'Ideas on the state of the British navy made by the Captain of HMS *Cleopatra*', 7 June 1797, [f. 2].

perspective was also put forward. As a pamphlet reminded British sailors after the mutinies of 1797, were there not 'thousands of FOREIGN SEAMEN who enter VOLUNTARILY into the BRITISH SERVICE, in Peace and in War, in preference to the Pay and the Service of the Countries to which they belong'?[22] British sailors were invited to 'look to the NAVY and the MERCHANTS' SERVICE of *other Countries*, and see where Seamen have been so well paid, so well fed, or so well treated, as in this Country': would they be provided, elsewhere, with 'so many HOSPITALS, PUBLIC AND PRIVATE CHARITABLE FUNDS AND INSTITUTIONS, for themselves and families, in case of Old Age, Accident, or Death'?[23] Of course, it would be unwise to rely on pro-government propaganda to establish the attractiveness of naval life. What is clear, however, is that a man's position in the international marketplace could make a substantial difference to his perception of the service.

7.2.2   'So Well Paid': Wages and Monetary Rewards

Neoclassical economic theories of labour migration tie it to individual workers' search for 'income maximisation', and the demand and supply differential across geographic labour markets, which in turn drives wage disparities.[24] This model fits well with the decisions of many sailors who ended up joining the British Navy. The heightened demand for seamen during wartime did not immediately drive up Royal Navy wages themselves – they had remained infamously stationary since 1653.[25] This was because ultimately the state had alternative means to procure additional men, including coercion via press gangs, or recruitment of British landsmen – 'raising productivity levels' and 'utilising the marginal areas of supply', in economic terminology.[26] However, wartime demand did induce spectacularly inflated bounties for joining, which were often available to recruits from anywhere. On 21 May 1803, the Admiralty Board sent directions never to pay the bounty to men joining abroad, but these were revoked the following year, when the Navy Board pointed out that the Royal Proclamation of 16 May 1803, instituting such bounties, did not contain any geographical restrictions; 'much inconvenience' had

[22] *An Address to the Seamen in the British Navy* (London: W. Richardson, 1797), 5.

[23] Ibid.

[24] Douglas S. Massey et al., 'Theories of International Migration: A Review and Appraisal', *Population and Development Review* 19:3 (1993), 431–66, at 432–3.

[25] Rodger, *Command*, 618–25; Anthony G. Brown, 'The Nore Mutiny – Sedition or Ships' Biscuits? A Reappraisal', *The Mariner's Mirror* 92:1 (2006), 60–74, at 60–1.

[26] For an overview of these mechanisms, see Starkey, 'War and the Market', 32–3.

'arisen', indeed, from the Admiralty's prohibition.[27] As early as March 1793, the American minister in London had complained that seamen were lured away from American shipping by the high bounties offered by the British Navy.[28] The profitability of serving in a powerful fleet was also augmented, in wartime, by prize money, a share of the value of captured shipping to which each seaman present at an action was entitled.[29] Finally, by the end of the eighteenth century, Britain's Navy far outstripped in size, and therefore in number of available berths, those of other European powers. As such, it constituted a ready source of employment for skilled men everywhere: some of them may have struggled to find any suitable job at all, in countries whose military fleets were small, and maritime trade depressed by the risks, losses, and insurance costs brought by war. 'Probability' of employment is an important factor, next to 'earnings', in microeconomic models of migration returns.[30]

Wages per se, therefore, were not the sole or most important consideration. However, it seems worthwhile to examine them briefly. The comparisons that follow use nominal wages (the raw amounts paid) rather than real wages. Real wages reflect the actual local value, extrapolated from the cost of life in different places, but they are only truly measurable in the case of sedentary occupations. The mobility of sailors makes it extremely complicated to assess the spending power of their pay.[31] The focus of this section is on navies, because their standardised salaries are easier to reconstruct than those of merchantmen, and more directly comparable to those of the Royal Navy. This might also lead to broader inferences regarding the cost of labour in the shipping markets of different countries, but a systematic comparison in this sense is beyond the scope of this book.[32]

In some cases, the British Navy did not pay more than other fleets. In 1805, for example, a Spanish *marinero* would have earned about a quarter more than a British able seaman, even though the payments were notoriously irregular (**Appendix 4**). This, alongside cultural factors, could help us to explain why so few Spanish sailors appear in Royal Navy crew samples. British wages were also broadly similar to those of the Dutch

---

[27] NMM, ADM/B/215, Board of Admiralty, In-Letters, May–June 1804, Navy Office, 27 June 1804. The note revoking the order is dated 17 August.

[28] *British and Foreign State Papers – 1812–1814, Volume I*, II, 1377.

[29] Starkey, 'War and the Market', 33–4.   [30] Massey, 'Theories', 434–5, 455.

[31] On this point, see also van Lottum et al., 'Sailors', 328; van Lottum, *Across the North Sea*, 122–3.

[32] For a survey, see van Royen et al., *'Those Emblems of Hell?'*. For examples of comparisons, see Andersen and Voth, 'Grapes of War', 20–1; Van Lottum et al., 'Sailors', 328–31.

Orangist Navy (depending on the rating equivalences one applies). A British able seaman only received between 8% and 16% more than a Dutch full *matroos*, and warrant officers sometimes were actually better off in the Dutch Navy, depending on ship rate (**Appendix 4**). By the late 1790s, the old Dutch fleet had ceased to exist, so questions of loyalty and practicality, rather than mere wage differentials, may have dictated Dutch seamen's choice between the French/Batavian or (where permitted) the British Navy. The Dutch maritime labour market, in general, is deemed to have come to permanent decline at the end of the eighteenth century.[33]

In other fleets, however, not only were berths limited in number, but the overall earnings for a sailor would be significantly lower. During the early modern period, the southern European shipping sector came to lag behind the northern, in terms of standards of living and economic prosperity.[34] Salaries were substantially higher in British than in Neapolitan and Sicilian shipping, as evidenced by the problem of desertions, which was a constant scourge for southern Italian ships touching British ports.[35] A rough comparison between the wages in the two navies helps to conclude that, in monetary terms at least, joining the British rather than the Sicilian could be an advantageous financial choice. In 1800, a carpenter or a boatswain in the Sicilian service earned about twice as much as their British counterparts in the smallest rated ships, and about the same as those aboard first rates. However, the nominal wages of ordinary seamen in the Royal Navy were at least 19% and possibly 34% higher than in the Sicilian Navy (depending on whether we compare them to '*marinari di seconda classe*' or '*marinari di terza classe*', second- or third-class seamen), and 55% higher for landsmen, or seamen at the bottom of the skill ladder ('*marinari di quarta classe*', fourth-class). A quick look at another southern European fleet, that of the Knights of the Order of Malta (which existed autonomously until 1798), confirms this pattern. In fact, wages in the British service were in this case about six times as high (**Appendix 4**). In short, what was not much money in Britain could be deemed a handsome wage abroad, and vice versa.

Historians have demonstrated that portraying early modern sailors simply as salaried proletariat ignores the many ways in which, aboard merchant vessels, they integrated their wages with 'hybrid' and autonomous forms of

---

[33] van Rossum et al., 'National and International Labour Markets', 52.

[34] Richard W. Unger, 'Overview. Trades, Ports and Ships: The Roots of Difference in Sailors' Lives', in Fusaro et al., *Law, Labour and Empire*, 1–17, esp. 16–17.

[35] Lo Sardo, *Napoli e Londra*, 169, 171.

trade and profit-making, including further payments and victuals.[36] This argument mostly relates to the long seventeenth century, but some elements of this complexity certainly survived: other economic factors, beyond cash payments, played into a sailor's choice to join. Whilst nominally the same for everyone, these too carried different worth, depending on a man's provenance and personal situation.

7.2.3 'So Well Treated': The Perks of Naval Service

Naval victuals may have been 'better' than common narratives have portrayed them. However, 'better' or 'worse' need some qualification. Especially in an age preceding a 'scientific' calorie-based understanding of diets, the perception of the nutritiousness of various types of food was highly subjective: it was both a 'form of embodied knowledge' and culturally specific.[37] To this, we need to add the simple factors of taste and habit, which vary widely within and across societies. During World War II, even in the neighbouring island of Trinidad, Caymanian Royal Navy reservists found themselves unable to eat the 'badly prepared' 'foreign' food provided to them, and the same was true of Trinidadians when Caymanian cooks were in charge.[38] In the eighteenth century, diverse traditions of alimentary consumption and agricultural, farming, fishing, and trading supply systems coexisted even within Europe (or indeed Britain and Ireland).[39] The cultural values attached to food probably mean that what the Navy provided could not simultaneously satisfy more than a portion of the men, given their disparate origins and backgrounds.

---

[36] See, for example, Richard J. Blakemore, 'Pieces of Eight, Pieces of Eight. Seamen's Earnings and the Venture Economy of Early Modern Seafaring', *The Economic History Review* 70:4 (2017), 1153–84, esp. at 1168–80; Philippe Haudrère, 'Heurs et malheurs des voyages maritimes sur la route des Indes orientales au XVIIIᵉ siècle', *Annales de Bretagne et des Pays de l'Ouest* 121:3 (2014), 165–75, at 172–5.

[37] Rebecca Earle, 'The Political Economy of Nutrition in the Eighteenth Century', *Past & Present* 242 (2019), 79–117.

[38] Daniel Owen Spence, '"They Had the Sea in Their Blood": Caymanian Naval Volunteers in the Second World War', in Arielli and Collins, *Transnational Soldiers*, 105–23, at 111, 113.

[39] For some case studies, see, for example, Melissa Calaresu, 'Thomas Jones' Neapolitan Kitchen: The Material Cultures of Food on the Grand Tour', *Journal of Early Modern History* 24:1 (2020), 84–102; Angela Jianu and Violeta Barbu (eds.), *Earthly Delights: Economies and Cultures of Food in Ottoman and Danubian Europe, c. 1500–1900* (Leiden and Boston, MA: Brill, 2018). On the links between materiality and cultural construction in local food traditions, see Alison K. Smith, 'National Cuisines', in Jeffrey M. Pilcher (ed.), *The Oxford Handbook of Food History* (Oxford: Oxford University Press, 2012), 444–58.

At the same time, there were some further factors at play. As in the case of 'low' wages, 'poor' victuals were perhaps not perceived as such by many seamen coming from foreign markets. Because of the distinctive storage and provisioning requirements, the substance of the sailor's diet would have been broadly similar in most contemporary navies, while even in the same navy it varied from station to station. Depending on the country, options included ship's biscuit, pasta or rice, cheese, meat and fish, legumes, and spirits (rum, beer, red wine, bourbon, brandy, or aquavit).[40] The same problems were also shared across fleets: in particular, the paucity of fresh fruit and vegetables caused frequent scurvy epidemics everywhere.[41] Yet some navies, like the French, struggled even more than the British to keep their provision to a healthy standard.[42] In 1808, the Swedish fleet was all but incapacitated by scurvy,[43] and a few years later British observers described the food in the Russian Navy as 'much inferior in quality, if not in quantity'.[44] For someone coming from a navy where people systematically died of malnutrition, even the much-maligned fare of the British naval mess would perhaps have seemed attractive, and a slight step up. Niklas Frykman has shown that 'foreigners' in the Navy could be a source of mutiny and protest.[45] However, it is also the case that some of them would have found the British Navy an unusually safe and advantageous haven. A transnational history of the Royal Navy need not be exclusively a history of rebellion and resistance.

In general, many of the supposed disadvantages or perks of naval life did not apply to all seamen equally, and an important divide was between men based in Britain or abroad. This was for reasons of both habit and logistics. First, some features of the British naval service and

---

[40] For various navies, see Macdonald, *Feeding Nelson's Navy*, 140–50; Martine Acerra and André Zysberg, *L'essor des marines de guerres européennes (vers 1680 – vers 1790)* (Paris: SEDES, 1997), 245–53; Michel Vergé-Franceschi, *La marine française au XVIIIᵉ siècle : Guerres – administration – exploration* (Paris: SEDES, 1996), 278–9; Seerup, 'Søetaten', 361–9; Joseph M. Wismayer, *The Fleet of the Order of St John 1530–1798* (Valletta: Midsea Books Ltd., 1997), 240–44; Radogna, *Storia della marina militare*, 38–9.

[41] The literature is vast. See, for example, Pat Crimmin, 'The Sick and Hurt Board and the Problem of Scurvy', *Journal for Maritime Research* 15:1 (2013), 47–53; Brian Vale, 'The Conquest of Scurvy in the Royal Navy 1793–1800: A Challenge to Current Orthodoxy', *The Mariner's Mirror* 94:2 (2008), 160–75.

[42] Macdonald, *Feeding Nelson's Navy*, 147–9; Acerra and Zysberg, *Essor des marines*, 250–2.

[43] A. N. Ryan (ed.), *The Saumarez Papers: Selections from the Baltic Correspondence of Vice-Admiral Sir James Saumarez 1808–1812* (London: Navy Records Society, 1968), Valentine Duke to Saumarez, 12 September 1808, 46–7; James Davey, 'Within Hostile Shores: Victualling the Royal Navy in European Waters during the French Revolutionary and Napoleonic Wars', *International Journal of Maritime History* 21:2 (2009), 241–60, at 241, 255.

[44] *Voyage to St. Petersburg*, 25.   [45] Frykman, 'Connections'; Frykman, 'Mutiny'.

environment may not have been ideal, culturally or physically, for men used to different lifestyles. Medical provision aboard Royal Navy ships was probably quite effective by the standards of the day.[46] Yet contemporary accounts show that the attitudes of seamen from different countries towards their own health, and medical treatment more generally, varied immensely: British naval surgeons, for example, observed that Russian sailors were culturally averse to seeking medical help.[47] Moreover, as naval surgeons recognised, the wet and cold climate of the Channel, North Sea or North Atlantic waters, where many British ships were stationed, would have been disastrous for the health of men who had always lived in warmer climates.[48] At the same time, British ships also travelled to tropical zones, hotbeds of high-mortality diseases, which many European sailors, particularly from nations without overseas colonies, would never have encountered in their home services. If scurvy was tackled relatively well by the British, at least by the end of the century, it was still a problem that seamen hardly faced, for example, on short-haul voyages in the Mediterranean.[49] Overall, different types and zones of seafaring carried radically different mortality rates for seamen,[50] and this must have played a part in their employment choices.

Second, besides previous habits and acclimatisation, logistics and bureaucracy caused problems. Sailors who were in the Navy as a result of transnational migration could be settled in Britain, or uncertain about their future, but also still domiciled abroad and aiming to return to their homes.[51] A large proportion of these men would not have family or a stable home on British territory. This had crucial implications for the applicability of commonly understood 'advantages' of British naval service.

For example, the Navy's provision for wages and pensions to be paid to the seamen's families, or to the seamen themselves after retirement, could be a perk of naval employment.[52] It was intended as such by the state, as a way of encouraging enlistment.[53] However, it only made sense if a sailor's domicile was within range of the British administrative machine, either directly or through allied governments. Invalidity pension

---

[46] Cardwell, 'Royal Navy Surgeons'.   [47] *Voyage to St. Petersburg*, 13–15.
[48] Section 4.2.   [49] Acerra and Zysberg, *Essor des marines*, 254–5.
[50] Cabantous, *Ciel dans la mer*, 101–6.   [51] Van Lottum, 'Some Thoughts', 651–2.
[52] Rodger, *Wooden World*, 131–5; Dancy, *Myth*, 95–6, 100.
[53] Patricia Y. C. E. Lin, 'Caring for the Nation's Families: British Soldiers' and Sailors' Families and the State, 1793–1815', in Alan Forrest, Karen Hagemann, and Jane Rendall (eds.), *Soldiers, Citizens and Civilians: Experiences and Perceptions of the Revolutionary and Napoleonic Wars, 1790–1820* (Basingstoke: Palgrave Macmillan, 2009), 99–117, at 101–2.

benefits, and the much-coveted spaces at Greenwich Hospital, were far less accessible to men who resided outside Britain, because of mere geographical distance.[54] At the moment, we only have data from the first half of the century, but the trend is clear: out of a sample of Greenwich pensioners, only 2.5% were found to be born abroad, and 0.4% as last resident abroad. These figures were 14.3% and 1% for Ireland, and a good 12.7% born but only 1% resident for Scotland.[55] Being born outside England but still in Britain or Ireland, then, made relatively little difference to a man's chance of securing a Greenwich pension; yet residence was a different matter. Families had similar difficulties: the widow of a Spanish pilot who had been lethally wounded in the service in 1813 only received a pension in 1821. This was after a thick file of documentation in Spanish and English translation was forwarded to the Admiralty via two attorneys, one in Bilbao, near her village, and one in Bristol acting on his behalf.[56]

If pensions were difficult to claim for non-residents, so were wages themselves. By Act of Parliament, a seaman's relatives could receive their proportion of his wages from the Treasurer of the Navy if in London, Clerks of the Cheque at Portsmouth, Plymouth, and Chatham, elsewhere in Britain either from the Receiver General of the Land Tax or from Collectors of Customs or Excise, and in Ireland from a Collector of the Revenue or Revenue Officer: nothing was explicitly said of other places.[57] Aside from lacking this security for his family whilst he was away, a sailor who was not a resident often could not claim his wages tout court. The very system of pay by ticket intrinsically depended on having trusty agents ashore in Britain, and not everyone could rely on this.[58] Foreigners who were discharged as 'unserviceable', the Navy Office reported in 1801, 'appear to be in great distress from not being able to obtain their Wages', presumably because of their lack of local connections.[59] In 1802, the Dutch official van Lelyveld was still negotiating to be paid, as an intermediary, the wages due to some Dutchmen for their service in HMS *Monmouth* two years earlier: they had since joined the Dutch Brigade and, being 'scattered in different Quarters' across Jersey,

---

[54] Foy, 'Royal Navy's Employment', 17–18.
[55] Wilcox, '"Poor Decayed Seamen"', 71–3. See also Section 4.1.
[56] TNA, ADM 106/1549, Navy Board In-Letters Promiscuous Letters I.J., 1814–1822, Pension of widow of J. I. de Ybarraran, 8 May 1821.
[57] 35 Geo. III c. 28 § iii, xxii.
[58] Margaret Hunt, 'Credit, Crime and Gender in English Maritime Communities 1650–1750', The Eighteenth-Century Seminar, University of Cambridge, 23 October 2018.
[59] NMM, ADM/B/203, Board of Admiralty, In-Letters, December 1801–February 1802, Navy Office, 29 December 1801.

Guernsey, and Lymington, 'will perhaps never be enabled to receive in person the benefit of their Tickets'.[60]

Navy officials were aware of these problems and tried to compensate for them as far as possible. For example, in January 1804, the Navy Board asked the Board of Admiralty to arrange for Indian and Chinese seamen to be paid directly by naval officers at Madras and Bombay, when discharged there, rather than being given a pay ticket. These seamen were not allowed to reach Britain in person: the Admiralty, unwilling to take responsibility for them, had mandated their discharge in Indian ports before their ships undertook the return journey. In this way, the ordinary system would have forced them to sell their ticket on to profiteering middlemen, which was both illegal and 'a great loss'. The Admiralty's solution was, in turn, modelled on arrangements made by Admiral Keith in the Mediterranean, in April 1802: when he discharged there all the Italians and Maltese serving in his ships, he had the naval storekeepers pay their wages in loco.[61]

Alternatively, if a substantial number of men came from the same country, their relatives at home could be paid directly. From 1803 onwards, for example, half of Maltese sailors' monthly wages could be automatically delivered to their families.[62] In order to be legally valid, British seamen's letters of attorney and wills had to be drawn in a specific format and probated, but in the spring of 1808 the Navy decided to dispense with this in the case of Sicilian and Maltese seamen who had died in the service: it would simply pay any due wages if the 'representatives' of the deceased had a ticket to show for them, and were 'swearing themselves according to the Laws of their respective Countries, to be entitled to the same'.[63] Even in the Revolutionary Wars, before the British occupation, similar arrangements were provided via diplomatic channels. The British consul in Malta, William England, transmitted complete lists of all the local men in the British service between 1793 and 1798, and received their pay to be redistributed to the families, a process which was overseen and countersigned by two Maltese

[60] TNA, ADM 106/1559, Navy Board In-Letters Promiscuous Letters L., 1790–1804, B. P. van Lelyveld to Commissioner Hartwell, 11 January 1802; B. P. van Lelyveld to the Commissioners of the Navy, 19 February 1802.
[61] NMM, ADM/B/213, Board of Admiralty, In-Letters, January–February 1804, Navy Office, 18 January 1804.
[62] NMM, ADM/B/221, Board of Admiralty, In-Letters, December 1805–March 1806, Navy Office, 5 February 1806, and attachments.
[63] NMM, ADM/B/231, Board of Admiralty, In-Letters, April–May 1808, Navy Office, 27 May 1808; ADM/B/232, Board of Admiralty, In-Letters, June–July 1808, Navy Office, 8 June 1808. For the legislation on British seamen's letters of attorney and wills, see, for example, 26 Geo. III c. 63.

merchants acting as witnesses to the Admiralty.[64] The operation was not smooth, as the consul complained at the beginning that he had received poor and unclear instructions, and he was unable to reconstruct in which ships the men on his list were serving; moreover, he had to front the costs, which were initially charged as an imprest against him and Admiral Hood.[65] At the end of these men's service, difficulties also arose, as some of them returned to the island without 'proper discharge tickets' from their captains, meaning that England was unable to pay them their remaining due.[66]

The Maltese were lucky enough to be in this safeguarded position. However, theirs was a special case: they were recruited in a structured and systematic manner, through clear agreements with their local authorities. Seamen coming from other parts of the world, who joined on an individual basis, would not have benefited from a similar advantage. Importantly, again, these points also apply to men originating from more remote parts of Britain and Ireland: the 'foreignness' discussed here is merely situational and geographical, rather than legal. In 1802, frauds were discovered in Ireland, where the wages remitted to seamen's families were paid in Irish rather than British currency, and in this way surreptitiously reduced.[67]

Travelling distance from a man's domicile not only prevented him from accessing some benefits and rewards of service, but often it left him worse off than before entering the Navy. At the turn of the nineteenth century, the East India Company regularly brought Chinese and Lascar sailors to Britain, and was responsible for their return journeys and temporary housing in London, which caused much controversy because of poor living conditions and public affrays.[68] The Navy also took South and East Asian seamen to Britain, but the difference was that it did not have systematic means to send them back. In 1802, the East India Company reported to the Admiralty that, 'from motives of humanity', it had so far paid for the return journey of Indian and Chinese ex-naval sailors, but that, as their number had grown, it could no longer afford to do so, unless

---

[64] TNA, ADM 30/63/6, Pay Lists of Maltese Seamen, 1793–8. These lists contain up to 433 names at any given time, which dropped to 171 in May 1798, in the final days of Malta's independence.

[65] Ibid., William England to the Principal Officers & Commissioners of His Majesty's Navy, 11 September, 7 November 1794.

[66] Ibid., William England to the Principal Officers & Commissioners of His Majesty's Navy, 2 September 1797.

[67] NMM, ADM/B/205, Board of Admiralty, In-Letters, June–September 1802, Navy Office, 16 August 1802.

[68] Yu Po-ching, 'Chinese Seamen in London and St Helena in the Early Nineteenth Century', in Fusaro et al., *Law, Labour and Empire*, 287–303.

the government paid.[69] Precedents existed, as shown by correspondence from 1798, with the Admiralty at first trying to get the Company to hire these sailors and thus make them 'work their passage' 'free of expense to Government', and eventually relenting and disbursing £14 per man.[70] This time, however, the Lords Commissioners instructed Admiral Rainier, commander in chief in the East Indies, 'not to allow any men of this Description to be brought to England in the ships of war returning home'.[71] Some of these seamen asked for their return passages to be paid for even when, it was discovered, the ships they were serving in had never been to India, so the Admiralty refused;[72] however, it is unclear whether the sailors were simply trying to play the system, or whether they had indeed been initially brought to Europe in another British ship. Service in the Navy, overall, could ultimately leave a man stranded thousands of miles from home.

Sometimes, if the Navy was in particular need of people, non-British seamen could be recruited under different terms altogether, which tried to supply for their geographical displacement. We saw how Neapolitans and Sicilians in theory could not be taken outside the Mediterranean. Similarly, in 1795, Admiral Murray at Halifax asked that a discharged crew's wages be paid there, since they were 'all Inhabitants of this country'. He was pressed to find enough hands, so he also suggested 'that a number of Seamen could be raised here and at Newfoundland, to serve in the Squadron on this Station, if they were insured to be discharged in this country again, in a Peace', and paid off there.[73] After 1803, Maltese seamen who enlisted on the island were offered very special conditions of service: they would receive one month advance pay, and thereafter be paid every two months; they could not be taken from the station 'against their Will'; they could leave the service at any time giving two months' advance notice to their captains; if, after two years, they decided to remain, they would be paid a bounty of 50 *scudi* the able seamen and 25 *scudi* the others, and only then would they be 'bound to serve' until the end of the war.[74] It would have been

---

[69] NMM, ADM/B/205, Board of Admiralty, In-Letters, June–September 1802, Navy Office, 10 August 1802.

[70] TNA, ADM 106/1559, Navy Board In-Letters Promiscuous Letters L., 1790–1804, W. A. Ramsay to R. A. Nelson, 23, 25, 31 May, 2 June 1798.

[71] NMM, ADM/B/205, Board of Admiralty, In-Letters, June–September 1802, Navy Office, 10 August 1802.

[72] Ibid., 21 August 1802.

[73] TNA, ADM 1/493, Letters from Commanders-in-Chief, North America, 1795–6, G. Murray to Evan Nepean, 24 June 1795, ff. 154–5.

[74] NMM, ADM/B/221, Board of Admiralty, In-Letters, December 1805–March 1806, Navy Office, 5 February 1806, and attachments.

impossible for a British sailor to negotiate service only around his hometown, or quitting at will.

Special treatment was not only available in the terms of service, but also in case of individual discharges through diplomatic pressure. By Act of Parliament, British naval seamen could only be paid the balance of their wages when they were invalided or transferred to another ship, or when their ship was eventually paid off. The Admiralty, however, introduced the system of 'Pay Lists', at first for discharged Americans, and then extended to all aliens: Pay Lists allowed a man, if he had been initially impressed, to receive his wages 'immediately' upon discharge, regardless of when the rest of the ship's company was paid.[75] This was an important concession for people who were likely to find themselves on the other side of the world, and perhaps with no intention to return to British territory, when their ships were finally paid off years later. It was not much of a concession, however, if we consider that it did not apply to men who had initially volunteered into the Navy, but only to those who had been illegally pressed to begin with, and thus potentially removed from their usual trade routes and communities.

Sometimes, we may conclude, a foreign domicile could result in advantages, like preferential terms of service. Much more often, it caused delays, injustices, and distress. Where it could, the Admiralty intervened to redress problems and abuses, but its reach and control grew increasingly limited the further away from England, and even more so from British territories. Even in the cases in which issues were eventually solved, what looked like administrative glitches on paper would have had, in the meantime, a severe impact on the lives of seamen and their families.

7.3   Beyond the Impressed/Volunteer Dichotomy

Market differentials and practical considerations all played into a seaman's choice to join the service, or refuse to do so. Enlistment, however, was often not a matter of choice. British naval historiography has recently been torn by a heated debate between historians who argue that around half of the Navy's seamen were brutally pressed and those who put this figure at a mere fifth, and stress that press gangs were overall reasonably

---

[75] NMM, ADM/B/216, Board of Admiralty, In-Letters, July–October 1804, Navy Office, 12 July 1804; ADM/B/220, Board of Admiralty, In-Letters, September–November 1805, Navy Office, 22 September, 1 October 1805; TNA, ADM 1/1052, Letters from Commanders-in-Chief, Portsmouth, 1802, nn. 201–400, 381, Mark Milbanke to Evan Nepean, 21 April 1802.

tolerated.[76] This, however, obscures the fact that naval recruits were not always either pressed or volunteers.

To be sure, we saw that impressment could target aliens as well as British subjects. This was clearly the case, even more so, for those who were 'immigrants' but not foreign by British law. The category included men from British overseas territories, and Britons who had long settled abroad. Mid-century impressment in the American colonies was frequent and disruptive, and may have been a factor in precipitating the American Revolution.[77] However, the simple volunteer/impressed dichotomy fails to capture the significance of certain important forms of enlistment.

We know from previous chapters that Maltese, southern Italians, and Dutchmen were sometimes recruited 'in block', through diplomatic agreements with their sovereigns. Does this make them volunteers or coerced workforce? Had they agreed to serve, and, most importantly, had they agreed to serve in the British Navy? This is a form of recruitment that we routinely forget, although it arguably bears some similarities with the quota system trialled during the Revolutionary Wars, by which local British authorities had to supply a set number of men.[78] An even more striking case of recruitment via third-party contracting is that of enslaved workforce. In 1795, for example, Admiral Murray temporarily manned vessels on the North American station using Black men 'belonging' to the inhabitants of Bermuda, 'with a positive agreement to be discharged when the owners wish it, and on no account to be sent from the Station'.[79] These men were neither pressed nor volunteers, but volunteer*ed* by someone else. At the same time, in the Caribbean, piloting and diving skills in particular allowed enslaved people to carve out spaces of 'privileged exploitation', as Kevin Dawson has aptly put it, often by serving for the Royal Navy itself.[80] Their negotiated experiences find no place in our analysis of naval employment, if we assimilate all sailors to the contemporary stereotype of the free-born British 'sons of the waves', on a clear spectrum between willing labourer and

---

[76] Dancy, *Myth*, 155–6, 187–8.   [77] Brunsman, *Evil Necessity*; Magra, *Poseidon's Curse*.

[78] On the Quota Acts, see Lewis, *Social History*, 87–90, 116–27; Dancy, *Myth*, 157–85.

[79] TNA, ADM 1/493, Letters from Commanders-in-Chief, North America, 1795–6, G. Murray to Francis Pender, 12 July 1795, ff. 179–80.

[80] Kevin Dawson, 'Enslaved Ship Pilots in the Age of Revolutions: Challenging Notions of Race and Slavery between the Boundaries of Land and Sea', *Journal of Social History* 47:1 (2013), 71–100; idem, 'Enslaved Swimmers and Divers in the Atlantic World', *The Journal of American History* 92:4 (2006), 1327–55; idem, 'History Below the Waterline: Enslaved Salvage Divers Harvesting Seaports' Hinter-Seas in the Early Modern Atlantic', *International Review of Social History* 64 (2019), 43–70.

conscripted recruit. There are at least two more types of entry that fit imperfectly with this model.

7.3.1   'A Last Expedient': Prisoners of War

The recruitment of prisoners of war was controversial, but common, throughout the long eighteenth century, both in Britain and in other countries.[81] The 1793–1815 period was no exception. In the case of war captives, the two categories of alien and man coming from abroad overlap almost perfectly. Yet, by taking them into the service, the Admiralty regularly ignored legal status. Alienhood, once again, mattered little, but the specific circumstance of having been taken aboard enemy shipping, displaced and incarcerated, led to a distinctive channel of entry into the Navy.

Patterns of recruitment of prisoners of war oscillated with the ebb and flow of conflict. Nonetheless, they seem to reflect the theory that British elites were increasingly alarmed about revolutionary ideas and internal disloyalty throughout the 1790s, but much less so when the war resumed in 1803, and the prominent concern became the threat of invasion.[82] In parallel, we can probably see the effect of the growing mobilisation and demand for manpower. Thus, it appears that the recruitment of prisoners was more liberal in 1793–4, increasingly stricter from then until the end of the Revolutionary War, and relatively lax again (sometimes even eager) from 1803, with smaller oscillations linked to wartime necessity, diplomatic agreements, ministerial directions, and Admiralty management. These changes, in turn, dictate where the majority of prisoner recruits would fall if we wanted to apply a scale to measure their willingness to serve.

In the first few years, the service was rather open to prisoners, especially willing neutrals.[83] Much depended on informal channels and the flexibility of prison officials. Writing from Kinsale, in October 1794,

---

[81]   See, for example, Morieux, *Society*, 40–4; Olive Anderson, 'The Treatment of Prisoners of War in Britain during the American War of Independence', *Historical Research* 28:77 (1955), 63–83, at 71–2.

[82]   For a nuanced discussion of this evolution, see Mark Philp, 'Introduction: The British Response to the Threat of Invasion, 1797–1815', in idem (ed.), *Resisting Napoleon: The British Response to the Threat of Invasion, 1797–1815* (Aldershot: Ashgate, 2006), 1–17.

[83]   See, for example, TNA, ADM 98/16, Sick and Hurt Board to the Admiralty, 1793–4, 17 July, 11 November 1793, 6 October 1794, ff. 10–11, 127, 399–400; ADM 12/63, Admiralty Digest 1794 – Part 2, 79.16, summary of letter from Colonel Souter, 29 August 1794; ADM 1/2128, Letters from Captains, Surnames M., 1794, 199, J. N. Morris, 14 March 1794; ADM 1/2679, Letters from Captains, Surnames W., 1794, 63, Captain Wemyss, 7 June 1794.

Captain Sylvester Moriarty requested permission to take all the neutral prisoners that should be found in future, and asked the Sick and Hurt Board 'to instruct their Agent at Kinsale (who is prodigiously tenacious of adhering to the black letter of His orders) not to throw any obstacles in the way'.[84] Moriarty voiced a perfect excuse:

most certainly, it must be more to the advantage of the States they are Subjects of, that they should be employed in His Majesty's fleet to strengthen the Common Cause: than that they should be sufferd [sic] to remain among rank Republica[n]s, active and Zealous in recommending their infamous Sistem [sic], and indefatigable in corrupting the Morals of their associates.[85]

These justifications were a superficial veneer, as even enemy Frenchmen were frequently taken: non-combatants like stewards, cooks, and bakers, and a large number of boys,[86] but also fighting men.[87] The Army, too, actively scouted for royalist prisoners.[88] Amidst political considerations and patronising arguments, the men's own perspective is sometimes hard to discern. In particular, the issue of the extensive recruitment of boys needs to be investigated further. Were they accepted, or harvested? The formulation of letters concerning them is striking, as it is often the ship captain or admiral who is the subject, 'desirous' to have them discharged.

In subsequent years, Admiralty policy slowly tightened. Some slight adjustments were already visible in 1795, when prisoners were still entered but often excluded from harbour service, or bounty money.[89]

---

[84] TNA, ADM 1/2128, Letters from Captains, Surnames M., 1794, 188, Sylvester Moriarty, 25 October 1794.

[85] Ibid.

[86] See, for example, TNA, ADM 98/16, Sick and Hurt Board to the Admiralty, 1793–4, 17 July, 26 August, 23 October, 4 and 11 November 1793, 14 and 21 February, 20 June, 14 November 1794, ff. 10–11, 57, 111–12, 122–3, 128–9, 212–13, 223, 293–4, 421–2; ADM 1/2679, Letters from Captains, Surnames W., 1794, 76–7, G. B. Westcott to Philip Stephens, 14, 19 June 1794; ADM 1/3062, Letters from Lieutenants, Surnames P., 1793–4, Richard Mansel Philipps to Philip Stephens, 29 January 1794.

[87] TNA, ADM 1/1715, Letters from Captains, Surnames D., 1794, 142, J. Drury to Philip Stephens, 14 January 1794; ADM 12/63, Admiralty Digest 1794 – Part 2, 79.16, summary of letter from R. Murray, 4 March 1794.

[88] See, for example, TNA, ADM 98/16, Sick and Hurt Board to the Admiralty, 1793–4, 28 May, 4, 6, 27, 30 June, 24 November, 15 December 1794, ff. 277–8, 284, 287–8, 297–8, 300, 428–9, 467–8.

[89] TNA, ADM 12/67, Admiralty Digest 1795 – Part 2, 79.16, summary of letters from Sir Richard King, 9 January 1795, and Captain Montagu, 9 January 1795; ADM 1/3167, Letters from Lieutenants, Surnames T., 1793–6, 33 and 34, John Thomson to Evan Nepean, 10 and 14 October 1795; ADM 12/75, Admiralty Digest 1797 – Part 2, 79.16, summary of letter by Captain Essington, 11 November 1797; ADM 1/2495, Letters from Captains, Surnames S., 1797, nn. 1–150, 137, Joseph Short to Evan Nepean, 3 August 1797.

The strictest change concerned enemies. Whilst several Dutchmen, ex-prisoners from the Cape, fought against their country at Camperdown, their compatriots captured in that engagement faced different rules. Both Captain Mitchel of HMS *Isis* and Captain Walker of HMS *Monmouth* reported of a few prisoners whom they had 'found very useful' or 'all good Seamen', but the Admiralty only allowed them to keep those who were neutrals – not 'natives of Holland' or French.[90] A Frenchman who claimed to be a loyalist and have 'fought against his Country' applied to enter in Bristol in May 1798, but the Admiralty replied that 'no Frenchmen of any description in [*sic*] allowed to enter for H.M. Navy'.[91] In 1800, Captain John Burn of HMS *Blonde* received the same sharp answer when he naively asked the Admiralty to pay the bounty for one of his men, 'a native of France'.[92]

At this point, we come across prisoners of war who are closest to being 'volunteers'. Many Frenchmen and Dutchmen even tried to pass as neutrals in order to enter.[93] The Navy was also flooded with keen prisoners who were in fact physically unfit for service, leading to stricter directions for their selection.[94] Several were still recruited, including, contradictorily, a few Frenchmen and Dutchmen.[95] However, as more and more men were captured, and diffidence grew, perhaps the supply was starting to exceed the demand.

After the war resumed, in 1803, there were once again more prisoners willing to serve than the Navy would accept: sometimes, the 'impropriety' of a request to recruit French or otherwise suspect volunteers was

---

[90] TNA, ADM 1/2134, Letters from Captains, Surnames M., 1797, nn. 201–363, 236–7, William Mitchel to Evan Nepean, 19 and 21 November 1797; ADM 1/2684, Letters from Captains, Surnames W., 1797, nn. 1–200, 17–18, James Walker to Evan Nepean, 22 and 27 November 1797.

[91] Captain Thomas Hawker to Evan Nepean, 13 May 1798, reproduced in Nicholas Rogers (ed.), *Manning the Royal Navy in Bristol: Liberty, Impressment and the State, 1739–1815* (Bristol: Bristol Record Society, 2014), 158.

[92] TNA, ADM 1/1524, Letters from Captains, Surnames B., 1800, nn. 251–485, 459a, John Burn to Evan Nepean, 24 March 1800.

[93] See, for example, TNA, ADM 1/1041, Letters from Commanders-in-Chief, Portsmouth, 1800, nn. 401–600, 456, Mark Milbanke to Evan Nepean, 26 May 1800; MacDougall, *All Men Are Brethren*, 468.

[94] See, for example, TNA, ADM 1/732, Letters from Commanders-in-Chief, Nore, 1800, 174, Alexander Graeme to Evan Nepean, 3 April 1800.

[95] See, for example, TNA, ADM 1/2501, Letters from Captains, Surnames S., 1800, nn. 1–200, 110–16, Joseph Short to Evan Nepean, 24 February, 2, 9, 16, 27, 30 March, 6 April 1800; ADM 1/2066, Letters from Captains, Surnames L., 1800, nn. 1–200, 3, Charles Henry Lane, 2 January 1800. On Frenchmen and Dutchmen: ADM 12/93, Admiralty Digest 1801 – Part 3, 79.16, summary of letters from Admiral Romley, 23 May, 13, 15, 26 June, 7 July 1801.

still reasserted.[96] In 1811, the Admiralty asked the Transport Board whether it could in some way 'prevent' some prisoners' 'frequent and vexatious Applications' to join.[97] At the same time, we distinguish hints of a softer approach. In July 1806, when a captain requested approval for thirteen French recruits, the Admiralty did not simply turn him down, but checked 'whether in his opinion they can be relied upon'.[98] Danes continued to be recruited even when they became enemies, albeit with heavy limitations in the merchant or transport service.[99] After 1812, Americans who wished to serve were also often allowed, especially if they were 'Bona fide' Americans, rather than naturalised 'and really British subjects'[100] – although parallel directives were also issued, confusingly, stating that 'no American born' could be taken.[101] Sir Home Popham explained in 1811 that he had used prisoners 'as a last expedient': 'there was little to apprehend from the Enemy and much from the Elements at that season'.[102] As the reserves of seafarers were increasingly eroded by the ongoing conflict, and the main concern was remaining afloat, the Navy could no longer afford to be too particular.

This, however, did not stop at the stage of an allowance. It seems that many prisoners were heavily pressured to join or rejoin. Some Americans, discharged from their original ships to go to prison, were directly put on board others 'by the force of Arms', or so it was claimed.[103] Even when not explicitly coerced, were recruits from war prisons truly volunteers? In theory, the Admiralty explicitly instructed

---

[96] See, for example, TNA, ADM 1/1943, Letters from Captains, Surnames H., 1811, nn. 496–700, 574, Captain Hanchett, 21 March 1811; ADM 1/1113, Letters from Commanders-in-Chief, Portsmouth, 1807, nn. 1801–1947, 1905, George Montagu to W. W. Pole, 16 November 1807.

[97] TNA, ADM 12/147, Admiralty Digest 1810–11 – Part 3, 79.16, summary of report from the Transport Board, 4 April 1811.

[98] NMM, ADM/B/223, Board of Admiralty, In-Letters, July–September 1806, Navy Office, 5 July 1806.

[99] TNA, ADM 12/129, Admiralty Digest 1807 – Part 3, 79.16, summary of letters from Colonel Anderson, 12 November 1807 and from the Transport Board, 1 December 1807; ADM 1/3760, Letters from the Transport Board, January–September 1810, 30 January 1810, ff. 22–4.

[100] TNA, ADM 12/168, Admiralty Digest 1814 – Part 3, 79.16, summary of letter from the Secretary of State, 5 January 1814; ADM 1/3766, Letters from the Transport Board, January–August 1814, 5 February 1814, f. 216.

[101] ADM 12/168, Admiralty Digest 1814 – Part 3, 79.16, summary of letter from the Transport Board, 10 May 1814.

[102] TNA, ADM 1/2338, Letters from Captains, Surnames P., 1811, nn. 349–500, 376, Home Popham to J. W. Croker, 2 February 1811.

[103] National Archives at College Park, Maryland [henceforth USNA], RG 59 Entry A1 928 (1227194), Letters Received Regarding Impressed Seamen, 1794–1815, American seamen to James Madison, 24 July 1813. I am greatly indebted to Professor Nicholas Guyatt for all USNA records.

recruitment captains working with prisoners that they could not take 'any measures with a view of persuading \or inducing/ them to enter; but that it must be a complete act of their own'.[104] That many American captives, even under duress, refused to enlist in the British Navy, during both the American and the French War, has been frequently remarked upon: peer pressure, threats, patriotism, and codes of justice and honour all played a role.[105] Post-1807 Danish and Norwegian prisoners showed similar patterns of behaviour.[106] The menaces of French fellow prisoners could even deter keen neutrals from entering the Navy, as captains who made the mistake of temporarily sending volunteers back to prison soon found out.[107] We also have evidence of naval bounties being a crucial consideration: in 1794, sixteen Flemings, who had entered HMS *Alexander* from the *Hero* Prison Ship, requested to be returned to prison when they did not receive the bounty which they had been promised by the *Hero* commander.[108] Similarly, the following year, a group of eighteen Dutch prisoners applied to enter the service, but eleven of them, 'understanding no bounty money will be paid them', later refused.[109]

Moreover, across the period, prisoners were sometimes allowed to choose *which* service to enter. In December 1793, some of them at Stapleton were willing to join the merchant marine, but 'not inclined to go on board Men of War'.[110] After a Dutch frigate was wrecked on the Scottish coast in 1807, seventy-two of its crew volunteered for the Royal Marines. Twenty-seven of them 'were detained on board the *Winchelsea*' prison ship 'under a Supposition that they wished to remain in the Navy',

---

[104] TNA, ADM 1/2497, Letters from Captains, Surnames S., 1798, nn. 1–200, 178, Joseph Short to Evan Nepean, 28 November 1798.

[105] Lemisch, 'Listening to the "Inarticulate"'; Francis D. Cogliano, '"We All Hoisted the American Flag": National Identity among American Prisoners in Britain during the American Revolution', *Journal of American Studies* 32:1 (1998), 19–37; Robin F. A. Fabel, 'Self-Help in Dartmoor: Black and White Prisoners in the War of 1812', *Journal of the Early Republic* 9:2 (1989), 165–90, at 175, 179–80; Perl-Rosenthal, *Citizen Sailors*, 73–6. For a sophisticated analysis of social dynamics among American prisoners of war, see also Nicholas Guyatt, *The Hated Cage: An American Tragedy in Britain's Most Terrifying Prison* (New York: Basic Books, 2022). I am very grateful to him for letting me read an early draft of this.

[106] Glenthøj and Ottosen, *Experiences of War*, 105.

[107] See, for example, TNA, ADM 1/2497, Letters from Captains, Surnames S., 1798, nn. 1–200, 178, Joseph Short to Evan Nepean, 28 November 1798; ADM 12/147, Admiralty Digest 1810–11 – Part 3, 79.16, summary of letter from Admiral Otway, 11 January 1811.

[108] TNA, ADM 1/2679, Letters from Captains, Surnames W., 1794, 67, Thomas West to Philip Stephens, 3 February 1794.

[109] TNA, ADM 1/3167, Letters from Lieutenants, Surnames T., 1793–6, 33 and 34, John Thomson to Evan Nepean, 10 and 14 October 1795.

[110] TNA, ADM 98/16, Sick and Hurt Board to the Admiralty, 1793–4, 11 December 1793, ff. 164–5.

but they 'declared that they only volunteered for the Marine [*sic*]', and their wish was complied with.[111] The same happened in the North Sea squadron in 1811.[112] This acquiescence often even went directly against the Navy's practical requirements: in 1795, of a group of Dutch prisoners at Chatham, fourteen chose to serve in the Navy, thirty-two in the Marines, and forty-three in the Army. Admiral Buckner was instructed to 'concert with' the commanding officer of the Marines, as it would 'be advisable that means should be taken to influence those who are desirous of entering into the Land Service to go into the Marine'. It was acknowledged as a possibility that this might not work.[113] The prisoners, then, often enjoyed some level of choice at the point of enlistment.

Still, these recruits' situation cannot be compared to that of free men who volunteered. Historians disagree on their assessment of living conditions in British war prisons and hulks: the topic was politically charged and instrumentalised at the time, and the prisoners' fare varied across locations, groups, and periods.[114] However, it is easy to see that for many men captivity would have been intolerable. Some of the prisoners sent over into the Navy were found to be in poor conditions, 'very ragged and dirty', to the point that rendezvous captains requested permission to allow them the 'entering shilling', so that they could buy soap to wash themselves and get a haircut.[115] A few were allowed to enter as a consequence of their informing on fellow prisoners' escape attempts, which meant that their life was in danger.[116] In July 1813, ex-Navy Americans in Chatham complained that they were refused exchange until the end of the war if they could not prove citizenship, scattered among French prisoners in an attempt to make them rejoin the Navy, and exposed to lethal winter conditions, 'neglected by the american agent and not having clothiltg and neeeasaries [*sic*] of life'. 'We must all indiscriminately', they wrote to President Madison, 'in Preterrence [*sic*] to the Confines of

[111] TNA, ADM 1/3751, Letters from the Transport Board, February–June 1807, 4 June 1807, ff. 390–1.
[112] TNA, ADM 12/147, Admiralty Digest 1810–11 – Part 3, 79.16, summary of letters from Admiral Young, 21 July 1811, and from the Transport Board, 31 July 1811.
[113] TNA, ADM 12/67, Admiralty Digest 1795 – Part 2, 79.16, summary of letters from Admiral Buckner, 8 and 14 October 1795.
[114] For a more positive account, see Tim Leunig, Jelle van Lottum, and Bo Poulsen, 'Surprisingly Gentle Confinement: British Treatment of Danish and Norwegian Prisoners of War during the Napoleonic Wars', *Scandinavian Economic History Review* 66:3 (2018), 282–97.
[115] TNA, ADM 1/2497, Letters from Captains, Surnames S., 1798, nn. 1–200, 174, Joseph Short to Evan Nepean, 9 November 1798; ADM 1/2501, Letters from Captains, Surnames S., 1800, nn. 1–200, 111, Joseph Short to Evan Nepean, 2 March 1800.
[116] MacDougall, *All Men Are Brethren*, 451, 471.

another Winter in the Cold confines of a dreary Prison \Ship/ Must take refuge under the British Flag Horrid Idea – after so Arduous a Struggle to emancipate ourselves from the Bowels and tyranny of a British Man of War'. 'We have no Country to Claim us (the World is our Country)', they complained, feeling abandoned by all.[117] Rhetorical addresses of this sort may need careful handling. However, it is clear that, for prisoners of war, the choice of serving could be dictated by a desire to pick the lesser evil between paid naval employment (which came with good opportunities for desertion) and indefinite and deadly confinement.[118] As such, even 'voluntary' enlistment was often more a forced decision than an act of genuine volunteering.

Free seamen, too, could be pushed to volunteer by personal and economic circumstances, but they were rarely faced with similar pressure. The Navy has been represented, sometimes, as a receptacle of criminals and the dredges of His Majesty's prisons. However, Clive Emsley has shown that in fact only limited numbers of petty offenders were offered enlistment as an alternative to gaol, hard labour, or other punishments.[119] Moreover, imprisoned or convicted Britons often were not volunteering under pressure: they were plainly coerced, like press-ganged men.[120] The situation of war captives becoming Royal Navy sailors or Marines was, thus, a uniquely grey area.

7.3.2   'The Touch of the Royal Colours Gave Him Freedom': Fugitives from Enslavement and the Navy

Whilst the famous Somerset ruling of 1772 did not actually forbid a state of bondage on British soil, as many contemporaries believed, it still made Britain the Holy Land of hopeful fugitives from everywhere.[121] Royal Navy decks could bring some of that hope a bit closer in range, and become a refuge and a ticket to freedom. In the Caribbean, political considerations and the influence of local enslavers often secured the return of those who had fled into the service.[122] In May 1800, for

---

[117] USNA, RG 59 Entry A1 928 (1227194), Letters Received Regarding Impressed Seamen, 1794–1815, various American seamen to James Madison, 20 and 24 July 1813.

[118] Cf. Morieux, *Society*, 43, 155–9. On prisoners entering with the goal of deserting, see, for example, TNA, ADM 12/162, Admiralty Digest 1813 – Part 3, 79.16, summary of letter from Edward Pellew, 17 December 1813.

[119] Clive Emsley, 'The Recruitment of Petty Offenders during the French Wars 1793–1815', *The Mariner's Mirror* 66:3 (1980), 199–208; Rodger, *Wooden World*, 170–1.

[120] Emsley, 'Recruitment', 201–6; Rogers, *Press Gang*, 10–11.

[121] Foy, '"Unkle Sommerset's" Freedom'.   [122] Rogers, *Press Gang*, 92–3.

example, the captain's steward John Ashley, who had volunteered aboard HMS *Squirrell* in Jamaica, was discovered to have escaped enslavement, and 'belong' to a lady in Barbados. The ship was by then at Woolwich, and the Board of Admiralty authorised the captain to discharge him, 'on condition of finding an able Seaman to Serve in his stead': they all knew that the service 'would be liable to lose' Ashley if the *Squirrell* was ever in Barbados again.[123] However, especially when the enslavers were not British subjects, but enemies, no further concerns intervened. The British squadron in the Chesapeake during the War of 1812 welcomed and protected thousands of fugitives from enslavement, who flocked to it with their families.[124] In April 1814, Admiral Cochrane issued a proclamation encouraging these refugees, and offering the alternative between British service or resettlement as free men in British colonies.[125]

Elsewhere, too, especially under officers who were either morally opposed to slavery or stubborn about national rights and indifferent to the finesses of diplomacy, enslaved men could find a haven in British men-of-war. In 1806, a fugitive at the Cape of Good Hope volunteered incognito into Sir Francis Beaufort's ship, travelled to England and back, and became fully integrated into the crew. When his identity emerged, the following year, and the enslaver applied for his return, Beaufort 'replied at once that had I known he was a slave, I would not have taken him in the first instance, but that now after being a year a free man, and receiving the K. bounty, and depending on me for protection, I would not give him up.' He did not hesitate to oppose both the Cape Governor and his own admiral; when, under orders, he was forced to receive the enslaver on board, the sailor had disappeared, and a 'real search' (the double underlining is Beaufort's) conducted by officers yielded no results. The fugitive emerged from his hiding when the ship was at sea again ('I wish you could have seen the honest joy displayed by my brave crew, when poor Blacky first peeped up – and looked round to see if he was clear out at sea', Sir Francis wrote to his sister). The man was promptly discharged to a ship headed to the West Indies, thus escaping re-enslavement: after two years in the service, slaves were legally 'enfranchised'. Once in England, Beaufort's conduct was validated by the Admiralty, although he had taken a significant risk challenging orders and the Cape elites, and was 'accused of imprudence and foolish good nature'. As he told the Governor,

---

[123] TNA, ADM 1/1922, Letters from Captains, Surnames H., 1800, nn. 1–350, 121, J. Hamstead to Evan Nepean, 1 May 1800.
[124] Malcomson, 'Freedom'.   [125] Ibid., 369.

I had hoped to find it the pride and boast of Englishmen whether Governors or Captains to share their freedom with the inhabitants of every climate where their influence extended, to protect the adopted sons of G. Britain as well as her native subjects, and to make the abolition of slavery a fact as well as a law.[126]

Beaufort's conduct was not unique. In 1798, some Maltese enslavers complained about this. 'From the days of the renowned Blake to this hour', Lord St Vincent boasted, after the Admiralty enquired on the matter, 'it has been the Pride & Glory of the Officers of His Maj.'s navy to give Freedom to Slaves, wherever they carried the British Flag': in all Mediterranean ports, local authorities warned slave holders to secure their men whilst a British ship was in the harbour. St Vincent recalled an episode happened aboard HMS *Alarm*, at Genoa, when two enslaved Tunisian men had suddenly jumped into the ship's launch. One of them 'wrapped the Pendant round his waist', claiming the protection of Britain, but they were still dragged ashore by the guard. St Vincent had then intervened, obtaining from the Doge and Senate of the city the restitution of the two men and the torn pendant, the punishment of the guard, and 'an apology made on the Quarter Deck of the Alarm under the Kings Colours, for the outrage offer'd to the rights of the British Nation'. When he asked the fugitive 'what were his Sensations when the Guard tore him from the Pendant Staff, his reply was, that he felt no dread, for he knew that the touch of the Royal Colours gave him Freedom'.[127]

In cases like these, the attraction of the British Navy was not in the details of wage, victualling or pension differentials, but simply in the escape and protection it could offer. However, we should avoid giving too much weight to saviour-like self-portrayals of British might. The transition from enslavement to naval service was often even more constrained than a choice made under duress. Historians have highlighted the unsavoury aspects of the status of post-1807 'liberated Africans', which simply led them into new forms of disempowerment and coerced labour.[128] A clause of the 1807 Act for the Abolition of the Slave Trade stated that, when a slaving vessel was captured, the enslaved men aboard

---

[126] HL, Sir Francis Beaufort Papers, 1710–1953, Box 18, mssFB 798, Beaufort to Frances Anne Edgeworth, 3 February 1814.

[127] TNA, FO 49/2, Consul William England, Captain Alexander John Ball, and the Grand Master, April 1789–1800, St Vincent to Evan Nepean, 31 May 1798, ff. 123–4.

[128] Padraic Xavier Scanlan, 'The Rewards of Their Exertions: Prize Money and British Abolitionism in Sierra Leone, 1808–1823', *Past & Present* 225 (2014), 113–42. On the ways in which liberated Africans fought back exploiting the ambiguities of the system, especially into the nineteenth century, see Jake Christopher Richards, 'Anti-Slave-Trade Law, "Liberated Africans" and the State in the South Atlantic World, c.1839–1852', *Past & Present* 241 (2018), 179–219.

were of course not to be sold, but it was 'lawful' 'either to enter and enlist the same, or any of them, into His Majesty's Land or Sea Service, as Soldiers, Seamen, or Marines, or to bind the same, or any of them, whether of full Age or not, as Apprentices, for any Term not exceeding Fourteen Years'. What is more, the Act continued, 'every such Native of *Africa* who shall be so enlisted or entered as aforesaid into any of His Majesty's Land or Sea Forces as a Soldier, Seaman, or Marine, shall be considered, treated, and dealt with in all Respects as if he had voluntarily so enlisted or entered himself'.[129] The bounty money for these 'volunteers' went to the officers and seamen who had captured them, apportioned in the same way as prize money.[130] The 'volunteering' of the enslaved was a qualitatively different form of entry, born of the peculiar pressures of displacement and oppression.

7.4 Mercenaries? Allegiances in Doubt

There is one final question that needs to be raised, if we want to avoid overly materialist interpretations of transnationality, and a complete erasure of the difference between military and non-military institutions. Seafaring work was always dangerous, but once in a navy a man must be contractually prepared to fight (however rarely), kill, and be killed, and not simply in immediate self-defence. In some senses, *all* naval sailors in the French Wars were mercenaries: they were professional mariners, serving for pay. However, this does not negate one further layer of considerations, which we may be unable to pin down in full, as the abundant literature on 'popular patriotism' has demonstrated, but which we must certainly take into account – because contemporaries very much did.

Lack of direct stakes in the British nation, some contemporaries assumed, naturally made a man less committed to the British cause and, therefore, less trustworthy in the service. In 1813, for example, the West India merchant Joseph Marryat attributed the defeat of HMS *Java* in its engagement against the American USS *Constitution* to the fact that the crew had a high proportion of 'foreigners', who 'refused to obey the orders of the captain to repair the ship in the intermission of the action, whereas the American frigate was ready in an hour to renew the engagement'. His bias was evident, as he was trying to expose the evils of foreign shipping.[131] Still, some officers also shared this view. At the beginning of

---

[129] 47 Geo. III sess. 1 c. 36 § vii.   [130] Ibid., § viii–x.
[131] Hansard, House of Commons, vol. 26, 'American Licence Trade', 18 May 1813, cc. 240–1 https://parlipapers.proquest.com/parlipapers.

his career, William Dillon noticed repeated cases of 'foreigners' hiding away or abandoning their guns during actions; this, he wrote,

made a lasting impression on my mind, never to employ them in any ship I might command. Consequently, when I rose in the Service, my first object in taking the command of any ship of war was to get rid of all of them that happened to be serving on board.[132]

Because of this strong conviction, he was completely baffled to come across a brave Swedish sailor, who, in his view, seemed to be of a higher social class than that of common seaman, and 'had a romantic attachment for everything English'.[133]

As a result of such voices, the assumption that 'foreigners' lacked commitment also appears in the historiography. In his social history of the Navy, Michael Lewis, after listing Dillon's and some other examples of desertions and betrayals, simplistically concludes that this was common and 'hardly surprising': 'without loyalty to Britain (which presumably most foreigners did not possess) what indeed *did* sailors 'owe the Royal Navy?'.[134] This kind of interpretation ignores basic aspects of servicemen's psychology, like loyalty to comrades, corps spirit and professional self-definition, above and beyond vague national identifications.[135] Moreover, it perpetuates an all-too-easy, unlifelike dichotomy between members of a national community, by blood and by spirit, and 'others'. Nonetheless, some men did wrestle with allegiances, if in much more complex terms.

The question of Jack Tar's 'patriotism' assumes a completely different light when we consider that the main personal and social attachments of many naval seamen were not rooted in the British Isles. Traditional images of seamen's uncomplicated loyalty to King and Country have been questioned by Nicholas Rogers, but in his view even protests remained at least rhetorically and opportunistically framed by reference to British free-birth rights.[136] Similarly, for Isaac Land, British sailors fought a long 'campaign' to be recognised and treated as full members of the nation, morally, racially, and in their masculinity.[137] Niklas Frykman, instead, has argued for the development of a transnational 'lower-deck republicanism', which did not take the shape of an 'explicit consciousness' or shake the structure of national loyalty in combat, but was nonetheless emerging as a shared 'ideology'.[138] Finally, we cannot forget that many men would have not

---

[132] Dillon, *Narrative*, I, 131, 135, 142 (quote), 160; II, 293.   [133] Ibid., I, 142.
[134] Lewis, *Social History*, 129–33.   [135] Arielli and Collins, 'Introduction', 8.
[136] Rogers, *Press Gang*, 103–26; Nicholas Rogers, 'The Sea Fencibles, Loyalism and the Reach of the State', in Philp, *Resisting Napoleon*, 41–59.
[137] Land, 'Customs of the Sea'.   [138] Frykman, 'Connections'.

concerned themselves with ideologies or attachments. Yet, for some seamen in the Royal Navy, matters of loyalty transcended the simple choice between allegiance to Britain, to a maritime radical transnationalism, and to nobody: there were third parties towards which they also directed their investment and allegiance. Sometimes, this was or became altogether incompatible with British service.

An individual's allegiance is a very blurry concept, tinged with fear, prudence, convenience, or social pressure. 'Third-party' loyalties were often not just a matter of subjecthood law, cultural difference, or generic patriotic sentiment, but rather, they depended on the social conundrum of personal and moral connections across geographical distance and state boundaries, and of how these connections were construed and interpreted by both the individuals and the Navy.

Some men certainly did not rank Britain very high on their scale of devotion. In 1810, a few French soldiers who had deserted the French Army in Spain to join the British service were discovered (by some Germans who had also volunteered) plotting to seize the ship and take it to France.[139] Among the men who were already in the Navy, a clash of allegiances, or an opportunity to quit the service, often came to the fore when they were asked to fight their other country. In 1810, Otta [?] Barrolds [sic], a Dutchman in HMS *Defence*, expressed some 'Scruples' 'to serve against his Country' (he was told that 'he must continue to serve, or go to Prison').[140] In 1801, after the outbreak of hostilities with the northern powers, some Danes and Swedes in the service 'signified... their aversion to serve against their respective nations'.[141] The same happened after 1807 and 1810, and when the War of 1812 broke out a true flood of American sailors serving aboard British men-of-war applied to be transferred to prison – whether out of patriotism, fear of repercussions, or simple dislike of a naval life into which they had often been pressed[142] Allegiance provided both excuses and concerns, very tightly entangled.

---

[139] TNA, ADM 12/147, Admiralty Digest 1810–11 – Part 3, 79.16, summary of letter from Captain Sotheby, 29 September 1810[?].

[140] TNA, ADM 12/147, Admiralty Digest 1810–11 – Part 3, 79.16, summary of letter from Sir Edward Pellew, 28 October 1810. Note that the quote is from the summary, not from the original text of the letter.

[141] TNA, ADM 12/93, Admiralty Digest 1801 – Part 3, 79.16, summary of letter by Captain S. T. Digby, 3 April 1801.

[142] See, for example, Danes: TNA, ADM 12/147, Admiralty Digest 1810–11 – Part 3, 79.16, summary of letters from Louis Hutchinson and Peter Holstrom, 8 May 1811, and Christian Whildfoard, 25 August 1811; ADM 1/1180, Letters from Commanders-in-Chief, Portsmouth, 1811, nn. 3501–3600, 3537, J. S. Hulbert to the Admiralty, 27 August 1811; on Americans: ADM 12/162, Admiralty Digest 1813 – Part 3, 79.16, summary of dozens of letters, including, for example, from R. Bickerton, 31 December 1812[?] and 1 January 1813, Admiral Murray, 31 December 1812[?], Captain Rainier,

By the same token, the choice itself of joining the British Navy could be in fact dictated by stakes in another cause. At the end of 1796, French seamen in the Channel were reported by (admittedly not impartial) émigré intelligence 'to desert every day to come into our Service in Ships of War, on any Station that it might be thought proper to employ them, such is their repugnantcy [*sic*] to every part of the Republican Service'.[143] We have already encountered the Sicilian and Dutch Orangist sailors who saw the British Navy as a way to defend their country or their prince, even when they had to risk their lives or forego months of pay. Their service may have been inspired by duty, but not towards Britain.

During wartime, anyway, doubtful allegiance hardly ever resulted in blanket policies of mistrust targeting 'non-British' seamen. In fact, country-specific expertise could provide a pool of men for extraordinary tasks. In July 1814, at Plymouth, the order was sent out to select, among the common seamen in the service, one or two Prussians, 'steady Men and of good character', for a special mission to Prussia.[144] The safety of His Majesty's ships was routinely entrusted to pilots from every corner of the world's coastlines (including France): local, minute geographical expertise was indispensable in a global war, and handsomely remunerated.[145] The Admiralty could be reluctant to discharge even enemy aliens who wished to go to prison. In 1814, Francis Rodrigo, a Frenchman, was told that if he wanted that he needed to prove his

10 January 1813; ADM 1/1229, Letters from Commanders-in-Chief, Portsmouth, 1814, nn. 1–99, 13 and 23, R. Bickerton to John W. Croker, 2 and 4 January 1814; ADM 1/1230, Letters from Commanders-in-Chief, Portsmouth, 1814, nn. 101–200, 136, 139, 155, R. Bickerton to John Wilson Croker, 24, 25, 27 January 1814; ADM 106/1549, Navy Board In-Letters Promiscuous Letters I.J., 1814–1822, Richard Johnson, 14 May 1818. See also: Fabel, 'Self-Help in Dartmoor', 174–5; Ira Dye, 'American Maritime Prisoners of War, 1812–1815', in Timothy J. Runyan (ed.), *Ships, Seafaring, and Society: Essays in Maritime History* (Detroit, MI: Wayne State University Press, 1987), 293–320, at 302.

[143] TNA, WO 1/921, j. Intelligence: Prince de Bouillon: Correspondence, 1794–6, Captain D'Auvergne Prince of Bouillon, 13 December 1796, f. 821.

[144] TNA, ADM 1/834, Letters from Commanders-in-Chief, Plymouth, 1814, nn. 1–876, 873, W. Domett to J. W. Croker, 16 July 1814.

[145] *Regulations and Instructions Relating to His Majesty's Service at Sea* (London: W. Winchester and Son, 1808), 202; Dawson, 'Enslaved Ship Pilots'. For specific examples, see NMM, ADM/B/205, Board of Admiralty, In-Letters, June–September 1802, Navy Office, 12 July 1802; ADM/B/216, Board of Admiralty, In-Letters, July–October 1804, Navy Office, 18 September 1804; ADM/B/206, Board of Admiralty, In-Letters, October–December 1802, Navy Office, 1 December 1802; ADM/B/229, Board of Admiralty, In-Letters, November 1807 – January 1808, Navy Office, 10 January 1808, and attachments.

origin.[146] After their country had become an enemy in 1810, many Swedes also faced resistance and attempts to lure them into remaining in the Navy: Frederick Peterson from HMS *Thisbe*, after applying for discharge, was sent to the flagship at the Nore, as 'disposable', in case he changed his mind.[147] When three others in HMS *Rosario* wrote to the Admiralty, in early February 1811, saying that they had 'been informed that a war had commenced with Sweden' and that they wanted to be sent home or to prison, they were 'Informed their Information is not correct, and that they must remain where they are'.[148] The war had in fact commenced on 17 November. Americans asking to be sent to prison after 1812 even received 'very bad usage' in some ships, they alleged, and faced 'the greatst [*sic*] difficulty and emba[rrassm]ent', including 'threats of Hanging', 'confinement in Irons and in Some instances of flogging'.[149] The Navy was often equally possessive of all its workforce: if the systematic xenophobic purges of a Dillon had been commonplace, the fleet would have simply lost a substantial chunk of its hands. There was only so much coerced swapping of personnel that could occur with merchantmen.

What did happen was that *ad hoc* precautions were taken, even for the men's own sake. Before the North Sea fleet engaged in the Battle of Copenhagen, in 1801, Scandinavian sailors aboard were prudently redeployed in other squadrons.[150] In February 1814, Admiral Domett signalled the case of some Americans who had 'served with much credit', 'pointing out the hardship which must occur by continuing them in the Spencer, should she be sent to America': the Admiralty allowed them the option to go to prison or be transferred to a ship in the home service.[151]

Serving in the British Navy, it must be said, did not always burn bridges with other homelands. Some seamen, when captured in the act, promptly claimed to have been impressed. American sailors were routinely reintegrated into their national community and fleet through

---

[146] TNA, ADM 1/1229, Letters from Commanders-in-Chief, Portsmouth, 1814, nn. 1–99, 52, R. Bickerton to John W. Croker, 9 January 1814.

[147] TNA, ADM 12/147, Admiralty Digest 1810–11 – Part 3, 79.16, summary of letter from Sir C. Hamilton, 21 January 1811, and see also Sir Edward Pellew, 9 January 1811.

[148] TNA, ADM 12/147, Admiralty Digest 1810–11 – Part 3, 79.16, summary of letter from 3 Swedes on board the Rosario, 7 February 1811.

[149] USNA, RG 59 Entry A1 928 (1227194), Letters Received Regarding Impressed Seamen, 1794–1815, various American seamen to James Madison, 20 and 24 July 1813.

[150] Dudley Pope, *Life in Nelson's Navy*, 2nd ed. (London: Chatham Publishing, 1997), 109.

[151] TNA, ADM 12/168, Admiralty Digest 1814 – Part 3, 79.16, summary of letter from Admiral Domett, 25 February 1814.

narratives of continued loyalty in the face of forced service.[152] In 1810, the French-controlled Neapolitan Navy was eager to take back the Neapolitan sailors captured aboard British vessels. To this end, Neapolitan officials themselves insisted on the interpretation that these men had been in the Royal Navy against their will, left stranded in Sicily when the two kingdoms had broken apart, and then impressed.[153] Again, in the eyes of the state, seamen constituted a valuable national commodity: while it was almost impossible to prevent them from enlisting in the fleets of other countries, they often had a strong tide in their favour if they ever decided that returning home had become the best option.[154] Their service for the enemy could then be conveniently erased.

Not everyone, however, was so lucky. In June 1797, HMS *Cumberland* was stationed at Spithead, and an alarmed letter which its captain wrote to the Admiralty must be read in the context of the very recent fleet mutinies in that station.[155] He sent the names of 'four discontented Frenchmen' in his crew who were 'extremely sollicitos [*sic*]' to be discharged; 'the service', he believed, 'will be much benefited by their requisition being comply'd with', especially given that only a few days before 'a man of a similar description' in the ship 'was taken up and convey'd to Winchester for Treasonable expressions'. The four sailors were paid the wages that they were due, minus any bounty which they had received, and discharged to prison.[156] Three of them then wrote to the Admiralty, hoping to be considered 'as Loyallists', after four years of service in the British Navy, and expressing their terror at the idea of being exchanged with 'Repulicans': 'if wee are what will be our doom when wee [?] to France'. They hoped that their Lordships would do them the 'Charity' to 'Set us at Liberty so as wee might pass to a Neutral

---

[152] Myra C. Glenn, 'Forging Manhood and Nationhood Together: American Sailors' Accounts of their Exploits, Sufferings, and Resistance in the Antebellum United States', *American Nineteenth Century History* 8:1 (2007), 27–49, at 33–7.

[153] ASN, Ministero degli affari esteri – Decennio Francese, Busta 5338, 397 (5359/7), Correspondence relative to Neapolitan seamen found aboard British vessels, 1810, Marchese di Gallo to the Minister of Marine, 6 June 1810; Duca di Campochiaro to Duc de Cadore, 1 July 1810.

[154] Morieux, *Society*, 41.

[155] There is a vast literature on the 1797 fleet mutinies at Spithead and the Nore. See, for example, Ann Veronica Coats and Philip MacDougall (eds.), *The Naval Mutinies of 1797: Unity and Perseverance* (Woodbridge: The Boydell Press, 2011); Frykman, 'Mutiny', 175–6; N. A. M. Rodger, 'Mutiny or Subversion? Spithead and the Nore', in Thomas Bartlett, David Dickson, Dáire Keogh, and Kevin Whelan (eds.), *1798: A Bicentenary Perspective* (Dublin: Four Courts Press, 2003), 549–64; Callum Easton, 'Counter-Theatre during the 1797 Fleet Mutinies', *International Review of Social History* 64:3 (2019), 389–414.

[156] TNA, ADM 1/2134, Letters from Captains, Surnames M., 1797, nn. 201–363, 283, Robert Montagu to Evan Nepean, 20 June 1797.

Country'.[157] In an international context where national allegiances were interwoven with political beliefs, civil war, and class tensions, displacement created tangled knots of all these strands. In most countries, Britain included, the law condemned national seamen caught serving in enemy fleets to be executed for high treason.[158] This may not have always been applied in practice, but it also reflected more pervasive forms of social condemnation.

In short, some seamen's problems went far beyond those common to normal veterans, either celebrated as heroes or utterly neglected on their return home. By being in the British Navy, some men were conventionally out of place, and this thought must have been well present to their minds. British law did not pose substantial obstacles to their enlistment, but it could or would not overcome the fact that they were economically, socially, and politically displaced, and that this displacement could have catastrophic personal consequences. The maritime profession undoubtedly offered opportunities to navigate, ignore, and exploit allegiances. However, in a world ablaze with war, the situation of 'partial uprootedness' of many migrant seafarers, with each of their feet on different, clashing tectonic plaques, at best forced them into difficult choices, and at worst simply ripped their lives apart.

7.5   Conclusion

Navy policies towards men who enlisted as immigrants or refugees were not substantially divergent, in many ways, from those towards men who were aliens, spoke a different language, practised a different religion, or were assumed to belong to a different 'race'. Good hands were always needed in the service, and accommodations would be made, as far as convenient, to secure their entry and permanence in it. Such accommo dations, however, could not go as far as physically bridging geographical distance and social uprooting. The Navy had the power to ignore legal or cultural differences, and the men might learn to do so as well, but material issues were another matter. In this sense, we can say that at least one type of 'foreigner' would have been in the service under radically different circumstances to 'British' comrades: the man who was, for whatever reason, displaced.

By definition, naval service displaces everyone, because most people live ashore. However, strong cultural, economic, and administrative links

---

[157] Ibid., Jean Jugla [Jouglas], Andrew Petter [Petry] and Francis Elliot [Alliot] to the Admiralty, n.d.

[158] MacDougall, *All Men Are Brethren*, 466–7; Johnsen, *Han sad*, 132–3.

existed between the British fleet and mainland Britain, and this was obviously not the case for any other territory. People from abroad who chose British naval employment often saw it as an option in a completely different landscape of opportunities and values. What on a British marketplace were low wages, elsewhere may have seemed high. Disadvantages of the service might also become perks, and vice versa: the very structure of employer–employee contractual relations often had to be reframed ad hoc for immigrants, or be desperately irrelevant. Sailors from Britain, however coerced or oppressed, would never have entered the Royal Navy as rented slaves or diplomatic commodities, from prisons of war, or running away from enslavement. Moreover, the allegiances of those who did not 'belong', or belonged to multiple places, had to be renegotiated, engendering their own forms of disruption and compulsion. All these conditions were peculiar to men who had in common not primarily legal or cultural foreignness, however defined, but simply being outsiders to the material, geographical, or political sphere of Britain and its Navy. In turn, their case helps us to reconsider the way in which we understand *all* naval sailors. Displacement often proceeded by gradations, rather than sharp dichotomies.

This chapter aimed to study the Navy not as a standalone institution taking centre stage, or as an employer in the *British* maritime market, but as part of an international labour marketplace, and as a nodal point where various currents of global mobility encountered each other. This perspective allows us to examine it under a transnational lens, through the movement of the men who crossed borders, land, and sea in order to join it – or leave it. The Navy's openness to global workers helps us to question an often self-referential national portrayal, which is accurate if we consider the fleet as a political and military tool, but not necessarily if we observe the social dynamics or cultural outlook of the men who composed it. This framework also leads us to better understand the Navy's functioning, by broadening the scale of comparison. In particular, it begins to outline, beyond long-standing narratives, which traits of the Navy as an institution were common in the eighteenth-century Atlantic and European maritime world, and which were indeed exceptional.

Conclusion

Filthy and indolent, hardy and brave, a less than desirable supplement to a crew or in everything as good as British sailors: the whole spectrum of value judgements was applied by British officers to those whom they termed 'foreign' sailors. This is because the term 'foreign' hid and hides a very composite group. The historian needs to be careful not to fall into the same trap. The Jamaican Black fugitive and the southern Italian nobleman, the Irish Catholic peasant and the old Norwegian sea wolf, the Highlander Marine speaking only Erse, and the Swede speaking fluent English with a Scottish accent deserve a more nuanced treatment than the blunt label of 'foreigner'. This can be achieved by splitting apart the specific traits which earned them that label.

Observing all these traits separately allows us to go beyond officers' individual comments and prejudices, praising or disparaging, and describe the overall administrative trends of the wartime Navy. These led it to transcend, in its recruitment, the very national boundaries that it was its task to defend and represent. The edges and legal delimitations of the nation-state were the most striking form of boundary that the Navy ignored, with its indiscriminate enlistment and naturalisation of aliens. This makes it qualify as a proper subject for transnational history – a history that looks beyond and across nation-states. Yet there were other types of differences and assumed differences, more or less aligned with national definitions, over which Navy officers also trampled in their search for men. The Navy of the French Wars, in its recruitment, straddled linguistic and religious barriers and transcended racial prejudices, even though English and Anglicanism remained the official standards in use, and racism could be rife among the crews. 'Inclusiveness' was not an official policy and did not necessarily result in fairness of rights or individual treatment. Rather, it was a collective, pragmatic attitude, which was only possible when each man was conceptualised as a useful pair of hands. One does encounter, in the sources, examples of charitable officers and actions, but in general accommodation was granted especially when and insofar as it helped to maximise efficiency.

In this sense, two extremes need to be navigated, in a study like this. On the one hand, it is easy to fall into a moral narrative, personifying the Navy, and casting it as a 'good', solicitous, and enlightened employer. It is important to remember, however, that the attitudes and policies described in this book all aimed at achieving strategic and combat effectiveness with the scarce resources available. Some individual decisions may have stemmed from humanity or compassion, but these are not what this study is aiming to investigate. Seamen, willing or coerced, 'British' or not, skilled or landlubbers, Black or white, Protestant or Catholic, were all absorbed and used up in a ruthless, violent game of states at war, transcending any individual experience. On the other hand, the Navy as an institution can also be excessively depersonalised, leading us to forget that each decision was made by an individual officer at a specific time, and as such it may not have been fully 'objective', or pragmatically the most efficient move. Again and again, we have encountered the influence of attitudes, prejudices, and worldviews. Widely held beliefs surrounding southern and northern European seamen and their navies resulted in different paths to their incorporation into the British fleet. Different cultural habits, like the perceived unruliness of southern Italians, inspired spite in British officers, whereas a failure to conform to expectations, as when a 'foreign' northern European spoke English like an Englishman, provoked mistrust. Various ideas surrounding 'foreignness', in all its different forms, still had an impact on the shape and extent of recruitment policies, even when these policies programmatically ignored 'foreignness' as such.

The perspective of the individual sailors is also very easy to neglect, partly because it does not survive often enough to escape the danger of undue generalisations. Most of this book, then, has not dwelled extensively on the men's experience. That legal, linguistic, religious, or racialised physical difference did not mean exclusion from the Navy still does not indicate that they lacked implications on a social and personal level. Being an alien could save a man from impressment, or cause him to be executed when he returned to his original country; not speaking fluent English could mean isolation aboard, and an impossibility to reach petty officer rank; a devout Jew or Muslim (and in fact Christian) in a Navy ship would have to make heavy compromises on observance of his faith; most of all, a man could be despised and mistreated merely because of the colour of his skin. Accommodation on the part of the Navy did not always suffice, especially when it clashed with concrete circumstances, rather than conventions or preconceptions. Differences in how employment is evaluated when put on a larger, international scale of options; the practical consequences of physical and social displacement; the pressures and recruitment channels that are peculiar to men 'belonging' to another sovereign, or deprived of their freedom; the attachment to place of origin which in wartime crystallises into loyalty, or is deemed to do so: these were all material realities mostly independent of national and cultural labels, but rather grounded in the very experience of migration and geographical removal. As we have seen, they often exceeded even the ability of states to compensate for or erase them.

Looking further in time beyond the end of the French Wars highlights this point most clearly. After 1815, the whole system of 'pragmatic inclusiveness' collapsed, and these very practical aspects of displacement were the trigger for legal and cultural forms of discrimination that had been suppressed by the Navy during the war. This helps us to see how far the acceptance and relatively fair treatment of men who were aliens, seen as culturally 'other', or coming from abroad had been the result of a coincidental alignment with utilitarian management principles.

The end of the conflict brought momentous change. The men borne for wages in the Navy went down sharply from 126,400 in 1814 to 78,900 in 1815, 35,200 in 1816, and a mere 22,900 in 1817.[1] At the same time, the numbers employed in the merchant service remained steady or even saw a slight decrease, from 172,800 men registered as paying Greenwich hospital duties in 1814 to 171,000 in 1817, after a brief spike at 178,800 in 1816.[2] Thus, merchantmen could not have absorbed much of the Navy's leftovers: over 100,000 blue water seamen suddenly found themselves unemployed. Many would have been fishermen or landsmen, happy to return to their previous lives, but many others did not have such a ready solution. The main issue was that, with the decommissioning of the Navy, seamen abruptly lost much of their worth and usefulness to the state, and therefore much of their personal leverage. This was true of every man, including Britons: British Army and Navy veterans faced hard times after 1815, in a phase of economic depression.[3]

It must also be stated at the outset that not all foreigners were let off from the Navy when the war ended: the musters of the vessels that took part in the bombardment of Algiers in August 1816 show crews that were still around 8.5% foreign-born, with a fairly even split between

---

[1] Morriss, *Foundations*, 227. I have rounded all figures to the nearest hundred.   [2] Ibid.
[3] N. Gash, 'After Waterloo: British Society and the Legacy of the Napoleonic Wars', *Transactions of the Royal Historical Society* 28 (1978), 145–57, at 150–2. This situation was not wholly unprecedented, of course: for the end of the American War, see Margarette Lincoln, *Trading in War: London's Maritime World in the Age of Cook and Nelson* (New Haven, CT, and London: Yale University Press, 2018), 172–3.

non-subjects and imperial subjects.[4] It is true that, at the end of July 1815, the Admiralty had decided to emit circular orders 'to discharge all foreigners from the Service, but particularly such as wish it, altho' they may have received bounty'.[5] In particular, there seems to have been a new resistance to recruiting unskilled non-Britons: there are orders from mid-1817 clearly stating that 'no Foreign Boys ought to be entered'.[6] However, in October 1815, when the Commander-in-Chief at Plymouth asked the Admiralty what he was to do with some foreigners in his ships (and in particular two Americans who had 'been a considerable time in His Majesty's Service, and profess great attachment to it'), the answer was clear:

> altho' their Lordships do not wish to encourage foreigners to enter into the Navy in time of peace, yet if any able bodied seaman fit for the service and who may have already served in the Navy should wish to enter, their Lordships see no objection to their being received.[7]

This may seem counterintuitive, but the Navy, having just discharged over half of its manpower, did not find what ad hoc recruitment it needed especially easy. In October 1815, the Admiralty was chiding rendezvous captains: their Lordships were 'very much surprized at the little exertion which has been used in procuring Volunteer Seamen for His Majesty's Fleet', and threatened to scrap the rendezvous if they failed to procure more men.[8] Throughout most of the nineteenth century, and especially until the proper establishment of continuous service in the 1850s, the need for skilled naval manpower remained, and a handful of foreign seamen's services – again from both the Empire and Europe – continued to be cyclically required, for example when the fleet suddenly remobilised

---

[4] TNA, ADM 37/5682, Muster Book of HMS *Queen Charlotte*, July–December 1816; ADM 37/5665, Muster Book of HMS *Impregnable*, July–October 1816; ADM 37/5762, Muster Book of HMS *Leander*, July 1816–February 1817; ADM 37/5747, Muster Book of HMS *Hebrus*, September 1815–December 1816; ADM 37/5919, Muster Book of HMS *Prometheus*, August 1815–December 1816; ADM 37/5826, Muster Book of HMS *Britomart*, August 1815–April 1817.

[5] TNA, ADM 3/185, Admiralty Rough Minutes, June–August 1815, 26 July 1815. See also summary of this note in ADM 12/174, Admiralty Digest 1815 – Part 3, 83.15. This went against another circular order which they had issued in May, instructing port commanders 'not to discharge any foreigners who have volunteered into H M Service': ADM 3/184, Admiralty Rough Minutes, January–May 1815, 27 May 1815.

[6] TNA, ADM 12/185, Admiralty Digest 1817 – Part 2, 83 and 83.30, summary of letter from and instructions to Sir John Duckworth, 6 July 1817.

[7] TNA, ADM 1/837, Letters from Commanders-in-Chief, Plymouth, 1815, nn. 501–1269, 1068, John Duckworth to J. W. Croker, 17 October 1815.

[8] TNA, ADM 3/186, Admiralty Rough Minutes, September–December 1815, 16 October 1815.

for the Crimean War.[9] Into the Victorian era, then, despite the growing 'anti-mercenary' sentiments and the claims of national (or even imperial) self-sufficiency, the foreign Jack Tar remained a relatively familiar, if decreasing, presence on Royal Navy decks.[10] This is even without mentioning the merchant marine, where the recruitment of both aliens and imperial subjects boomed after the repeal of the Navigation Laws in 1849 – opening a new phase of large-scale labour exploitation and systematic racial discrimination in Britain's maritime world.[11] As a twentieth-century historian aptly puts it, foreign and colonial seamen were to remain a '"reserve"' resource 'that could be wheeled in and out of the British economy as conditions dictated'.[12] In practice, then, the change was far more gradual than one might expect: the French Wars and eighteenth-century immigration policies more generally project their long shadow far into the nineteenth century, and beyond.

What did change abruptly in 1814–15, however, was the weight of the term 'foreigner', and the attitudes of the British government, Admiralty, seamen, and society at large towards it and towards the men to whom it was now prominently attached. Prejudice fomented by economic crisis is not conducive to long-term practical thinking: at the end of the war, circumstances and tensions that had been back-staged jumped to the fore, and people enjoying lower legal, cultural, or social integration were naturally among the worst off. With thousands of British subjects unemployed and starving, the state overall displayed little interest in or compassion for alien seamen.

As we saw in Chapter 6, concerns about the prudency of training up men belonging to rival powers had already been voiced in Parliament during the war itself. Countries without large fleets, indeed, had much to gain from allowing their young men to train abroad, and then bring back

---

[9] I explore this point in statistical detail in a forthcoming study, together with the musters just mentioned in footnote 4: Sara Caputo, '"Contriving to Pick Up Some Sailors": The Royal Navy and Foreign Manpower, 1815–1865', in Thomas Dodman and Aurélien Lignereux (eds.), *From the Napoleonic Empire to the Age of Empire – Empire after the Emperor* (Palgrave Macmillan, forthcoming 2023).

[10] On the rise of anti-mercenarism in nineteenth-century Britain, see Percy, *Mercenaries*, 148–64.

[11] For some literature on the matter, see Frost, *Ethnic Labour*; G. Balachandran, 'Recruitment and Control of Indian Seamen: Calcutta, 1880–1935', *International Journal of Maritime History* 9:1 (1997), 1–18; Ravi Ahuja, 'Mobility and Containment: The Voyages of South Asian Seamen, c.1900–1960', *International Review of Social History* 51:S14 (2006), 111–41; Dixon, 'Lascars', 268; Sherwood, 'Race'; Bruijn, 'Seafarers', 8, 16.

[12] Diane Frost, 'Racism, Work and Unemployment: West African Seamen in Liverpool 1880s–1960s', in Frost, *Ethnic Labour*, 22–33, at 32.

home their skills.[13] 'Our commerce [h]as now become too much the nursery for seamen of other countries, and unless care was taken hereafter, most of our British sailors would become Americans', the wealthy East Indian merchant John Prinsep had warned in the Commons in 1806. Even if deemed less efficient, he continued, forecasting what would become imperial policy in the following century, 'the British Lascar ought in policy to be preferred to Danish or American sailors'.[14] West Indian merchants, too, incensed by the competition offered by the 'encouragement exclusively given to foreign shipping', tried to blame it for the 'decrease of British seamen', who were replaced in the Navy by foreign crews.[15] 'Thus do we supply the sinews of war, to the ruler of continental Europe', lamented Lord Cochrane in 1810.[16] If legal distinctions and merchants' complaints had not mattered much during wartime, when any sailors were desperately needed, now the situation was different, and precious helpers had turned into a resource drain for everyone concerned. Since they had been suspended 'during the Continuance of this present Hostilities, and no longer', the Navigation Laws came back into full force, shutting out alien seamen from most berths in the merchant navy.[17]

Many British seamen, terrified of being left jobless, also turned hostile. This was a familiar pattern from previous wars, and one that was to have a long subsequent history. Still in the twentieth century, the demobbing at the end of large conflicts like the two World Wars led to bursts of anti-immigrant riots in ports across Britain. Sustained activity on the part of the National Sailors' and Firemen's Union contributed to racist legislation like the Special Restriction (Coloured Alien Seamen) Order of 1925, in which constructions of both race and alienhood intersected to create powerful forms of exclusion.[18] At the end of the American War in 1783, British sailors had used both official petitioning channels and brutal

---

[13] See the Norwegian example: Sætra, 'International Labour Market', 201.

[14] Hansard, House of Commons, vol. 7, 'India Budget', 18 July 1806, cc. 1194–1220, at 1215 https://api.parliament.uk/historic-hansard/commons/1806/jul/18/india-budget#column_1194.

[15] Hansard, HC, vol. 26, 'American Licence Trade', 18 May 1813, cc. 240–1.

[16] Hansard, House of Commons, vol. 17, '[Court of Admiralty]', 13 June 1810, cc. 624–41, at 625 https://parlipapers.proquest.com/parlipapers. See also vol. 21, 'Mr. Brougham's Motion relating to the Orders in Council and the Licence Trade', 3 March 1812, cc. 1092–1163 https://api.parliament.uk/historic-hansard/commons/1812/mar/03/mr-broughams-motion-relating-to-the.

[17] 43 Geo. III c. 64 § i.

[18] Lane, 'Political Imperatives'; Neil Evans, 'Across the Universe: Racial Violence and the Post-War Crisis in Imperial Britain, 1919–1925', in Frost, Ethnic Labour, 59–88; Dick Lawless, 'The Role of Seamen's Agents in the Migration for Employment of Arab Seafarers in the Early Twentieth Century', ibid., 34–58, at 40–1.

intimidation to deter their foreign colleagues from 'stealing' their jobs.[19] In 1815, they tried to compel masters of ships anchored in the Thames to lay off all foreigners, accused of agreeing to lower wages, and then proceeded to organise parades and petitions on the matter.[20] 'English employment... should be given to Englishmen, who are willing to work', protested a few hundred discharged sailors who marched on the Admiralty singing 'God Save the King'.[21] Cultural echoes of the nation now chimed with legal distinctions, reinforcing them. As has been pointed out by Isaac Land and Nicholas Rogers, Marcus Rediker's transnational working class solidarity only worked up to a point:[22] if racial prejudice could be one of its limits, job scarcity was another. Under the influence of broader social upheaval, the elusively defined 'Foreign Jack Tars' now crystallised into a 'group'.

In theory, at the end of the war, the Admiralty 'undertook to send home to their own Countries all Foreigners discharged from His Majesty's Naval Service', the same provision that was offered to British seamen.[23] In practice, the reduced peacetime establishment lacked the physical 'means' to convey everyone home, so several men were eventually left to 'use their own exertions or apply to their respective Consuls'.[24] By the spring of 1816, all remaining Navy ships had already sailed away to their stations, and no special transports could be equipped; moreover, foreign seamen who only stepped forward a long time after their initial discharge often had, in the meantime, undertaken voyages in merchantmen: the Navy categorically refused to take any further responsibility for them.[25] Stranded in a foreign country, enjoying little sympathy or support networks, many seamen were reduced to desperate conditions, especially with the arrival of winter. Newspapers from November 1816 return a dire picture of 'poor half-naked creatures', 'foreign and other sailors, who herd at night about the bridges, from absolute inability to procure better shelter from the cold'.[26] Out of charity, and very grudgingly, the Admiralty at last agreed to equip two ships, the *Batavier* and the *Helder*, which, moored in the Thames, helped a few

---

[19] Lincoln, *Trading*, 94–6.   [20] Rogers, *Press Gang*, 122.

[21] *Morning Post*, 25 July 1815, 3.

[22] Rogers, *Press Gang*, 93, 99–100; Land, 'Many-Tongued Hydra'; Land, 'Customs'; Land, *War*, esp. 25–6.

[23] TNA, HO 28/45, Home Office Admiralty Correspondence: Letters and Papers, 1816–18, J. W. Croker to J. Beckett, 12 January 1816, ff. 3–4; Lord Melville to the Lord Mayor of London, 5 November 1816, ff. 78–9.

[24] Ibid., John Barrow to J. Beckett, 29 April 1816, ff. 29–30.

[25] Ibid., Admiralty Office to J. H. Addington, 30 October and 6 November 1816, ff. 69–73; Lord Melville to the Lord Mayor of London, 5 November 1816, ff. 78–9.

[26] *The Times*, 18 November 1816, 2; 30 November 1816, 2.

hundred of these men to survive until the spring. It was never acknowledged, however, that this was due to them: at least half of those sailors,
the Board stated, had never been in the naval service. Additionally, they
argued, given that British consuls abroad were legally obliged to provide
for 'destitute' British seamen, 'the principle of analogy and reciprocity
would seem to authorize an expectation that the consuls of foreign
powers should take measures of the same nature for the relief of their
Countrymen here'.[27] Yet, as the Mayor of Bristol pointed out, the
foreign consuls also rarely helped, despite repeated applications.[28]
They claimed that these seamen, by serving Britain, had 'forfeited all
claims on their Native Country & violated the Allegiance they owed it'.[29]
The legal categories that were twisted in one direction during wartime
now further proved their flimsiness by being twisted in the opposite
direction. Caught in between states, the same men who were previously
wanted by all were now rejected by all.

Thus, the somewhat exceptional bubble created within the wartime
Navy, which has been the object of this study, eventually burst. Different
types of labels and demarcations, which had been proven and treated as
utterly unimportant, suddenly became a convenient framework for both
individuals and the state to harken onto. Once again, 'foreignness'
defined as being an immigrant and social outsider proved the most
relevant form of foreignness in these men's lives. Yet all the other
definitions – from alienhood to cultural prejudice and racial character-
isations – now came forcefully in its wake.

[27] TNA, HO 28/45, Home Office Admiralty Correspondence: Letters and Papers,
1816–18, J. W. Croker to John Beckett, 2 April 1817, ff. 135–9.
[28] Ibid., John Haythorne to Viscount Sidmouth, 6 November 1816, ff. 74–5.
[29] Ibid., Matthew Word (Lord Mayor of London) to Lord Melville, 1 November 1816, ff.
80–1; *Morning Chronicle*, 14 January 1820, 3.

Appendix 1: Sampling Limitations

The analysis carried out in Chapter 1 takes the information found in muster books at face value. This can present some problems, in a context where manual annotation, difficult circumstances, low accountability, and high potential benefit of deception magnified human error. Sometimes, the clerks might misplace a man out of mere ignorance: in 1804, Charles Hendricksen appeared on HMS *Leviathan*'s books as born in Norway, but he stated that he was actually from 'Gottenburgh'.[1] Seamen could also lie about their origin, casting themselves as foreign to obtain a discharge, or as coming from a different – neutral – country, if they were French or Dutch, to avoid imprisonment.[2]

These problems are compounded by the challenges of transcription. Sometimes, place names were illegible, or did not seem to correspond to any known toponyms, even allowing for phonetic and orthographical variations, or misspellings. Therefore, I had to exclude an average one or two seamen per ship. Moreover, several towns all over the Atlantic world often shared the same name. Thus, unless this was followed by further clarifications, like 'N. A.', or 'North America', it was impossible to establish, for example, whether a man from 'Boston' or 'Halifax' would be from Britain or North America, whether a man from 'Charlestown' would be English, Scottish, American, or West Indian, and whether a man from 'Baltimore' would be American or Irish. Unfortunately, all these persons have had to be expunged from the database. When the ambiguity was only within Britain, however, or between Britain and Ireland (e.g. 'Milford'), the men were retained in the sample (except where Britons and Irishmen were treated separately), because the fact that they were not born abroad was still deemed precious

---

[1] TNA, ADM 1/1065, Letters from Commanders-in-Chief, Portsmouth, 1804, H. W. Bayntun to George Montagu, 12 January 1804.

[2] See the case of some prisoners of war, suspected Dutch, claiming that they were Danes: TNA, ADM 12/105, Admiralty Digest 1803 – Special, 478. See also Section 7.3.1.

information. In certain cases, where the surrounding context seemed to justify it, calculated choices were made: for instance, 'Lynn' has been classed as British/Irish, leaving out the less likely North American port, and men from 'Boston' marked as having joined via the Lincolnshire quota were put down as English.

Appendix 2: Rating by Origin

Figure 1.9 in Chapter 1 shows the results of post-hoc testing, plotting the relative percentage contribution of each cell to the final result.[1] The raw data extracted from the musters, and on which the chi-square test was based, are in the contingency table (**Table A2.1**). The expected values in brackets show the numbers of men that would have been expected to fall under each rating and origin category if only chance was at play.

---

[1] This percentage derives from a division performed between each cell's chi-square value and the omnibus chi-square value. Cell chi-square values are obtained by squaring the standardised residuals for each cell. In turn, standardised residuals are calculated by subtracting the expected value from the observed value, and dividing by the square root of the expected value. See T. Mark Beasley and Randall E. Schumacker, 'Multiple Regression Approach to Analysing Contingency Tables: Post Hoc and Planned Comparison Procedures', *The Journal of Experimental Education* 64:1 (1995), 79–93, at 90–1. For the code used, see 'Chi-Square Test of Independence in R', *STHDA: Statistical Tools for High-Throughput Data Analysis* www.sthda.com/english/wiki/chi-square-test-of-independence-in-r. For some literature on post-hoc chi-square testing and the avoidance of inflated type I error, see Myron K. Cox and Coretta H. Key, 'Post Hoc Pair-Wise Comparisons for the Chi-Square Test of Homogeneity of Proportions', *Educational and Psychological Measurement* 53 (1993), 951–62; Anyela Camargo, Francisco Azuaje, Haiying Wang, and Huiru Zheng, 'Permutation-based Statistical Tests for Multiple Hypotheses', *Source Code for Biology and Medicine* 3 (2008), 15.

Table A2.1. *Rank and rating by origin, contingency table (observed values, expected values in brackets, and percentages by column)*

	Boy	Landsman	Ordinary seaman	Able seaman	Young gentleman	Petty/warrant officer, idler, artisan	Total
Britain	151	286	464	1,357	255	555	3,068
	(134.765)	(341.825)	(533.443)	(1351.155)	(207.762)	(499.050)	
	78.65%	58.73%	61.053%	70.49%	86.15%	78.06%	
Ireland	19	121	146	295	24	82	687
	(30.177)	(76.543)	(119.451)	(302.557)	(46.523)	(111.749)	
	9.9%	24.846%	19.21%	15.33%	8.11%	11.53%	
Abroad	22	80	150	273	17	74	616
	(27.058)	(68.632)	(107.106)	(271.288)	(41.715)	(100.200)	
	11.46%	16.43%	19.74%	14.18%	5.74%	10.41%	
Total	192	487	760	1,925	296	711	4,371[1]

H_0: There is no significant association between origin and rank or rating aboard the ships.

$\chi^2(1) = 133.5369$

$p < .01$

$\varphi_c = 0.124$

[1] The difference between this figure and the sample total (4,392) is due to the 21 men whose birthplace was such that it could have been either in Britain or in Ireland (e.g., 'Milford').

Appendix 3: Rating by Foreign Origin

Table A3.1. *Rank and rating of foreign groups, contingency table (observed values, expected values in brackets, and percentages by row)*

	Boy	Landsman	Ordinary seaman	Able seaman	Young gentleman	Petty/warrant officer, idler, artisan	Total
North America	1	27	30	92	3	36	**189**
	(6.86)	(24.64)	(44.91)	(84.52)	(5.3)	(22.77)	**31.19%**
	0.53%	14.29%	15.87%	48.68%	1.59%	19.05%	
West Indies	5	14	14	22	6	2	**63**
	(2.29)	(8.21)	(14.97)	(28.17)	(1.77)	(7.59)	**10.4%**
	7.94%	22.22%	22.22%	34.92%	9.52%	3.18%	
Northern Europe	1	23	63	101	5	24	**217**
	(7.88)	(28.29)	(51.56)	(97.04)	(6.09)	(26.14)	**35.81%**
	0.46%	10.6%	29.03%	46.54%	2.3%	11.06%	
Southern Europe	3	7	25	38	1	9	**83**
	(3.01)	(10.82)	(19.72)	(37.12)	(2.33)	(10)	**13.7%**
	3.61%	8.43%	30.12%	45.78%	1.21%	10.84%	
Eastern Europe	0	3	1	2	0	1	**7**
	(0.25)	(0.91)	(1.66)	(3.13)	(0.2)	(0.84)	**1.16%**
	0%	42.86%	14.29%	28.57%	0%	14.29%	
Asia	10	3	7	11	2	1	**34**
	(1.23)	(4.43)	(8.08)	(15.21)	(0.95)	(4.1)	**5.61%**
	29.41%	8.82%	20.59%	32.35%	5.88%	2.94%	
Africa	2	2	4	5	0	0	**13**
	(0.47)	(1.7)	(3.09)	(5.81)	(0.37)	(1.57)	**2.15%**
	15.39%	15.39%	30.77%	38.46%	0%	0%	
Total	22	79	144	271	17	73	**606**

Appendix 4: Wage Comparisons across Fleets

Table A4.1. *Comparison between wages in the British Navy and in the Spanish Navy (1790 and 1805)*

Spanish Navy (wages of a *marinero*)[1]		Spanish Navy (pound sterling equivalent)[2]	British Navy[3]		British Navy wages to Spanish Navy
1790	70 rs.	1£ 5s 6d (306d)	Landsman	18s (216d)	**70.6%**
			Ordinary seaman	19s (228d)	**74.5%**
			Able seaman	1£ 4s (288d)	**94.1%**
1800	87 rs.	N/A	Landsman	1£ 1s 6d (258d)	**N/A**
			Ordinary seaman	1£ 3s 6d (282d)	
			Able seaman	1£ 9s 6d (354d)	
1805	100 rs.	1£ 16s 6d (438d)	Landsman	1£ 1s 6d (258d)	**58.9%**
			Ordinary seaman	1£ 3s 6d (282d)	**64.4%**
			Able seaman	1£ 9s 6d (354d)	**80.8%**

[1] The data for 1790 and 1805 come from J. M. Vázquez Lijó, '*La Matrícula de Mar y sus repercusiones en la Galicia del siglo XVIII*' (unpublished PhD thesis, Universidad de Santiago de Compostela, 2005), 1032, 1045. The figure for 1800 is reported as 3 *reales* per day in Carla Rahn Phillips, 'The Labour Market for Sailors in Spain, 1570–1870', in van Royen et al., '*Those Emblems of Hell*'?, 329–48, at 341–2. Other than *marinero*, the Spanish ratings were too different from the British (task-focused more than experience-focused) to allow meaningful comparisons. They were, in descending order of pay, *artillero de preferencia*, *artillero ordinario, marinero, grumete, paje* (Lijó, ibid.).
[2] The Spanish *peso* (8 *reales*) oscillated significantly, but I have approximated the conversion rate to 35 pound sterling pence: Rafael Torres Sánchez, Javier Gómez Biscarri, and Fernando Pérez de Gracia, 'Exchange Rate Behavior and Exchange Rate Puzzles: Why the Eighteenth Century Might Help', *Revista de Historia Económica/Journal of Iberian and Latin American Economic History* 23:1 (2005), 143–74, at 157. The data for 1800 are missing in this study.
[3] Data from Rodger, *Command*, 623–5. The wages are for lunar (28-day) rather than calendar months, and it is unclear what other navies used, but the difference seems minimal for our purposes anyway.

Table A4.2. *Comparison between wages in the British Navy (1797–1802) and in the pre–Batavian Republic Dutch Navy*

Pre-1795 Dutch Navy[1]		Dutch Navy (pound sterling equivalent)[2]	British Navy		British Navy wages to Dutch Navy
Matroos/ Lichtmatroos	f14 / f11	305d / 240d	Landsman	1£ 1s 6d (258d)	**84.6%/107.5%**
Matroos/ Lichtmatroos	f14 / f11	305d / 240d	Ordinary seaman	1£ 3s 6d (282d)	**92.5%/117.5%**
Matroos	f14 / f15	305d / 327d	Able seaman	1£ 9s 6d (354d)	**116.1%/108.3%**
Bootsman	f26	567d	Boatswain	3£ (720d)	**127%**
Eerste timmerman	f48	1,047d	Carpenter[3]	3£ (720d)	**68.8%**

[1] These figures relate to the four Dutch ships taken into British service in 1800. Rates of pay were identical across ship rates, and those for a *matroos* were in theory all averaged at f 14 regardless of the level of skill, but in practice paid on a decreasing rate starting at f 14 for able seamen: KH, 2271, Stukken betreffende de Nederlandse marineschepen, B. P. van Lelyveld to Evan Nepean, 13 June 1800. Wages remained essentially unchanged in the first half of the nineteenth century, and the later values are inserted in the table as an alternative to differentiate between landsmen and experienced sailors: Bruijn, 'Zeevarenden', 171.

[2] The conversion rate is the one applied by mutual agreement in 1800 by the Prince of Orange and the British government to pay the four Dutch ships: 11 guilders to the pound sterling. See KH, 2271, Stukken betreffende de Nederlandse marineschepen, Willem Van Voss, 'Supletoire Rolle der Manschappen van Zijne Doorlugtige Hoogh.[ds] Fregat Hector en derselver verdiende en te goed hebbende Gagie tot 21 Maart 1800 Incluis', 23 April 1800, Litt:[a] A 1° loco.

[3] Both the boatswain's and the carpenter's wages varied depending on the rate of the ship, going from £2 to £4 until 1802. Here, I have chosen the middle option (third-rate ships), since the Dutch vessels are of mixed size,

Table A4.3. *Comparison between wages in the British Navy and in the Sicilian Navy (c.1800)*

Sicilian Navy[1]		Sicilian Navy (pound sterling equivalent)[2]	British Navy		British Navy wages to Sicilian Navy
Marinaro di quarta classe	3 D 80g	13s 11d (167d)	Landsman	1£ 1s 6d (258d)	154.5%
Marinaro di terza classe	4 D 80g	17s 7d (211d)	Ordinary seaman	1£ 3s 6d (282d)	133.6%
Marinaro di seconda classe	5 D 40g	19s 10d (238d)	Ordinary seaman	1£ 3s 6d (282d)	118.5%
Marinaro di prima classe	N/A	N/A	Able seaman	1£ 9s 6d (354d)	N/A
Capomastro di corda	19 D	3£ 9s 8d (836d)	Boatswain	2£ (480d)	57.4%
Capomastro costruttore	24 D	4£ 8s (1,056d)	Carpenter[3]	2£ (480d)	45.5%

[1] These are the wages owed to the crews of the gunboats deployed at Palermo, in June 1800: ASN, Affari Esteri, 3664, Marina Real Ministero – Giugno 1800, 'Richiesta per il pagamento de' soldi dell'intero mese di Giugno corrente anno 1800, spettanti agli Ufficiali di guerra, e Politici distaccati in Palermo per la direzione, ed armamento delle Lance Cannoniere ed alla Marineria assent:[a] sulle med.[e]'.

[2] John Jackson, *Reflections on the Commerce of the Mediterranean* (London: W. Clarke and Sons, 1804), 161–2. According to Jackson, the pound sterling oscillated in value between 41 and 52 Sicilian *terri*, but for the purposes of this study the conversion rate adopted is the one he reports further on, of 44 British pence to the ducat. One ducat consisted of 5 *terri*, or 100 grains.

[3] Here, I have chosen the lowest option for boatswains' and carpenters' wages, that for service on sixth rates and below, given that the data on Sicilian wages refer to small-size gunboats.

Table A4.4. *Comparison between wages in the British Navy (1798, 1803) and in the Maltese Navy (c.1789)*

Navy of the Order of St John[1]		Navy of the Order of St John (pound sterling equivalent)[2]	British Navy[3]		British Navy wages to Order's Navy
Marinaro di terza classe	1.10.10 (450 G, or 1.875 S)	3s 5d (41d) (3.375s)	Landsman *When paid in Maltese currency*	1£ 1s 6d (258d) 9.6 *(2,280 grani)*	**629.3%** ***506.7%***
Marinaro di seconda classe	2.4.10 (570 G, or 2.375 S)	4s 3d (51d) (4.275s)	Ordinary seaman *When paid in Maltese currency*	1£ 3s 6d (282d) 11.3 *(2,700 grani)*	**552.9%** ***473.7%***
Marinaro di prima classe	2.10.10 (690 G, or 2.875 S)	5s 2d (62d) (5.175s)	Able seaman *When paid in Maltese currency*	1£ 9s 6d (354d) 14	**571%** ***487%***
Nocchiere	N/A		Boatswain	3£ (720d)	**N/A**
Maestro d'ascia	5.10.10 (1,410 G, or 5.875 S)	10s 7d (127d) (10.575s)	Carpenter	3£ (720d)	**566.9%**

[1] NLM, AOM, 1817, 'Nave S. Zaccaria Com.^te Lista di paga fatta all'Equipag. della med. li 28. Aple 1789', ff. 589–601.

[2] The main currency in Malta was the scudo (oeud), equivalent to 12 tarì, 1 tarì being in turn worth 20 grani. According to Joseph Grima, 1 scudo was equivalent to 1.5 British shillings: Grima, *Fleet of the Knights*, 406. The British, however, determined it to be 1.8 shillings in 1800 (which means approximately 11 scudi to the pound), and this value is assumed here for conversion. See Anthony Luttrell, 'Eighteenth-Century Malta: Prosperity and Problems', *Hyphen* 3:2 (1982), 37–51, at 38.

[3] The values in Maltese currency are what Maltese seamen in the British service were paid according to the conditions presented in Sir Alexander Ball's Proclamation of 25 August 1803. These wages were subsequently lowered even further by Admiralty warrant, but the figures used here are those in the original document. See NMM, ADM/B/221, Board of Admiralty, In-Letters, December 1805–March 1806, Navy Office, 5 February 1806, and attachments. Maltese seamen in the British service during the 1790s were paid even less, as the conversion rate then was 9 scudi and 4 tarì to the pound, reduced to 9 scudi by May 1795: TNA, ADM 30/63/6, Pay Lists of Maltese Seamen, 1793–8. In these cases, the wages received were effectively less than those of equivalent British ratings. We saw that this type of recruitment, however, came with special conditions of payment, service, and discharge, and as such is an exception. Generally speaking, in the eighteenth-century British Navy, non-British sailors were paid the same as Britons, according to their rating.

Bibliography

Manuscript Primary Sources

Archives of the Metropolitan Cathedral, Mdina, Malta

AIM Processi criminali 137.

Archivio di Stato, Naples

Affari Esteri, Raccolta di trattati diplomatici estratti dall'Archivio del Ministero degli affari esteri, Volume 5: *Trattati diplomatici dal 1791 al 1799*.
Affari Esteri, 3662, Marina Real Ministero – 1793–9.
Affari Esteri, 3663, Marina Real Ministero – Gennaio–Maggio 1800.
Affari Esteri, 3664, Marina Real Ministero – Giugno 1800.
Affari Esteri, 3666, Marina Real Ministero – Agosto 1800.
Affari Esteri, 3668, Marina Real Ministero – Novembre e Dicembre 1800.
Affari Esteri, 4333, Generi Somministrati agli Inglesi dai Regj Arsenali 1800–13.
Affari Esteri, 4339, Tolone. Spedizione delle truppe di Sua Maestà Siciliana. Carteggio fra Acton e il generale Bartolomeo Forteguerri, capo della squadra napoletana e carteggio di lord Hamilton, 1793–94.
Affari Esteri, 4377, Viaggio del re Francesco I in Spagna, 1829–30 – Suppliche.
Ministero degli affari esteri – Decennio Francese, Busta 5338.

Archivio di Stato – Sezione militare, Naples (Pizzofalcone)

Ruoli Regie Navi Registri di Marina, Busta 3, n. 5, Frag.ª Minerva, January 1810.
Ruoli Regie Navi Registri di Marina, Busta 3, n. 6, Frag.ª Sirena, 1810.
Segreteria antica, 377, Accademia di Marina (Sicilia), 1809–12.
Segreteria antica, 378, Accademia di Marina (Sicilia), 1813–15.

The British Library, London

Egerton MS 2639, General Sir John Francis Edward Acton, 6th Baronet Neapolitan Prime Minister: Correspondence with Sir W. Hamilton, vol. i., 1781–98.
Egerton MS 2640, General Sir John Francis Edward Acton, 6th Baronet Neapolitan Prime Minister: Correspondence with Sir W. Hamilton, vol. ii., 1797–1800.

Caird Library, National Maritime Museum, Greenwich

ADL/J/9, Impressment Exemption Form for Reyer Torsen, 25 April 1807.
ADM/B/202, Board of Admiralty, In-Letters, August–November 1801.
ADM/B/203, Board of Admiralty, In-Letters, December 1801–February 1802.
ADM/B/205, Board of Admiralty, In-Letters, June–September 1802.
ADM/B/206, Board of Admiralty, In-Letters, October–December 1802.
ADM/B/212, Board of Admiralty, In-Letters, November–December 1803.
ADM/B/213, Board of Admiralty, In-Letters, January–February 1804.
ADM/B/215, Board of Admiralty, In-Letters, May–June 1804.
ADM/B/216, Board of Admiralty, In-Letters, July–October 1804.
ADM/B/219, Board of Admiralty, In-Letters, June–August 1805.
ADM/B/220, Board of Admiralty, In-Letters, September–November 1805.
ADM/B/221, Board of Admiralty, In-Letters, December 1805–March 1806.
ADM/B/222, Board of Admiralty, In-Letters, April–June 1806.
ADM/B/223, Board of Admiralty, In-Letters, July–September 1806.
ADM/B/225, Board of Admiralty, In-Letters, January–March 1807.
ADM/B/229, Board of Admiralty, In-Letters, November 1807–January 1808.
ADM/B/231, Board of Admiralty, In-Letters, April–May 1808.
ADM/B/232, Board of Admiralty, In-Letters, June–July 1808.
ADM/B/235, Board of Admiralty, In-Letters, January–February 1809.
CRK/7/43, Lord Hood to Sir William Hamilton, 20 November 1793.
CRK/7/44, Lord Hood to Sir William Hamilton, 22 November 1793.
CRK/7/45, Lord Hood to Sir William Hamilton, 3 December 1793.
CRK/7/49, Lord Hood to Sir William Hamilton, 24 December 1793.
CRK/7/55, Lord Hood to Sir William Hamilton, 30 January 1794.
CRK/7/57, Lord Hood to Sir William Hamilton, 19 February 1794.
CRK/7/60, Lord Hood to Sir William Hamilton, 15 March 1794.

Cambridge University Library: British and Foreign Bible Society's Library

BSA/D1/5/4, Bible Society Correspondence Books (Home and Foreign), vol. 4, June 1810–September 1812.

Devon Archives and Local Studies, Devon Heritage Centre, Exeter

152M/C/1798/ON, Political and Personal Papers of Henry Addington, 1st Viscount Sidmouth, 1705–1824, Correspondence & Papers for the Year 1798, Naval Correspondence.

The Edinburgh City Archive

SL115/2/1, Aliens Register, 1798–1803.

The Huntington Library, San Marino, California

mssHM81125–81166, Robert Saunders Dundas, Viscount Melville Papers, 1812–14.
mssFB 1-1920, Sir Francis Beaufort Papers, 1710–1953.

Koninklijk Huisarchief, The Hague

Willem V A 31 Inv.nr. 2241, Notities over de organisatie en de staat van de Engelse marine, 1799.

Willem V A 31 Inv.nr. 2267, Stukken betreffende Nederlandse troepen en marineschepen in Engelse dienst, 1799–1800.

Willem V A 31 Inv.nr. 2271, Stukken betreffende de Nederlandse marineschepen en hun bemanningen in Engeland en de daarbij behorende briefwisseling tussen Willem V en B.P. van Lelyveld, commissaris van de prins voor het contact met de Engelse overheid, 1796, 1800–2.

Willem V A 31 Inv.nr. 2272, Stukken betreffende de Nederlandse marineschepen en hun bemanningen in Engeland en de daarbij behorende briefwisseling tussen Willem V en B.P. van Lelyveld, commissaris van de prins voor het contact met de Engelse overheid, 1803–4.

The National Archives, Kew

ADM 1/392, Letters from Commanders-in-Chief, Mediterranean, 1794.

ADM 1/493, Letters from Commanders-in-Chief, North America, 1795–6.

ADM 1/725, Letters from Commanders-in-Chief, Nore, 1795.

ADM 1/732, Letters from Commanders-in-Chief, Nore, 1800.

ADM 1/733, Letters from Commanders-in-Chief, Nore, 1801, nn. 2–600.

ADM 1/734, Letters from Commanders-in-Chief, Nore, 1801, nn. 615–909.

ADM 1/736, Letters from Commanders-in-Chief, Nore, 1803.

ADM 1/815, Letters from Commanders-in-Chief, Plymouth, 1800.

ADM 1/834, Letters from Commanders-in-Chief, Plymouth, 1814, nn. 1–876.

ADM 1/837, Letters from Commanders-in-Chief, Plymouth, 1815, nn. 501–1269.

ADM 1/1041, Letters from Commanders-in-Chief, Portsmouth, 1800, nn. 401–600.

ADM 1/1043, Letters from Commanders-in-Chief, Portsmouth, 1800, nn. 801–999.

ADM 1/1052, Letters from Commanders-in-Chief, Portsmouth, 1802, nn. 201–400.

ADM 1/1065, Letters from Commanders-in-Chief, Portsmouth, 1804, nn. 1–150.

ADM 1/1066, Letters from Commanders-in-Chief, Portsmouth, 1804, nn. 153–300.

ADM 1/1113, Letters from Commanders-in-Chief, Portsmouth, 1807, nn. 1801–1947.

ADM 1/1180, Letters from Commanders-in-Chief, Portsmouth, 1811, nn. 3501–3600.

ADM 1/1229, Letters from Commanders-in-Chief, Portsmouth, 1814, nn. 1–99.

ADM 1/1230, Letters from Commanders-in-Chief, Portsmouth, 1814, nn. 101–200.

ADM 1/1236, Letters from Commanders-in-Chief, Portsmouth, 1814, nn. 802–900.

ADM 1/1248, Letters from Commanders-in-Chief, Portsmouth, 1815, nn. 153–300.

ADM 1/1249, Letters from Commanders-in-Chief, Portsmouth, 1815, nn. 301–450.

ADM 1/1524, Letters from Captains, Surnames B., 1800, nn. 251–485.

ADM 1/1660, Letters from Captains, Surnames C., 1811, nn. 579–800.

ADM 1/1715, Letters from Captains, Surnames D., 1794.

ADM 1/1922, Letters from Captains, Surnames H., 1800, nn. 1–350.

ADM 1/1943, Letters from Captains, Surnames H., 1811, nn. 496–700.

ADM 1/1945, Letters from Captains, Surnames H., 1812.

ADM 1/2066, Letters from Captains, Surnames L., 1800, nn. 1–200.

ADM 1/2128, Letters from Captains, Surnames M., 1794.

ADM 1/2134, Letters from Captains, Surnames M., 1797, nn. 201–363.

ADM 1/2338, Letters from Captains, Surnames P., 1811, nn. 349–500.

ADM 1/2495, Letters from Captains, Surnames S., 1797.

ADM 1/2497, Letters from Captains, Surnames S., 1798, nn. 1–200.

ADM 1/2501, Letters from Captains, Surnames S., 1800, nn. 1–200.

ADM 1/2679, Letters from Captains, Surnames W., 1794.

ADM 1/2684, Letters from Captains, Surnames W., 1797, nn. 1–200.

ADM 1/3062, Letters from Lieutenants, Surnames P., 1793–4.

ADM 1/3167, Letters from Lieutenants, Surnames T., 1793–6.

ADM 1/3740, Letters from the Transport Board, July 1800–March 1801.

ADM 1/3751, Letters from the Transport Board, February–June 1807.

ADM 1/3760, Letters from the Transport Board, January–September 1810.

ADM 1/3766, Letters from the Transport Board, January–August 1814.

ADM 1/3850, Letters from Foreign Consuls, 1796–8.

ADM 1/3851, Letters from Foreign Consuls, 1799–1800.

ADM 1/4183, Admiralty, Letters from Secretaries of State, January–April 1800.

ADM 1/4185, Admiralty, Letters from Secretaries of State, September–December 1800.

ADM 1/4232, Admiralty, Letters from Secretaries of State, January–March 1815.

ADM 1/5364, Courts Martial Papers, August–September 1798.

ADM 1/5486, Courts Martial Papers: Nore Mutiny, 1797.

ADM 3/184, Admiralty Rough Minutes, January–May 1815.

ADM 3/185, Admiralty Rough Minutes, June–August 1815.

ADM 3/186, Admiralty Rough Minutes, September–December 1815.

ADM 7/303, Law Officers' Opinions, 1796–7.

ADM 7/305, Law Officers' Opinions, 1800–2.

ADM 7/307, Law Officers' Opinions, 1805–8.

ADM 7/308, Law Officers' Opinions, 1809–10.

ADM 7/313, Law Officers' Opinions, 1816–19.

ADM 7/398, Register of Protections from Being Pressed – Apprentices, Foreigners and Others, 1795–1801.

ADM 8/69, The Present Disposition of His Majesty's Ships and Vessels in Sea Pay, 1793.

ADM 8/83, The Present Disposition of His Majesty's Ships and Vessels in Sea Pay, 1802.

ADM 8/100, The Present Disposition of His Majesty's Ships and Vessels in Sea Pay, 1813.

ADM 12/26, Analysis and digest of court martial convictions, arranged by offence: SI-W, 1755–1806.

ADM 12/63, Admiralty Digest 1794 – Part 2.

ADM 12/67, Admiralty Digest 1795 – Part 2.

ADM 12/75, Admiralty Digest 1797 – Part 2.

ADM 12/79, Admiralty Digest 1798 – Part 2.

ADM 12/86, Admiralty Digest 1800 – Part 1.

ADM 12/87, Admiralty Digest 1800 – Part 2.

ADM 12/93, Admiralty Digest 1801 – Part 3.

ADM 12/99, Admiralty Digest 1802 – Part 3.

ADM 12/105, Admiralty Digest 1803 – Special.

ADM 12/129, Admiralty Digest 1807 – Part 3.

ADM 12/147, Admiralty Digest 1810–11 – Part 3.

ADM 12/162, Admiralty Digest 1813 – Part 3.

ADM 12/168, Admiralty Digest 1814 – Part 3.

ADM 12/174, Admiralty Digest 1815 – Part 3.

ADM 12/185, Admiralty Digest 1817 – Part 2.

ADM 30/63/6, Pay Lists of Maltese Seamen, 1793–8.

ADM 35/2948, Pay Book of HMS *Nassau*, 1 May 1807–24 November 1809.

ADM 36/8615, Muster Books of HMS *Marlborough*, April 1780–January 1781.

ADM 36/8616, Muster Books of HMS *Marlborough*, June 1779–August 1780.

ADM 36/8962, Muster Books of HMS *Marlborough*, February–November 1781.

ADM 36/11194, Muster Book of HMS *Minerva*, November–December 1793.

ADM 36/11578, Muster Book of HMS *Victory*, May–October 1794.

ADM 36/11981, Muster Book of HMS *Penelope*, November–December 1793.

ADM 36/12177, Muster Book of HMS *Blanche*, August–December 1793.

ADM 36/12279, Muster Book of HMS *Circe*, September–October 1797.

ADM 36/12756, Muster Book of HMS *Montagu*, September–October 1797.

ADM 36/14336, Muster Book of HMS *Alexander*, July–August 1800.

ADM 36/14389, Muster Book of HMS *Santa Dorotea*, January 1801–May 1802.

ADM 36/14781, Muster Book of HMS *Quebec*, March–April 1802.

ADM 36/15330, Muster Book of HMS *Jupiter*, March–April 1802.

ADM 36/15379, Muster Book of HMS *Centurion*, February–March 1802.

ADM 36/15834, Muster Books of HMS *Leviathan*, January–April 1804.

ADM 36/16370, Muster Book of HMS *Termagant*, October–November 1804.

ADM 36/16809, Muster Book of HMS *Phoebe*, September–October 1805.

ADM 37/32, Muster Book of HMS *Nassau*, 1–20 September 1807.

ADM 37/280, Muster Book of HMS *Arethusa*, November–December 1805.

ADM 37/3109, Muster Book of HMS *Nightingale*, September–October 1811.

ADM 37/3701, Muster Book of HMS *Bucephalus*, June–July 1813.

ADM 37/4214, Muster Book of HMS *Astrea*, July–August 1813.

ADM 37/4303, Muster Book of HMS *Garland*, June–July 1813.

ADM 37/5665, Muster Book of HMS *Impregnable*, July–October 1816.

ADM 37/5682, Muster Book of HMS *Queen Charlotte*, July–December 1816.

ADM 37/5747, Muster Book of HMS *Hebrus*, September 1815–December 1816.

ADM 37/5762, Muster Book of HMS *Leander*, July 1816–February 1817.

ADM 37/5826, Muster Book of HMS *Britomart*, August 1815–April 1817.

ADM 37/5919, Muster Book of HMS *Prometheus*, August 1815–December 1816.

ADM 51/577, Captains' Logs, Including MARLBOROUGH (18 June 1779–22 July 1783).

ADM 52/1858, Master's Log HMS *Marlborough*, 18 June 1779–30 June 1781.

ADM 98/16, Sick and Hurt Board to the Admiralty, 1793–4.

ADM 98/17, Sick and Hurt Board to the Admiralty, 1795–6.

ADM 98/24, Sick and Hurt Board to the Admiralty, 1806–8.

ADM 101/84/6A, Medical journal HMS *Ambuscade* for 26 August 1800 to 27 August 1801 by Thomas Hendry.

ADM 101/86/1, Journal of HMS *Arethusa* by Thomas Simpson, Surgeon, 14 May 1805–14 June 1806.

ADM 101/91/4, Journal of HMS *Bombay* by John Knox, Surgeon, 14 May 1808–13 May 1809.

ADM 101/93/1, Medical and surgical journal of HMS *Canopus* for 17 June 1806–16 June 1807 by A. Martin, Surgeon.

ADM 101/112/5, Medical journal of His Majesty's Prison Hospital ship *Le Pegaze* [*Le Pegase*] from the 25 January 1804 to 14 January 1805 by [William Bickley Smith?], Surgeon.

ADM 101/120/3, Medical and Surgical Journal of HMS *Shannon* by Alexander Jack, 30 July 1812–29 July 1813.

ADM 101/121/3B, Medical journal of HMS *Swiftsure* for 8 July 1798 to 9 July 1799 by James Dalziel.

ADM 101/121/3C, Medical journal of HMS *Swiftsure* for 9 July 1799 to 9 July 1800 by James Dalziel.

ADM 101/123/1, Medical journal of HMS *Theban* for 16 November 1813 to 16 November 1814 by William Ure, Surgeon.

ADM 101/125/3, Medical and surgical journal of HMS *Ville de Paris* for 25 March 1813 to 24 March 1814 by William Warner, Surgeon.

ADM 106/1549, Navy Board In-Letters Promiscuous Letters I.J., 1814–22.

ADM 106/1559, Navy Board In-Letters Promiscuous Letters L., 1790–1804.

ADM 106/1569, Navy Board In-Letters Promiscuous Letters M., 1790–1801.

FO 49/2, Consul William England, Captain Alexander John Ball, and the Grand Master, April 1789–1800.

FO 70/1, General correspondence before 1906: Sicily and Naples – Sir William Hamilton and Consuls, 1780–1.

FO 70/7, General correspondence before 1906: Sicily and Naples – Sir William Hamilton, and Consuls, 1794.

HO 28/45, Home Office Admiralty Correspondence: Letters and Papers, 1816–18.

HO 44/47, Home Office: Domestic Correspondence, 1814–38.

PROB 11/1933/71, Will of Philip otherwise Filippo Thovez of Bronte, Sicily, 4 August 1840.

WO 1/921, j. Intelligence: Prince de Bouillon: Correspondence, 1794–6.

National Archives at College Park, MD

RG 59 Entry A1 928 (1227194), Letters Received Regarding Impressed Seamen, 1794–1815.

National Library of Malta, Valletta

AOM, 1817, 'Nave S. Zaccaria Com.^te Lista di paga fatta all'Equipag. della med. li 28. Aple 1789'.

AOM 1927, [Comm. Manso], 'Instruzione per il Cappellano di Galera', n.d.

AOM 1931, '[Ruolo dell'equipaggio della] "S. Giovanni"', 1712–35.

The National Library of Scotland, Edinburgh

GB233/MS.3599, Lynedoch Papers.

GB233/MS.9232, Robert Ritchie, Journal of Voyages, 1811–12.

National Museum of the Royal Navy, Portsmouth

1988/417(1) 621, Press Warrants, 1793–7.
1988/500, The Papers of the Penrose and Coode Families, 1772–*c.*1880.
1977/301, Officers' Letters, 1688–1900.

Parliamentary Archives, London

HL/PO/JO/10/7/965, Records of the House of Lords: Main Papers, British
     Mariners Bill – Amendments and Clauses, 3 April 1794.

University of Nottingham, Manuscripts and Special Collections

Pw Jd 751/1, '*Memorie* relative to the Health of the Army in Sicily, submitted to
     His Excellency Lt. General Lord William Bentinck', 1812.
Pw Jd 4028, Plan for Discharged Men from Foreign Corps, n.d.
Pw Jd 5564, Papers relating to the Sicilian flotilla.
Pw Jd 5660, Instructions to Brig. Genl. Hall commanding the combined flotilla,
     1812.
Pw Jd 5940, State of the royal flotilla, 1814.

Printed Primary Sources

Parliamentary Sources

Hansard 1803–2005, House of Commons, https://api.parliament.uk/historic-han
     sard/index.html.
The History and Proceedings of the House of Commons, 14 vols. (London: Richard
     Chandler, 1742–4).
Journals of the House of Lords, Beginning Anno Tricesimo Quarto Georgii Tertii, 1794.
The Parliamentary Debates from the Year 1803 to the Present Time, ed. T. C.
     Hansard (London: Longman et al., 1812).
The Parliamentary History of England, from the Earliest Period to the Year 1803, 36
     vols. (London: T. C. Hansard, 1819).
ProQuest U.K. Parliamentary Papers https://parlipapers.proquest.com/parlipapers.
Tomlins, Thomas Edlyne and Raithby, John (eds.), *The Statutes at Large, of England
     and of Great-Britain: From Magna Carta to the Union of the Kingdoms of Great
     Britain and Ireland*, 20 vols. (London: George Eyre and Andrew Strahan, 1811).
Tomlins, Thomas Edlyne, Raithby, John, and Simons, N. (eds.), *The Statutes of
     the United Kingdom of Great Britain and Ireland*, multiple vols. (London:
     George Eyre and Andrew Strahan, 1804–57).

Periodicals

Courier and Evening Gazette, London.
The Edinburgh Advertiser.
The Edinburgh Evening Courant.
The Herald and Chronicle, Edinburgh.
The London Gazette.

The London Packet, or New Lloyd's Evening Post.
The Morning Chronicle, London.
The Morning Post and Daily Advertiser [later *The Morning Post*], London.
The Naval Chronicle.
The Sun, London.
The Times.
The Universal Magazine of Knowledge and Pleasure, London.

Other Printed Primary Sources

An Address to the Seamen in the British Navy (London: W. Richardson, 1797).
Blackstone, William, *Commentaries on the Laws of England, in Four Books*, 13th ed.
    (London: A. Strahan, 1800).
Bowers, William, *Naval Adventures during Thirty-Five Years' Service*, 2 vols.
    (London: Richard Bentley, 1833).
[Brauw, J. de Vaandrig], *Mijne emigratie in Duitschland, Engeland en Ierland, in de
    jaren 1799–1802* (Utrecht: N. van der Monde, 1837).
British and Foreign State Papers – 1812–1814, Volume I, 170 vols. (London: James
    Ridgway and Sons, 1841).
Bromley, J. S. (ed.), *The Manning of the Royal Navy: Selected Public Pamphlets
    1693–1873* (London: Navy Records Society, 1974).
Byrn, John D. (ed.), *Naval Courts Martial, 1793–1815* (Farnham and Burlington,
    VT: Routledge, 2009).
Chitty, Joseph, *A Treatise on the Law of the Prerogatives of the Crown* (London:
    Joseph Butterworth and Son and Dublin: John Cooke, 1820).
*Convention between His Britannick Majesty and His Sicilian Majesty. Signed at
    Naples, the 12th of July, 1793.* (London: Edward Johnston, 1793).
Cuoco, Vincenzo, 'La politica inglese e l'Italia', in *Scritti vari – Parte prima: Periodo
    milanese (1801–1806)*, eds. Nino Cortese and Fausto Nicolini (Bari: Gius.
    Laterza e figli, 1924), 201–13 [*Giornale Italiano*, 5–8 January 1806].
D'Ayala, Mariano, *Le vite de' più celebri capitani e soldati napoletani dalla giornata di
    Bitonto fino a' dì nostri* (Naples: Stamperia dell'Iride, 1843).
De Boisgelin, Louis, *Travels through Denmark and Sweden*, 2 vols. (London:
    Wilkie and Robinson, 1810).
De Divitiis, Gigliola Pagano (ed.), *Il commercio inglese nel Mediterraneo dal '500 al
    '700: Corrispondenza consolare e documentazione britannica tra Napoli e Londra*
    (Naples: Guida Editori, 1984).
Dillon, William Henry, *A Narrative of My Professional Adventures (1790–1839)*,
    ed. Michael A. Lewis, 2 vols. (London: Navy Records Society, 1953–6).
Gutteridge, H. C. (ed.), *Nelson and the Neapolitan Jacobins: Documents Relating to
    the Suppression of the Jacobin Revolution at Naples June 1799* (London: Navy
    Records Society, 1903).
Hall, Basil, *Fragments of Voyages and Travels: Chiefly for the Use of Young Persons*,
    9 vols. (Edinburgh: R. Cadell and London: Whittaker & Co., 1831–3).
Hay, Robert, *Landsman Hay: The Memoirs of Robert Hay 1789–1847*, ed. M. D.
    Hay (London: Rupert Hart-Davis, 1953).
Historical Manuscripts Commission, *Report on the Manuscripts of J. B. Fortescue,
    Esq., Preserved at Dropmore*, 10 vols. (London: His Majesty's Stationery
    Office, 1892–1927).

Hitchcock, Tim et al., *The Old Bailey Proceedings Online, 1674–1913*, version 7.0, www.oldbaileyonline.org.

Hoffman, Frederick, *A Sailor of King George*, ed. A. Beckford Bevan and H. B. Wolryche-Whitmore (London: John Murray, 1901).

Home, Henry, Lord Kames, *Sketches of the History of Man*, 4 vols., 2nd ed. (London: W. Strahan and T. Cadell and Edinburgh: W. Creech, 1778).

Hume, David, *Essays Moral, Political, and Literary*, ed. Eugene F. Miller (Indianapolis, IN: Liberty Fund, 1987 [1777]).

Hunter, William, *An Essay on the Diseases Incident to Indian Seamen, or Lascars, on Long Voyages* (Calcutta: The Honorable Company Press, 1804).

The Impress, Considered as the Cause Why British Seamen Desert from Our Service to the Americans (London, 1810).

Jackson, John, *Reflections on the Commerce of the Mediterranean* (London: W. Clarke and Sons, 1804).

Johnson, Samuel, *A Dictionary of the English Language*, 10th ed. (London: various, 1792).

[Johnson, Samuel], *Johnson's Dictionary of the English Language in Miniature* (London: S. Jordan, 1795).

Lloyd, Christopher (ed.), *The Keith Papers*, 2 vols. (London: Navy Records Society, 1950).

Mangin, Edward, 'Some Account of the Writer's Situation as Chaplain in the British Navy', in *Five Naval Journals 1789–1817*, ed. H. G. Thursfield (London: Navy Records Society, 1951).

Meyer, J. D., *Esprit, origine et progrès des institutions judiciaires des principaux pays de l'Europe*, 2 vols. (Paris: G. Dufour et Ed. D'Ocagne, 1823).

Montesquieu, *De l'esprit des lois, par Montesquieu. Précédé de l'analyse de cet ouvrage par D'Alembert*, 2 vols. (Paris: P. Pourrat Fres, 1831).

Narrative of the Travels and Voyages of Davis Bill (Brattleborough, VT: William Fessenden, [1810]).

The Navy List, Corrected to the End of December, 1819 (London: John Murray, [1820]).

Nicol, John, *Life and Adventures 1776–1801*, ed. Tim Flannery (Melbourne: The Text Publishing Company, 1997 [Edinburgh, 1822]).

Nicolas, Nicholas Harris (ed.), *The Dispatches and Letters of Vice Admiral Lord Viscount Nelson*, 2 vols. (London: Henry Colburn, 1845).

The Register of the Times – Volume 4 (London, 1795).

Regulations and Instructions Relating to His Majesty's Service at Sea, 13th ed. (London, 1790).

Regulations and Instructions Relating to His Majesty's Service at Sea (London: W. Winchester and Son, 1808).

Rodger, N. A. M. (ed.), *Articles of War: The Statutes Which Governed Our Fighting Navies 1661, 1749 and 1886* (Havant: Kenneth Mason, 1982).

Rogers, Nicholas (ed.), *Manning the Royal Navy in Bristol: Liberty, Impressment and the State, 1739–1815* (Bristol: Bristol Record Society, 2014).

Ryan, A. N. (ed.), *The Saumarez Papers: Selections from the Baltic Correspondence of Vice-Admiral Sir James Saumarez 1808–1812* (London: Navy Records Society, 1968).

Scott, Robert, *The History of England; During the Reign of George III Designed as a Continuation of Hume and Smollett*, 4 vols. (London: J. Robins and Co., 1824).

Sheridan, Thomas, *A Complete Dictionary of the English Language, both with regard to Sound and Meaning*, 2nd ed. (London: Charles Dilly, 1789).

Smyth, James Carmichael, *An Account of the Experiment Made at the Desire of the Lords Commissioners of the Admiralty, on Board the Union Hospital Ship, to Determine the Effect of the Nitrous Acid in Destroying Contagion, and the Safety with Which It May Be Employed* (London: J. Johnson, 1796).

Spavens, William, *Memoirs of a Seafaring Life*, ed. N. A. M. Rodger (London: The Folio Society, 2000 [1796]).

Supplementary Treaty between His Majesty and the King of the Two Sicilies; Signed at Palermo the 12th of September 1812 (London: R. G. Clarke, 1812).

Treaty of Alliance and Subsidy between His Majesty the King of the United Kingdom of Great Britain and Ireland, and His Majesty the King of the Two Sicilies; Signed at Palermo, the 13th May 1809 (London: A. Strahan, 1811).

Vernon, Francis V., *Voyages and Travels of a Sea Officer* (London, 1792).

Volunteers... Let Us, Who Are Englishmen, Protect and Defend Our Good King and Country against the Attempts of All Republicans and Levellers, and against the Designs of Our Natural Enemies... ([Lewes]: W. & A. Lee, c.1797) (Caird Library, 659.133.1:355.216:094, Item PBB7084).

A Voyage to St. Petersburg in 1814, with Remarks on the Imperial Russian Navy. By a Surgeon in the British Navy (London: Sir Richard Phillips & Co., 1822).

Walsh, E., *A Narrative of the Expedition to Holland, in the Autumn of the Year 1799* (London: G. G. and J. Robinson, 1800).

Watt, Helen and Hawkins, Anne (eds.), *Letters of Seamen in the Wars with France 1793–1815*, (Woodbridge: The Boydell Press, 2016).

Wildman, Richard, *Institutes of International Law*, 2 vols. (London: William Benning & Co., 1850).

Reference Materials and Archival Guides

Colledge, J. J., *Ships of the Royal Navy: An Historical Index*, 2 vols. (Newton Abbot: David & Charles, 1969).

Colledge, J. J. and Warlow, Ben, *Ships of the Royal Navy: The Complete Record of All Fighting Ships of the Royal Navy* (Philadelphia, PA and Newbury: Casemate, 2010).

Pappalardo, Bruno, *Royal Navy Lieutenants' Passing Certificates (1691–1902)*, 2 vols. (Kew: List and Index Society, 2001).

'Trafalgar Ancestors', The National Archives www.nationalarchives.gov.uk/trafalgarancestors/advanced_search.asp.

Rodger, N. A. M., *Naval Records for Genealogists* (Kew: PRO Publications, 1998).

Sheldon, Matthew, *Guide to the Manuscript Collections of the Royal Naval Museum* (Portsmouth: Royal Naval Museum, 1997).

Syrett, David and DiNardo, R. L. (eds.), *The Commissioned Sea Officers of the Royal Navy 1660–1815* (Aldershot and Brookfield, VT: Scolar Press, 1994).

Woelderink, Bernard, *Inventaris van de archieven van stadhouder Willem V 1745–1808 en de Hofcommissie van Willem IV en Willem V 1732–1794* (Hilversum: Verloren, 2005).

Secondary Sources

Abulafia, David, 'Mediterraneans', in W. V. Harris (ed.), *Rethinking the Mediterranean* (Oxford: Oxford University Press, 2005), 64–93.

Acerra, Martine and Zysberg, André, *L'essor des marines de guerres européennes (vers 1680 – vers 1790)* (Paris: SEDES, 1997).

Ackerknecht, Erwin H., 'Anticontagionism between 1821 and 1867', *Bulletin of the History of Medicine* 22 (1948), 562–93.

Adkins, Roy and Adkins, Lesley, *Jack Tar: The Extraordinary Lives of Ordinary Seamen in Nelson's Navy*, 2nd ed. (London: Abacus, 2009).

A'Hearn, Brian, Baten, Jörg, and Crayen, Dorothee, 'Quantifying Quantitative Literacy: Age Heaping and the History of Human Capital', *The Journal of Economic History* 69:3 (2009), 783–808.

Ahuja, Ravi, 'Mobility and Containment: The Voyages of South Asian Seamen, c.1900–1960', *International Review of Social History* 51:S14 (2006), 111–41.

Allardyce, Alexander, *Memoir of the Honourable George Keith Elphinstone K. B. Viscount Keith, Admiral of the Red* (Edinburgh and London: William Blackwood and Sons, 1882).

Allen, W. O. B. and McClure, Edmund, *Two Hundred Years: The History of the Society for Promoting Christian Knowledge, 1698–1898* (London: Society for Promoting Christian Knowledge, 1898).

Alsop, J. D., 'Warfare and the Creation of British Imperial Medicine, 1600–1800', in Geoffrey L. Hudson (ed.), *British Military and Naval Medicine, 1600–1830* (Amsterdam and New York: Rodopi, 2007), 23–50.

Ambrosini, Filippo, *L'albero della libertà: Le Repubbliche Giacobine in Italia 1796–1799* (Turin: Edizioni del Capricorno, 2013).

Andersen, Dan H. and Voth, Hans-Joachim, 'The Grapes of War: Neutrality and Mediterranean Shipping under the Danish Flag, 1747–1807', *Scandinavian Economic History Review* 48:1 (2000), 5–27.

Anderson, Benedict, *Imagined Communities: Reflections on the Origin and Spread of Nationalism*, 2nd ed. (London and New York: Verso, 1991).

Anderson, Olive, 'The Treatment of Prisoners of War in Britain during the American War of Independence', *Historical Research* 28:77 (1955), 63–83.

Anderson, Warwick, 'Disease, Race, and Empire', *Bulletin of the History of Medicine* 70:1 (1996), 62–7.

'Immunities of Empire: Race, Disease, and the New Tropical Medicine, 1900–1920', *Bulletin of the History of Medicine* 70:1 (1996), 94–118.

Arielli, Nir and Collins, Bruce, 'Introduction: Transnational Military Service Since the Eighteenth Century', in Nir Arielli and Bruce Collins (eds.), *Transnational Soldiers: Foreign Military Enlistment in the Modern Era* (Basingstoke: Palgrave Macmillan, 2013), 1–12.

Atkins, Gareth, 'Christian Heroes, Providence, and Patriotism in Wartime Britain, 1793–1815', *The Historical Journal* 58:2 (2015), 393–414.

'Religion, Politics and Patronage in the Late Hanoverian Navy, c.1780–c.1820', *Historical Research* 88:240 (2015), 272–90.

Atwood, Rodney, *The Hessians: Mercenaries from Hessen-Kassel in the American Revolution* (Cambridge: Cambridge University Press, 1980).

Avallone, Paola, 'Il controllo dei "forestieri" a Napoli tra XVI e XVIII secolo. Prime note', *Mediterranea* 3 (2006), 169–78.

Badham, F. P., 'Nelson and the Neapolitan Republicans', *The English Historical Review* 13:50 (1898), 261–82.

Balachandran, G., 'Recruitment and Control of Indian Seamen: Calcutta, 1880–1935', *International Journal of Maritime History* 9:1 (1997), 1–18.

Balkin, David B. and Schjoedt, Leon, 'The Role of Organizational Cultural Values in Managing Diversity: Learning from the French Foreign Legion', *Organizational Dynamics* 41 (2012), 44–51.

Ball, Philip, *A Waste of Blood and Treasure: The 1799 Anglo-Russian Invasion of the Netherlands* (Barnsley: Pen & Sword, 2017).

Bartlett, C. J., *Great Britain and Sea Power 1815–1853* (Oxford: Clarendon Press, 1963).

Bartlett, Roger P., *Human Capital: The Settlement of Foreigners in Russia 1762–1804* (Cambridge: Cambridge University Press, 1979).

Basilica Pontificia Santa Maria del Lauro, *Storie di tempeste e di fede: Gli ex voto nel Santuario Santa Maria del Lauro* (Castellammare di Stabia: Eidos, 1998).

Basker, James G., 'Scotticisms and the Problem of Cultural Identity in Eighteenth-Century Britain', in John Dwyer and Richard B. Sher (eds.), *Sociability and Society in Eighteenth-Century Scotland* (Edinburgh: Mercat Press, 1993), 81–95.

Battaglini, Mario, *Francesco Caracciolo: La misteriosa tragica avventura del grande ammiraglio di Napoli* (Naples: Generoso Procaccini, 1998).

Baugh, Daniel A., *British Naval Administration in the Age of Walpole* (Princeton, NJ: Princeton University Press, 1965).

Bayly, C. A. et al., '*AHR* Conversation: On Transnational History', *The American Historical Review* 111:5 (2006), 1441–64.

Beasley, T. Mark and Schumacker, Randall E., 'Multiple Regression Approach to Analysing Contingency Tables: Post Hoc and Planned Comparison Procedures', *The Journal of Experimental Education* 64:1 (1995), 79–93.

Beck, Catherine, 'Patronage and Insanity: Tolerance, Reputation and Mental Disorder in the British Navy 1740–1820', *Historical Research* 94:263 (2021), 73–95.

Beerbühl, Margrit Schulte, 'British Nationality Policy as a Counter-Revolutionary Strategy During the Napoleonic Wars: The Emergence of Modern Naturalisation Regulations', in Andreas Fahrmeir, Olivier Faron, and Patrick Weil (eds.), *Migration Control in the North Atlantic World: The Evolution of State Practices in Europe and the United States from the French Revolution to the Inter-War Period* (New York and Oxford: Berghahn Books, 2003), 55–70.

Behrman, Cynthia Fansler, *Victorian Myths of the Sea* (Athens, OH: Ohio University Press, 1977).

Belich, James, *Making Peoples: A History of the New Zealanders from Polynesian Settlement to the End of the Nineteenth Century* (Auckland: Penguin Books, 1996).

Bell, David, *The First Total War: Napoleon's Europe and the Birth of Modern Warfare* (London: Bloomsbury, 2007).

Benton, Lauren, *Law and Colonial Cultures: Legal Regimes in World History, 1400–1900* (Cambridge: Cambridge University Press, 2002).

Bianco, Giuseppe, *La Sicilia durante l'occupazione inglese (1806–1815)* (Palermo: Alberto Reber, 1902).

Blake, Lauren E. and Garcia-Blanco, Mariano A., 'Human Genetic Variation and Yellow Fever Mortality during 19th Century U.S. Epidemics', *mBio* 5:3 (2014), 1–6.

Blake, Nicholas, 'The Complements of Four Dutch Ships Taken at the Texel in 1799', *The Mariner's Mirror* 106:3 (2020), 349–55.

Blake, Richard, *Evangelicals in the Royal Navy 1775–1815: Blue Lights & Psalm-Singers* (Woodbridge: The Boydell Press, 2008).

Blakemore, Richard J., 'The Legal World of English Sailors, c. 1575–1729', in Maria Fusaro, Bernard Allaire, Richard J. Blakemore, and Tijl Vanneste (eds.), *Law, Labour and Empire: Comparative Perspectives on Seafarers, c. 1500–1800* (Basingstoke: Palgrave Macmillan, 2015), 100–20.

'Pieces of Eight, Pieces of Eight: Seamen's Earnings and the Venture Economy of Early Modern Seafaring', *The Economic History Review* 70:4 (2017), 1153–84.

Blum, Matthias and Krauss, Karl-Peter, 'Age Heaping and Numeracy: Looking behind the Curtain', *Economic History Review* 71:2 (2018), 464–79.

Bolster, W. Jeffrey, *Black Jacks: African American Seamen in the Age of Sail* (Cambridge, MA: Harvard University Press, 1997).

'Letters by African American Sailors, 1799–1814', *The William and Mary Quarterly* 3rd Series 64:1 (2007), 167–82.

Booker, John, *Maritime Quarantine: The British Experience, c.1650–1900* (Aldershot and Burlington, VT: Ashgate, 2007).

Bravo, Martino Ferrari, 'The Nautical School of Venice of 1739 and the English Teachers. Navigation Training in Venice: Between Seamanship and Science', *Transactions of the Naval Dockyards Society* 5 (2009), 39–49.

Brockliss, Laurence, Cardwell, John and Moss, Michael, *Nelson's Surgeon: William Beatty, Naval Medicine, and the Battle of Trafalgar* (Oxford: Oxford University Press, 2005).

Broderick, George, 'The Development of Insular Celtic', in Per Sture Ureland (ed.), *Entstehung von Sprachen und Völkern: Glotto- und ethnogenetische Aspekte europäischer Sprachen – Akten des 6. Symposions über Sprachkontakt in Europa, Mannheim 1984* (Tübingen: Max Niemeyer Verlag, 1985), 153–80.

Brown, Anthony G., 'The Nore Mutiny – Sedition or Ships' Biscuits? A Reappraisal', *The Mariner's Mirror* 92:1 (2006), 60–74.

Brown, Christopher L., 'From Slaves to Subjects: Envisioning an Empire without Slavery, 1772–1834', in Philip D. Morgan and Sean Hawkins (eds.), *Black Experience and the Empire* (Oxford: Oxford University Press, 2006), 111–40.

Brubaker, Rogers, *Ethnicity without Groups* (Cambridge, MA and London: Harvard University Press, 2004).

'In the Name of the Nation: Reflections on Nationalism and Patriotism', *Citizenship Studies* 8:2 (2004), 115–27.

Brubaker, Rogers and Cooper, Frederick, 'Beyond "Identity"', *Theory and Society* 29 (2000), 1–47.

Bruijn, Jaap, 'Zeevarenden', in G. Asaert et al. (eds.), *Maritieme Geschiedenis der Nederlanden – Deel 3: Achttiende eeuw en eerste helft negentiende eeuw, van ca. 1680 tot 1850–1860* (Bussum: Uitgeverij De Boer Maritiem, 1976–8), 146–90.

'Seafarers in Early Modern and Modern Times: Change and Continuity', *International Journal of Maritime History* 17:1 (2005), 1–16.

The Dutch Navy of the Seventeenth and Eighteenth Centuries (St John's, Newfoundland: International Maritime Economic History Association, 2011).

Zeegang: Zeevarend Nederland in de achttiende eeuw (Zutphen: WalburgPers, 2016).

Brunsman, Denver, *The Evil Necessity: British Naval Impressment in the Eighteenth-Century Atlantic World* (Charlottesville, VA and London: University of Virginia Press, 2013).

Buchanan, Ian (ed.), *A Dictionary of Critical Theory*, 2nd ed. (Oxford: Oxford University Press, 2018).

Buchet, Christian, 'La Royal Navy et les levées d'hommes aux Antilles (1689–1763) : Difficultés rencontrées et modalités évolutives', *Histoire, économie et société* 4 (1990), 521–43.

Burg, B. R., *Boys at Sea: Sodomy, Indecency, and Courts Martial in Nelson's Navy* (Basingstoke: Palgrave Macmillan, 2007).

Burke, Peter, *Languages and Communities in Early Modern Europe* (Cambridge: Cambridge University Press, 2004).

Burroughs, Robert and Huzzey, Richard (eds.), *The Suppression of the Atlantic Slave Trade: British Policies, Practices and Representations of Naval Coercion* (Manchester: Manchester University Press, 2017).

Cabantous, Alain, *Le ciel dans la mer : Christianisme et civilisation maritime, XVIᵉ-XIXᵉ siècles* (Paris: Fayard, 1990).

Calaresu, Melissa, 'Looking for Virgil's Tomb: The End of the Grand Tour and the Cosmopolitan Ideal in Europe', in Jaś Elsner and Joan-Pau Rubiés (eds.), *Voyages and Visions: Towards a Cultural History of Travel* (London: Reaktion Books, 1999), 138–61.

'From the Street to Stereotype: Urban Space, Travel and the Picturesque in Late Eighteenth-Century Naples', *Italian Studies* 62:2 (2007), 189–203.

'Thomas Jones' Neapolitan Kitchen: The Material Cultures of Food on the Grand Tour', *Journal of Early Modern History* 24:1 (2020), 84–102.

Calaresu, Melissa and Hills, Helen, 'Between Exoticism and Marginalization: New Approaches to Naples', in Melissa Calaresu and Helen Hills (eds.), *New Approaches to Naples c.1500–c.1800: The Power of Place* (Farnham and Burlington, VT: Ashgate, 2013), 1–8.

Callister, Graeme, *War, Public Opinion and Policy in Britain, France and the Netherlands, 1785–1815* (Cham: Palgrave Macmillan, 2017).

Camargo, Anyela, Azuaje, Francisco, Wang, Haiying, and Zheng, Huiru, 'Permutation-based Statistical Tests for Multiple Hypotheses', *Source Code for Biology and Medicine* 3 (2008), 15.

Caputo, Sara, '*Scotland, Scottishness and the British Navy, c.1793–1815*' (unpublished MSc dissertation, The University of Edinburgh, 2015).

'Scotland, Scottishness, British Integration and the Royal Navy, 1793–1815', *The Scottish Historical Review* 97:1 (2018), 85–118.

'Alien Seamen in the British Navy, British Law, and the British State, *c.*1793–*c.*1815', *The Historical Journal* 62:3 (2019), 685–707.

'Vers une histoire transnationale de la marine Britannique au XVIIIe siècle', *Annales historiques de la Révolution Française* 397 (2019), 13–32.

'Mercenary Gentlemen? The Transnational Service of Foreign Quarterdeck Officers in the Royal Navy of the American and French Wars, 1775–1815', *Historical Research* 94:266 (2021), 806–26.

'Treating, Preventing, Feigning, Concealing: Sickness, Agency, and the Medical Culture of the British Naval Seaman at the End of the Long Eighteenth Century', *Social History of Medicine* (advance article, 2021).

'"Contriving to Pick Up Some Sailors": The Royal Navy and Foreign Manpower, 1815–1865', in Thomas Dodman and Aurélien Lignereux (eds.), *From the Napoleonic Empire to the Age of Empire – Empire after the Emperor* (Palgrave Macmillan, forthcoming 2023).

Carastro, Mario, 'E dopo Graefer? Gli amministratori della Ducea sino al 1873', *Bronte Insieme – La ducea inglese ai piedi dell'Etna (1799–1981)*, 2005 www.bronteinsieme.it/2st/nelson_graefer1.htm.

Cardwell, M. John, 'Royal Navy Surgeons, 1793–1815: A Collective Biography', in David Boyd Haycock and Sally Archer (eds.), *Health and Medicine at Sea, 1700–1900* (Woodbridge: The Boydell Press, 2009), 38–62.

Carpenter, Kirsty and Mansel, Philip (eds.), *The French Émigrés in Europe and the Struggle against Revolution, 1789–1814* (Basingstoke: Macmillan Press Ltd, 1999).

Carretta, Vincent, 'Naval Records and Eighteenth-Century Black Biography', *Journal for Maritime Research* 5:1 (2003), 143–58.

Carus, A. W. and Ogilvie, Sheilagh, 'Turning Qualitative into Quantitative Evidence: A Well-Used Method Made Explicit', *Economic History Review* 62:4 (2009), 893–925.

Cavell, S. A., *Midshipmen and Quarterdeck Boys in the British Navy, 1771–1831* (Woodbridge: The Boydell Press, 2012).

Cerutti, Simona, *Étrangers: Étude d'une condition d'incertitude dans une société d'Ancien Régime* (Montrouge Cedex: Bayard, 2012).

Charters, Erica, *Disease, War, and the Imperial State: The Welfare of the British Armed Forces during the Seven Years' War* (Chicago, MI and London: The University of Chicago Press, 2014).

Chase-Levenson, Alex, *The Yellow Flag: Quarantine and the British Mediterranean World, 1780–1860* (Cambridge: Cambridge University Press, 2020).

Chesterman, John, 'Natural-Born Subjects? Race and British Subjecthood in Australia', *Australian Journal of Politics and History* 51:1 (2005), 30–9.

'Chi-Square Test of Independence in R', *STHDA: Statistical Tools for High-Throughput Data Analysis*, www.sthda.com/english/wiki/chi-square-test-of-independence-in-r.

Chin, Aimee, Juhn, Chinhui, and Thompson, Peter, 'Technical Change and the Demand for Skills during the Second Industrial Revolution: Evidence from the Merchant Marine, 1891–1912', *The Review of Economics and Statistics* 88:3 (2006), 572–8.

Chircop, John, 'The Narrow-Sea Complex: A Hidden Dimension in Mediterranean Maritime History', in Gordon Boyce and Richard Gorski (eds.), *Resources and Infrastructures in the Maritime Economy, 1500–2000* (St. John's, Newfoundland: International Maritime Economic History Association, 2002), 43–61.

Churchill, Wendy D., 'Efficient, Efficacious and Humane Responses to Non-European Bodies in British Military Medicine, 1780–1815', *The Journal of Imperial and Commonwealth History* 40:2 (2012), 137–58.

Clarke, Joseph, 'Encountering the Sacred: British and French Soldiers in the Revolutionary and Napoleonic Mediterranean', in Joseph Clarke and John Horne (eds.), *Militarized Cultural Encounters in the Long Nineteenth Century: Making War, Mapping Europe* (Basingstoke: Palgrave Macmillan, 2018), 49–73.

Clemente, Alida, *Il Mestiere dell'incertezza. La pesca nel Golfo di Napoli tra XVIII e XX secolo* (Napoli: Alfredo Guida, 2005).

Coats, Ann Veronica and MacDougall, Philip (eds.), *The Naval Mutinies of 1797: Unity and Perseverance* (Woodbridge: The Boydell Press, 2011).

Cobley, Alan, 'Black West Indian Seamen in the British Merchant Marine in the Mid Nineteenth Century', *History Workshop Journal* 58 (2004), 259–74.

Cockburn, Alexander, *Nationality: or the Law Relating to Subjects and Aliens, Considered with a View to Future Legislation* (London: William Ridgway, 1869).

Cogliano, Francis D., '"We All Hoisted the American Flag": National Identity among American Prisoners in Britain during the American Revolution', *Journal of American Studies* 32:1 (1998), 19–37.

Cohen, Paul, 'Langues et pouvoirs politiques en France sous l'Ancien Régime : Cinq anti-lieux de mémoire pour une contre-histoire de la langue française', in Serge Lusignan et al. (eds.), *L'introuvable unité du français. Contacts et variations linguistiques en Europe et en Amérique (XIIe- XVIIIe siècle)* (Quebec City: Presses de l'Université Laval, 2012), 109–43.

Colville, Quintin and Davey, James (eds.), *A New Naval History* (Manchester: Manchester University Press, 2018).

Connor, Walker, *Ethnonationalism: The Quest for Understanding* (Princeton, NJ: Princeton University Press, 1994).

Constable, Marianne, *The Law of the Other: The Mixed Jury and Changing Conceptions of Citizenship, Law, and Knowledge* (Chicago, IL, and London: The University of Chicago Press, 1994).

Convertito, Coriann, *'The Health of British Seamen in the West Indies, 1770–1806'* (unpublished PhD thesis, University of Exeter, 2011).

Conway, Stephen, 'Continental Connections: Britain and Europe in the Eighteenth Century', *History* 90:299 (2005), 353–74.

   Britain, Ireland, and Continental Europe in the Eighteenth Century: Similarities, Connections, Identities (Oxford: Oxford University Press, 2011).

   'Continental European Soldiers in British Imperial Service, c.1756–1792', *English Historical Review* 129:536 (2014), 79–106.

   'Another Look at the Navigation Acts and the Coming of the American Revolution', in John McAleer and Christer Petley (eds.), *The Royal Navy and the British Atlantic World, c. 1750–1820* (London: Palgrave Macmillan, 2016), 77–96.

Britannia's Auxiliaries: Continental Europeans and the British Empire, 1740–1800 (Oxford: Oxford University Press, 2017).

Cordingly, David, *Billy Ruffian – The Bellerophon and the Downfall of Napoleon: The Biography of a Ship of the Line, 1782–1836* (London: Bloomsbury, 2003).

Cortese, Nino, 'Bausan, Giovanni', *Dizionario biografico degli Italiani – Volume 7*, Treccani, 1970 www.treccani.it/enciclopedia/giovanni-bausan_(Dizionario-Biografico)/.

Cox, Myron K. and Key, Coretta H., 'Post Hoc Pair-Wise Comparisons for the Chi-Square Test of Homogeneity of Proportions', *Educational and Psychological Measurement* 53 (1993), 951–62.

Craies, W. F., 'The Right of Aliens to Enter British Territory', *Law Quarterly Review* 6 (1890), 27–41.

Cressy, David, 'Levels of Illiteracy in England, 1530–1730', *The Historical Journal* 20:1 (1977), 1–23.

Crimmin, Pat, 'The Sick and Hurt Board and the Problem of Scurvy', *Journal for Maritime Research* 15:1 (2013), 47–53.

Cross, Anthony, 'The Elphinstones in Catherine the Great's Navy', in Mark Cornwall and Murray Frame (eds.), *Scotland and the Slavs: Cultures in Contact 1500–2000* (Newtonville, MA: Oriental Research Partners, 2001), 55–71.

Curtin, P. D., '"The White Man's Grave:" Image and Reality, 1780–1850', *Journal of British Studies* 1:1 (1961), 94–110.

Daae, Ludvig, *Nordmænds Udvandringer til Holland of England i nyere tid* (Christiania: Alb. Cammermeyer, 1880).

Dainotto, Roberto M., 'Does Europe Have a South? An Essay on Borders', *The Global South* 5:1 (2011), 37–50.

Dakhlia, Jocelyne, *Lingua Franca : Histoire d'une langue métisse en Méditerranée* (Arles: Actes Sud, 2008).

Dancy, J. Ross, *The Myth of the Press Gang: Volunteers, Impressment and the Naval Manpower Problem in the Late Eighteenth Century* (Woodbridge: The Boydell Press, 2015).

'Sources and Methods in the British Impressment Debate', *The International Journal of Maritime History* 30:4 (2018), 733–46.

D'Angelo, Michela, 'Oltre lo stretto. "Viva lu 'ngrisi, mannaja la Franza!"', in Renata De Lorenzo (ed.), *Ordine e disordine. Amministrazione e mondo militare nel Decennio francese – Atti del sesto seminario di studi "Decennio francese (1806–1815)"* (Napoli: Giannini Editore, 2012), 309–32.

Davey, James, 'Within Hostile Shores: Victualling the Royal Navy in European Waters during the French Revolutionary and Napoleonic Wars', *International Journal of Maritime History* 21:2 (2009), 241–60.

'The Royal Navy and the War with Denmark, 1808–1814', in Knut Arstad (ed.), *Krig på sjø og land: Norden i Napoleonskrigene* (Oslo: Forsvarsmuseet, 2014), 97–124.

Davey, James and Johns, Richard, *Broadsides: Caricature and the Navy 1756–1815* (Barnsley: Seaforth Publishing, 2012).

Davids, Karel, 'Maritime Labour in the Netherlands, 1570–1870', in Paul van Royen, Jaap Bruijn, and Jan Lucassen (eds.), *'Those Emblems of Hell'?*

European Sailors and the Maritime Labour Market, 1570–1870 (St John's, Newfoundland: International Maritime Economic History Association, 1997), 41–71.

Davies, J. D., *Britannia's Dragon: A Naval History of Wales* (Stroud: The History Press, 2013).

Davis, John A., 'The Neapolitan Revolution of 1799', *Journal of Modern Italian Studies* 4:3 (1999), 350–8.

Naples and Napoleon: Southern Italy and the European Revolutions (1780–1860) (Oxford: Oxford University Press, 2006).

Dawson, Kevin, 'Enslaved Swimmers and Divers in the Atlantic World', *The Journal of American History* 92:4 (2006), 1327–55.

'Enslaved Ship Pilots in the Age of Revolutions: Challenging Notions of Race and Slavery between the Boundaries of Land and Sea', *Journal of Social History* 47:1 (2013), 71–100.

Undercurrents of Power: Aquatic Culture in the African Diaspora (Philadelphia, PA: University of Pennsylvania Press, 2018).

'History Below the Waterline: Enslaved Salvage Divers Harvesting Seaports' Hinter-Seas in the Early Modern Atlantic', *International Review of Social History* 64 (2019), 43–70.

Dempsey, Guy C., Jr., *Napoleon's Mercenaries: Foreign Units in the French Army under the Consulate and Empire, 1799–1814* (London and Mechanicsburg, PA: Greenhill Books and Stackpole Books, 2002).

Desrosières, Alain, *The Politics of Large Numbers: A History of Statistical Reasoning*, trans. Camille Naish (Cambridge, MA and London: Harvard University Press, 1998).

Dixon, Conrad, 'Lascars: The Forgotten Seamen', in Rosemary Ommer and Gerald Panting (eds.), *Working Men Who Got Wet: Proceedings of the Fourth Conference of the Atlantic Canada Shipping Project July 24–July 26, 1980* (St. John's, Newfoundland: Memorial University of Newfoundland, 1980), 263–81.

Duffy, Michael, 'British Naval Intelligence and Bonaparte's Egyptian Expedition of 1798', *The Mariner's Mirror* 84:3 (1998), 278–90.

Duncan, James S., *In the Shadows of the Tropics: Climate, Race and Biopower in Nineteenth Century Ceylon* (Aldershot: Ashgate, 2007).

Dursteler, Eric R., 'Speaking in Tongues: Language and Communication in the Early Modern Mediterranean', *Past & Present* 217 (2012), 47–77.

Dye, Ira, 'American Maritime Prisoners of War, 1812–1815', in Timothy J. Runyan (ed.), *Ships, Seafaring, and Society: Essays in Maritime History* (Detroit, MI: Wayne State University Press, 1987), 293–320.

Earle, Rebecca, 'The Political Economy of Nutrition in the Eighteenth Century', *Past & Present* 242 (2019), 79–117.

Easton, Callum, 'Counter-Theatre during the 1797 Fleet Mutinies', *International Review of Social History* 64:3 (2019), 389–414.

Eder, Markus, *Crime and Punishment in the Royal Navy of the Seven Years' War, 1755–1763* (Aldershot and Burlington, VT: Ashgate, 2004).

Elias, Norbert and Scotson, John L., *The Established and the Outsiders: A Sociological Enquiry into Community Problems*, 2nd ed. (London: SAGE, 1994).

Elliott, Marianne, *Partners in Revolution: The United Irishmen and France* (New Haven, CT and London: Yale University Press, 1982).

Emsley, Clive, 'The Recruitment of Petty Offenders during the French Wars 1793–1815', *The Mariner's Mirror* 66:3 (1980), 199–208.

Enea, Maria Rosaria and Gatto, Romano, *Matematica e marineria: Accademia e Scuole di Marina nel Regno di Napoli* (Naples: La Città del Sole, 2013?).

Evans, Neil, 'Across the Universe: Racial Violence and the Post-War Crisis in Imperial Britain, 1919–1925', in Diane Frost (ed.), *Ethnic Labour and British Imperial Trade: A History of Ethnic Seafarers in the UK* (London: Frank Cass, 1995), 59–88.

Evans, Robin, *The Fabrication of Virtue: English Prison Architecture, 1750–1840* (Cambridge: Cambridge University Press, 1982).

Fabel, Robin F. A., 'Self-Help in Dartmoor: Black and White Prisoners in the War of 1812', *Journal of the Early Republic* 9:2 (1989), 165–90.

Fahrmeir, Andreas, *Citizens and Aliens: Foreigners and the Law in Britain and the German States, 1789–1870* (New York and Oxford: Berghahn Books, 2000).

Falck, Oliver, Heblich, Stephan, Lameli, Alfred, and Südekum, Jens, 'Dialects, Cultural Identity, and Economic Exchange', *Journal of Urban Economics* 72 (2012), 225–39.

Falck, Oliver, Lameli, Alfred, and Ruhose, Jens, 'Cultural Biases in Migration: Estimating Non-Monetary Migration Costs', *Papers in Regional Science* 97:2 (2018), 411–38.

Fedosov, Dmitry, 'Under the Saltire: Scots and the Russian Navy, 1690s–1910s', in Mark Cornwall and Murray Frame (eds.), *Scotland and the Slavs: Cultures in Contact 1500–2000* (Newtonville, MA: Oriental Research Partners, 2001), 21–53.

Feinberg, H. M., 'New Data on European Mortality in West Africa: The Dutch on the Gold Coast, 1719–1760', *Journal of African History* 15:3 (1974), 357–71.

Ferreiro, Larrie D., 'Spies versus Prize: Technology Transfer between Navies in the Age of Trafalgar', *The Mariner's Mirror* 93:1 (2007), 16–27.

Field, Andy, Miles, Jeremy, and Field, Zoë, *Discovering Statistics Using R* (London: SAGE, 2012).

Field, Clive D., 'Counting Religion in England and Wales: The Long Eighteenth Century, c.1680–c.1840', *Journal of Ecclesiastical History* 63:4 (2012), 693–720.

Fiorini, Stanley, 'A Survey of Maltese Nicknames I: The Nicknames of Naxxar, 1832', *Journal of Maltese Studies* 16 (1986), 62–82.

Fisher, Michael H., 'Working across the Seas: Indian Maritime Labourers in India, Britain, and in Between, 1600–1857', *International Review of Social History* 51 (2006), 21–45.

'Indian Ghat Sarangs as Maritime Labour Recruiting Intermediaries during the Age of Sail', *Journal for Maritime Research* 16:2 (2014), 153–66.

Fitzgerald, Ian and Smoczynski, Rafal, 'Anti-Polish Migrant Moral Panic in the UK: Rethinking Employment Insecurities and Moral Regulation', *Sociologický Časopis/Czech Sociological Review* 51:3 (2015), 339–61.

Fothergill, Brian, *Sir William Hamilton: Envoy Extraordinary* (London: Faber and Faber, 1969).
Foy, Charles R., 'Uncovering Hidden Lives: Developing a Database of Mariners in the Black Atlantic', *Common-Place* 9:2 (2009) www.common-place-archives.org/vol-09/no-02/tales/.
'"Unkle Sommerset's" Freedom: Liberty in England for Black Sailors', *Journal for Maritime Research* 13:1 (2011), 21–36.
'Seamen "Love Their Bellies": How Blacks Became Ship Cooks', 10 August 2014, *Uncovering Hidden Lives: Eighteenth Century Black Mariners* https://uncoveringhiddenlives.com/.
'The Royal Navy's Employment of Black Mariners and Maritime Workers, 1754–1783', *The International Journal of Maritime History* 28:1 (2016), 6–35.
Frost, Diane, 'Racism, Work and Unemployment: West African Seamen in Liverpool 1880s–1960s', in Diane Frost (ed.), *Ethnic Labour and British Imperial Trade: A History of Ethnic Seafarers in the UK* (London: Frank Cass, 1995), 22–33.
Frykman, Niklas, 'Seamen on Late Eighteenth-Century European Warships', *International Review of Social History* 54 (2009), 67–93.
'The Mutiny on the Hermione: Warfare, Revolution, and Treason in the Royal Navy', *Journal of Social History* 44:1 (2010), 159–87.
'Connections between Mutinies in European Navies', in Clare Anderson, Niklas Frykman, Lex Heerma van Voss, and Marcus Rediker (eds.), *Mutiny and Maritime Radicalism in the Age of Revolution* (Cambridge: Press Syndicate of the University of Cambridge, 2013), 87–107.
The Bloody Flag: Mutiny in the Age of Atlantic Revolution (Oakland, CA: University of California Press, 2020).
Galani, Katerina, *British Shipping in the Mediterranean during the Napoleonic Wars: The Untold Story of a Successful Adaptation* (Leiden and Boston, MA: Brill, 2017).
Gallagher, John, 'The Italian London of John North: Cultural Contact and Linguistic Encounter in Early Modern England', *Renaissance Quarterly* 70 (2017), 88–131.
'Language-Learning, Orality, and Multilingualism in Early Modern Anglophone Narratives of Mediterranean Captivity', *Renaissance Studies* 33:4 (2019), 639–61.
Galster, Kjeld Hald, 'Den Britiske invasion i Danmark, terrorbombardementet af København og Flådens ran', in Knut Arstad (ed.), *Krig på sjø og land: Norden i Napoleonskrigene* (Oslo: Forsvarsmuseet, 2014), 73–95.
Garrett, Aaron and Sebastiani, Silvia, 'David Hume on Race', in Naomi Zack (ed.), *The Oxford Handbook of Philosophy and Race* (Oxford: Oxford University Press, 2017).
Gash, N., 'After Waterloo: British Society and the Legacy of the Napoleonic Wars', *Transactions of the Royal Historical Society* 28 (1978), 145–57.
Gellner, Ernest, *Nations and Nationalism* (Oxford: Blackwell Publishers, 1983).
Giardino, Antonio Ermanno and Rak, Michele, *Per grazia ricevuta: Le tavolette dipinte ex voto per la Madonna dell'Arco – Il Cinquecento* (Naples: Ci.esse.ti cooperativa editrice, 1983).

Gilje, Paul A., '"Free Trade and Sailors' Rights": The Rhetoric of the War of 1812', *Journal of the Early Republic* 30 (2010), 1–23.

Free Trade and Sailors' Rights in the War of 1812 (Cambridge: Cambridge University Press, 2013).

To Swear like a Sailor: Maritime Culture in America, 1750–1850 (Cambridge: Cambridge University Press, 2016).

Glenn, Myra C., 'Forging Manhood and Nationhood Together: American Sailors' Accounts of their Exploits, Sufferings, and Resistance in the Antebellum United States', *American Nineteenth Century History* 8:1 (2007), 27–49.

Glenthøj, Rasmus and Ottosen, Morten Nordhagen, *Experiences of War and Nationality in Denmark and Norway, 1807–1815* (Basingstoke: Palgrave Macmillan, 2014).

Glete, Jan, *Navies and Nations: Warships, Navies and State Building in Europe and America, 1500–1860*, 2 vols. (Stockholm: Almqvist & Wiksell International, 1993).

Golby, David J., 'Corri Family (per. c.1770–1860)', *Oxford Dictionary of National Biography*, online ed. (Oxford: Oxford University Press, 2014) www .oxforddnb.com/view/article/69602.

Gooskens, Charlotte and Swarte, Femke, 'Linguistic and Extra-Linguistic Predictors of Mutual Intelligibility between Germanic Languages', *Nordic Journal of Linguistics* 40:2 (2017), 123–47.

Gooskens, Charlotte et al., 'Mutual Intelligibility between Closely Related Languages in Europe', *International Journal of Multilingualism* (2017), 1–25.

Gould, Eliga H., 'Zones of Law, Zones of Violence: The Legal Geography of the British Atlantic, circa 1772', *The William and Mary Quarterly* 60:3 (2003), 471–510.

Gradish, Stephen F., *The Manning of the British Navy during the Seven Years' War* (London: Royal Historical Society, 1980).

Graf, Arturo, *L'anglomania e l'influsso inglese in Italia nel secolo XVIII* (Turin: Ermanno Loescher, 1911).

Grant, James, *Cassell's Old and New Edinburgh: Its History, Its People, and Its Places*, 6 vols. (London: Cassell, Petter, Galpin & Co., 1881–7).

Green, Geoffrey L., *The Royal Navy and Anglo-Jewry 1740–1820: Traders and Those Who Served* (London: Geoffrey Green [The Self Publishing Association], 1989).

Green, Nancy L., *The Limits of Transnationalism* (Chicago, IL, and London: The University of Chicago Press, 2019).

Green, Samuel G., *The Story of the Religious Tract Society for One Hundred Years* (London: The Religious Tract Society, 1899).

Greene, Molly, 'The Mediterranean Sea', in David Armitage, Alison Bashford, and Sujit Sivasundaram (eds.), *Oceanic Histories* (Cambridge: Cambridge University Press, 2017), 134–55.

Greenwood, Michael J., 'Research on Internal Migration in the United States: A Survey', *Journal of Economic Literature* 13:2 (1975), 397–433.

Gregory, Desmond, *Malta, Britain, and the European Powers, 1793–1815* (Cranbury, NJ: Associated University Presses, 1996).

Greiling, Meredith, 'Sacred Vessels: British Church Ship Models', *The International Journal of Maritime History* 27:4 (2015), 793–7.

Grima, Joseph F., *The Fleet of the Knights of Malta: Its Organisation during the Eighteenth Century* (San Ġwann: BDL Publishing, 2016).

Guyatt, Nicholas, *The Hated Cage: An American Tragedy in Britain's Most Terrifying Prison* (New York: Basic Books, 2022).

Haas, J. M., *A Management Odyssey: The Royal Dockyards, 1714–1914* (Lanham, MD: University Press of America, 1994).

Hailwood, Mark, '"The Rabble That Cannot Read"? Ordinary People's Literacy in Seventeenth-Century England', *The Many-Headed Monster*, 13 October 2014 https://manyheadedmonster.wordpress.com/2014/10/13/the-rabble-that-cannot-read-ordinary-peoples-literacy-in-seventeenth-century-england/.

Hamilton, Douglas, '"A Most Active, Enterprising Officer": Captain John Perkins, the Royal Navy and the Boundaries of Slavery and Liberty in the Caribbean', *Slavery & Abolition* 39:1 (2018), 80–100.

Hamilton, W. Mark, *The Nation and the Navy: Methods and Organization of British Navalist Propaganda, 1889–1914* (New York and London: Garland Publishing Inc., 1986).

Hammar, AnnaSara, 'How to Transform Peasants into Seamen: The Manning of the Swedish Navy and a Double-Faced Maritime Culture', *The International Journal of Maritime History* 27:4 (2015), 696–707.

Hanley, Will, *Identifying with Nationality: Europeans, Ottomans, and Egyptians in Alexandria* (New York: Columbia University Press, 2017).

Hansen, Kim Philip, *Military Chaplains and Religious Diversity* (New York and Basingstoke: Palgrave Macmillan, 2012).

Harland, John, *Seamanship in the Age of Sail: An Account of the Shiphandling of the Sailing Man-of-War 1600–1860, Based on Contemporary Sources* (London: Conway, 2015).

Harper, Lawrence A., *The English Navigation Laws: A Seventeenth-Century Experiment in Social Engineering* (New York: Columbia University Press, 1939).

Harrison, Mark, '"The Tender Frame of Man": Disease, Climate, and Racial Difference in India and the West Indies, 1760–1860', *Bulletin of the History of Medicine* 70:1 (1996), 68–93.

Haudrère, Philippe, 'Heurs et malheurs des voyages maritimes sur la route des indes orientales au XVIIIᵉ siècle', *Annales de Bretagne et des Pays de l'Ouest* 121:3 (2014), 165–75.

Haupt, Heinz-Gerhard, 'Une nouvelle sensibilité : la perspective "transnationale"', *Cahiers Jaurès* 200 (2011–12), 173–80.

Hay, Douglas, 'Property, Authority and the Criminal Law', in Douglas Hay et al., *Albion's Fatal Tree: Crime and Society in Eighteenth-Century England* (London: Allen Lane and New York: Pantheon, 1975), 17–63.

Hayman, John G., 'Notions on National Characters in the Eighteenth Century', *Huntington Library Quarterly* 35:1 (1971), 1–17.

Heimburger, Franziska, 'Of Go-Betweens and Gatekeepers: Considering Disciplinary Biases in Interpreting History through Exemplary Metaphors.

Military Interpreters in the Allied Coalition during the First World War', in Beatrice Fischer and Matilde Nisbeth Jensen (eds.), *Translation and the Reconfiguration of Power Relations. Revisiting Role and Context of Translation and Interpreting* (Zurich and Berlin: Lit Verlag, 2012), 21–34.

Hobsbawm, E. J., *Nations and Nationalism since 1780: Programme, Myth, Reality*, 2nd ed. (Cambridge: Cambridge University Press, 1990).

Hogarth, Rana A., *Medicalizing Blackness: Making Racial Difference in the Atlantic World, 1780–1840* (Chapel Hill, NC: University of North Carolina Press, 2017).

Horden, Peregrine and Purcell, Nicholas, *The Corrupting Sea: A Study of Mediterranean History* (Oxford: Blackwell Publishing, 2000).

'The Mediterranean and "the New Thalassology"', *The American Historical Review* 111:3 (2006), 722–40.

Hudson, Nicholas, 'From "Nation" to "Race": The Origin of Racial Classification in Eighteenth-Century Thought', *Eighteenth-Century Studies* 29:3 (1996), 247–64.

Hudson, Pat and Ishizu, Mina, *History by Numbers: An Introduction to Quantitative Approaches*, 2nd ed. (London and New York: Bloomsbury, 2017).

Hunt, Margaret, 'Credit, Crime and Gender in English Maritime Communities 1650–1750', The Eighteenth-Century Seminar, University of Cambridge, 23 October 2018.

Iermano, Toni, 'Forteguerri, Bartolomeo', *Dizionario biografico degli Italiani – Volume 49, Treccani*, 1997 www.treccani.it/enciclopedia/bartolomeo-forte guerri_(Dizionario-Biografico)/.

Immerwahr, John, 'Hume's Revised Racism', *Journal of the History of Ideas* 53:3 (1992), 481–6.

Jaffer, Aaron, *Lascars and Indian Ocean Seafaring, 1780–1860: Shipboard Life, Unrest and Mutiny* (Woodbridge: The Boydell Press, 2015).

James, William, *The Naval History of Great Britain, from the Declaration of War by France, in February 1793; to the Accession of George IV in January 1820*, 6 vols., new ed. (London: Richard Bentley, 1886).

Jenks, Timothy, *Naval Engagements: Patriotism, Cultural Politics, and the Royal Navy 1793–1815* (Oxford and New York: Oxford University Press, 2006).

Jianu, Angela and Barbu, Violeta (eds.), *Earthly Delights: Economies and Cultures of Food in Ottoman and Danubian Europe, c. 1500–1900* (Leiden and Boston, MA: Brill, 2018).

Johansen, Hans Chr., 'Scandinavian Shipping in the Late Eighteenth Century in a European Perspective', *The Economic History Review* 45:3 (1992), 479–93.

'Danish Sailors, 1570–1870', in Paul van Royen, Jaap Bruijn, and Jan Lucassen (eds.), *'Those Emblems of Hell'? European Sailors and the Maritime Labour Market, 1570–1870* (St John's, Newfoundland: International Maritime Economic History Association, 1997), 233–52.

Johnsen, Berit Eide, *Han sad i prisonen… Sjøfolk i engelsk fangenskap 1807–1814* (Oslo: Universitetsforlaget, 1993).

'Norske sjøfolk i prisonen', in Helge Gamrath et al (eds.), *Nordjylland under Englandskrigen 1807–1814* (Aalborg: Aalborg Universitetsforlag, 2009), 285–96.

Jones, Elin, 'Space, Sound and Sedition on the Royal Naval Ship, 1756–1815', *Journal of Historical Geography* 70 (2020), 65–73.

Juan y Ferragut, Mariano, 'Jorge Juan: Su misión en Londres y la construcción naval española', in *Cuaderno n. 68 del Instituto de Historia y Cultura Naval – Jorge Juan y la ciencia ilustrada en España* (Madrid: Ministerio de Defensa, 2013), 91–107.

Kert, Faye Margaret, *Prize and Prejudice: Privateering and Naval Prize in Atlantic Canada in the War of 1812* (St John's, Newfoundland: International Maritime Economic History Association, 1997).

Kidd, Colin, 'Race, Empire, and the Limits of Nineteenth-Century Scottish Nationhood', *The Historical Journal* 46:4 (2003), 873–92.

   The Forging of Races: Race and Scripture in the Protestant Atlantic World, 1600–2000 (Cambridge: Cambridge University Press, 2006).

Kikkert, J. G., *Geld, macht & eer: Willem I, Koning der Nederlanders en Belgen 1772–1843* (Utrecht: Scheffers, 1995).

King, Peter, 'Decision-Makers and Decision-Making in the English Criminal Law, 1750–1800', *The Historical Journal* 27:1 (1984), 25–58.

Kiple, Kenneth F. and Kiple, Virginia H., 'Black Yellow Fever Immunities, Innate and Acquired, as Revealed in the American South', *Social Science History* 1:4 (1977), 419–36.

Kirch, Max S., 'Non-Verbal Communication across Cultures', *The Modern Language Journal* 63:8 (1979), 416–23.

Knight, Roger, *The Pursuit of Victory: The Life and Achievement of Horatio Nelson* (London: Penguin Books, 2006).

   'Changing the Agenda: The "New" Naval History of the British Sailing Navy', *The Mariner's Mirror* 97:1 (2011), 225–42.

Knight, Roger and Wilcox, Martin, *Sustaining the Fleet, 1793–1815: War, the British Navy and the Contractor State* (Woodbridge: The Boydell Press, 2010).

Kostantaras, Dean, 'Perfecting the Nation: Enlightenment Perspectives on the Coincidence of Linguistic and "National" Refinement', *European Review of History: Revue européenne d'histoire* 24:5 (2017), 659–82.

Koziurenok, K. L., 'Голландске офицеры в Российском Военно-морском флоте (вторая половина XVIII – начало XIX в.)', in Yu. N. Bespiatykh, Ia. V. Veluvenkamp, and L. D. Popova (eds.), *Нидерланды и северная Россия* (Saint Petersburg: Русско–Балтийский информационный центр, 2003), 299–324.

Kverndal, Roald, *Seamen's Missions: Their Origin and Early Growth – A Contribution to the History of the Church Maritime* (Pasadena, CA: William Carey Library, 1986).

Lafi, Nora, 'La langue des marchands de Tripoli au XIXe siècle : Langue franque et langue arabe dans un port méditerranéen', in Jocelyne Dakhlia (ed.), *Trames de langues : Usages et métissages linguistiques dans l'histoire du Maghreb* (Paris: Maisonneuve & Larose, 2004), 215–22.

Land, Isaac, 'Customs of the Sea: Flogging, Empire, and the "True British Seaman" 1770 to 1870', *Interventions* 3:2 (2001), 169–85.

   'The Many-Tongued Hydra: Sea Talk, Maritime Culture, and Atlantic Identities, 1700–1850', *Journal of American & Comparative Cultures* 25:3–4 (2002), 412–17.

War, Nationalism, and the British Sailor, 1750–1850 (New York: Palgrave Macmillan, 2009).

'New Scholarship on the Press Gang – Part 2 of 2', *Port Towns & Urban Cultures*, 3 August 2015 http://porttowns.port.ac.uk/press-gang2/.

Lande, R. Gregory, *Madness, Malingering, and Malfeasance: The Transformation of Psychiatry and the Law in the Civil War Era* (Washington, DC: Brassey's, Inc., 2003).

Lane, Tony, 'The Political Imperatives of Bureaucracy and Empire: The Case of the Coloured Alien Seamen Order, 1925', in Diane Frost (ed.), *Ethnic Labour and British Imperial Trade: A History of Ethnic Seafarers in the UK* (London: Frank Cass, 1995), 104–29.

Langbein, John H., 'Albion's Fatal Flaws', *Past & Present* 98 (1983), 96–120.

Langley, Harold D., 'The Negro in the Navy and Merchant Service – 1789–1860 1798', *The Journal of Negro History* 52:4 (1967), 273–86.

Laughton, J. K., 'The National Study of Naval History', *Transactions of the Royal Historical Society* 12 (1898), 81–93.

Laughton, J. K. and Morris, R. O., 'Smyth, William Henry (1788–1865)', *Oxford Dictionary of National Biography*, online ed. (Oxford: Oxford University Press, 2015) www.oxforddnb.com/view/article/25961.

Lavery, Brian, *Nelson's Navy: The Ships, Men and Organisation 1793–1815* (London: Conway Maritime Press, 1989).

Shipboard Life and Organisation, 1731–1815 (Aldershot and Brookfield, VT: Ashgate, 1998).

Shield of Empire: The Royal Navy and Scotland (Edinburgh: Birlinn, 2007).

Lawless, Dick, 'The Role of Seamen's Agents in the Migration for Employment of Arab Seafarers in the Early Twentieth Century', in Diane Frost (ed.), *Ethnic Labour and British Imperial Trade: A History of Ethnic Seafarers in the UK* (London: Frank Cass, 1995), 34–58.

Lawrence, Christopher, 'Disciplining Disease: Scurvy, the Navy, and Imperial Expansion, 1750–1825', in David Philip Miller and Peter Hanns Reill (eds.), *Visions of Empire: Voyages, Botany, and Representations of Nature* (Cambridge: Cambridge University Press, 1996), 80–106.

Lemisch, Jesse, 'Jack Tar in the Streets: Merchant Seamen in the Politics of Revolutionary America', *The William and Mary Quarterly* 25:3 (1968), 371–407.

'Listening to the "Inarticulate": William Widger's Dream and the Loyalties of American Revolutionary Seamen in British Prisons', *Journal of Social History* 3:1 (1969), 1–29.

Lemmi, Francesco, *Nelson e Caracciolo e la Repubblica Napoletana (1799)* (Florence: G. Carnesecchi e figli, 1898).

Lemmings, David, 'Introduction: Law and Order, Moral Panics, and Early Modern England', in David Lemmings and Claire Walker (eds.), *Moral Panics, the Media and the Law in Early Modern England* (Basingstoke: Palgrave Macmillan, 2009), 1–21.

Leow, Rachel, *Taming Babel: Language in the Making of Malaysia* (Cambridge: Cambridge University Press, 2016).

Letters by Historicus on Some Questions of International Law (London and Cambridge: Macmillan and Co., 1863).

Leunig, Tim, van Lottum, Jelle, and Poulsen, Bo, 'How Bad Were British Prison Hulks in the Napoleonic Wars? Evidence from Captured Danish and Norwegian Seamen', *The London School of Economics and Political Science – Economic History Working Papers*, No: 232/20160 (January 2016).

'Surprisingly Gentle Confinement: British Treatment of Danish and Norwegian Prisoners of War during the Napoleonic Wars', *Scandinavian Economic History Review* 66:3 (2018), 282–97.

Lewis, Michael, *The Navy in Transition 1814–1864: A Social History* (London: Hodder and Stoughton, 1965).

A Social History of the Navy 1793–1815, new ed. (London and Mechanicsburg, PA: Chatham Publishing, 2004 [1960]).

Liauzu, Claude, 'Mots et migrants méditerranéens', *Cahiers de la Méditerranée* 54:1 (1997), 1–14.

Lijó, J. M. Vázquez, *'La Matrícula de Mar y sus repercusiones en la Galicia del siglo XVIII'* (unpublished PhD thesis, Universidad de Santiago de Compostela, 2005).

Lin, Patricia Y. C. E., 'Caring for the Nation's Families: British Soldiers' and Sailors' Families and the State, 1793–1815', in Alan Forrest, Karen Hagemann, and Jane Rendall (eds.), *Soldiers, Citizens and Civilians: Experiences and Perceptions of the Revolutionary and Napoleonic Wars, 1790–1820* (Basingstoke: Palgrave Macmillan, 2009), 99–117.

Linch, Kevin, 'The Politics of Foreign Recruitment in Britain during the French Revolutionary and Napoleonic Wars', in Nir Arielli and Bruce Collins (eds.), *Transnational Soldiers: Foreign Military Enlistment in the Modern Era* (Basingstoke: Palgrave Macmillan, 2013), 50–66.

Lincoln, Margarette, *Representing the Royal Navy: British Sea Power, 1750–1815* (Aldershot and Burlington, VT: Ashgate, 2002).

Naval Wives & Mistresses (London: National Maritime Museum, 2007).

Trading in War: London's Maritime World in the Age of Cook and Nelson (New Haven, CT and London: Yale University Press, 2018).

Linebaugh, Peter and Rediker, Marcus, *The Many-Headed Hydra: Sailors, Slaves, Commoners, and the Hidden History of the Revolutionary Atlantic* (London and New York: Verso, 2000).

Lloyd, Christopher, *The British Seaman 1200–1960. A Social Survey* (London: Collins, 1968).

Lo Basso, Luca, 'Lavoro marittimo, tutela istituzionale e conflittualità sociale a bordo dei bastimenti della Repubblica di Genova nel XVIII secolo', *Mediterranea* 12 (2015), 147–68.

Lo Sardo, Eugenio, *Napoli e Londra nel XVIII secolo: Le relazioni economiche* (Naples: Jovene, 1991).

Lockwood, Matthew, '"Love Ye Therefore the Strangers": Immigration and the Criminal Law in Early Modern England', *Continuity and Change* 29 (2014), 349–71.

López, Carolina et al., 'Mechanisms of Genetically-Based Resistance to Malaria', *Gene* 467 (2010), 1–12.

Loveman, Mara, 'Is "Race" Essential?', *American Sociological Review* 64:6 (1999), 891–8.

Lucassen, Jan and Penninx, Rinus, *Newcomers: Immigrants and Their Descendants in the Netherlands, 1550–1995* (Amsterdam: Het Spinhuis, 1997).

Lucker, Ivonne, 'Jacob Dirksen: A Norwegian Sailor in the Dutch Republic (1727–1754)', in Louis Sicking, Harry de Bles, and Erlend des Bouvrie (eds.), *Dutch Light in the 'Norwegian Night': Maritime Relations and Migration across the North Sea in Early Modern Times* (Hilversum: Uitgeverij Verloren, 2004), 81–91.

Luttrell, Anthony, 'Eighteenth-Century Malta: Prosperity and Problems', *Hyphen* 3:2 (1982), 37–51.

Macdonald, Janet, *Feeding Nelson's Navy: The True Story of Food at Sea in the Georgian Era* (London and Mechanicsberg, PA: Chatham Publishing and Stackpole Books, 2004).

MacDougall, Ian, *All Men Are Brethren: French, Scandinavian, Italian, German, Dutch, Belgian, Spanish, Polish, West Indian, American, and Other Prisoners of War in Scotland during the Napoleonic Wars, 1803–1814* (Edinburgh: Birlinn, 2008).

Mackesy, Piers, *Statesmen at War: The Strategy of Overthrow 1798–1799* (London and New York: Longman, 1974).

Macleod, Donald John, 'Hebridean Service with the Royal Navy', in *The Islands Book Trust, Island Heroes: The Military History of the Hebrides* (Isle of Lewis: Islands Book Trust, 2010), 73–90.

Magra, Christopher P., 'Faith at Sea: Exploring Maritime Religiosity in the Eighteenth Century', *International Journal of Maritime History* 19:1 (2007), 87–106.

Poseidon's Curse: British Naval Impressment and Atlantic Origins of the American Revolution (Cambridge: Cambridge University Press, 2016).

Mahan, A. T., *The Influence of Sea Power upon the French Revolution and Empire, 1793–1812*, 2 vols. (Boston, MA: Little, Brown, and Company, 1892).

The Life of Nelson the Embodiment of the Sea Power of Great Britain, 2nd ed. (Boston, MA: Little, Brown, and Company, 1899).

Malcomson, Thomas, 'Freedom by Reaching the Wooden World: American Slaves and the British Navy during the War of 1812', *The Northern Mariner/Le marin du nord* 22:4 (2012), 361–92.

[Maresca, Benedetto], 'I marinai napoletani nella spedizione del 1784 contro Algieri (da un diario contemporaneo)', *Archivio storico per le province napoletane* 17:1 (1892), 808–50.

Maresca, Massimo, *Il Museo navale Mario Maresca di Meta* (Castellammare di Stabia: Nicola Longobardi editore, 2008).

Maresca, Massimo and Passaro, Biagio, *La Marineria della Penisola Sorrentina e la cantieristica in legno da Marina d'Equa a Marina Grande: Shipowners, Shipping and Wooden Shipbuilding in the Sorrento Peninsula* (Sorrento: Con-fine edizioni, 2011).

Martin, Philip and Zürcher, Gottfried, 'Managing Migration: The Global Challenge', *Population Bulletin* 63:1 (2008), 3–20.

Marzagalli, Silvia, 'Négoce et politique des étrangers en France à l'époque moderne : discours et pratiques de rejet et d'intégration', in Mickaël Augeron and Pascal Éven (eds.), *Les Étrangers dans les villes-ports atlantiques : Expériences* *françaises et allemandes XVe-XIXe siècle* (Paris: Les Indes Savantes, 2011), 45–62.

'Maritimity: How the Sea Affected Early Modern Life in the Mediterranean World', in Mihran Dabag, Dieter Haller, Nikolas Jaspert, and Achim Lichtenberger (eds.), *New Horizons: Mediterranean Research in the Twenty-first Century* (Paderborn: Ferdinand Schöningh, 2016), 309–31.

Marzagalli, Silvia and Müller, Leos, '"In Apparent Disagreement with All Law of Nations in the World": Negotiating Neutrality for Shipping and Trade during the French Revolutionary and Napoleonic Wars', *The International Journal of Maritime History* 28:1 (2016), 108–17.

Massey, Douglas S. et al., 'Theories of International Migration: A Review and Appraisal', *Population and Development Review* 19:3 (1993), 431–66.

McCain, Stewart, *The Language Question under Napoleon* (Basingstoke: Palgrave Macmillan, 2017).

McCranie, Kevin, 'The Recruitment of Seamen for the British Navy, 1793–1815: "Why Don't You Raise More Men?"', in Donald Stoker, Frederick C. Schneid, and Harold D. Blanton (eds.), *Conscription in the Napoleonic Era: A Revolution in Military Affairs?* (London and New York: Routledge, 2009), 84–101.

McEvoy, Timothy, 'Finding a Teacher of Navigation Abroad in Eighteenth-Century Venice: A Study of the Circulation of Useful Knowledge', *History of Science* 51 (2013), 100–23.

McGerr, Michael, 'The Price of the "New Transnational History"', *The American Historical Review* 96:4 (1991), 1056–67.

McLachlan, N. D., 'Bathurst at the Colonial Office, 1812–1827: A Reconnaissance', *Australian Historical Studies* 13:52 (1969), 477–502.

McNeill, J. R., *Mosquito Empires: Ecology and War in the Greater Caribbean, 1620–1914* (Cambridge: Cambridge University Press, 2010).

Mifsud, A., *Knights Hospitallers of the Ven. Tongue of England in Malta* (Valletta: Herald Print. Off., 1914).

Miller, Marion S., 'Italian Jacobinism', *Eighteenth-Century Studies* 11:2 (1977–8), 246–52.

Miller, R. W. H., *One Firm Anchor: The Church and the Merchant Seafarer, an Introductory History* (Cambridge. The Lutterworth Press, 2012).

Molhuysen, P. C. and Blok, P. J. (eds.), *Nieuw Nederlandsch biografisch woorden-boek*, 10 vols. (Leiden: A. W. Sijthoff, 1911).

Morgan, Philip D., 'Black Experiences in Britain's Maritime World', in David Cannadine (ed.), *Empire, the Sea and Global History: Britain's Maritime World, c.1760–c.1840* (Basingstoke: Palgrave Macmillan, 2007), 105–33.

Morieux, Renaud, 'Des règles aux pratiques juridiques : Le droit des étrangers en France et en Angleterre pendant la Révolution (1792–1802)', in Ph. Chassaigne and J.-P. Genet (eds.), *Droit et société en France et en Grande-Bretagne (XIIe–XXe siècles). Fonctions, usages et représentations* (Paris: Publications de la Sorbonne, 2003), 127–47.

Une mer pour deux royaumes : La Manche, frontière franco-anglaise (XVIIe–XVIIIe siècles) (Rennes: Presses Universitaires de Rennes, 2008).

'Diplomacy from Below and Belonging: Fishermen and Cross-Channel Relations in the Eighteenth Century', *Past & Present* 202 (2009), 83–125.

'Patriotisme humanitaire et prisonniers de guerre en France et en Grande-Bretagne pendant la Révolution française et l'Empire', in Laurent Bourquin et al. (eds.), *La politique par les armes. Conflits internationaux et politisation, XVe–XIXe siècles* (Rennes: Presses Universitaires de Rennes, 2014), 301–16.

The Channel: England, France and the Construction of a Maritime Border in the Eighteenth Century (Cambridge: Cambridge University Press, 2016).

'Indigenous Comparisons', in John H. Arnold, Matthew Hilton, and Jan Rüger (eds.), *History after Hobsbawm: Writing the Past for the Twenty-First Century* (Oxford: Oxford University Press, 2017), 50–75.

The Society of Prisoners: Anglo–French Wars and Incarceration in the Eighteenth Century (Oxford: Oxford University Press, 2019).

Morriss, Roger, *The Royal Dockyards during the Revolutionary and Napoleonic Wars* (Leicester: Leicester University Press, 1983).

The Foundations of British Maritime Ascendancy: Resources, Logistics and the State, 1755–1815 (Cambridge: Cambridge University Press, 2011).

Morrow, John, *British Flag Officers in the French Wars, 1793–1815: Admirals' Lives* (London and New York: Bloomsbury Academic, 2018).

Mozzillo, Atanasio, *La frontiera del Grand Tour: Viaggi e viaggiatori nel Mezzogiorno borbonico* (Naples: Liguori Editore, 1992).

Munch-Petersen, Thomas, 'The Causes of the British Attack on Denmark in 1807 and the Danish Alliance with France', in Knut Arstad (ed.), *Krig på sjø og land: Norden i Napoleonskrigene* (Oslo: Forsvarsmuseet, 2014), 43–71.

Newman, Brooke N., 'Contesting "Black" Liberty and Subjecthood in the Anglophone Caribbean, 1730s–1780s', *Slavery & Abolition* 32:2 (2011), 169–83.

Noiriel, Gérard, *État, nation et immigration : Vers une histoire du pouvoir* (Paris: Belin, 2001).

Ojala, Jari and Pehkonen, Jaakko, 'Technological Changes, Wage Inequality and Skill Premiums: Evidence over Three Centuries', *Government Institute for Economic Research – VATT Working Papers 5* (Helsinki, 2009).

Ojala, Jari, Pehkonen, Jaakko, and Eloranta, Jari, 'Deskilling and Decline in Skill Premium during the Age of Sail: Swedish and Finnish Seamen, 1751–1913', *Explorations in Economic History* 61 (2016), 85–94.

Oldham, James C., 'The Origins of the Special Jury', *The University of Chicago Law Review* 50:1 (1983), 137–221.

Palermo, Daniele, *Dal feudo alla proprietà: Il caso della Ducea di Bronte*, electronic ed. (Palermo: Mediterranea – Ricerche Storiche, 2012).

Parry, Clive, *British Nationality Law and the History of Naturalisation* (Milan: Giuffrè, 1954).

Passaro, Biagio, 'Polacche, tartane e feluche. Navi e navigazione mercantile napoletane nel Settecento', in *Navis: Rassegna di studi di archeologia, etnologia e storia navale. Atti del II convegno nazionale, Cesenatico – Museo della Marineria (13–14 aprile 2012)* (Padua: libreriauniversitaria.it edizioni, 2014), 219–25.

Passaro, Biagio, Sirago, Maria, and Trizio, Pasquale Bruno, *Al servizio della Capitale e della Corte: La marineria napoletana nel Settecento* (Naples: Edizioni Scientifiche Italiane, 2019).

Paulino, Maria Clara, 'The "Alien" European: British Accounts of Portugal and the Portuguese, 1780–1850', in Martin Farr and Xavier Guégan (eds.), *The British Abroad since the Eighteenth Century, Volume 1: Travellers and Tourists* (Basingstoke: Palgrave Macmillan, 2013), 101–16.

Pavlenko, Alexander, 'On the Use of "Be" as a Perfective Auxiliary in Modern Shetland Dialect: Hybridization and Synctactic Change', in P. Sture Ureland and Iain Clarkson (eds.), *Language Contact across the North Atlantic: Proceedings of the Working Groups Held at University College, Galway (Ireland), August 29–September 3, 1992 and the University of Göteborg (Sweden), August 16–21, 1993* (Tübingen: Max Niemeyer Verlag, 1996), 75–82.

Pedemonte, Danilo, 'Deserters, Mutineers and Criminals: British Sailors and Problems of Port Jurisdiction in Genoa and Livorno during the Eighteenth Century', in Maria Fusaro, Bernard Allaire, Richard J. Blakemore, and Tijl Vanneste (eds.), *Law, Labour and Empire: Comparative Perspectives on Seafarers, c. 1500–1800* (Basingstoke: Palgrave Macmillan, 2015), 256–71.

Percy, Sarah V., 'Mercenaries: Strong Norm, Weak Law', *International Organization* 61 (2007), 367–97.

Mercenaries: The History of a Norm in International Relations (Oxford: Oxford University Press, 2007).

Perl-Rosenthal, Nathan, *Citizen Sailors: Becoming American in the Age of Revolution* (Cambridge, MA, and London: The Belknap Press of Harvard University Press, 2015).

Phillips, Carla Rahn, 'The Labour Market for Sailors in Spain, 1570–1870', in Paul van Royen, Jaap Bruijn, and Jan Lucassen (eds.), *'Those Emblems of Hell'? European Sailors and the Maritime Labour Market, 1570–1870* (St John's, Newfoundland: International Maritime Economic History Association, 1997), 329–48.

'"The Life Blood of the Navy": Recruiting Sailors in Eighteenth-Century Spain', *The Mariner's Mirror* 87:4 (2001), 420–45.

Philp, Mark, 'Introduction: The British Response to the Threat of Invasion, 1791–1815', in Mark Philp (ed.), *Resisting Napoleon: The British Response to the Threat of Invasion, 1797–1815* (Aldershot: Ashgate, 2006), 1–17.

Pieri, Piero, 'L'origine della dominazione inglese a Malta', *Archivio storico di Malta* 19:4 (1938), 377–410.

Pietsch, Roland, 'Ships' Boys and Youth Culture in Eighteenth Century Britain: The Navy Recruits of the London Marine Society', *The Northern Mariner/Le marin du nord* 14:4 (2004), 11–24.

Pitte, Jean-Robert, *French Gastronomy: The History and Geography of a Passion*, trans. Jody Gladding (New York: Columbia University Press, 2002).

Po-ching, Yu, 'Chinese Seamen in London and St Helena in the Early Nineteenth Century', in Maria Fusaro, Bernard Allaire, Richard J. Blakemore, and Tijl Vanneste (eds.), *Law, Labour and Empire: Comparative Perspectives on Seafarers, c. 1500–1800* (Basingstoke: Palgrave Macmillan, 2015), 287–303.

Pope, Dudley, *Life in Nelson's Navy*, 2nd ed. (London: Chatham Publishing, 1997).

Porcaro, Giuseppe, *Francesco Caracciolo* (Naples: Arturo Berisio editore, 1967).

Potter, David M., 'The Historian's Use of Nationalism and Vice Versa', *The American Historical Review* 67:4 (1962), 924–50.

Prins, A. H. J., *In Peril on the Sea: Marine Votive Paintings in the Maltese Islands* (Valletta: Said, 1989).

Prize Papers Online *Atlas*, Brill http://prize-papers-atlas-online.brillonline.com/moreinfo.

Pullicino, J. Cassar, 'Social Aspects of Maltese Nicknames', *Scientia* 12:2 (1956), 66–94.

Quilley, Geoff, '"All Ocean Is Her Own": The Image of the Sea and the Identity of the Maritime Nation in Eighteenth-Century British Art', in Geoffrey Cubitt (ed.), *Imagining Nations* (Manchester and New York: Manchester University Press, 1998), 132–52.

Radogna, Lamberto, *Storia della marina militare delle Due Sicilie (1734–1860)* (Milan: Mursia, 1978).

Rankin, John, 'Nineteenth-Century Royal Navy Sailors from Africa and the African Diaspora: Research Methodology', *African Diaspora* 6 (2013), 179–95.

Ransley, Jesse, 'Introduction: Asian Sailors in the Age of Empire', *Journal for Maritime Research* 16:2 (2014), 117–23.

Rao, Anna Maria, '"Missed Opportunities" in the History of Naples', in Melissa Calaresu and Helen Hills (eds.), *New Approaches to Naples c.1500 – c.1800: The Power of Place* (Farnham and Burlington, VT: Ashgate, 2013), 203–23.

Rapport, Michael, *Nationality and Citizenship in Revolutionary France: The Treatment of Foreigners 1789–1799* (Oxford: Clarendon Press, 2000).

Rediker, Marcus, *Between the Devil and the Deep Blue Sea: Merchant Seamen, Pirates, and the Anglo-American Maritime World 1700–1750* (Cambridge: Cambridge University Press, 1987).

'Afterword: Reflections on the Motley Crew as Port City Proletariat', *International Review of Social History* 64 (2019), 255–62.

Reid, Stuart, 'Acton, Sir John Francis Edward, Sixth Baronet (1736–1811)', *Oxford Dictionary of National Biography*, online ed. (Oxford: Oxford University Press, 2008) www.oxforddnb.com/view/article/76.

Riall, Lucy, *Under the Volcano: Revolution in a Sicilian Town* (Oxford: Oxford University Press, 2013).

Richards, Jake Christopher, 'Anti-Slave-Trade Law, "Liberated Africans" and the State in the South Atlantic World, c.1839–1852', *Past & Present* 241 (2018), 179–219.

Richter, Dieter, *Napoli cosmopolita: Viaggiatori e comunità straniere nell'Ottocento* (Naples: Electa Napoli, 2002).

Ried, Walter, *Deutsche Segelschiffahrt seit 1470* (Munich: J. F. Lehmanns Verlag, 1974).

Riionheimo, Helka, Kaivapalu, Annekatrin, and Härmävaara, Hanna-Ilona, 'Introduction: Receptive Multilingualism', *Nordic Journal of Linguistics* 40:2 (2017), 117–21.

Robertson, J. D. M., *The Press Gang in Orkney and Shetland* (Kirkwall: Orcadian (Kirkwall Press), 2011).

Rodger, N. A. M., *The Wooden World: An Anatomy of the Georgian Navy* (London: Fontana Press, 1988).

'The British View of the Functioning of the Anglo-Dutch Alliance, 1688–1795', in G. J. A. Raven and N. A. M. Rodger (eds.), *Navies and Armies: The Anglo-Dutch Relationship in War and Peace 1688–1988* (Edinburgh: John Donald Publishers Ltd, 1990), 12–32.

'"A Little Navy of Your Own Making": Admiral Boscawen and the Cornish Connection in the Royal Navy', in Michael Duffy (ed.), *Parameters of British Naval Power 1650–1850* (Exeter: University of Exeter Press, 1992), 82–92.

'The Naval Chaplain in the Eighteenth Century', *Journal for Eighteenth Century Studies* 18:1 (1995), 33–45.

'Honour and Duty at Sea, 1660–1815', *Historical Research* 75:190 (2002), 425–47.

'Form and Function in European Navies, 1660–1815', in Leo Akveld et al. (eds.), *In het kielzog: maritiem-historische studies aangeboden aan Jaap R. Bruijn bij zijn vertrek als hoogleraar zeegeschiedenis aan de Universiteit Leiden* (Amsterdam: De Bataafsche Leeuw, 2003), 85–97.

'Mutiny or Subversion? Spithead and the Nore', in Thomas Bartlett, David Dickson, Dáire Keogh, and Kevin Whelan (eds.), *1798: A Bicentenary Perspective* (Dublin: Four Courts Press, 2003), 549–64.

The Command of the Ocean: A Naval History of Britain, 1649–1815 (London: Allen Lane, 2004).

'Perkins, John [nicknamed Jack Punch] (c. 1745–1812)', *Oxford Dictionary of National Biography*, online ed. (Oxford: Oxford University Press, 2008) www.oxforddnb.com/view/10.1093/ref:odnb/9780198614128.001.0001/odnb-9780198614128-e-50232.

Roding, Juliette and van Voss, Lex Heerma (eds.), *The North Sea and Culture (1550–1800): Proceedings of the International Conference Held at Leiden 21–22 April 1995* (Hilversum: Verloren, 1996).

Rogers, Nicholas, 'The Sea Fencibles, Loyalism and the Reach of the State', in Mark Philp (ed.), *Resisting Napoleon: The British Response to the Threat of Invasion, 1797–1815* (Aldershot: Ashgate, 2006), 41–59.

The Press Gang: Naval Impressment and Its Opponents in Georgian Britain (London and New York: Continuum, 2007).

'British Impressment and Its Discontents', *The International Journal of Maritime History* 30:1 (2018), 52–73.

Rose, J. Holland, *Lord Hood and the Defence of Toulon* (Cambridge: Cambridge University Press, 1922).

Sætra, Gustav, 'The International Labour Market for Seamen, 1600–1900: Norway and Norwegian Participation', in Paul C. van Royen, Jaap R. Bruijn, and Jan Lucassen (eds.), *'Those Emblems of Hell'? European Sailors and the Maritime Labour Market, 1570–1870* (St John's, Newfoundland: International Maritime Economic History Association, 1997), 173–210.

Sahlins, Peter, 'The Eighteenth-Century Citizenship Revolution in France', in Andreas Fahrmeir, Olivier Faron, and Patrick Weil (eds.), *Migration Control in the North Atlantic World: The Evolution of State Practices in Europe and the United States from the French Revolution to the Inter-War Period* (New York and Oxford: Berghahn Books, 2003), 11–24.

  Unnaturally French: Foreign Citizens in the Old Regime and After (Ithaca, NY and London: Cornell University Press, 2004).

  'Sur la citoyenneté et le droit d'aubaine à l'époque moderne : Réponse à Simona Cerutti', *Annales. Histoire, Sciences Sociales* 63:2 (2008), 385–98.

Salvemini, Raffaella, 'A tutela della salute e del commercio nel Mediterraneo: La sanità marittima nel Mezzogiorno pre-unitario', in Raffaella Salvemini (ed.), *Istituzioni e traffici nel Mediterraneo tra età antica e crescita moderna* (Rome: Consiglio Nazionale delle Ricerche, Istituto di Studi sulle Società del Mediterraneo, 2009), 259–96.

Sampson, Helen, *International Seafarers and Transnationalism in the Twenty-First Century* (Manchester and New York: Manchester University Press, 2013).

Samuel, Raphael, 'Perils of the Transcript', *Oral History* 1:2 (1972), 19–22.

Sánchez, Rafael Torres, Biscarri, Javier Gómez, and de Gracia, Fernando Pérez, 'Exchange Rate Behavior and Exchange Rate Puzzles: Why the Eighteenth Century Might Help', *Revista de Historia Economica/Journal of Iberian and Latin American Economic History* 23:1 (2005), 143–74.

Saunier, Pierre-Yves, *Transnational History* (Basingstoke: Palgrave Macmillan, 2013).

Scanlan, Padraic Xavier, 'The Rewards of Their Exertions: Prize Money and British Abolitionism in Sierra Leone, 1808–1823', *Past & Present* 225 (2014), 113–42.

Schaffer, Simon, 'Introduction', in Simon Schaffer, Lissa Roberts, Kapil Raj, and James Delbourgo (eds.), *The Brokered World: Go-Betweens and Global Intelligence, 1770–1820* (Sagamore Beach, MA: Science History Publications, 2009), ix–xxxviii.

Schama, Simon, *Patriots and Liberators: Revolution in the Netherlands 1780–1813*, 2nd ed. (London: Fontana Press, 1992).

Schiller, Nina Glick, Basch, Linda, and Szanton Blanc, Cristina, 'From Immigrant to Transmigrant: Theorizing Transnational Migration', *Anthropological Quarterly* 68:1 (1995), 48–63.

Schmidt, H. D., 'The Hessian Mercenaries: The Career of a Political Cliché', *History* 43:149 (1958), 207–12.

Schofield, R. S., 'Dimensions of Illiteracy, 1750–1850', *Explorations in Economic History* 10:4 (1973), 437–54.

Schotte, Margaret E., *Sailing School: Navigating Science and Skill, 1550–1800* (Baltimore, MD: Johns Hopkins University Press, 2019).

Schüppert, Anja, Hilton, Nanna Haug, and Gooskens, Charlotte, 'Introduction: Communicating across Linguistic Borders', *Linguistics* 53:2 (2015), 211–17.

Schutte, G. J., 'Willem IV en Willem V', in C. A. Tamse (ed.), *Nassau en Oranje in de Nederlandse geschiedenis* (Alphen aan den Rijn: A. W. Sijthoff, 1979), 187–228.

Schwartz, Aba, 'Interpreting the Effect of Distance on Migration', *Journal of Political Economy* 81:5 (1973), 1153–69.

Sebastiani, Silvia, 'Race and National Characters in Eighteenth-Century Scotland: The Polygenic Discourses of Kames and Pinkerton', *Cromohs* 8 (2003), 1–14.

'Nations, Nationalism and National Characters' in Aaron Garrett (ed.), *The Routledge Companion to Eighteenth Century Philosophy* (London and New York: Routledge, 2014), 593–617.

Seerup, Joen Jakob, '*Søetaten i 1700-tallet: Organisation, personel og daglidag i 1700-tallets danske flåde*' (unpublished PhD thesis, University of Copenhagen, 2010).

Sen, Sudipta, 'Imperial Subjects on Trial: On the Legal Identity of Britons in Late Eighteenth-Century India', *Journal of British Studies* 45:3 (2006), 532–55.

Seth, Suman, *Difference and Disease: Medicine, Race, and the Eighteenth-Century British Empire* (Cambridge: Cambridge University Press, 2018).

Sherwood, Marika, 'Race, Nationality and Employment among Lascar Seamen, 1660 to 1945', *Journal of Ethnic and Migration Studies* 17:2 (1991), 229–44.

Slope, Nick, '*Serving in Nelson's Navy: A Social History of Three Amazon Class Frigates Utilising Database Technology*' (unpublished PhD thesis, The University of West London, 2006).

Smith, Alison K., 'National Cuisines', in Jeffrey M. Pilcher (ed.), *The Oxford Handbook of Food History* (Oxford: Oxford University Press, 2012), 444–58.

Sogner, Sølvi, 'Norwegian-Dutch Migrant Relations in the Seventeenth Century', in Louis Sicking, Harry de Bles, and Erlend des Bouvrie (eds.), *Dutch Light in the 'Norwegian Night': Maritime Relations and Migration across the North Sea in Early Modern Times* (Hilversum: Uitgeverij Verloren, 2004), 43–56.

Spence, Daniel Owen, '"They Had the Sea in Their Blood": Caymanian Naval Volunteers in the Second World War', in Nir Arielli and Bruce Collins (eds.), *Transnational Soldiers: Foreign Military Enlistment in the Modern Era* (Basingstoke: Palgrave Macmillan, 2013), 105–23.

Stark, Suzanne J., *Female Tars: Women aboard Ship in the Age of Sail*, 2nd ed. (London: Pimlico, 1998).

Starkey, David J., *British Privateering Enterprise in the Eighteenth Century* (Exeter: University of Exeter Press, 1990).

'War and the Market for Seafarers in Britain, 1736–1792', in Lewis R. Fischer and Helge W. Nordvik (eds.), *Shipping and Trade, 1750–1950: Essays in International Maritime Economic History* (Pontefract: Lofthouse Publications, 1990), 25–42.

Statt, Daniel, *Foreigners and Englishmen: The Controversy over Immigration and Population, 1660–1760* (Cranbury, NJ: Associated University Presses, 1995).

Stein, Tristan, 'Passes and Protection in the Making of a British Mediterranean', *Journal of British Studies* 54 (2015), 602–31.

Stock, Paul, '"Almost a Separate Race": Racial Thought and the Idea of Europe in British Encyclopaedias and Histories, 1771–1830', *Modern Intellectual History* 8:1 (2011), 3–29.

'Sustaining the Empire: War, the Navy and the Contractor State', University of Greenwich, 2006–9 www.gre.ac.uk/ach/gmc/research/projects/sustaining-the-empire.

Taylor, Gordon, *The Sea Chaplains: A History of the Chaplains of the Royal Navy* (Oxford: Oxford Illustrated Press, 1978).

Thomas, Keith, 'Introduction', in Jan Bremmer and Herman Roodenburg (eds.), *A Cultural History of Gesture: From Antiquity to the Present Day* (Cambridge: Polity Press, 1991), 1–14.

Thompson, Neville, *Earl Bathurst and the British Empire 1762–1834* (Barnsley: Leo Cooper, 1999).

Thomson, Janice E., *Mercenaries, Pirates, and Sovereigns: State-Building and Extraterritorial Violence in Early Modern Europe* (Princeton, NJ: Princeton University Press, 1994).

Torpey, John C., *The Invention of the Passport: Surveillance, Citizenship and the State*, 2nd ed. (Cambridge: Cambridge University Press, 2018).

Tozzi, Christopher J., *Nationalizing France's Army: Foreign, Black, and Jewish Troops in the French Military, 1715–1831* (Charlottesville, VA and London: University of Virginia Press, 2016).

Tsiamis, Costas, Thalassinou, Eleni, Poulakou-Rebelakou, Effie, and Hatzakis, Angelos, 'Quarantine and British "Protection" of the Ionian Islands, 1815–64', in John Chircop and Francisco Javier Martínez (eds.), *Mediterranean Quarantines, 1750–1915: Space, Identity and Power* (Manchester: Manchester University Press, 2018), 256–79.

Tzoref-Ashkenazi, Chen, 'German Auxiliary Troops in the British and Dutch East India Companies', in Nir Arielli and Bruce Collins (eds.), *Transnational Soldiers: Foreign Military Enlistment in the Modern Era* (Basingstoke: Palgrave Macmillan, 2013), 32–49.

Ulrich, Nicole, 'International Radicalism, Local Solidarities: The 1797 British Naval Mutinies in Southern African Waters', in Clare Anderson, Niklas Frykman, Lex Heerma van Voss, and Marcus Rediker (eds.), *Mutiny and Maritime Radicalism in the Age of Revolution* (Cambridge: Press Syndicate of the University of Cambridge, 2013), 61–85.

Unger, Richard W., 'Overview. Trades, Ports and Ships: The Roots of Difference in Sailors' Lives', in Maria Fusaro, Bernard Allaire, Richard J. Blakemore, and Tijl Vanneste (eds.), *Law, Labour and Empire: Comparative Perspectives on Seafarers, c. 1500–1800* (Basingstoke: Palgrave Macmillan, 2015), 1–17.

Vale, Brian, 'The Conquest of Scurvy in the Royal Navy 1793–1800: A Challenge to Current Orthodoxy', *The Mariner's Mirror* 94:2 (2008), 160–75.

Van Breda Vriesman, Dorothea Josephine Antoinette, *In woelig vaarwater: Marineofficieren in de jaren 1779–1802* (Amsterdam: De Bataafsche Leeuw, 1998).

Van Eyck van Heslinga, E. S., 'A Competitive Ally. The Delicate Balance of Naval Alliance and Maritime Competition between Great Britain and the Dutch Republic, 1674–1795', in G. J. A. Raven and N. A. M. Rodger (eds.), *Navies and Armies: The Anglo-Dutch Relationship in War and Peace 1688–1988* (Edinburgh: John Donald Publishers Ltd, 1990), 1–11.

Van Heuven, Vincent J., Gooskens, Charlotte S., and van Bezooijen, Renée, 'Introducing MICRELA: Predicting Mutual Intelligibility between Closely Related Languages in Europe', In J. Navracsics and S. Bátyi (eds.), *First and Second Language: Interdisciplinary Approaches – Studies in Psycholinguistics 6* (Budapest: Tinta könyvkiadó, 2015), 127–45.

Van Lottum, Jelle, *Across the North Sea: The Impact of the Dutch Republic on International Labour Migration, c. 1550–1850* (Amsterdam: Aksant, 2007).

'Some Thoughts about Migration of Maritime Workers in the Eighteenth-Century North Sea Region', *The International Journal of Maritime History* 27:4 (2015), 647–61.

Van Lottum, Jelle, Lucassen, Jan, and Heerma van Voss, Lex, 'Sailors, National and International Labour Markets and National Identity, 1600–1850', in Richard W. Unger (ed.), *Shipping and Economic Growth 1350–1850* (Leiden and Boston: Brill, 2011), 309–51.

Van Lottum, Jelle and Poulsen, Bo, 'Estimating Levels of Numeracy and Literacy in the Maritime Sector of the North Atlantic in the Late Eighteenth Century', *Scandinavian Economic History Review* 59:1 (2011), 67–82.

Van Lottum, Jelle and van Zanden, Jan Luiten, 'Labour Productivity and Human Capital in the European Maritime Sector of the Eighteenth Century', *Explorations in Economic History* 53 (2014), 83–100.

Van Rossum, Matthias and Kamp, Jeannette (eds.), *Desertion in the Early Modern World a Comparative History* (New York: Bloomsbury Academic, 2016).

Van Rossum, Matthias, van Voss, Lex Heerma, van Lottum, Jelle, and Lucassen, Jan, 'National and International Labour Markets for Sailors in European, Atlantic and Asian Waters, 1600–1850', in Maria Fusaro and Amélia Polónia (eds.), *Maritime History as Global History* (St. John's, Newfoundland: International Maritime Economic History Association, 2010), 47–72.

Van Royen, Paul C., 'Mariners and Markets in the Age of Sail: The Case of the Netherlands', in Lewis R. Fischer (ed.), *The Market for Seamen in the Age of Sail* (St John's, Newfoundland: International Maritime Economic History Association, 1994), 47–57.

Vergé-Franceschi, Michel, *La marine française au XVIIIe siècle : guerres – administration – exploration* (Paris: SEDES, 1996).

Walsh, Patrick, 'Ireland and the Royal Navy in the Eighteenth Century', in John McAleer and Christer Petley (eds.), *The Royal Navy and the British Atlantic World, c. 1750–1820* (London: Palgrave Macmillan, 2016), 51–76.

Walter, Bronwen, '"Shamrocks Growing out of Their Mouths": Language and the Racialisation of the Irish in Britain', in Anne J. Kershen (ed.), *Language, Labour and Migration* (Aldershot and Burlington, VT: Ashgate, 2000), 57–73.

Watts, A. D., 'The Protection of Alien Seamen', *The International and Comparative Law Quarterly* 7:4 (1958), 691–711.

Weiss Muller, Hannah, 'Bonds of Belonging: Subjecthood and the British Empire', *Journal of British Studies* 53:1 (2014), 29–58.

Subjects and Sovereign: Bonds of Belonging in the Eighteenth-Century British Empire (Oxford: Oxford University Press, 2017).

Wells, J. C., *Accents of English 2: The British Isles* (Cambridge: Cambridge University Press, 1986).

Wilcox, Martin, 'The "Poor Decayed Seamen" of Greenwich Hospital, 1705–1763', *International Journal of Maritime History* 25:1 (2013), 65–90.

Wilkinson, Clive, *The British Navy and the State in the Eighteenth Century* (Woodbridge: The Boydell Press, 2004).

Williams, Siân, 'The Royal Navy and Caribbean Colonial Society during the Eighteenth Century', in John McAleer and Christer Petley (eds.), *The Royal Navy and the British Atlantic World, c. 1750–1820* (London: Palgrave Macmillan, 2016), 27–50.

Wills, Mary, *Envoys of Abolition: British Naval Officers and the Campaign against the Slave Trade in West Africa* (Liverpool: Liverpool University Press, 2019).

Wilson, Evan, *A Social History of British Naval Officers, 1775–1815* (Woodbridge: Boydell Press, 2017).

Wilson, Evan, Hammar, AnnaSara, and Seerup, Jakob (eds.), *Eighteenth-Century Naval Officers: A Transnational Perspective* (Cham: Palgrave Macmillan, 2019).

Wilson, Kathleen, *The Sense of the People: Politics, Culture and Imperialism in England, 1715–1785* (Cambridge: Cambridge University Press, 1995).

The Island Race: Englishness, Empire and Gender in the Eighteenth Century (London and New York: Routledge, 2003).

Wilson, Peter H., '"Mercenary" Contracts as Fiscal-Military Instruments', in Svante Norrhem and Erik Thomson (eds.), *Subsidies, Diplomacy, and State Formation in Europe, 1494–1789: Economies of Allegiance* (Lund: Lund University Press, 2020), 68–92.

Wilson, Thomas M. and Donnan, Hastings, 'Nation, State and Identity at International Borders', in Thomas M. Wilson and Hastings Donnan (eds.), *Border Identities: Nation and State at International Frontiers* (Cambridge: Cambridge University Press, 1998), 1–30.

Wimmer, Andreas and Schiller, Nina Glick, 'Methodological Nationalism and Beyond: Nation-State Building, Migration and the Social Sciences', *Global Networks* 2:4 (2002), 301–34.

Wismayer, Joseph M., *The Fleet of the Order of St John 1530–1798* (Valletta: Midsea Books Ltd., 1997).

Wolf, Joshua, '"To Be Enslaved or Thus Deprived": British Impressment, American Discontent, and the Making of the *Chesapeake-Leopard* Affair, 1803–1807', *War & Society* 29:1 (2010), 1–19.

Wolff, Larry, 'La géographie philosophique des Lumières : L'Europe de l'Est et les Tartares de Sibérie au regard de la civilisation', in Antoine Lilti and Céline Spector (eds.), *Penser l'Europe au XVIIIᵉ siècle : Commerce, civilisation, empire* (Oxford: Voltaire Foundation, 2014), 167–80.

Zarate, Juan Carlos, 'The Emergence of a New Dog of War: Private International Security Companies, International Law, and the New World Disorder', *Stanford Journal of International Law* 34:75 (1998), 75–162.

Zimmerman, James Fulton, *Impressment of American Seamen* (New York: [N/A], 1925).

Present-day news and media outlets

Bloody Foreigners: The Untold Battle of Trafalgar, series 1, episode 3 (Channel 4, 28 June 2010).
Horrible Histories, series 4, episode 12, written by Laurence Ricard (BBC, 2012).

R Software packages

Meyer, David, Zeileis, Achim, and Hornik, Kurt, *vcd: Visualizing Categorical Data* (2021, version 1.4-9) https://cran.r-project.org/web/packages/vcd/index.html.
Warnes, Gregory R., Bolker, Ben, Lumley, Thomas, and Johnson, Randall C., *gmodels: Various R Programming Tools for Model Fitting* (2018, version 2.18.1) https://cran.r-project.org/web/packages/gmodels/index.html.
Wei, Taiyun and Simko, Viliam, *R Package 'corrplot': Visualization of a Correlation Matrix* (2021, Version 0.92) https://github.com/taiyun/corrplot.
Wickham, Hadley, *ggplot2: Elegant Graphics for Data Analysis* (New York: Springer-Verlag, 2016) https://ggplot2.tidyverse.org.

Index

CPSIA information can be obtained
at www.ICGtesting.com
Printed in the USA
LVHW081130091122
732715LV00006B/363

9 781009 199797